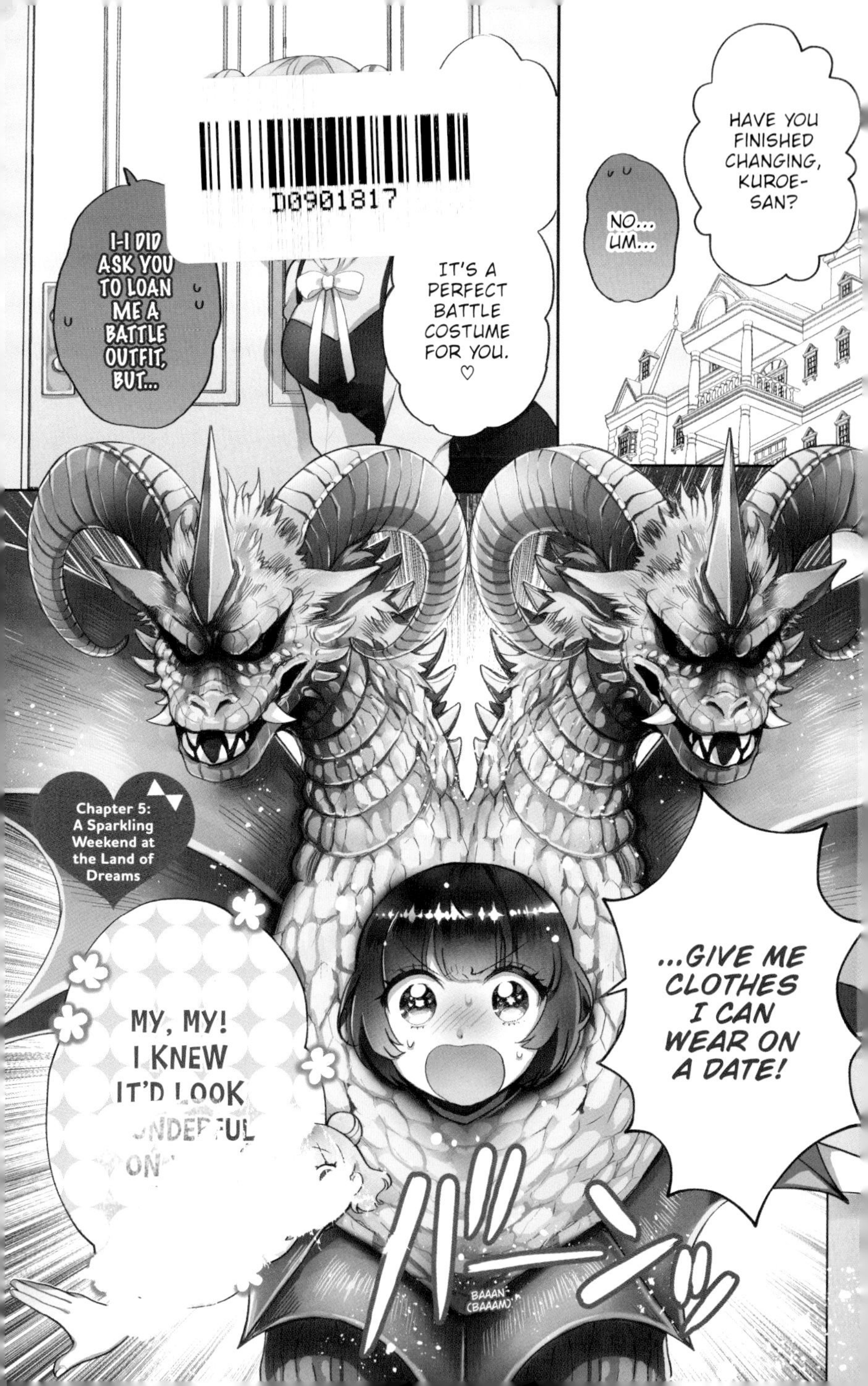
HAVE YOU FINISHED CHANGING, KUROE-SAN?
NO... UM...
IT'S A PERFECT BATTLE COSTUME FOR YOU. ♡
I-I DID ASK YOU TO LOAN ME A BATTLE OUTFIT, BUT...
...GIVE ME CLOTHES I CAN WEAR ON A DATE!
Chapter 5: A Sparkling Weekend at the Land of Dreams
MY, MY! I KNEW IT'D LOOK
BAAAN (BAAAM)

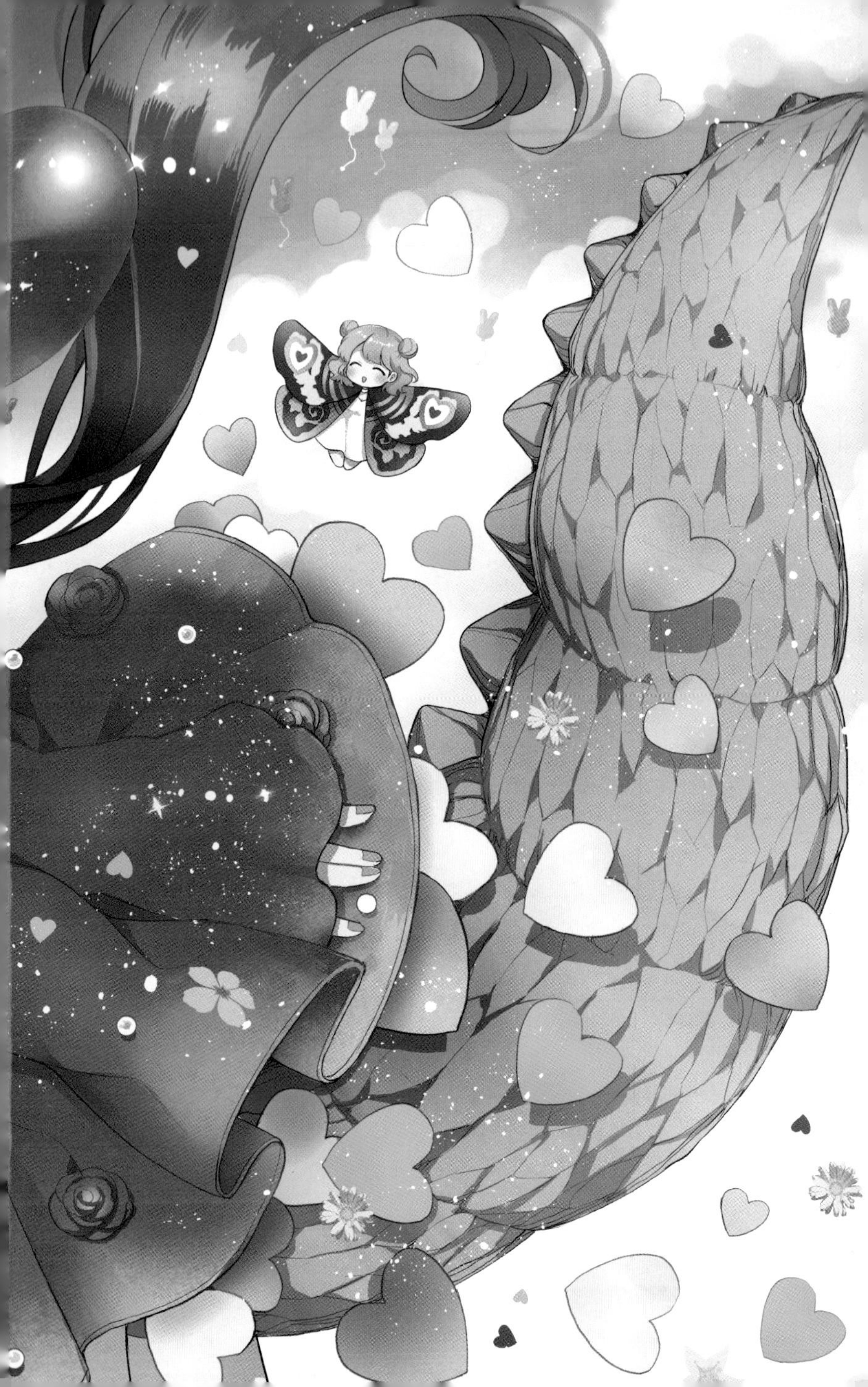

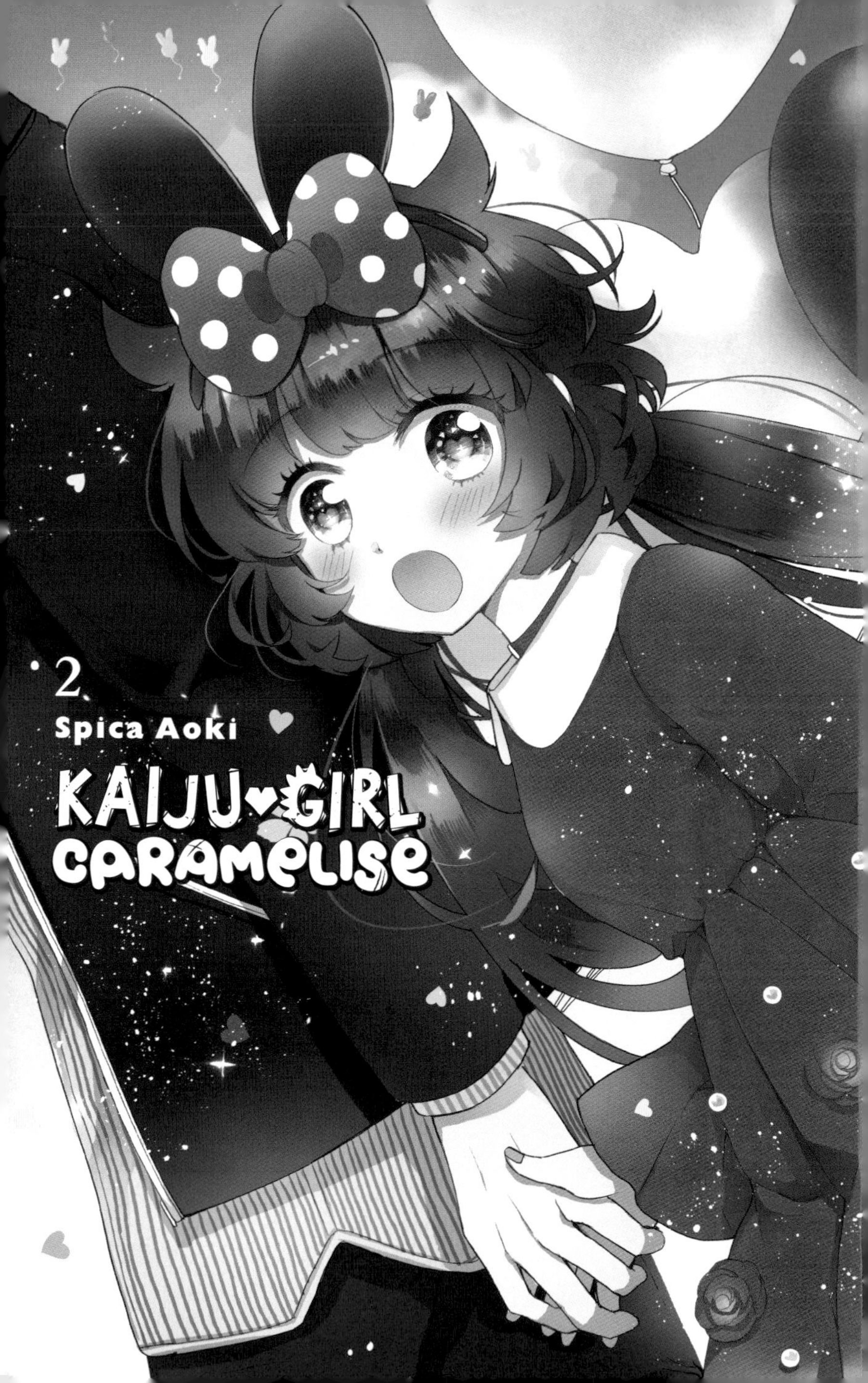
2
Spica Aoki
KAIJU GIRL
CARAMELISE

contents

ALL YOU NEED TO KNOW ABOUT KAIJU GIRL CARAMELISE

Kuroe Akaishi is a high school girl with a problem: When she gets excited, parts of her body transform. When Arata Minami, the class hottie, makes her heart beat, she turns into a giant kaiju. Upon seeing Kuroe suddenly getting chummy with Arata, a few girls from their class harass her by locking her in the gym storage room. Despite knowing that falling in love would only cause her to become a kaiju, she reveals her feelings to Arata when he appears to save her. Soon after, she turns into a huge kaiju a second time and ends up destroying the school gym......

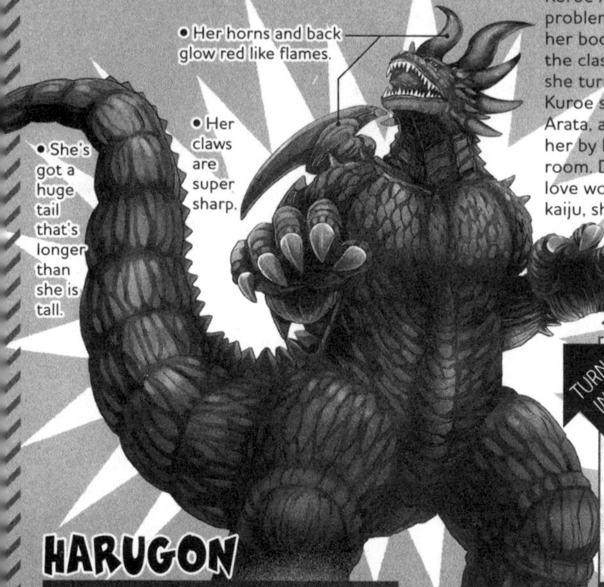
• Her horns and back glow red like flames.
• Her claws are super sharp.
• She's got a huge tail that's longer than she is tall.
• She's equipped with powerful legs to support that enormous body.

HARUGON

A huge, one-hundred-meter kaiju that appeared in Tokyo one day out of the blue. This is what Kuroe Akaishi looked like post-transformation when Arata Minami made her heart beat faster. A comedian on a morning variety show called her Harugon as a joke, and the name stuck. Kuroe still remains herself even in kaiju form.

TURNS INTO

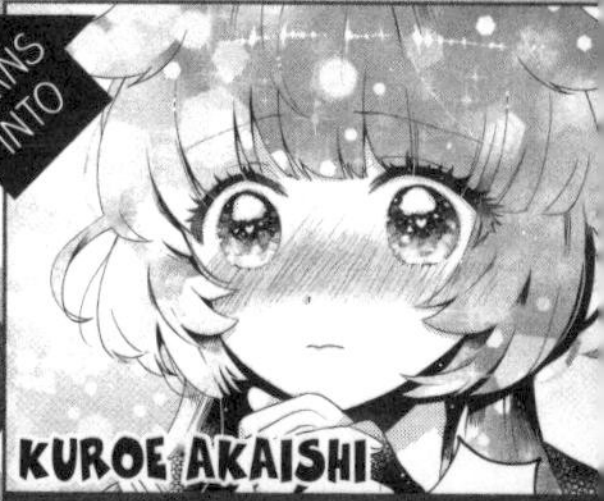

KUROE AKAISHI

The great kaiju Harugon's normal form. Fearing the physical changes that lead up to her kaiju transformation, she did everything she could when she was little to avoid interactions with people, and it's turned her into a gloomy high schooler. Her hobby is drawing, and she loves sweets.

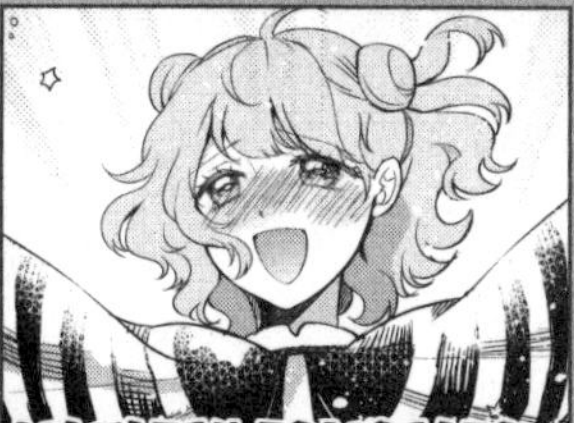

MANATSU TOMOSATO

A beautiful girl who loves kaiju and attends the same high school as Kuroe. She's somehow gotten the idea that Kuroe is Harugon's "priestess" and can communicate with it telepathically. She's got a large bust.

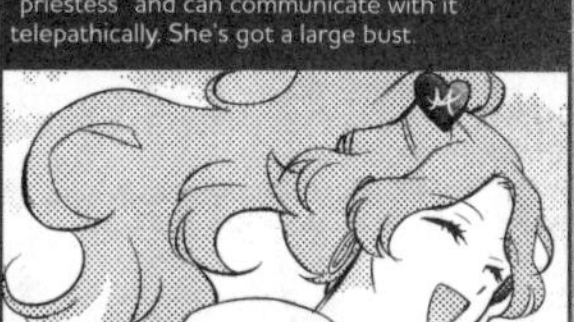

RINKO AKAISHI

Kuroe's rather overprotective mother. She's a huge fan of the singer Mayumi Hamasaki.

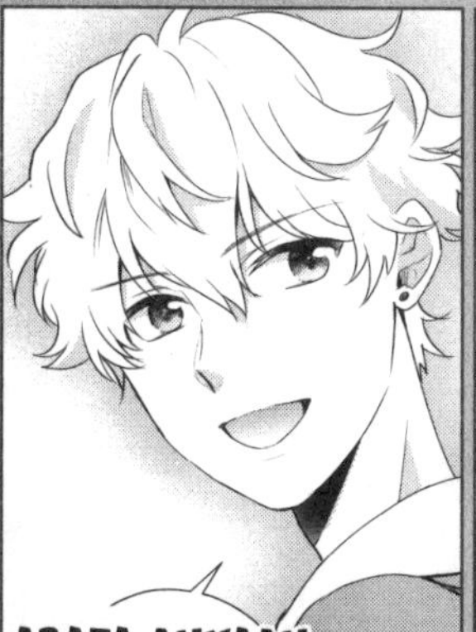

ARATA MINAMI

A handsome, photogenic guy in Kuroe's class. He was attracted to Kuroe because, unlike the other girls, she's always true to herself. Because he's rather clueless and tends to get physically close to people, he's been a handful for her to deal with. He was chubby back in middle school, so he never fails to stay on top of his calorie intake even to this day.

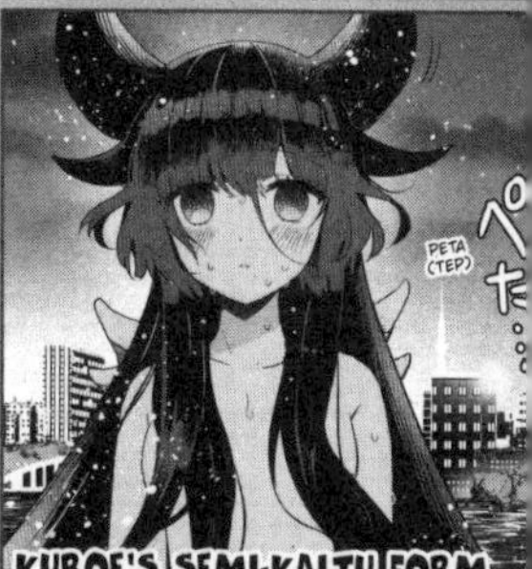
PETA (TEP)

KUROE'S SEMI-KAIJU FORM

What Kuroe looks like when she's partially turned into a kaiju. A variety of changes can occur: She can grow horns, her hands can get bigger, she can sprout a tail, etc.

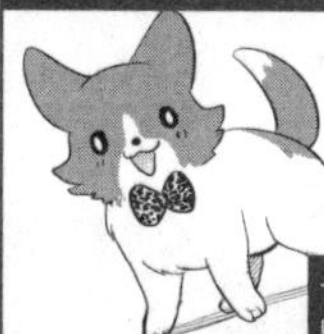

JUMBO KING

The Akaishi family pet. A clever dog.

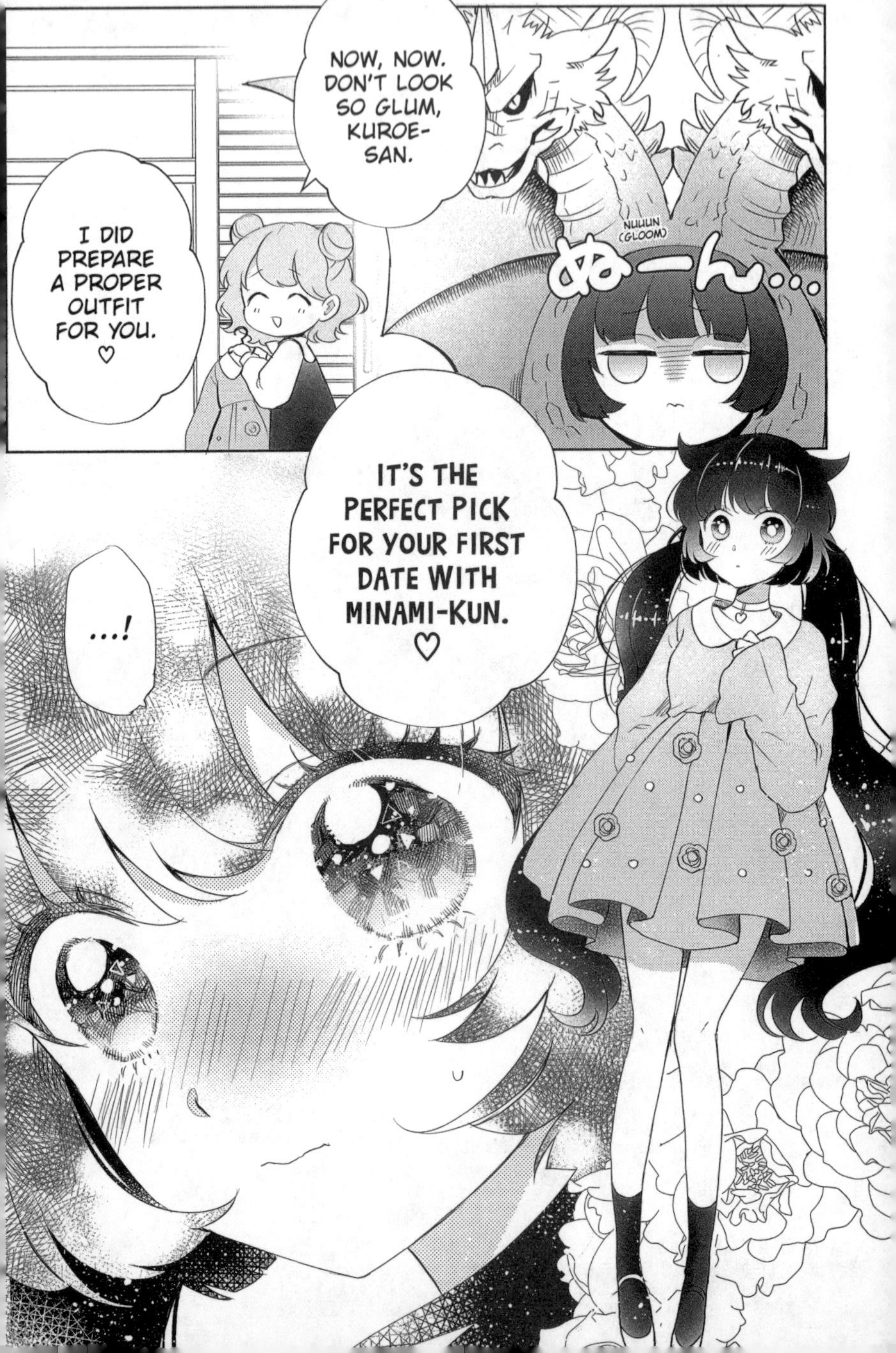
NOW, NOW. DON'T LOOK SO GLUM, KUROE-SAN.
NUUUN (GLOOM)
ぬーん…
I DID PREPARE A PROPER OUTFIT FOR YOU. ♡
IT'S THE PERFECT PICK FOR YOUR FIRST DATE WITH MINAMI-KUN. ♡
...!

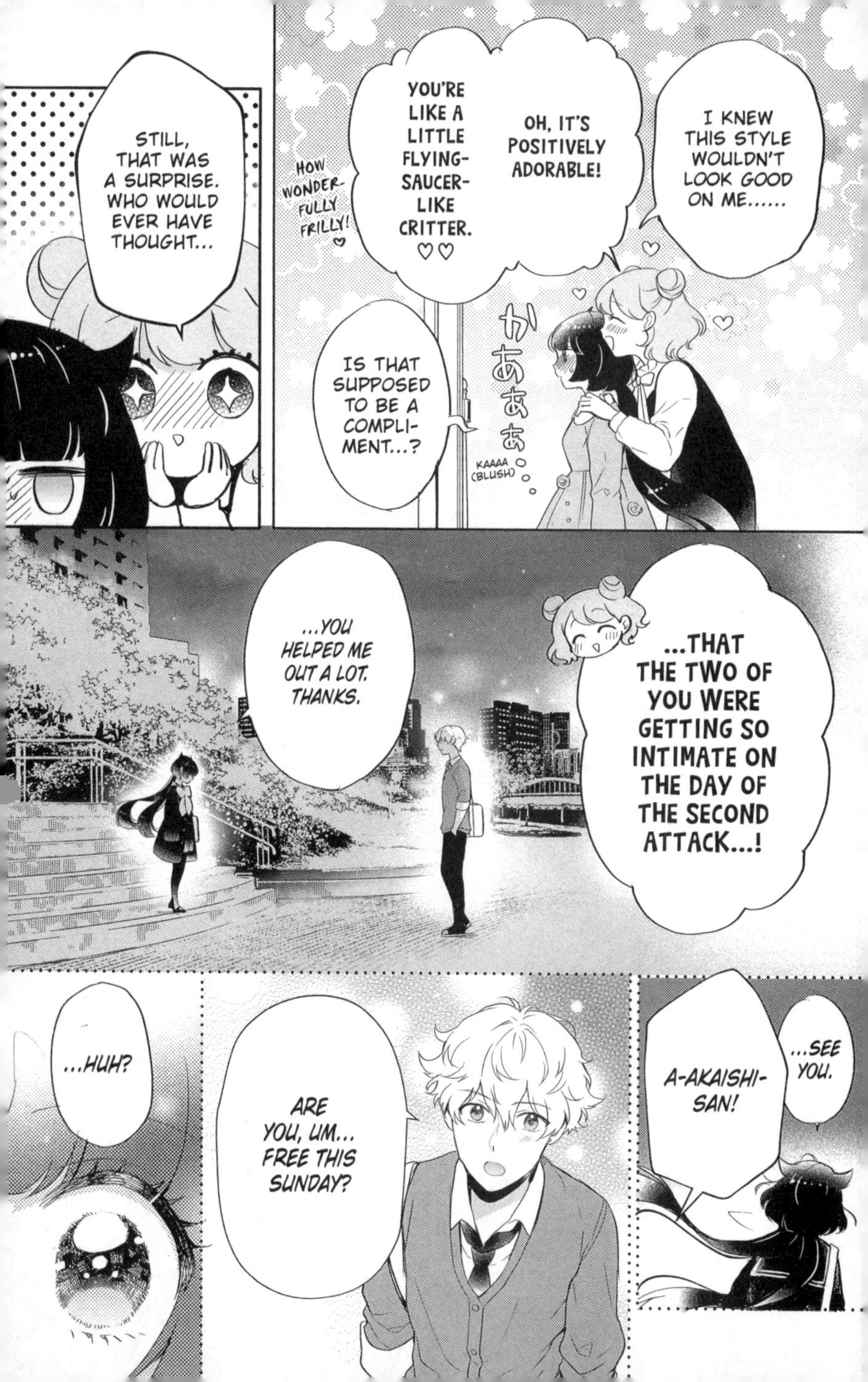
I KNEW THIS STYLE WOULDN'T LOOK GOOD ON ME......
OH, IT'S POSITIVELY ADORABLE!
YOU'RE LIKE A LITTLE FLYING-SAUCER-LIKE CRITTER. ♡♡
HOW WONDERFULLY FRILLY! ♡
かあああ
KAAAA (BLUSH)
IS THAT SUPPOSED TO BE A COMPLIMENT...?
STILL, THAT WAS A SURPRISE. WHO WOULD EVER HAVE THOUGHT...
...THAT THE TWO OF YOU WERE GETTING SO INTIMATE ON THE DAY OF THE SECOND ATTACK...!
...YOU HELPED ME OUT A LOT. THANKS.
...SEE YOU.
A-AKAISHI-SAN!
ARE YOU, UM... FREE THIS SUNDAY?
...HUH?

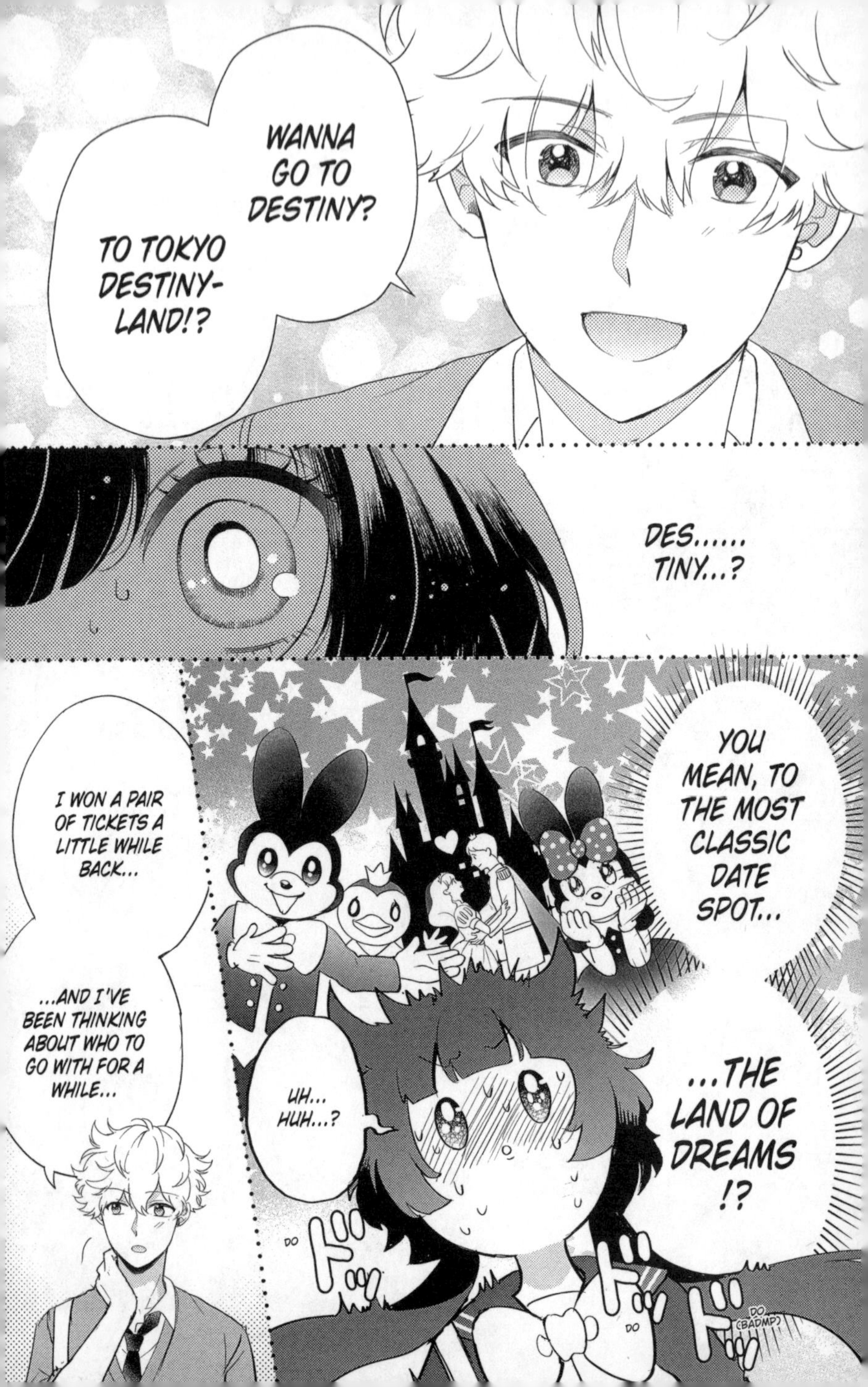
WANNA GO TO DESTINY?
TO TOKYO DESTINY-LAND!?
DES...... TINY...?
YOU MEAN, TO THE MOST CLASSIC DATE SPOT...
...THE LAND OF DREAMS !?
UH... HUH...?
DO
DO
DO (BADMP)
I WON A PAIR OF TICKETS A LITTLE WHILE BACK...
...AND I'VE BEEN THINKING ABOUT WHO TO GO WITH FOR A WHILE...

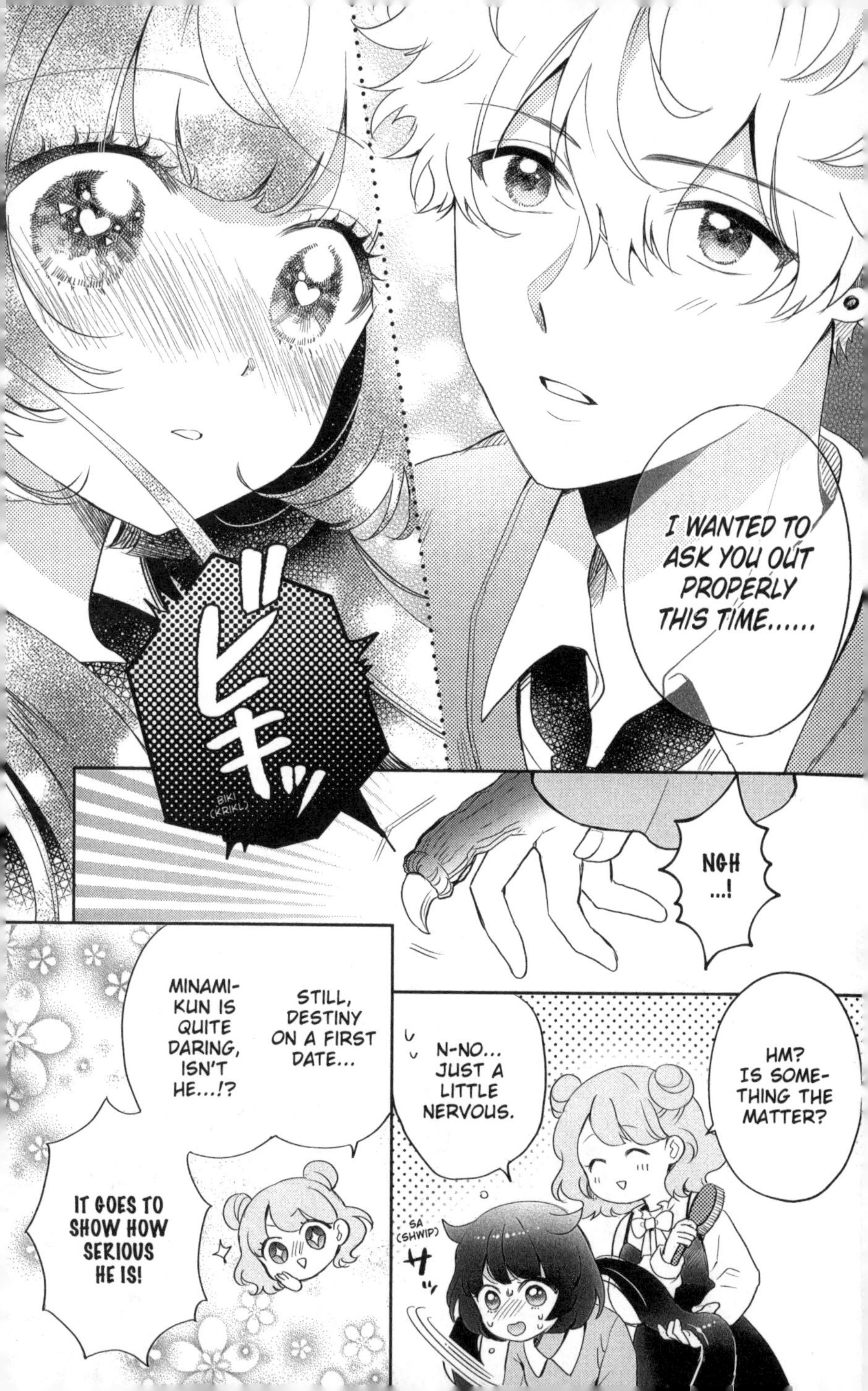
I WANTED TO ASK YOU OUT PROPERLY THIS TIME......
BIKI (KRIKL)
NGH ...!
HM? IS SOME-THING THE MATTER?
N-NO... JUST A LITTLE NERVOUS.
SA (SHWIP)
STILL, DESTINY ON A FIRST DATE...
MINAMI-KUN IS QUITE DARING, ISN'T HE...!?
IT GOES TO SHOW HOW SERIOUS HE IS!

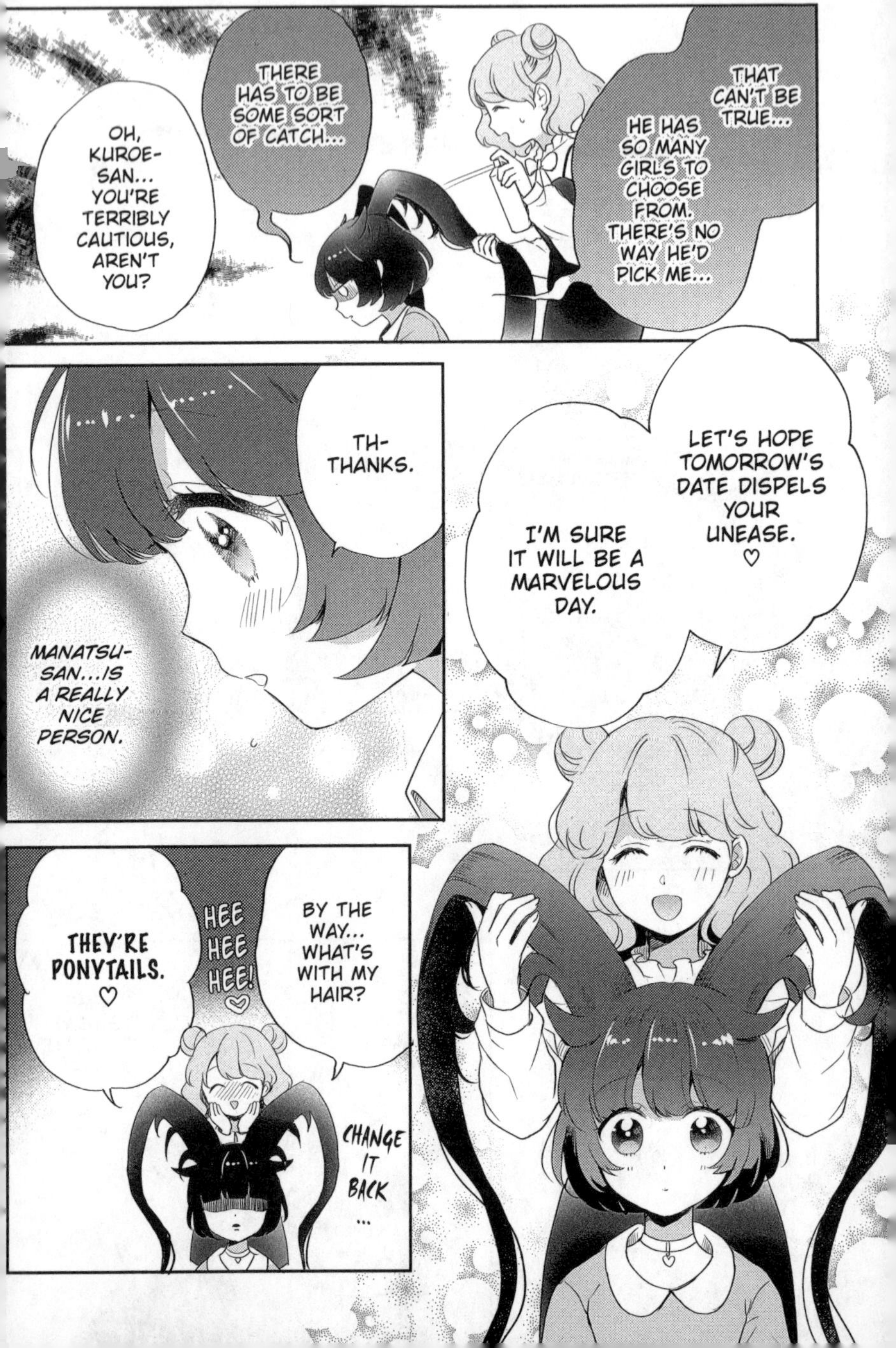
THAT CAN'T BE TRUE...
HE HAS SO MANY GIRLS TO CHOOSE FROM. THERE'S NO WAY HE'D PICK ME...
THERE HAS TO BE SOME SORT OF CATCH...
OH, KUROE-SAN... YOU'RE TERRIBLY CAUTIOUS, AREN'T YOU?
LET'S HOPE TOMORROW'S DATE DISPELS YOUR UNEASE. ♡
I'M SURE IT WILL BE A MARVELOUS DAY.
TH-THANKS.
MANATSU-SAN...IS A REALLY NICE PERSON.
BY THE WAY... WHAT'S WITH MY HAIR?
HEE HEE HEE! ♡
THEY'RE PONYTAILS. ♡
CHANGE IT BACK...

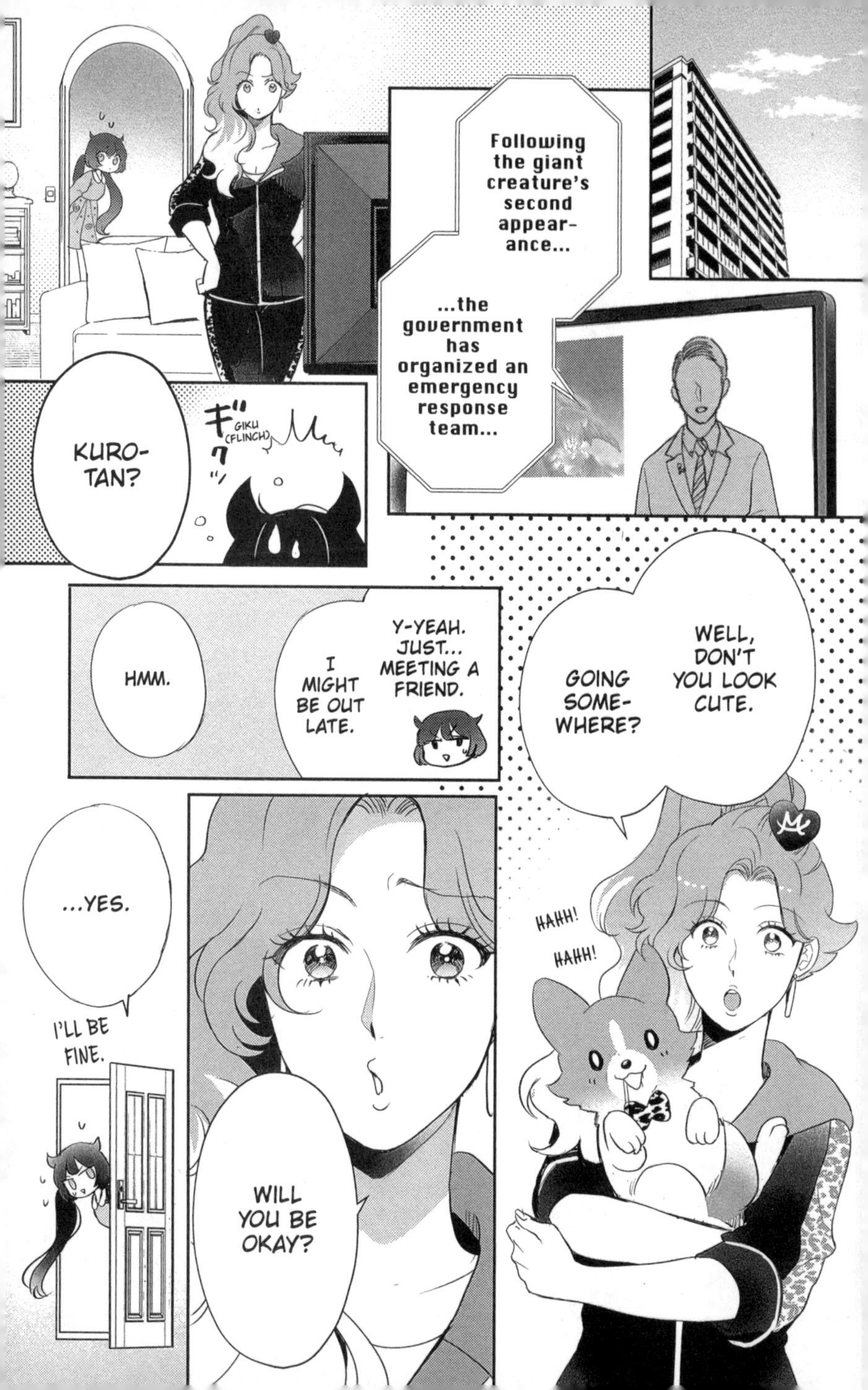

Following the giant creature's second appearance...
...the government has organized an emergency response team...
KURO-TAN?
GIKU (FLINCH)
WELL, DON'T YOU LOOK CUTE.
GOING SOME-WHERE?
HAHH!
HAHH!
Y-YEAH. JUST... MEETING A FRIEND.
I MIGHT BE OUT LATE.
HMM.
WILL YOU BE OKAY?
...YES.
I'LL BE FINE.

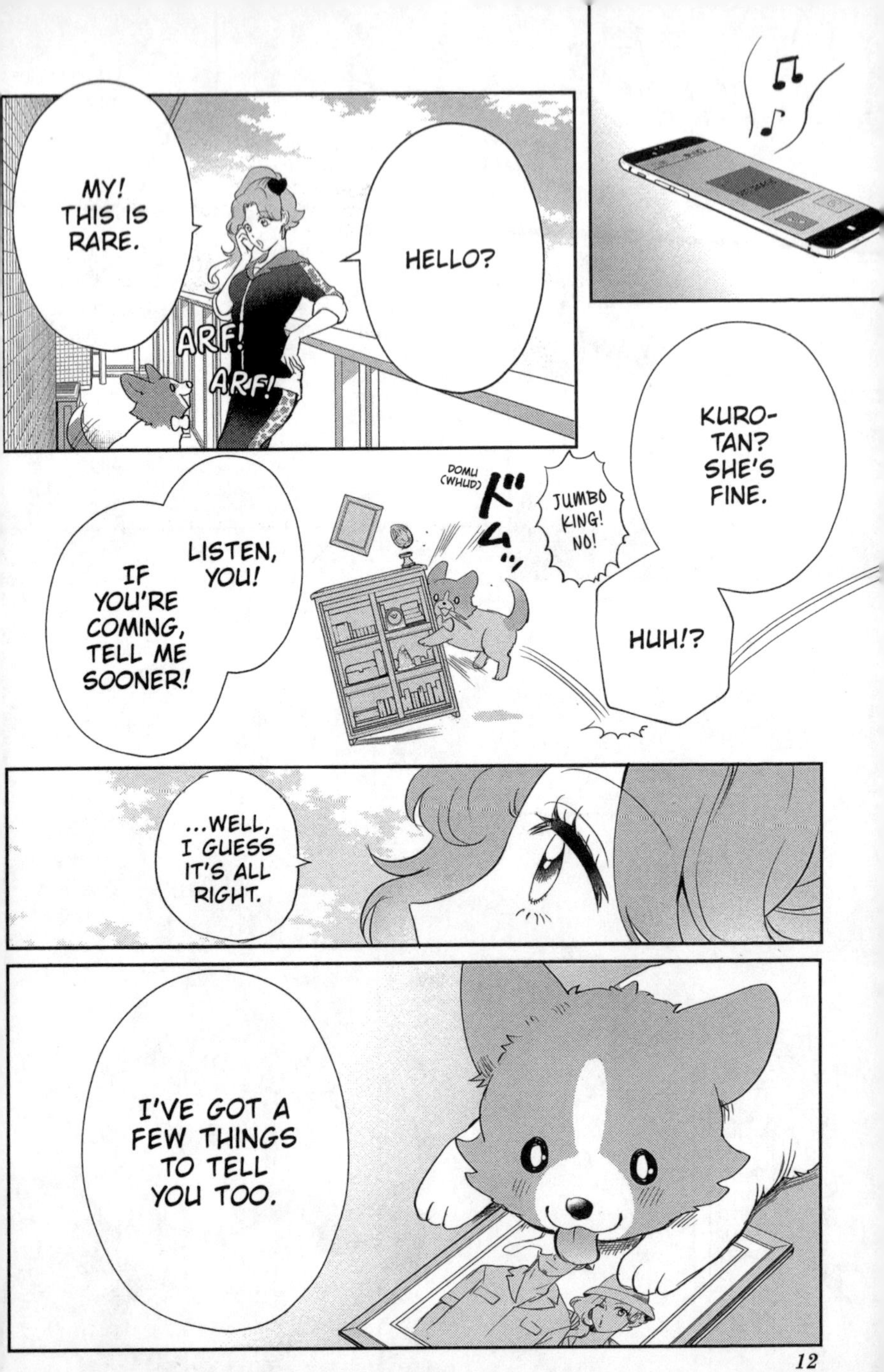
HELLO?
MY! THIS IS RARE.
ARF!
ARF!
KURO-TAN? SHE'S FINE.
HUH!?
JUMBO KING! NO!
DOMU (WHUD)
ドムッ
LISTEN, YOU!
IF YOU'RE COMING, TELL ME SOONER!
...WELL, I GUESS IT'S ALL RIGHT.
I'VE GOT A FEW THINGS TO TELL YOU TOO.

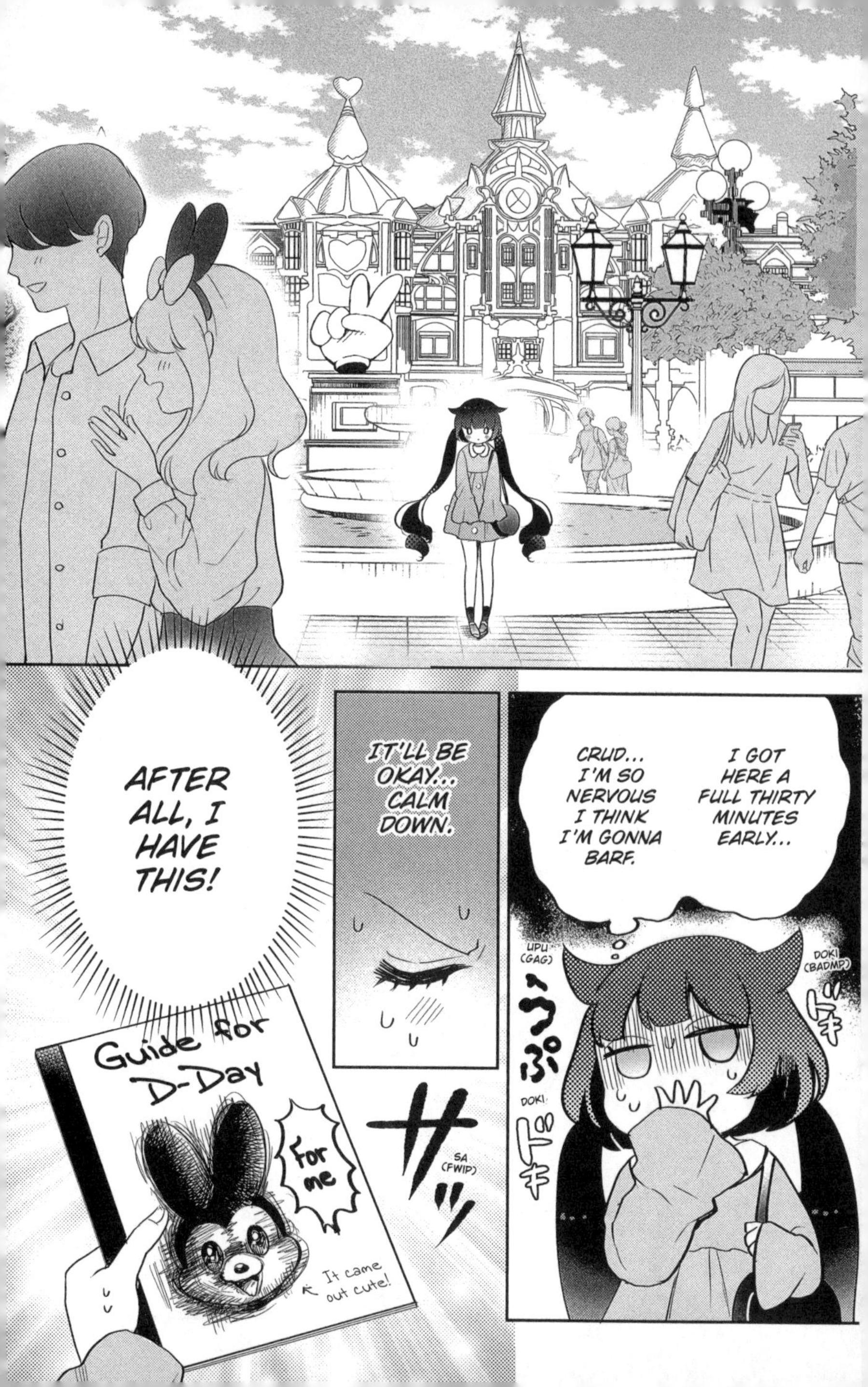
I GOT HERE A FULL THIRTY MINUTES EARLY...
CRUD... I'M SO NERVOUS I THINK I'M GONNA BARF.
DOKI (BADMP)
ドキ
UPU (GAG)
うぷ
DOKI
ドキ
IT'LL BE OKAY... CALM DOWN.
SA (FWIP)
ザッ
AFTER ALL, I HAVE THIS!
Guide for D-Day
for me
It came out cute!

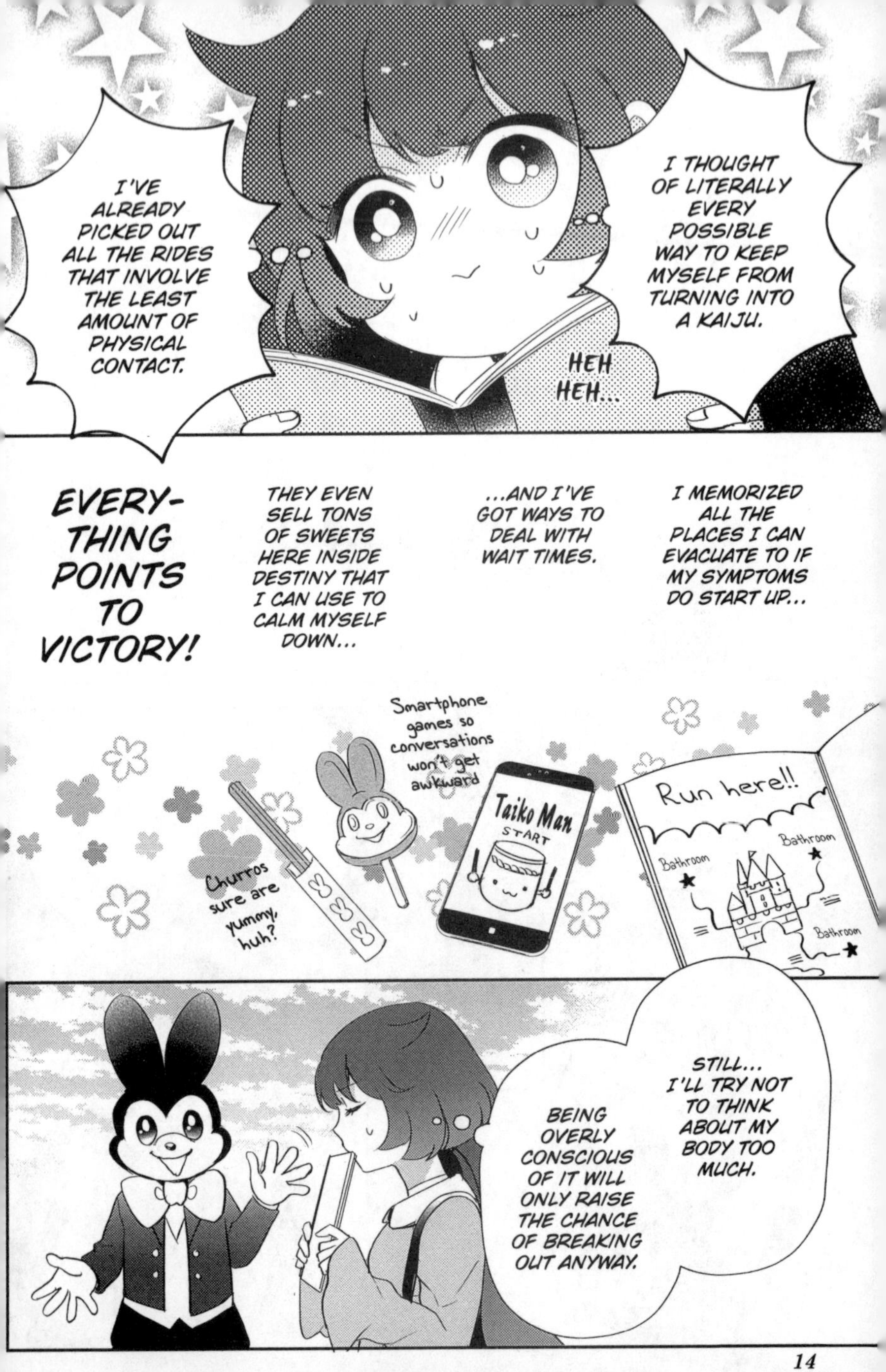
I THOUGHT OF LITERALLY EVERY POSSIBLE WAY TO KEEP MYSELF FROM TURNING INTO A KAIJU.
I'VE ALREADY PICKED OUT ALL THE RIDES THAT INVOLVE THE LEAST AMOUNT OF PHYSICAL CONTACT.
HEH HEH...
I MEMORIZED ALL THE PLACES I CAN EVACUATE TO IF MY SYMPTOMS DO START UP...
...AND I'VE GOT WAYS TO DEAL WITH WAIT TIMES.
THEY EVEN SELL TONS OF SWEETS HERE INSIDE DESTINY THAT I CAN USE TO CALM MYSELF DOWN...
EVERY-THING POINTS TO VICTORY!
Run here!!
Bathroom
Bathroom
Bathroom
Taiko Man
START
Smartphone games so conversations won't get awkward
Churros sure are yummy, huh?
STILL... I'LL TRY NOT TO THINK ABOUT MY BODY TOO MUCH.
BEING OVERLY CONSCIOUS OF IT WILL ONLY RAISE THE CHANCE OF BREAKING OUT ANYWAY.

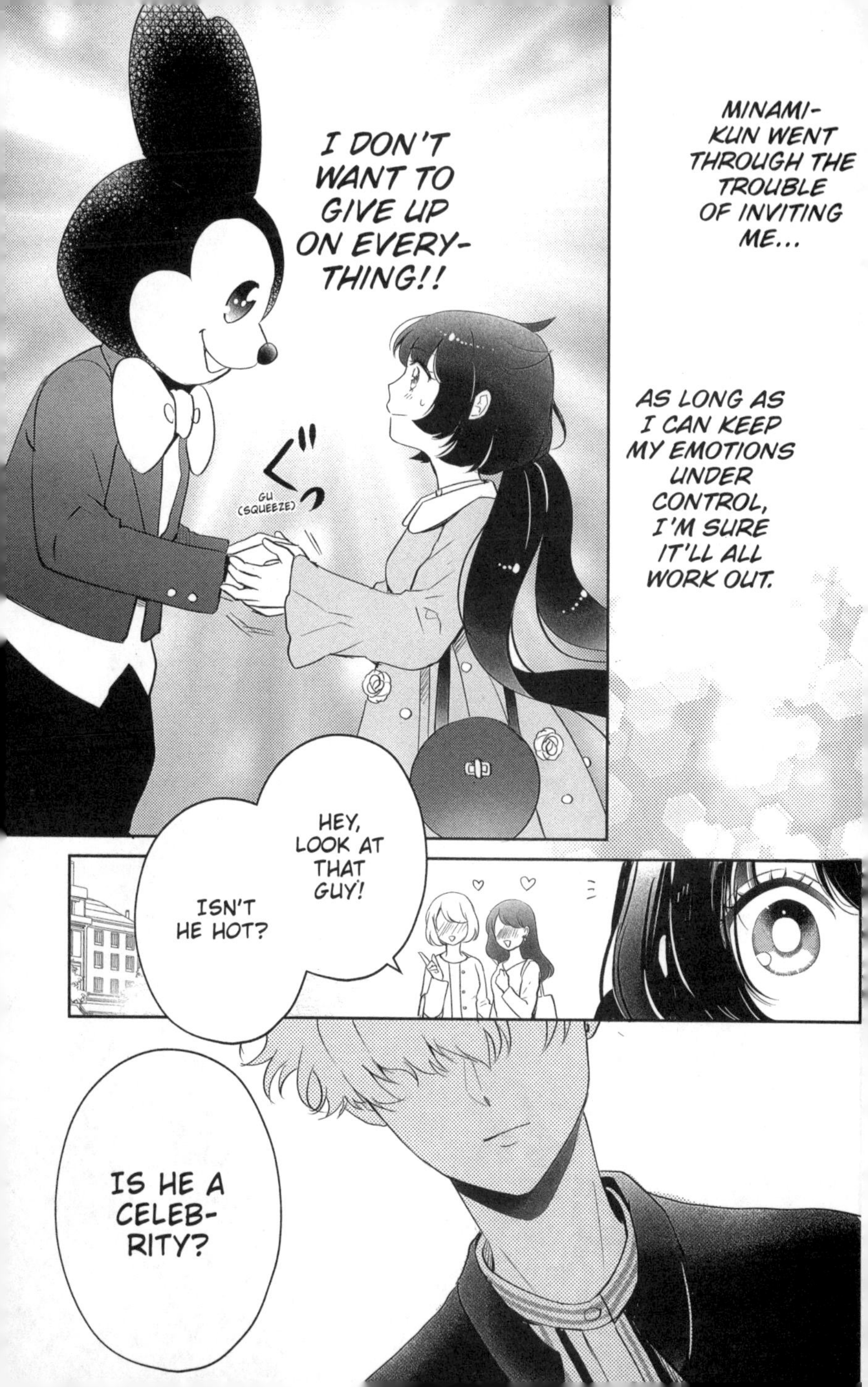
MINAMI-KUN WENT THROUGH THE TROUBLE OF INVITING ME...
I DON'T WANT TO GIVE UP ON EVERY-THING!!
GU (SQUEEZE)
AS LONG AS I CAN KEEP MY EMOTIONS UNDER CONTROL, I'M SURE IT'LL ALL WORK OUT.
HEY, LOOK AT THAT GUY!
ISN'T HE HOT?
IS HE A CELEB-RITY?

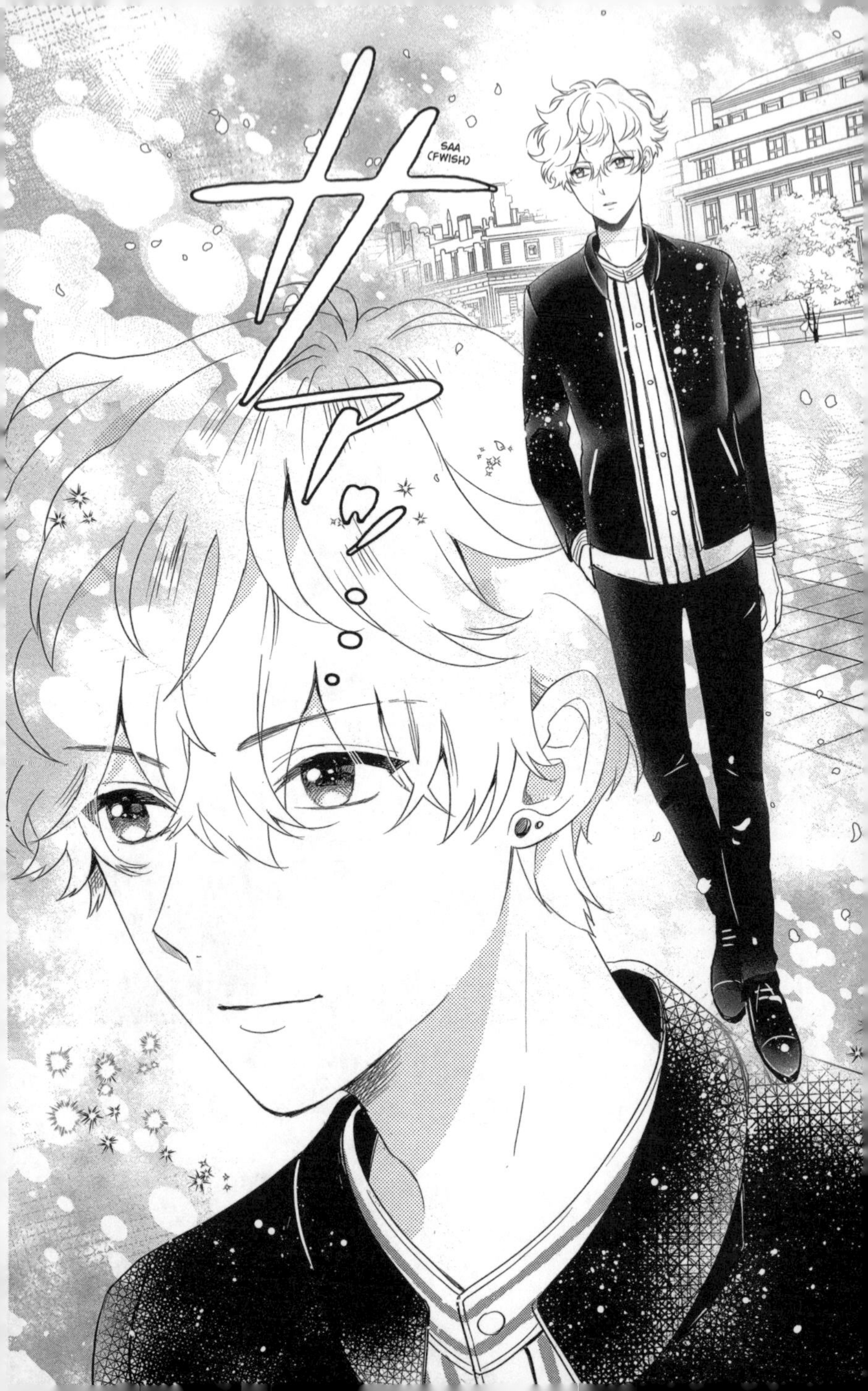
サァ
SAA
(FWISH)

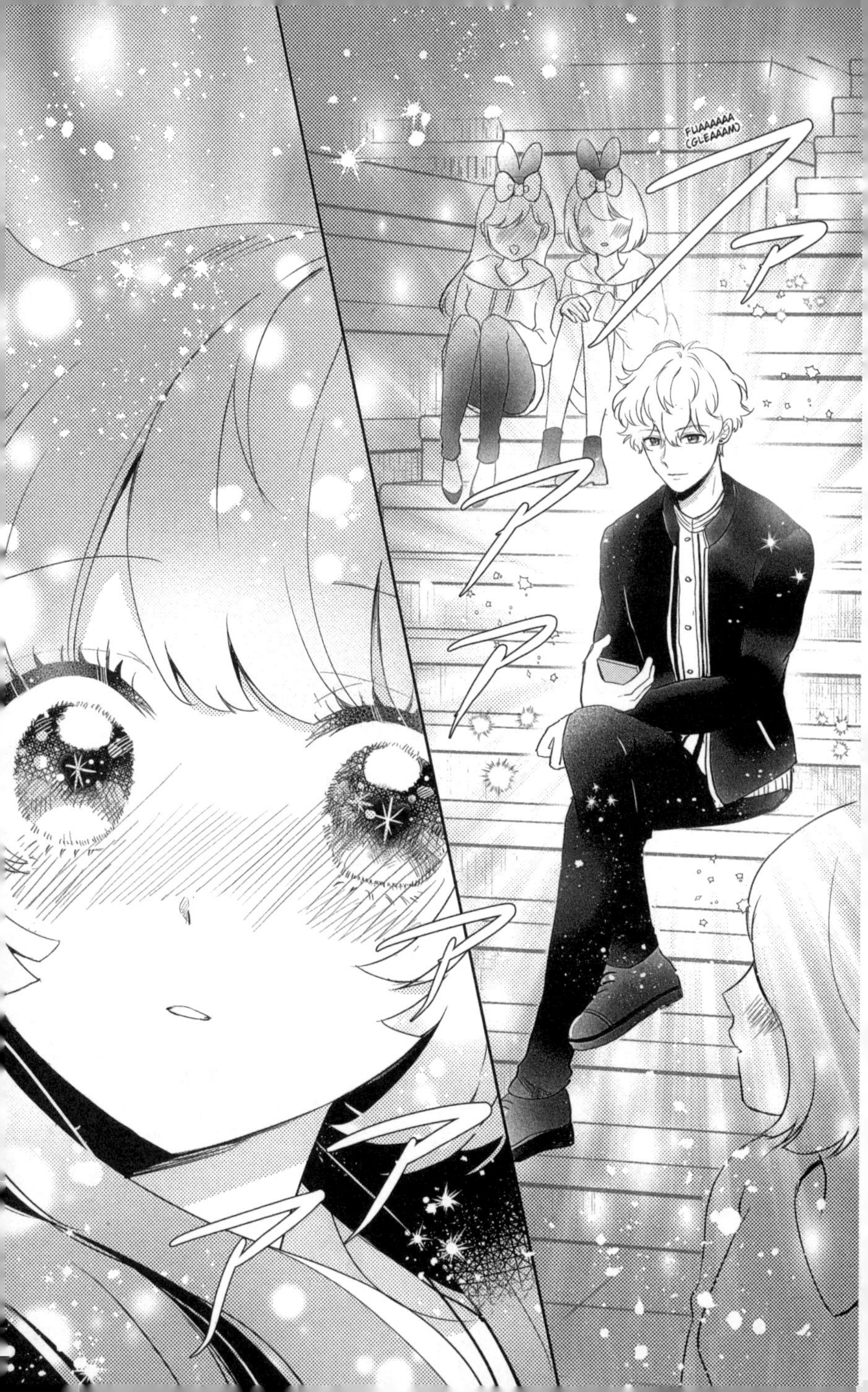
FUAAAAAA
(GLEAAAM)

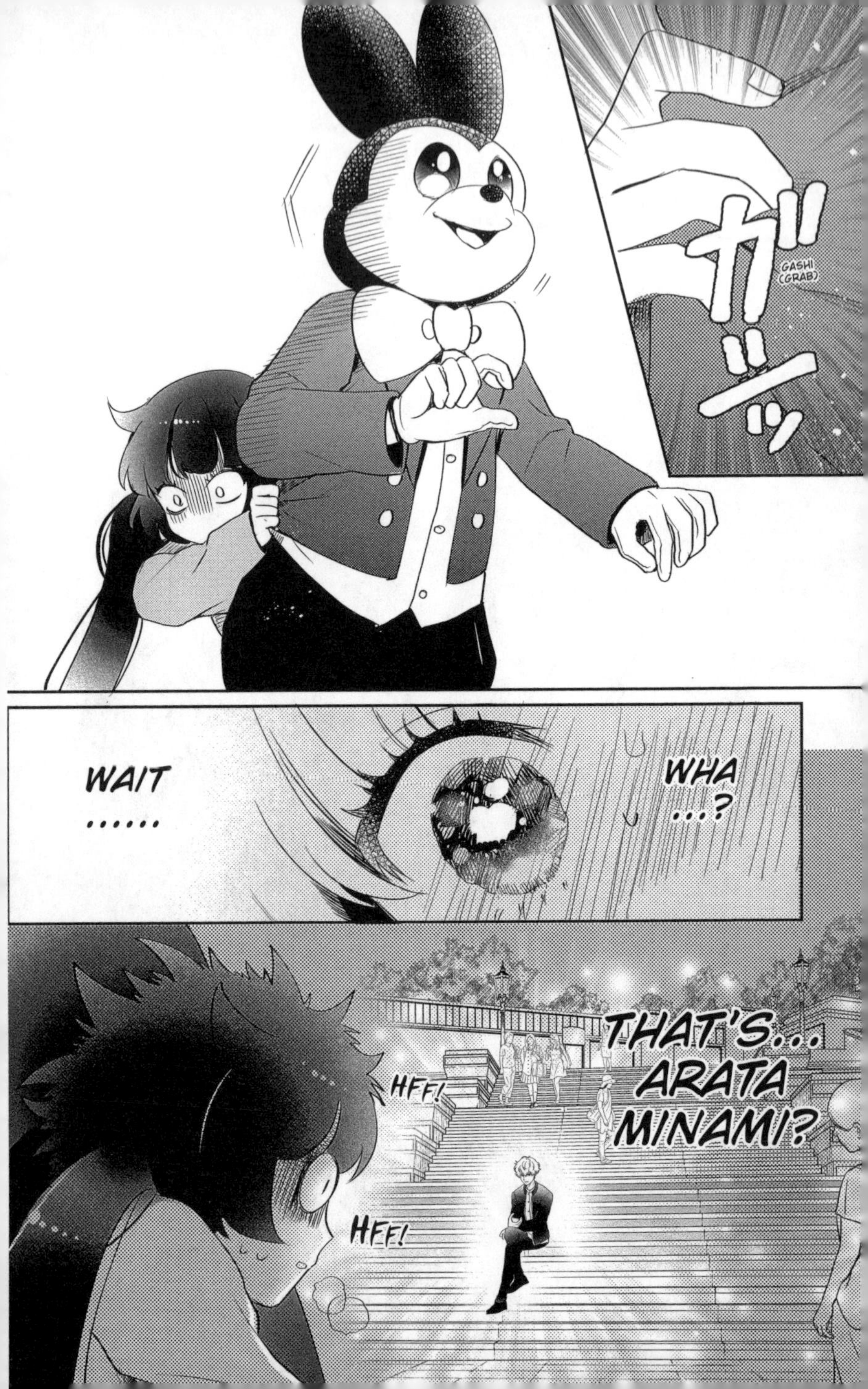
GASHI (GRAB)
WHA ...?
WAIT ......
THAT'S... ARATA MINAMI?
HFF!
HFF!

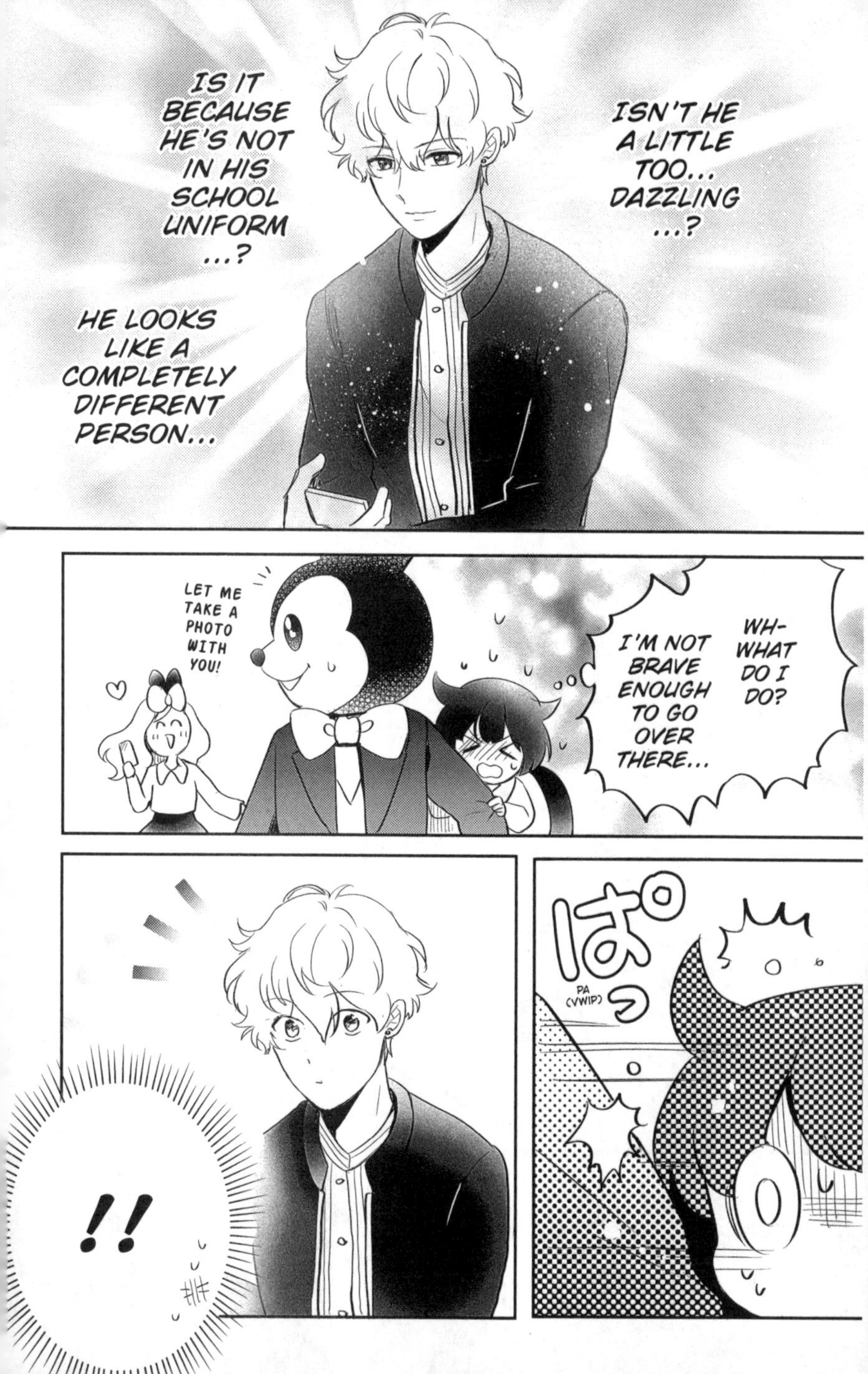
ISN'T HE A LITTLE TOO... DAZZLING ...?
IS IT BECAUSE HE'S NOT IN HIS SCHOOL UNIFORM ...?
HE LOOKS LIKE A COMPLETELY DIFFERENT PERSON...
WH- WHAT DO I DO?
I'M NOT BRAVE ENOUGH TO GO OVER THERE...
LET ME TAKE A PHOTO WITH YOU!
ぱっ
PA (VWIP)
!!

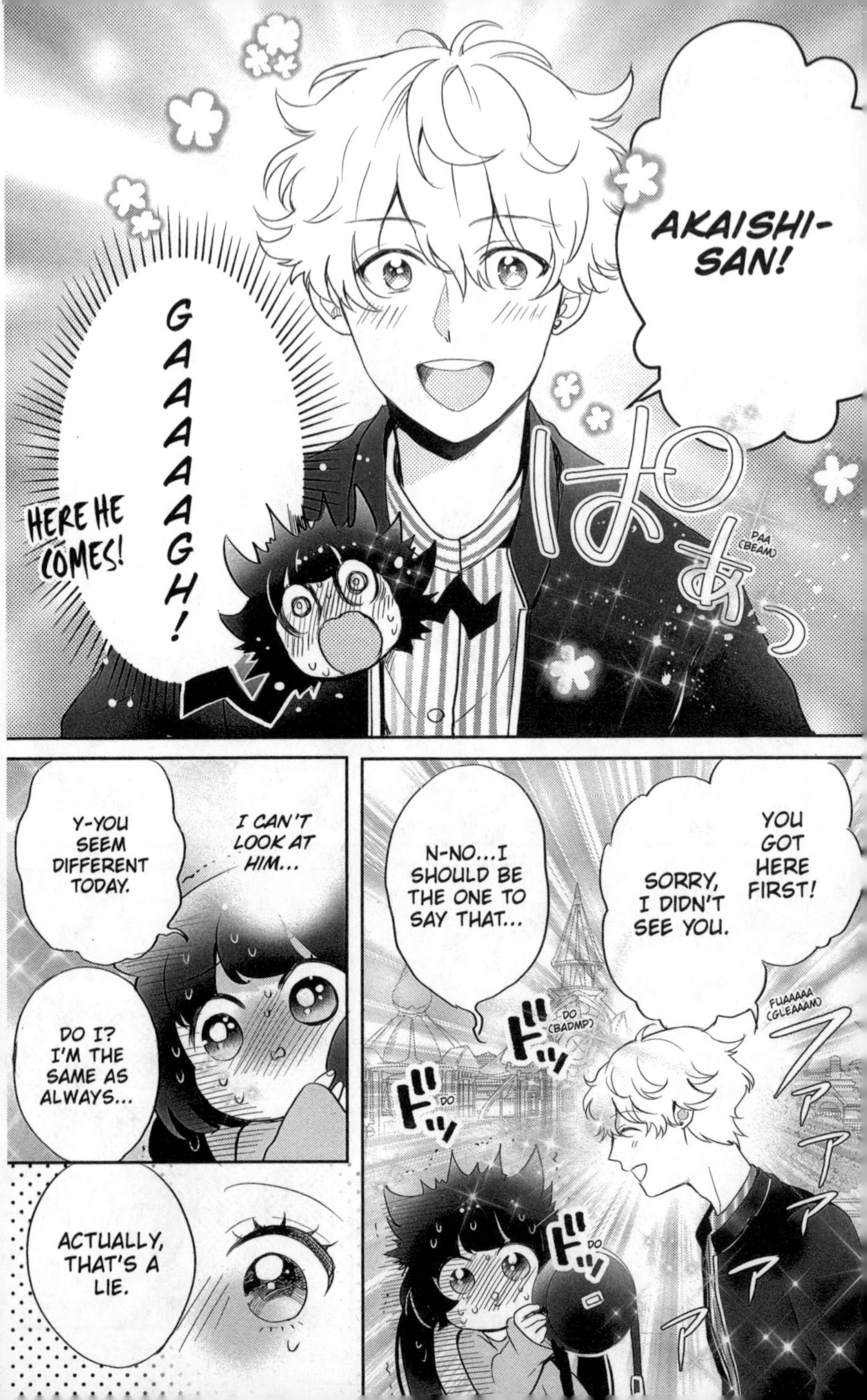
AKAISHI-SAN!
ぱあっ
PAA (BEAM)
GAAAAAAGH!
HERE HE COMES!
YOU GOT HERE FIRST!
SORRY, I DIDN'T SEE YOU.
ファアアア
FUAAAAA (GLEAAAM)
N-NO...I SHOULD BE THE ONE TO SAY THAT...
ドッ
DO (BADMP)
ドッ
DO
ドッ
DO
I CAN'T LOOK AT HIM...
Y-YOU SEEM DIFFERENT TODAY.
DO I? I'M THE SAME AS ALWAYS...
ACTUALLY, THAT'S A LIE.

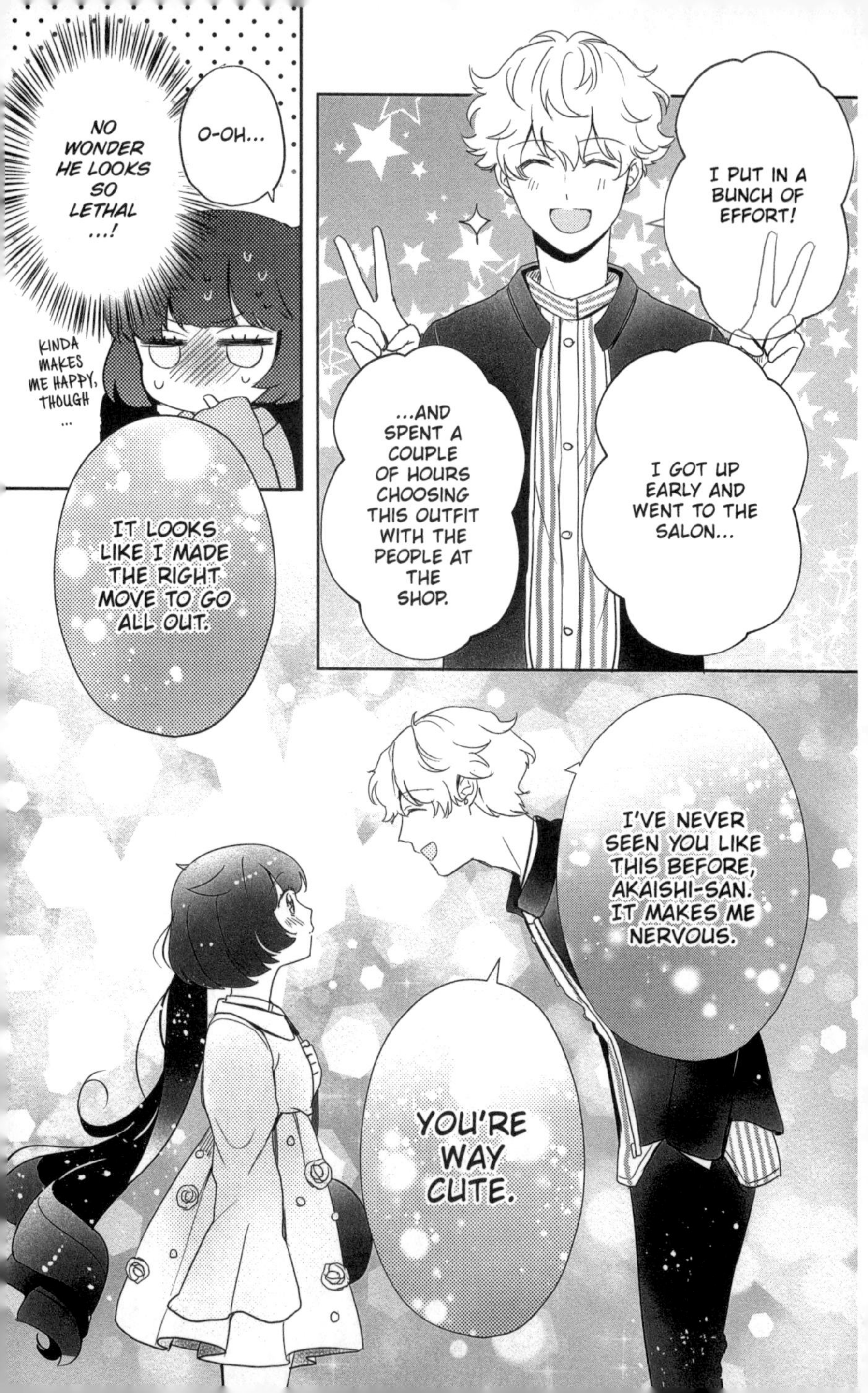
I PUT IN A BUNCH OF EFFORT!
I GOT UP EARLY AND WENT TO THE SALON...
...AND SPENT A COUPLE OF HOURS CHOOSING THIS OUTFIT WITH THE PEOPLE AT THE SHOP.
O-OH...
NO WONDER HE LOOKS SO LETHAL...!
KINDA MAKES ME HAPPY, THOUGH...
IT LOOKS LIKE I MADE THE RIGHT MOVE TO GO ALL OUT.
I'VE NEVER SEEN YOU LIKE THIS BEFORE, AKAISHI-SAN. IT MAKES ME NERVOUS.
YOU'RE WAY CUTE.

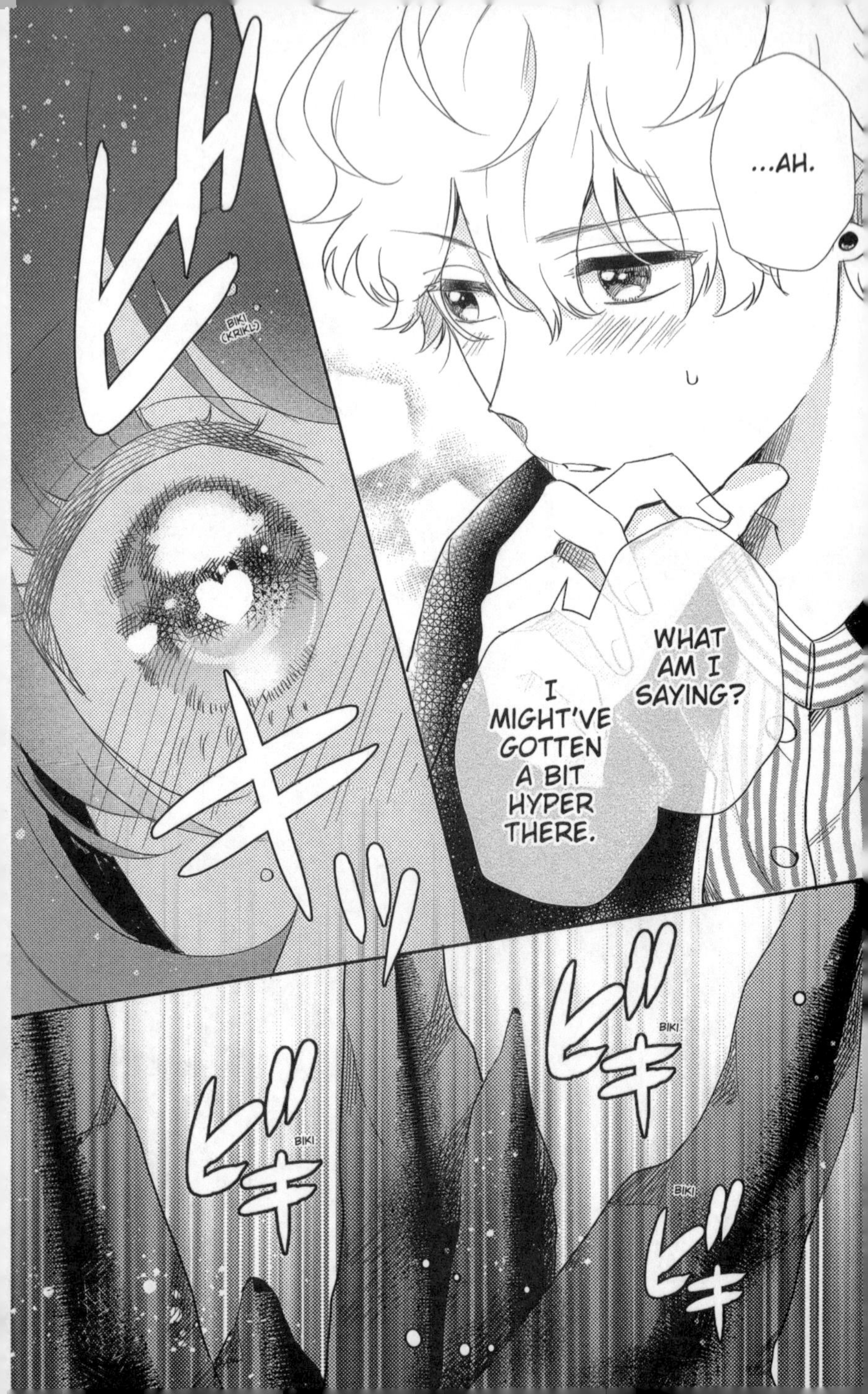
...AH.
WHAT AM I SAYING?
I MIGHT'VE GOTTEN A BIT HYPER THERE.
BIKI (KRIKL)
BIKI
BIKI
BIKI

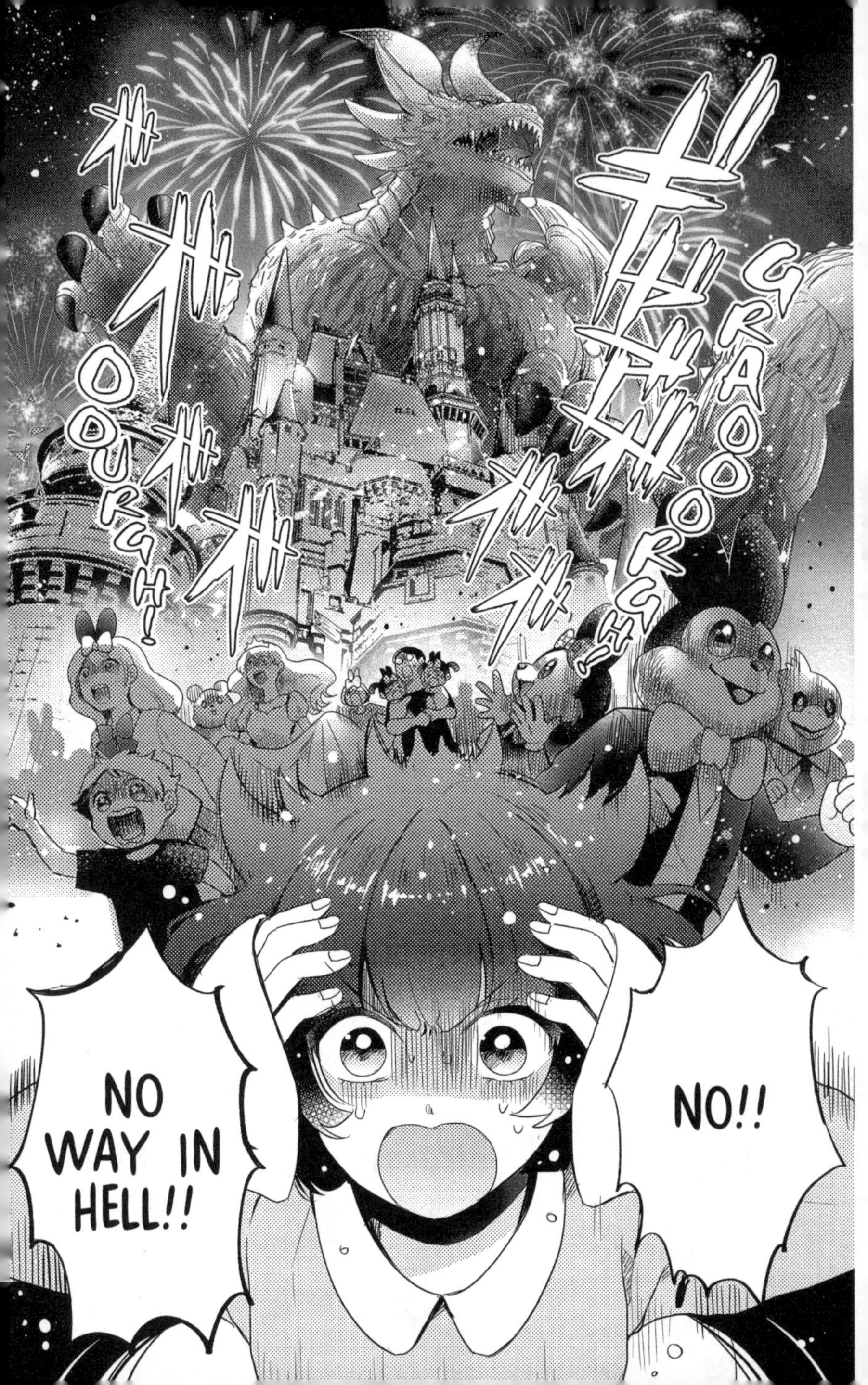
GRAOOORGH!
OOURGH!
NO!!
NO WAY IN HELL!!

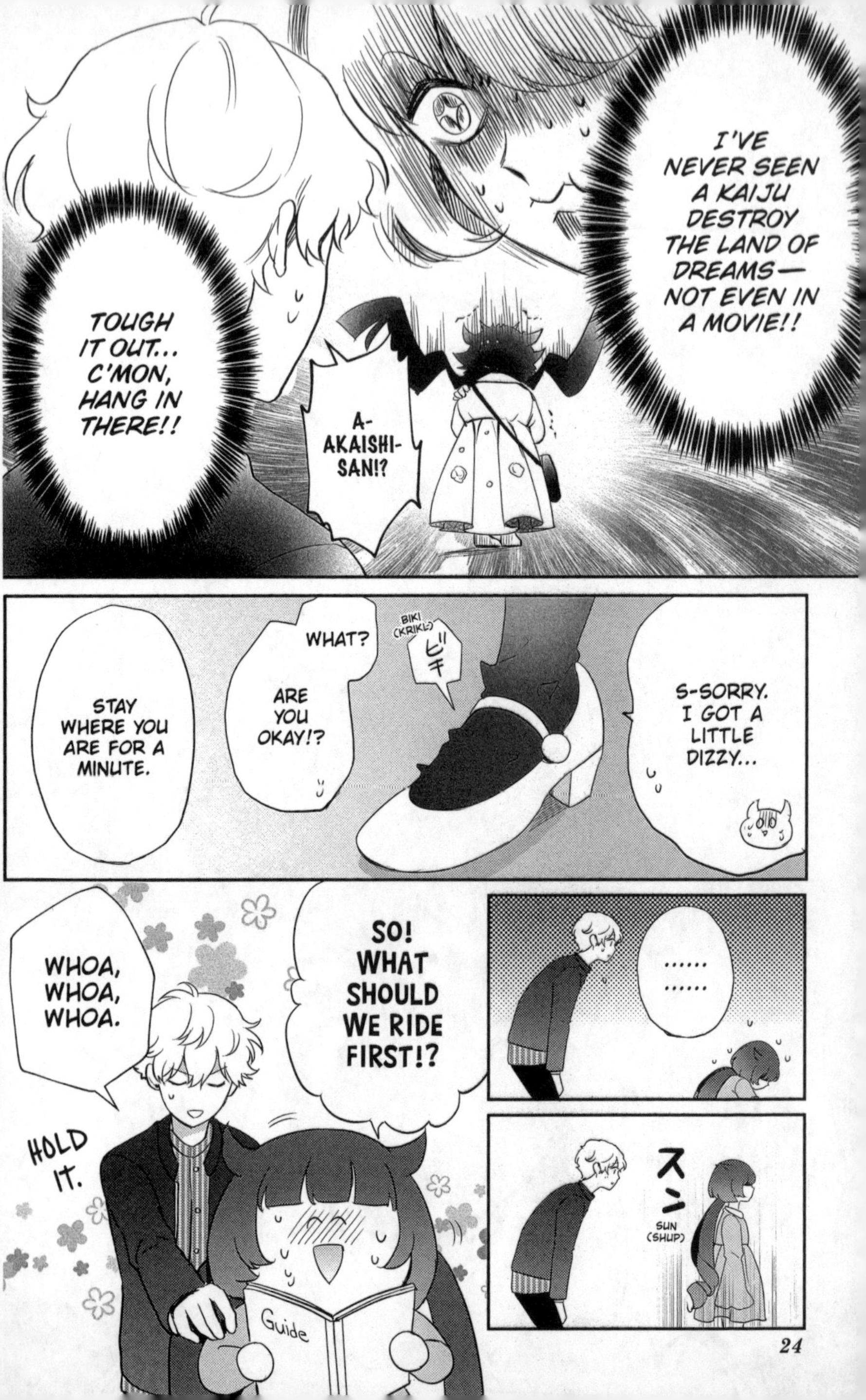
I'VE NEVER SEEN A KAIJU DESTROY THE LAND OF DREAMS— NOT EVEN IN A MOVIE!!
A-AKAISHI-SAN!?
TOUGH IT OUT... C'MON, HANG IN THERE!!
S-SORRY. I GOT A LITTLE DIZZY...
ビキ
BIKI (KRIKI)
WHAT?
ARE YOU OKAY!?
STAY WHERE YOU ARE FOR A MINUTE.
....
スン
SUN (SHUP)
SO! WHAT SHOULD WE RIDE FIRST!?
WHOA, WHOA, WHOA.
HOLD IT.
Guide

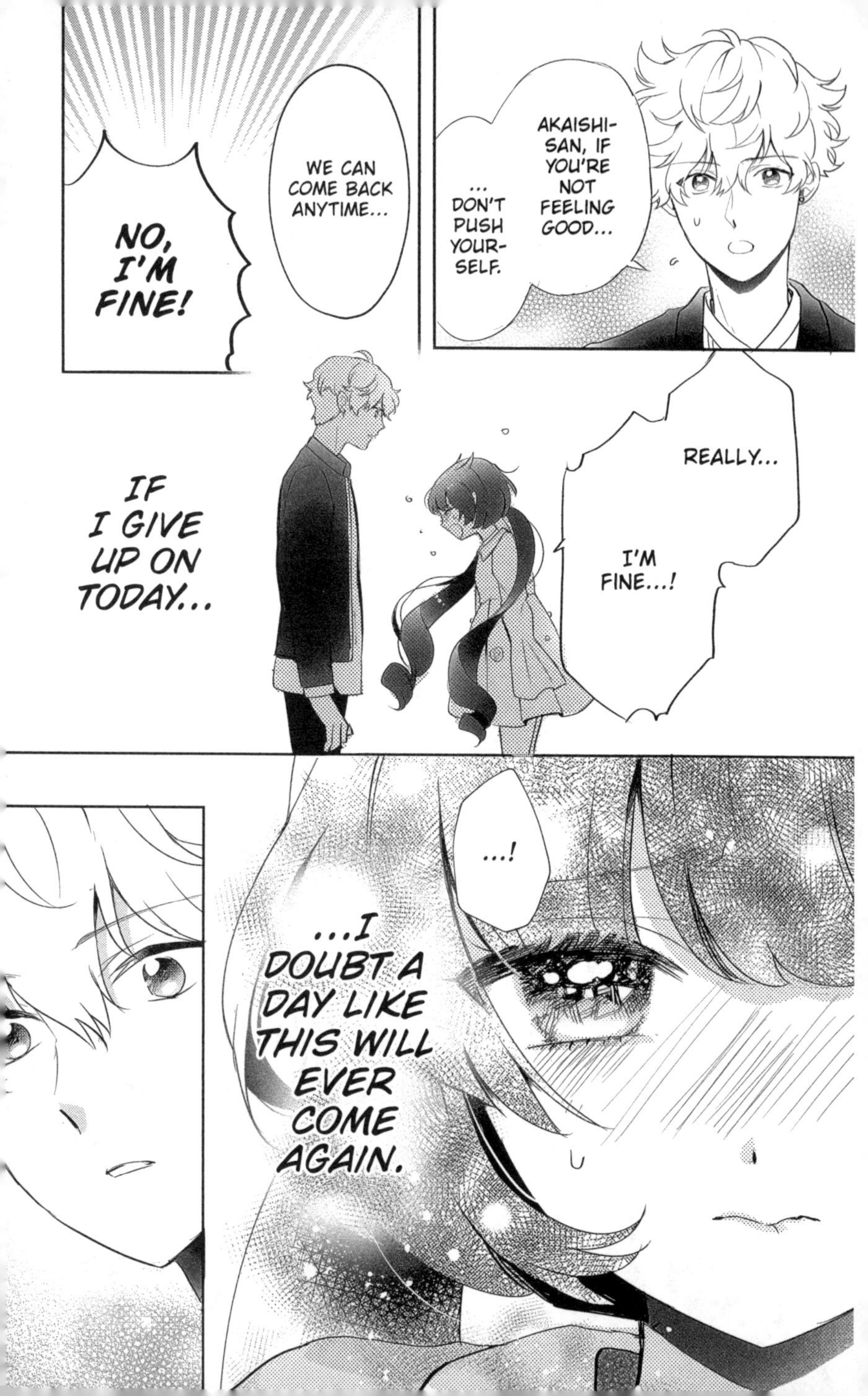
AKAISHI-SAN, IF YOU'RE NOT FEELING GOOD...
... DON'T PUSH YOURSELF.
WE CAN COME BACK ANYTIME...
NO, I'M FINE!
REALLY...
I'M FINE...!
IF I GIVE UP ON TODAY...
...!
...I DOUBT A DAY LIKE THIS WILL EVER COME AGAIN.

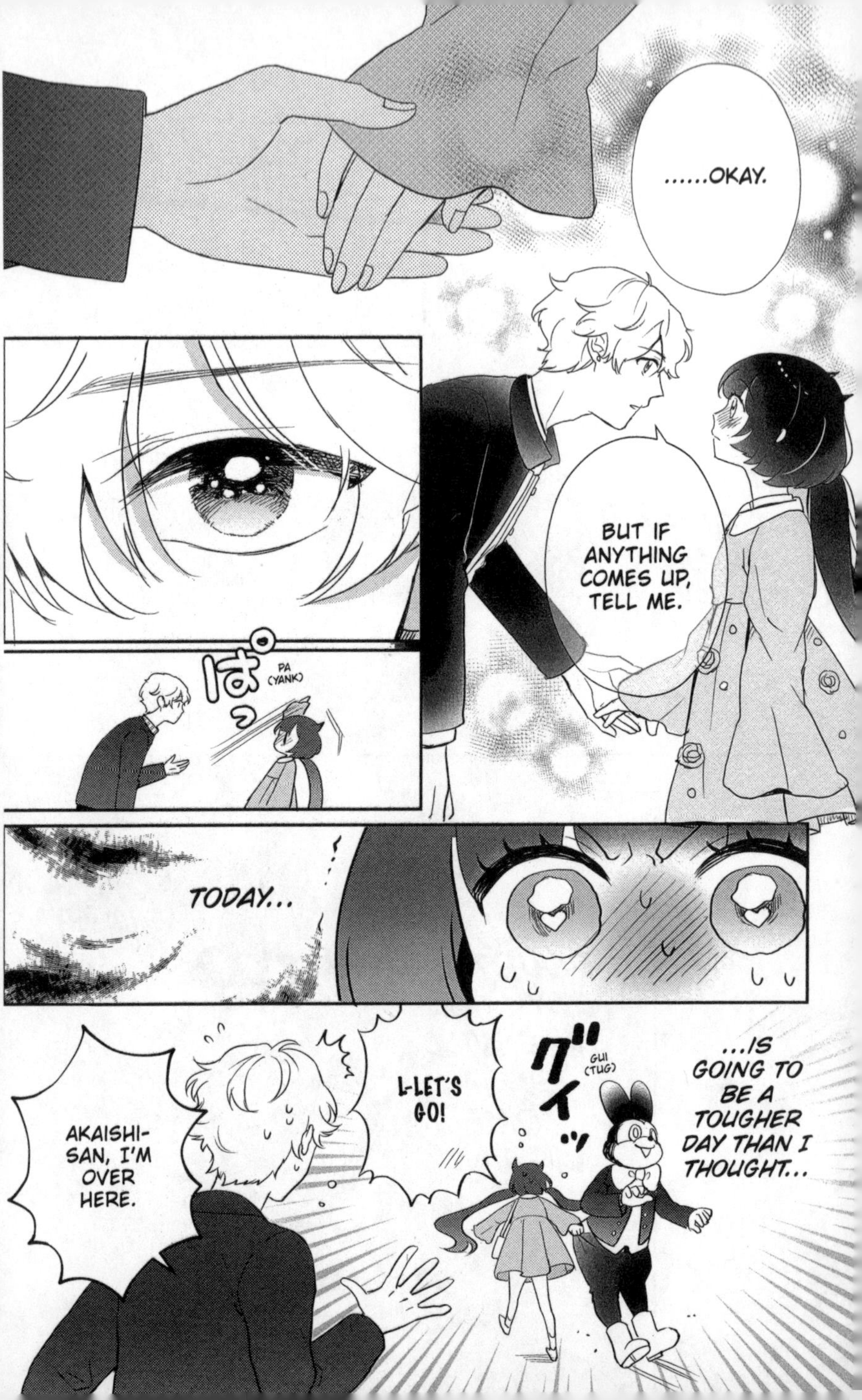
......OKAY.
BUT IF ANYTHING COMES UP, TELL ME.
ぱっ
PA (YANK)
TODAY...
...IS GOING TO BE A TOUGHER DAY THAN I THOUGHT...
グイッ
GUI (TUG)
L-LET'S GO!
AKAISHI-SAN, I'M OVER HERE.

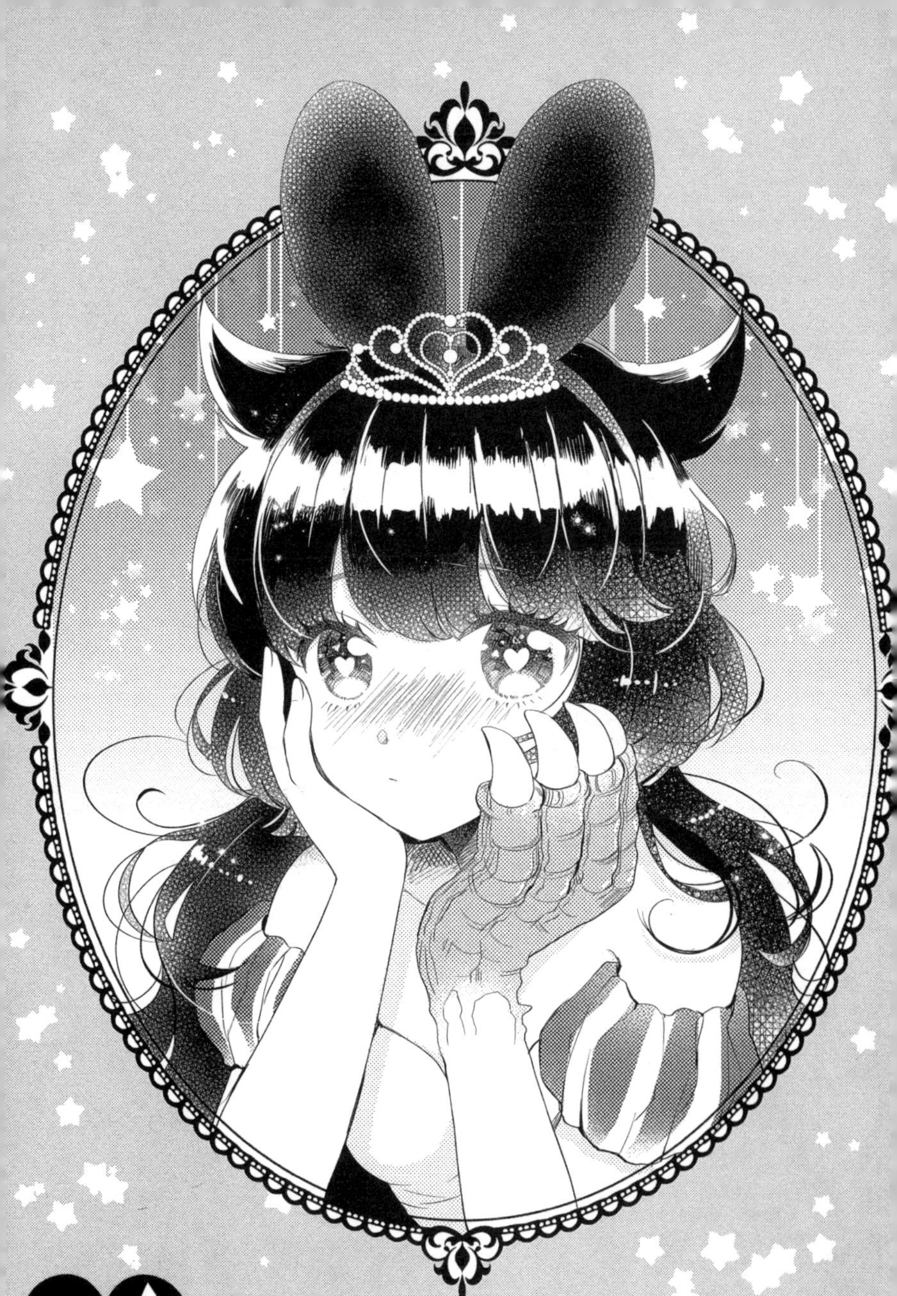

Chapter 6: Meanwhile, the Kaiju's Mom Was...

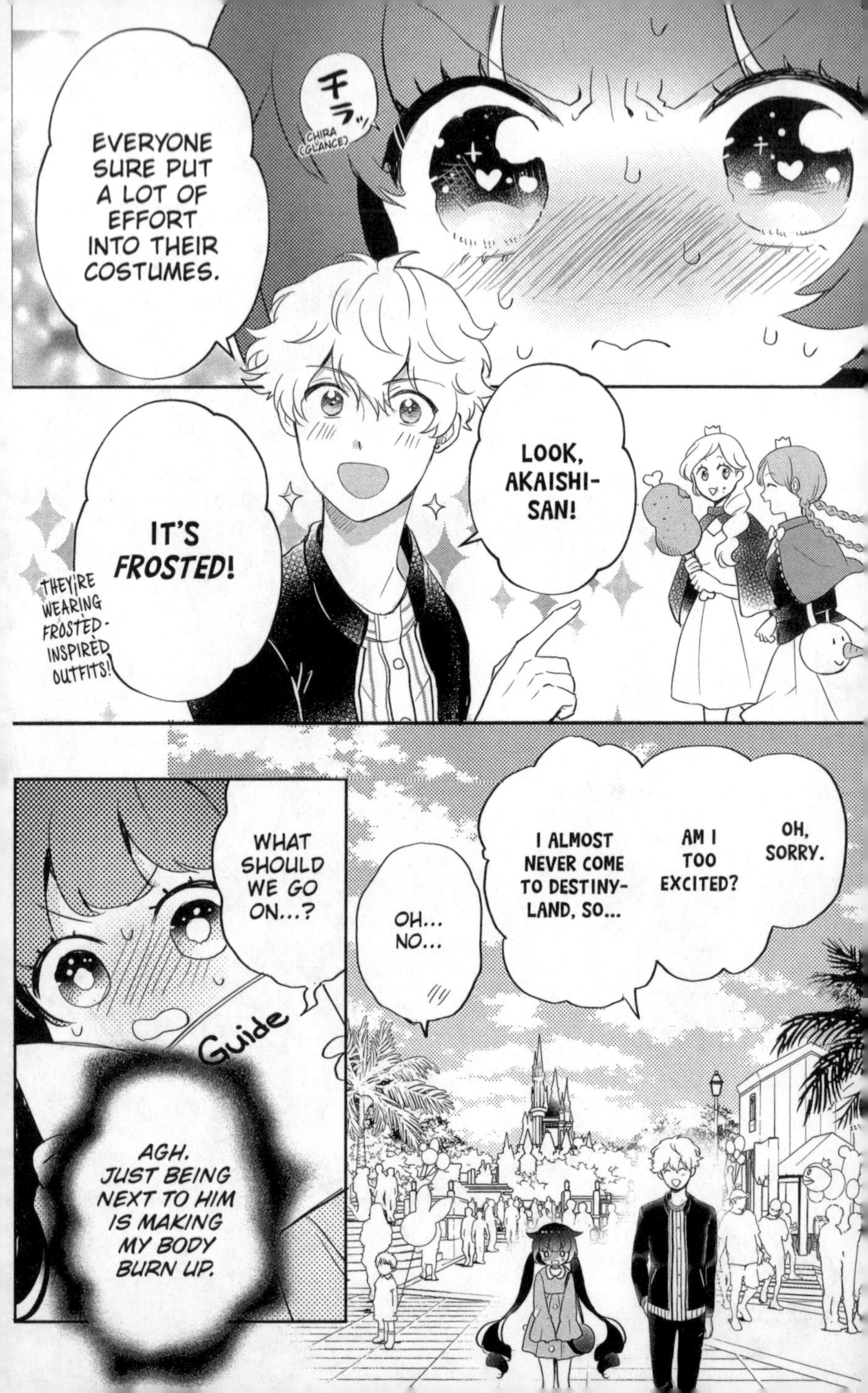
チラッ
CHIRA (GLANCE)
EVERYONE SURE PUT A LOT OF EFFORT INTO THEIR COSTUMES.
LOOK, AKAISHI-SAN!
IT'S *FROSTED*!
THEY'RE WEARING FROSTED-INSPIRED OUTFITS!
OH, SORRY.
AM I TOO EXCITED?
I ALMOST NEVER COME TO DESTINY-LAND, SO...
OH... NO...
WHAT SHOULD WE GO ON...?
Guide
AGH. JUST BEING NEXT TO HIM IS MAKING MY BODY BURN UP.

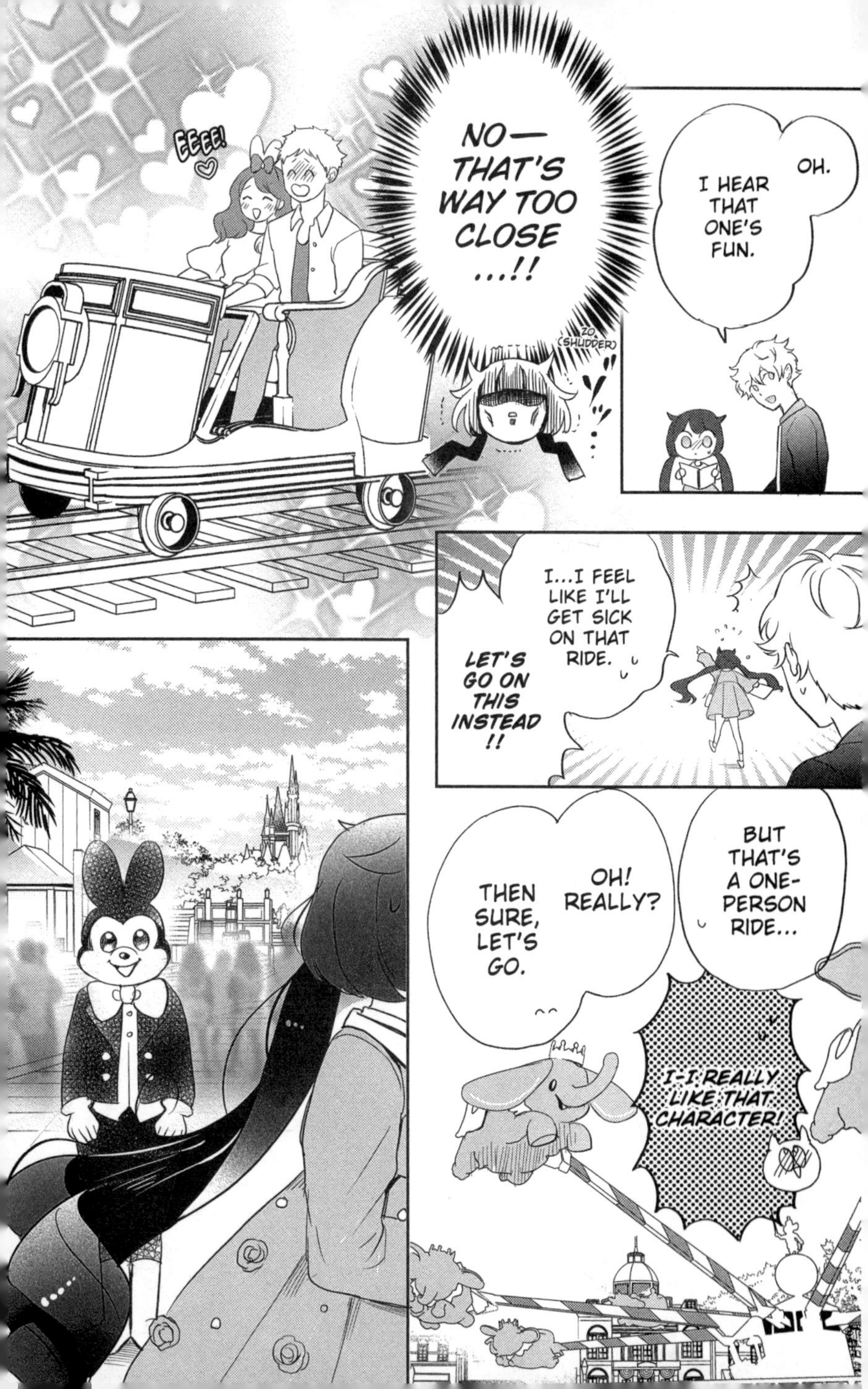
OH.
I HEAR THAT ONE'S FUN.
NO— THAT'S WAY TOO CLOSE ...!!
EEEE!
ZO (SHUDDER)
I...I FEEL LIKE I'LL GET SICK ON THAT RIDE.
LET'S GO ON THIS INSTEAD !!
BUT THAT'S A ONE-PERSON RIDE...
OH! REALLY?
THEN SURE, LET'S GO.
I-I REALLY LIKE THAT CHARACTER!

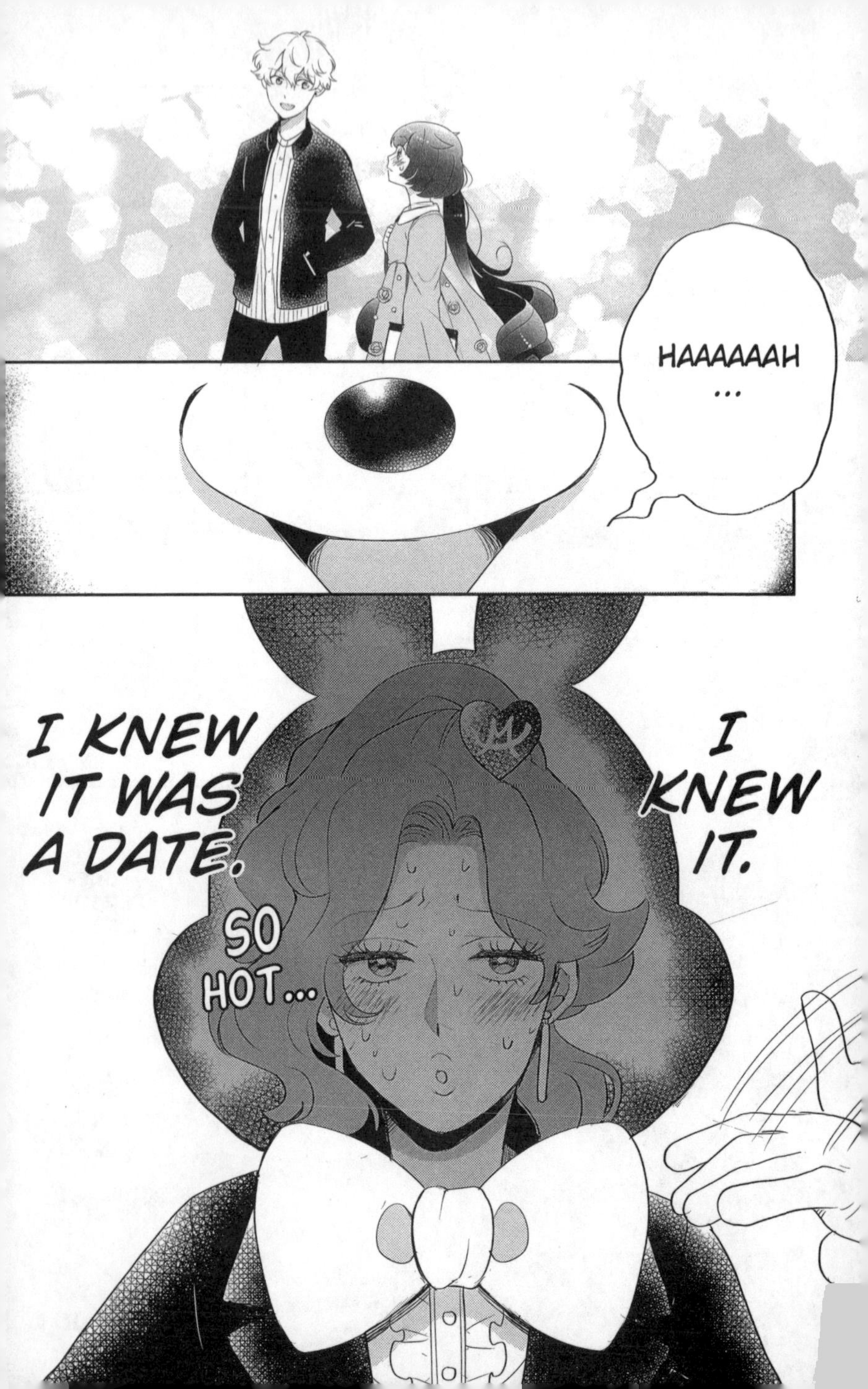
HAAAAAAH
…
I KNEW IT.
I KNEW IT WAS A DATE.
SO HOT…

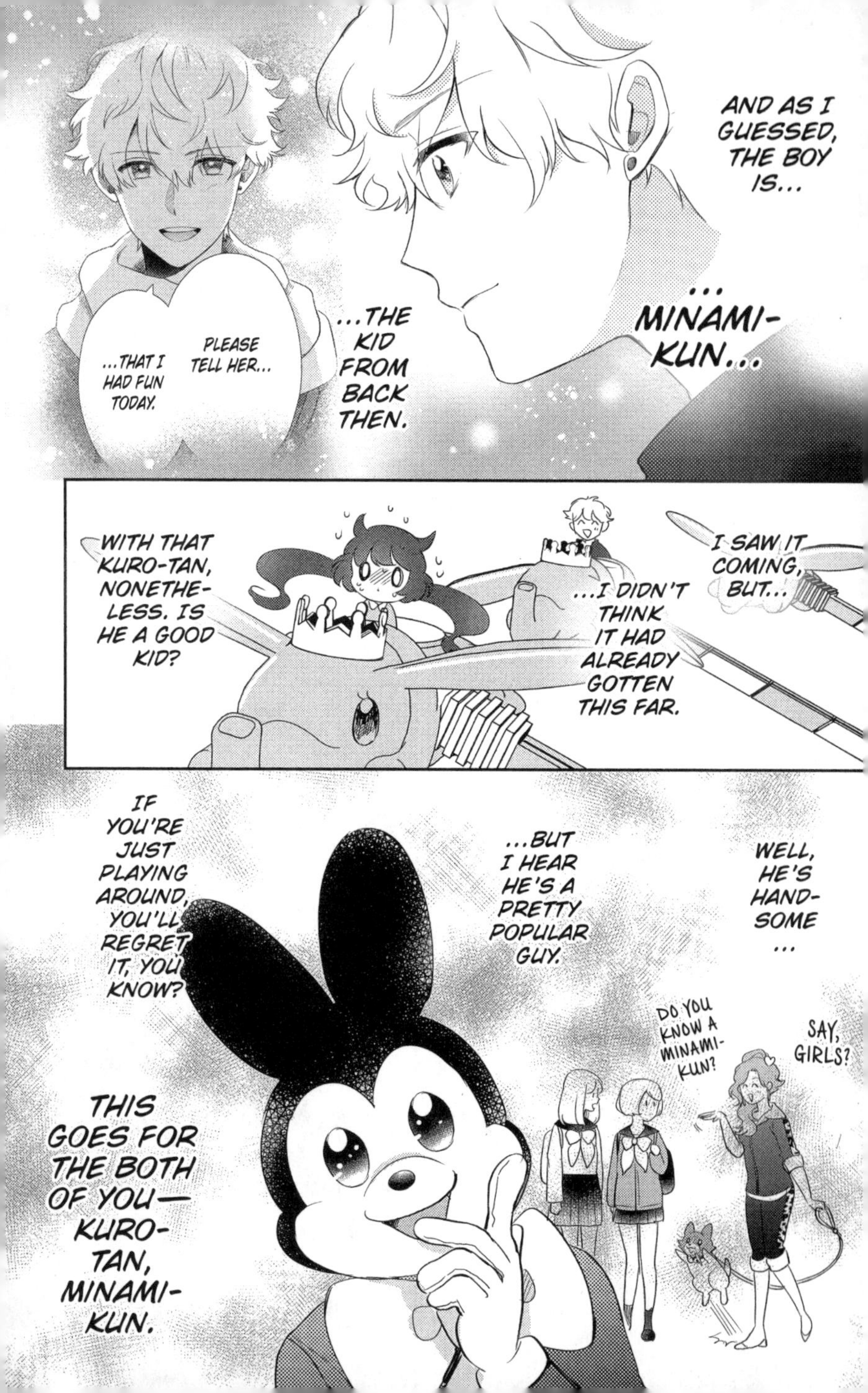
AND AS I GUESSED, THE BOY IS...
...MINAMI-KUN...
...THE KID FROM BACK THEN.
PLEASE TELL HER...
...THAT I HAD FUN TODAY.
I SAW IT COMING, BUT...
...I DIDN'T THINK IT HAD ALREADY GOTTEN THIS FAR.
WITH THAT KURO-TAN, NONETHELESS. IS HE A GOOD KID?
SAY, GIRLS?
DO YOU KNOW A MINAMI-KUN?
WELL, HE'S HANDSOME...
...BUT I HEAR HE'S A PRETTY POPULAR GUY.
IF YOU'RE JUST PLAYING AROUND, YOU'LL REGRET IT, YOU KNOW?
THIS GOES FOR THE BOTH OF YOU—KURO-TAN, MINAMI-KUN.

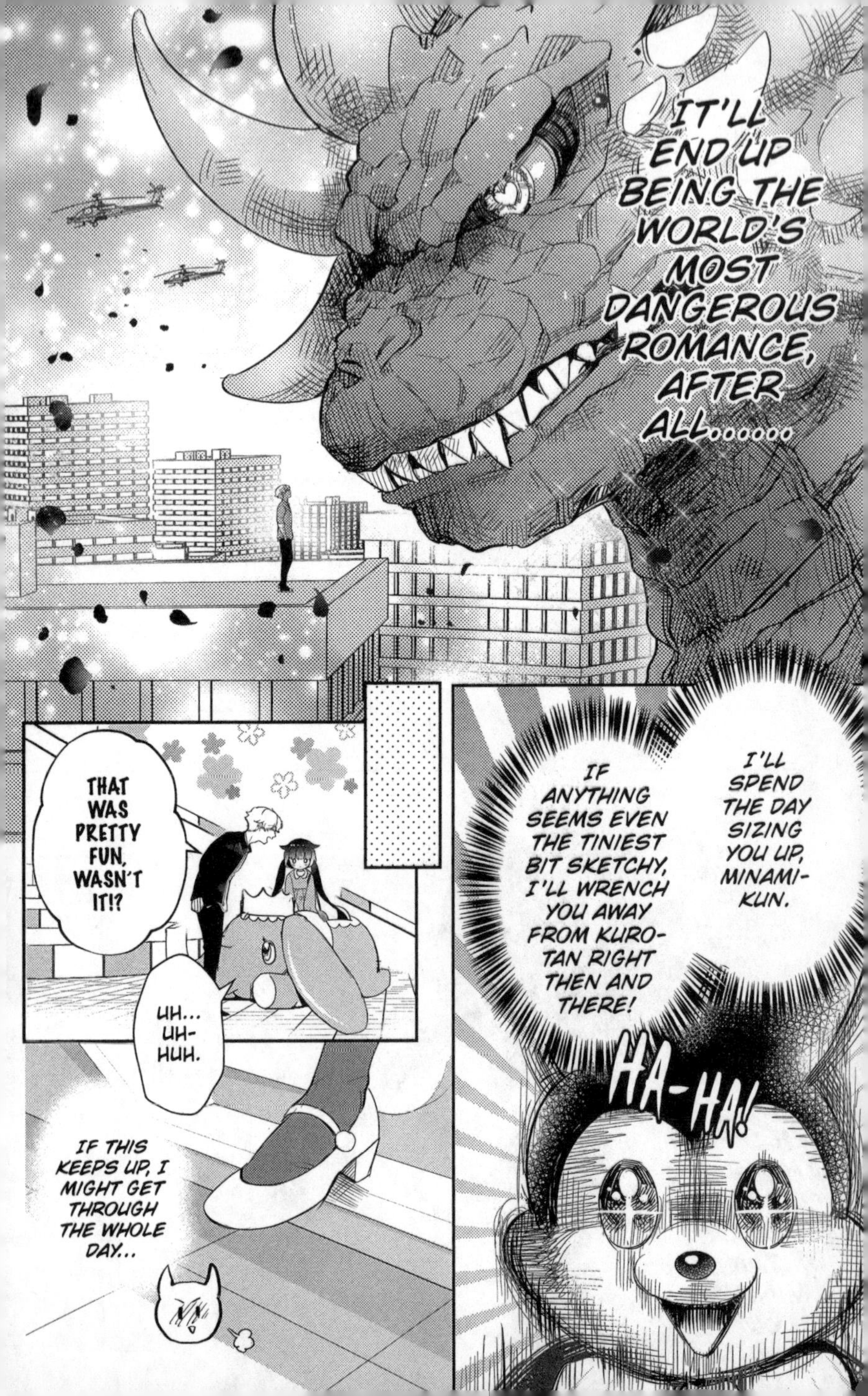
IT'LL END UP BEING THE WORLD'S MOST DANGEROUS ROMANCE, AFTER ALL......
I'LL SPEND THE DAY SIZING YOU UP, MINAMI-KUN.
IF ANYTHING SEEMS EVEN THE TINIEST BIT SKETCHY, I'LL WRENCH YOU AWAY FROM KURO-TAN RIGHT THEN AND THERE!
HA-HA!
THAT WAS PRETTY FUN, WASN'T IT!?
UH... UH-HUH.
IF THIS KEEPS UP, I MIGHT GET THROUGH THE WHOLE DAY...

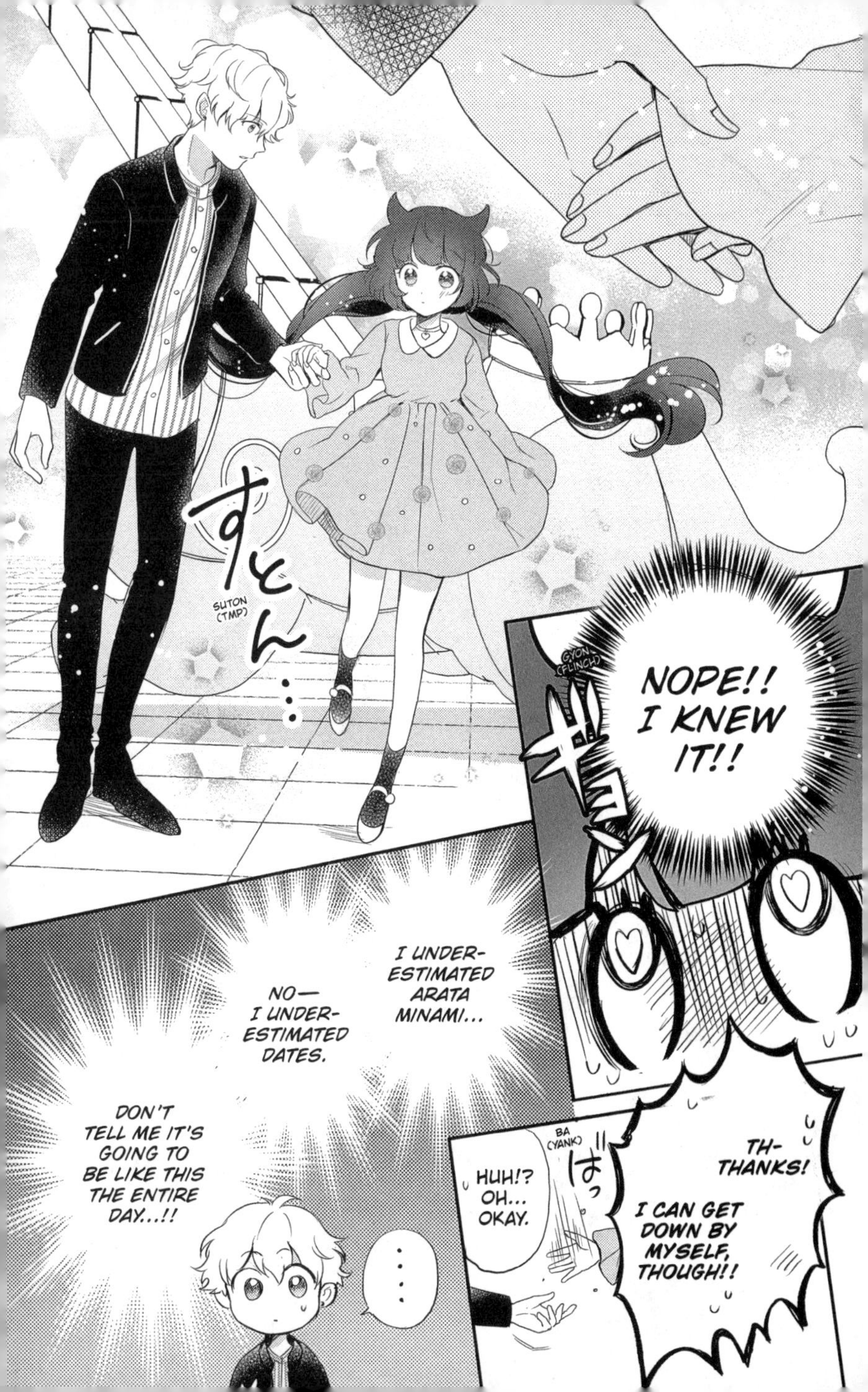
すとん…
SUTON (TMP)
GYON (FLINCH)
NOPE!! I KNEW IT!!
TH-THANKS!
I CAN GET DOWN BY MYSELF, THOUGH!!
ばっ
BA (YANK)
HUH!? OH... OKAY.
I UNDER-ESTIMATED ARATA MINAMI...
NO— I UNDER-ESTIMATED DATES.
DON'T TELL ME IT'S GOING TO BE LIKE THIS THE ENTIRE DAY...!!
....

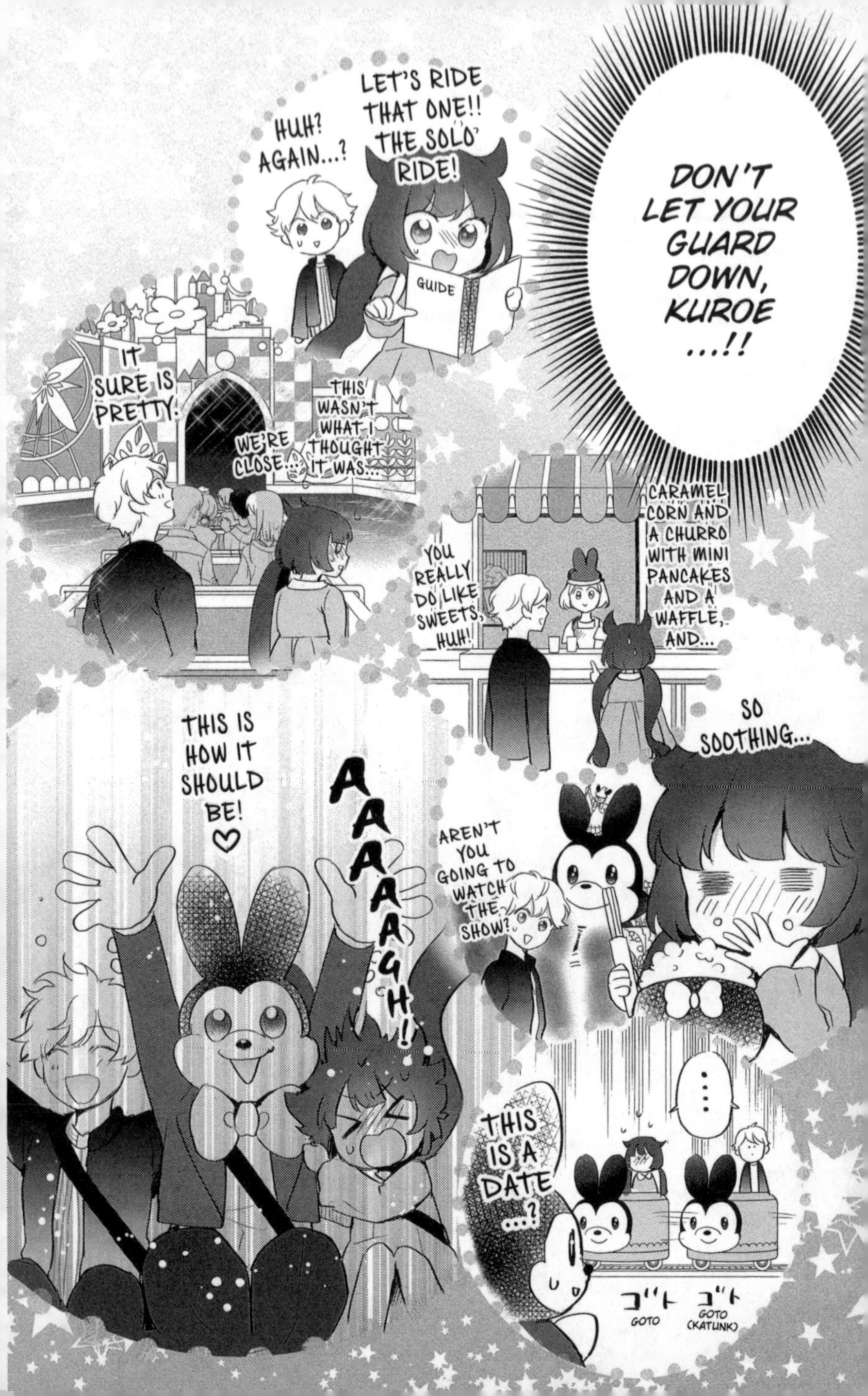
DON'T LET YOUR GUARD DOWN, KUROE...!!
LET'S RIDE THAT ONE!! THE SOLO RIDE!
HUH? AGAIN...?
GUIDE
CARAMEL CORN AND A CHURRO WITH MINI PANCAKES AND A WAFFLE, AND...
YOU REALLY DO LIKE SWEETS, HUH!
THIS WASN'T WHAT I THOUGHT IT WAS...
IT SURE IS PRETTY.
WE'RE CLOSE.
SO SOOTHING...
AREN'T YOU GOING TO WATCH THE SHOW?
....
THIS IS A DATE...?
ゴットゴット
GOTO GOTO (KATUNK)
THIS IS HOW IT SHOULD BE! ♡
AAAAAAGH!

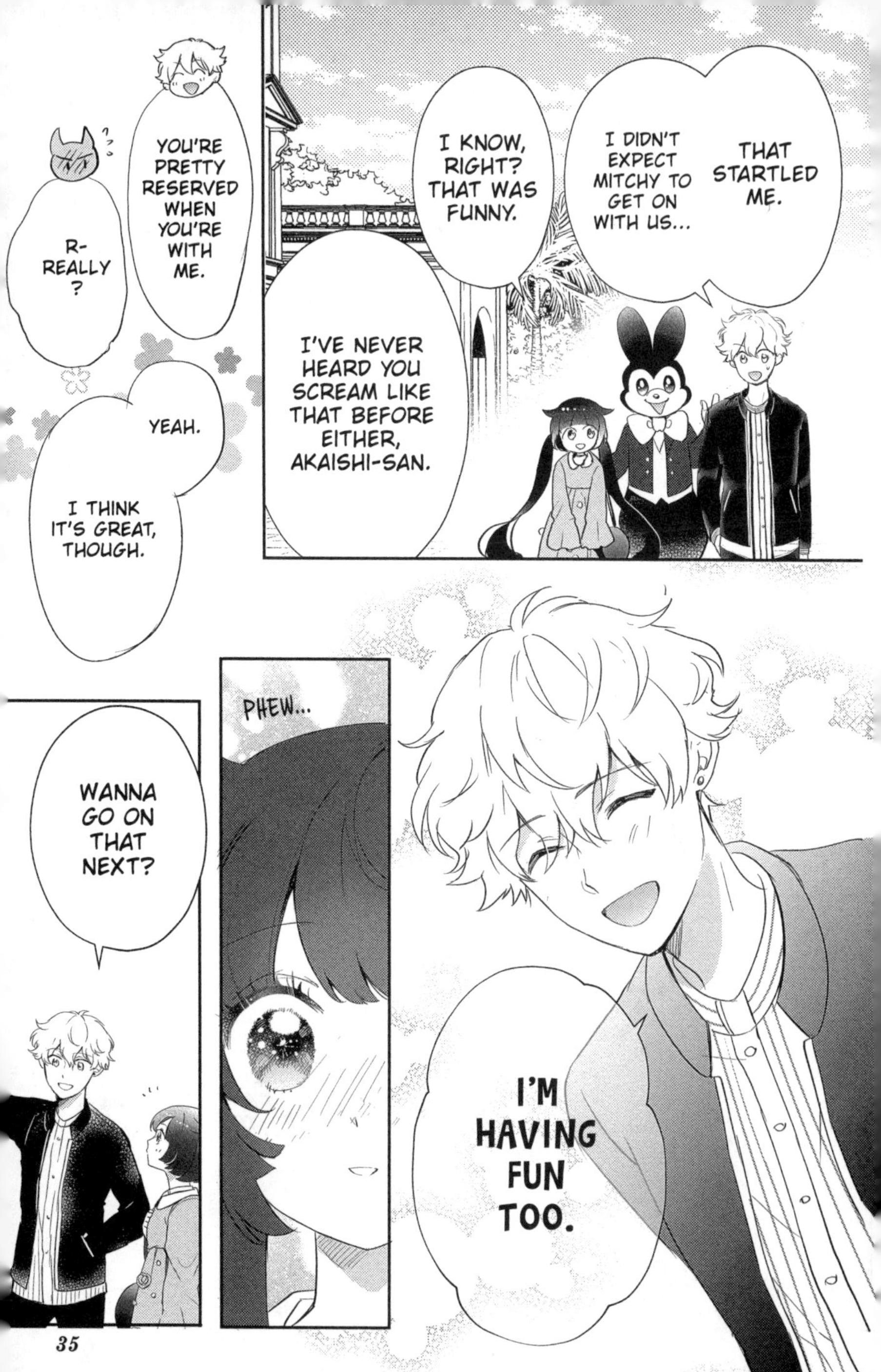
THAT STARTLED ME.
I DIDN'T EXPECT MITCHY TO GET ON WITH US...
I KNOW, RIGHT? THAT WAS FUNNY.
I'VE NEVER HEARD YOU SCREAM LIKE THAT BEFORE EITHER, AKAISHI-SAN.
YOU'RE PRETTY RESERVED WHEN YOU'RE WITH ME.
R-REALLY?
YEAH.
I THINK IT'S GREAT, THOUGH.
I'M HAVING FUN TOO.
PHEW...
WANNA GO ON THAT NEXT?

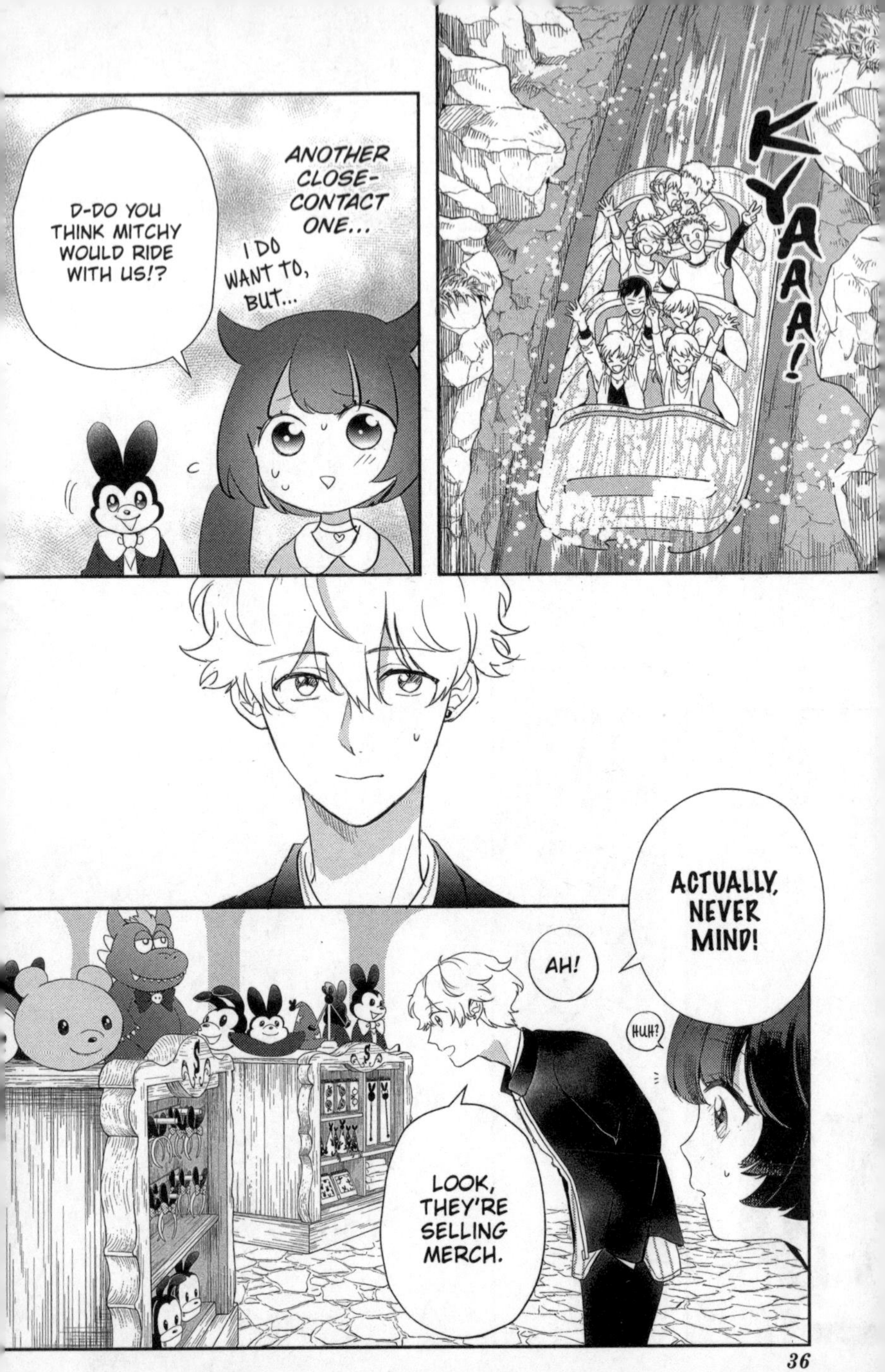
KYAAA!
ANOTHER CLOSE-CONTACT ONE...
I DO WANT TO, BUT...
D-DO YOU THINK MITCHY WOULD RIDE WITH US!?
ACTUALLY, NEVER MIND!
HUH?
AH!
LOOK, THEY'RE SELLING MERCH.

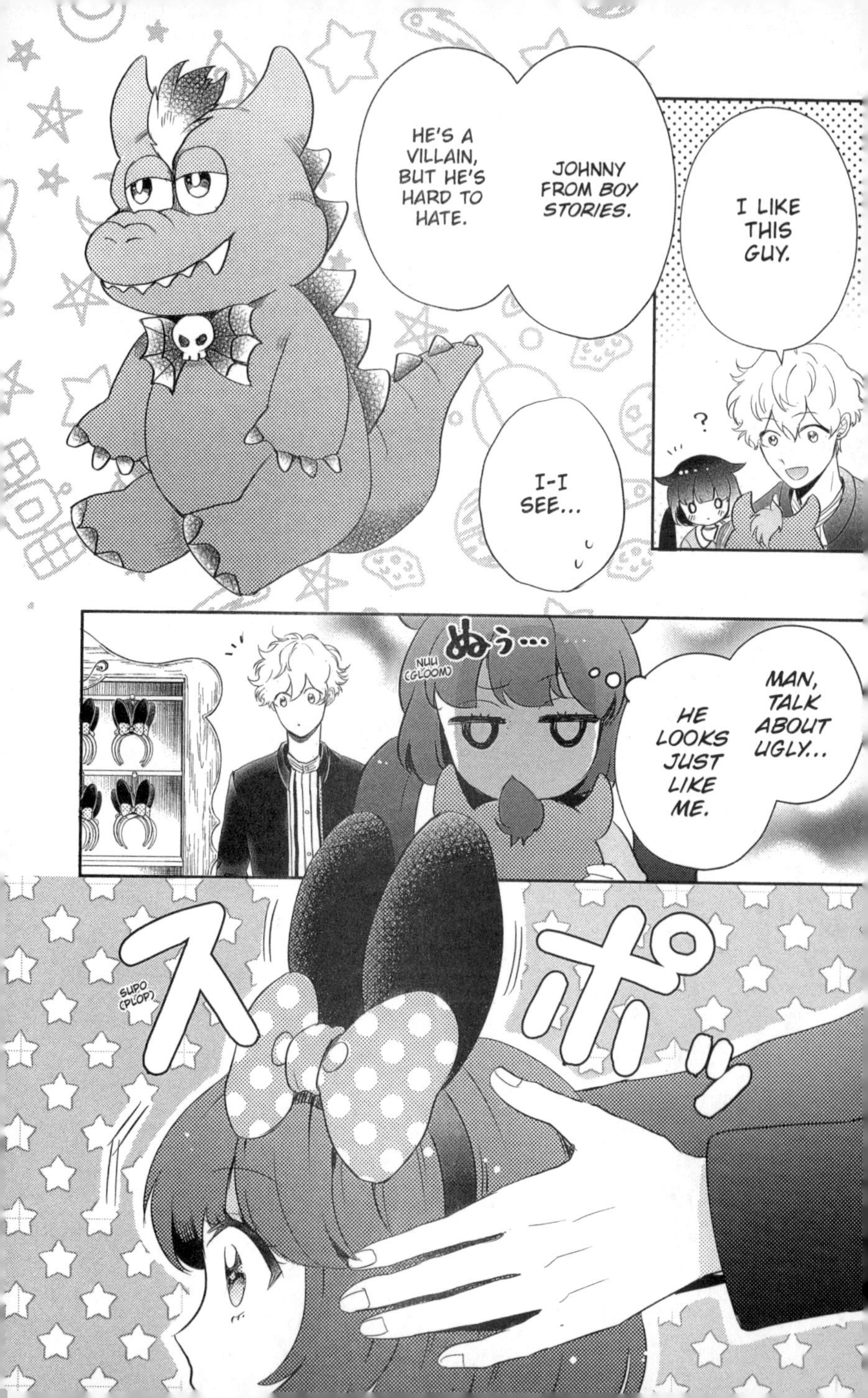
I LIKE THIS GUY.
JOHNNY FROM *BOY STORIES*.
HE'S A VILLAIN, BUT HE'S HARD TO HATE.
I-I SEE...
ぬぅ…
NUU (GLOOM)
MAN, TALK ABOUT UGLY...
HE LOOKS JUST LIKE ME.
スポッ
SUPO (PLOP)

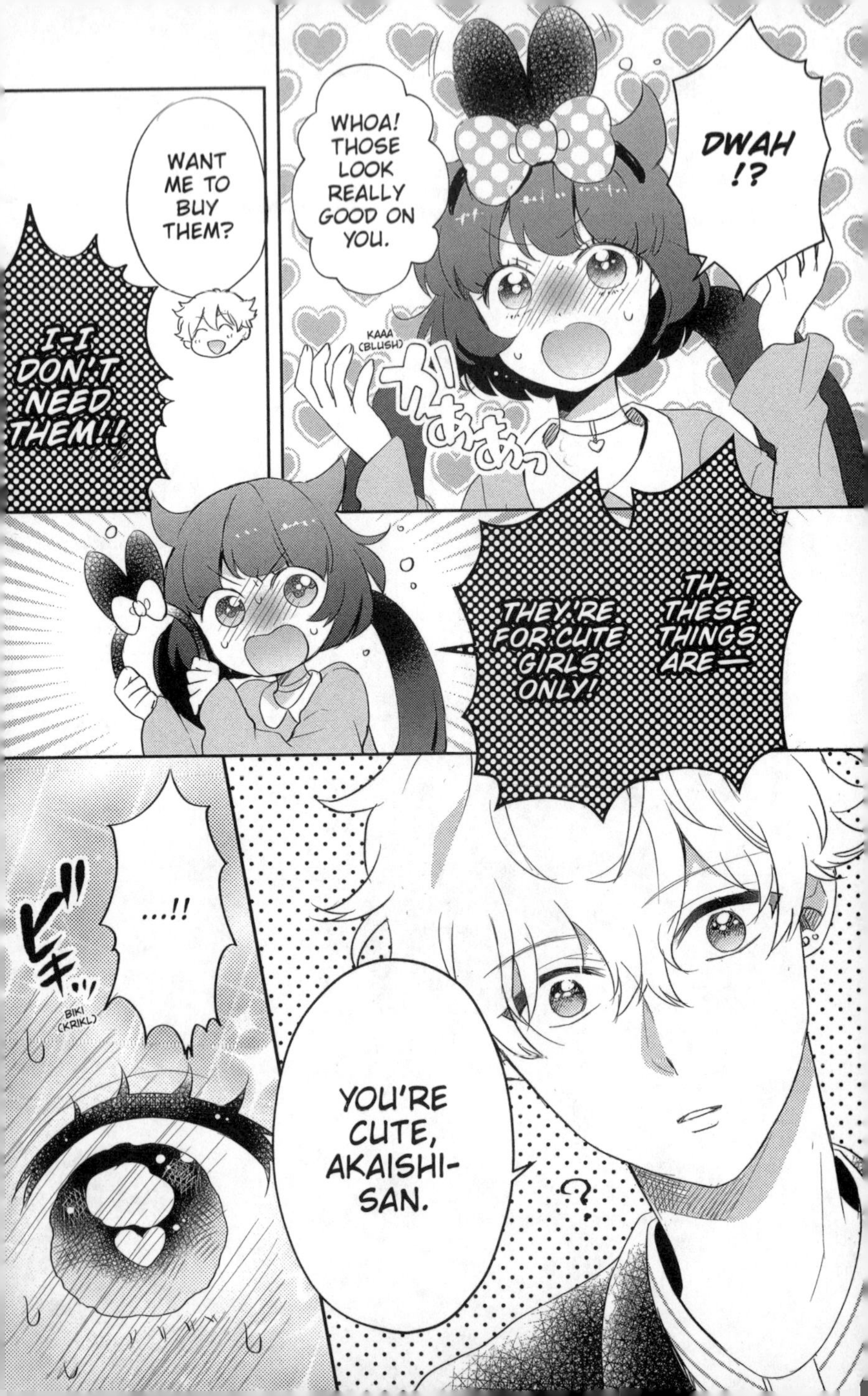
DWAH!?
WHOA! THOSE LOOK REALLY GOOD ON YOU.
KAAA (BLUSH)
WANT ME TO BUY THEM?
I-I DON'T NEED THEM!!
TH-THESE THINGS ARE—
THEY'RE FOR CUTE GIRLS ONLY!
YOU'RE CUTE, AKAISHI-SAN.
?
...!!
BIKI (KRIKL)

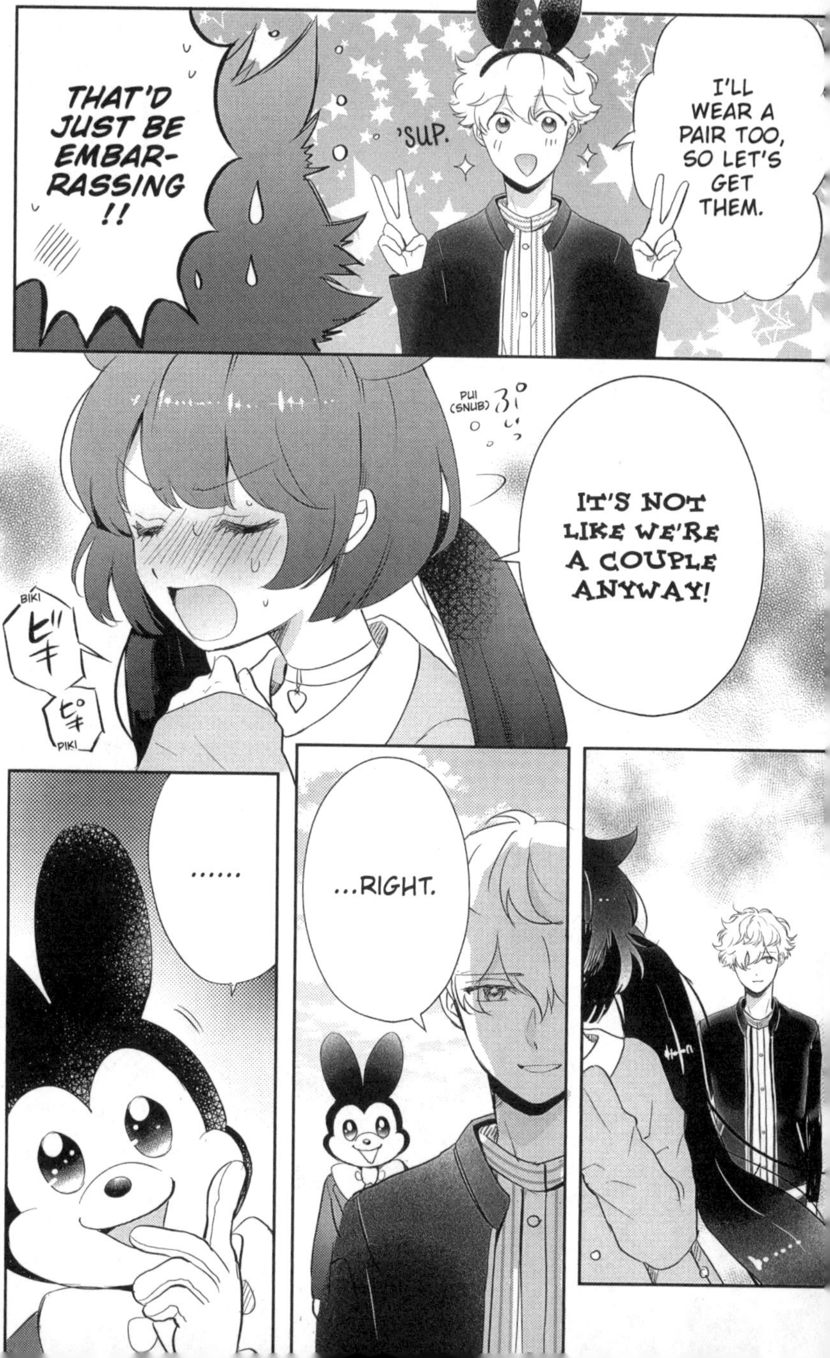
I'LL WEAR A PAIR TOO, SO LET'S GET THEM.
'SUP.
THAT'D JUST BE EMBARRASSING!!
PUI (SNUB)
ぷいっ
IT'S NOT LIKE WE'RE A COUPLE ANYWAY!
BIKI
ビキ
ピキ
PIKI
...RIGHT.
......

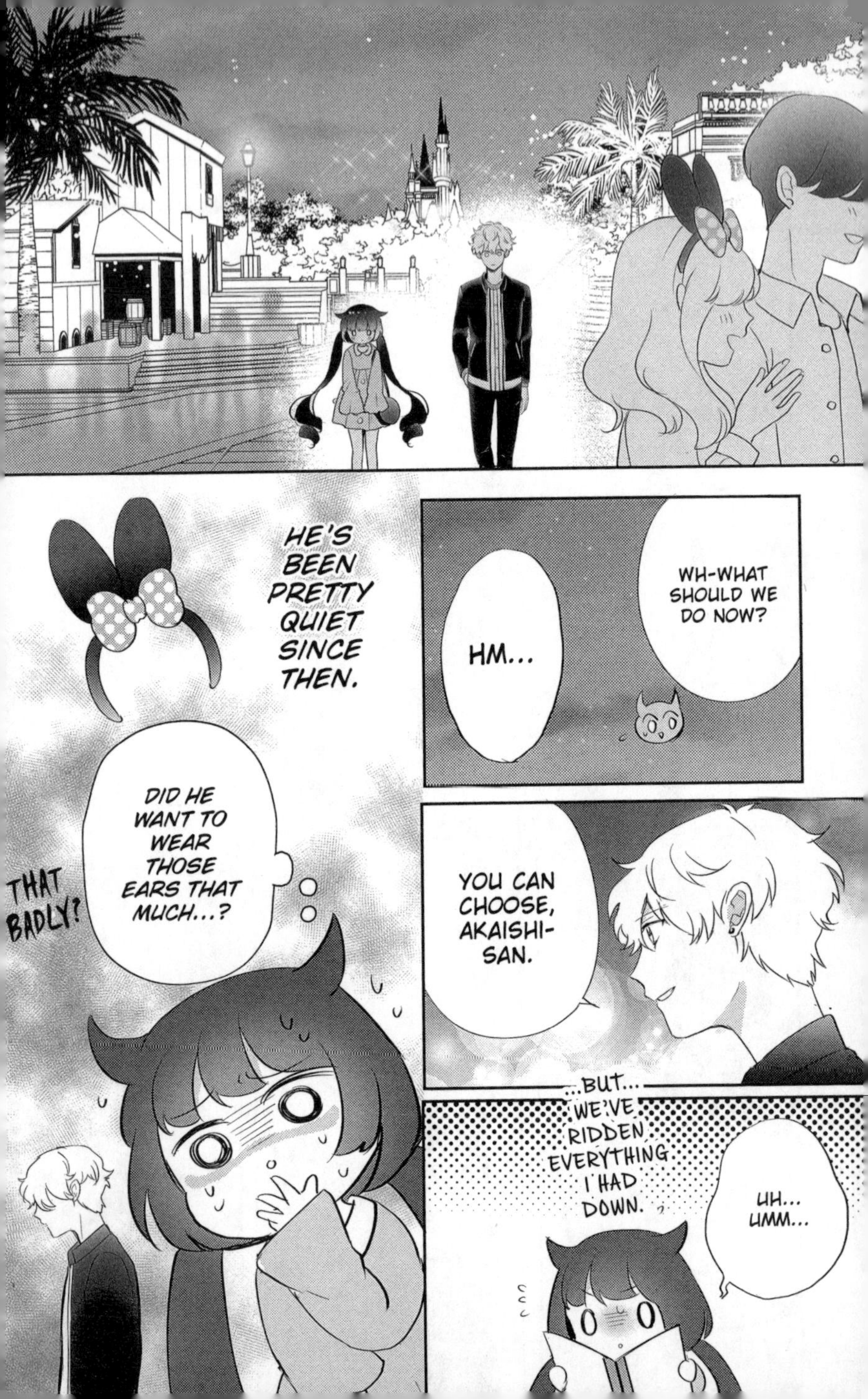
WH-WHAT SHOULD WE DO NOW?
HM...
YOU CAN CHOOSE, AKAISHI-SAN.
...BUT... WE'VE RIDDEN EVERYTHING I HAD DOWN.
UH... UMM...
HE'S BEEN PRETTY QUIET SINCE THEN.
DID HE WANT TO WEAR THOSE EARS THAT MUCH...?
THAT BADLY?

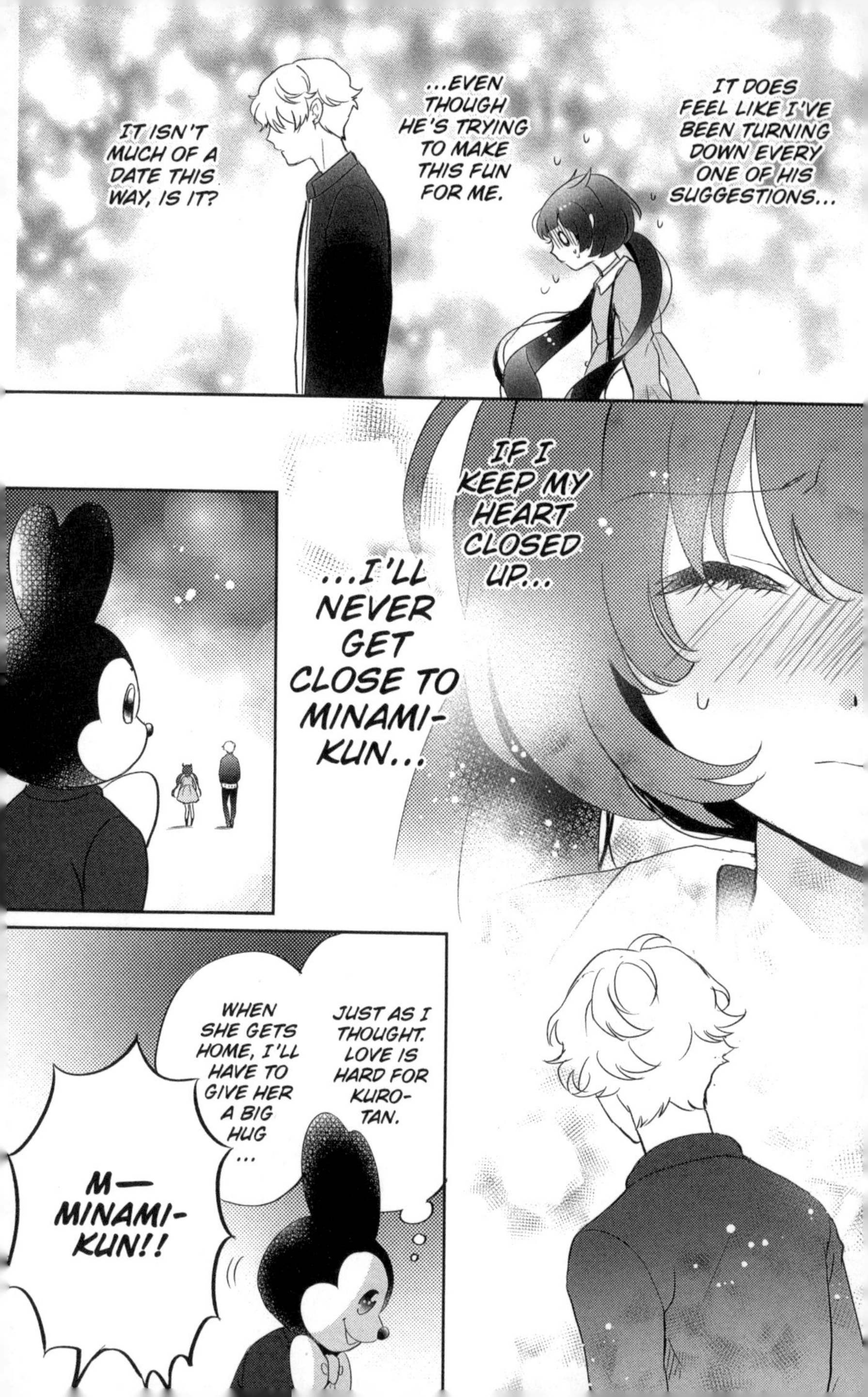
IT DOES FEEL LIKE I'VE BEEN TURNING DOWN EVERY ONE OF HIS SUGGESTIONS...
...EVEN THOUGH HE'S TRYING TO MAKE THIS FUN FOR ME.
IT ISN'T MUCH OF A DATE THIS WAY, IS IT?
IF I KEEP MY HEART CLOSED UP...
...I'LL NEVER GET CLOSE TO MINAMI-KUN...
JUST AS I THOUGHT. LOVE IS HARD FOR KURO-TAN.
WHEN SHE GETS HOME, I'LL HAVE TO GIVE HER A BIG HUG...
M—MINAMI-KUN!!

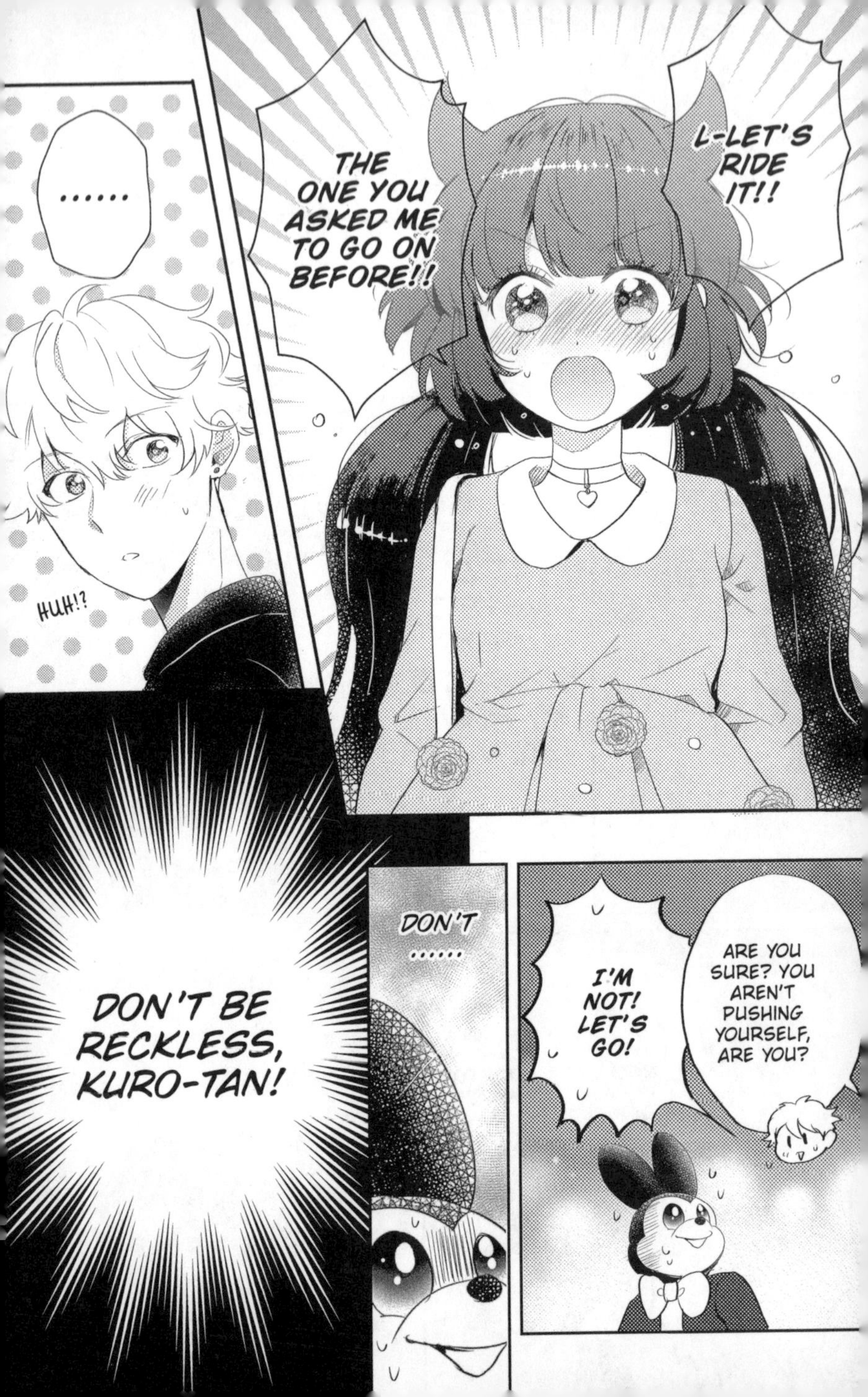
L-LET'S RIDE IT!!
THE ONE YOU ASKED ME TO GO ON BEFORE!!
......
HUH!?
ARE YOU SURE? YOU AREN'T PUSHING YOURSELF, ARE YOU?
I'M NOT! LET'S GO!
DON'T ......
DON'T BE RECKLESS, KURO-TAN!

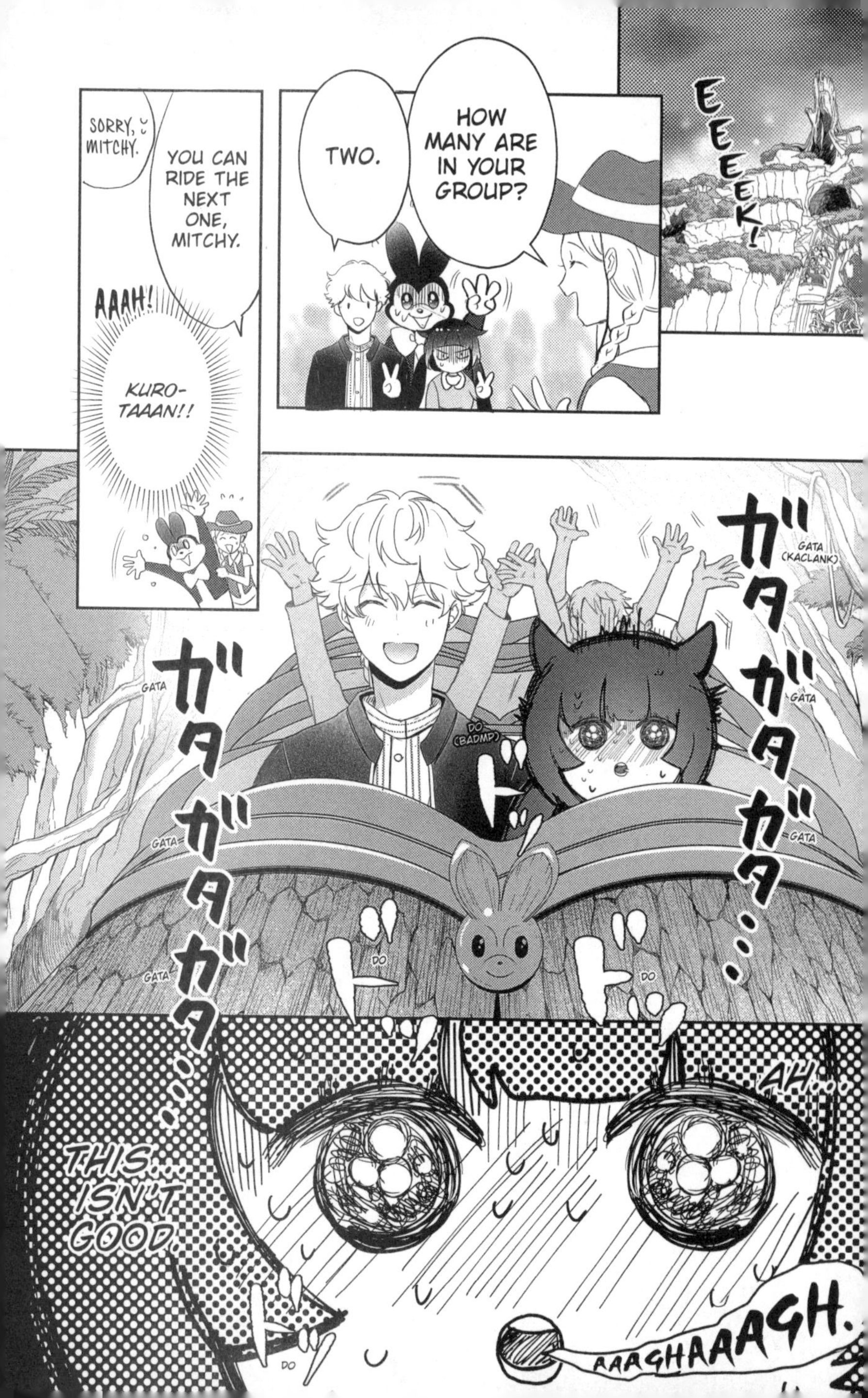
EEEEEK!
HOW MANY ARE IN YOUR GROUP?
TWO.
SORRY, MITCHY.
YOU CAN RIDE THE NEXT ONE, MITCHY.
AAAH!
KURO-TAAAN!!
GATA (KACLANK)
GATA
GATA
GATA
GATA
GATA
DO (BADMP)
DO
DO
AH...
THIS... ISN'T GOOD.
DO
AAAGHAAAAGH.

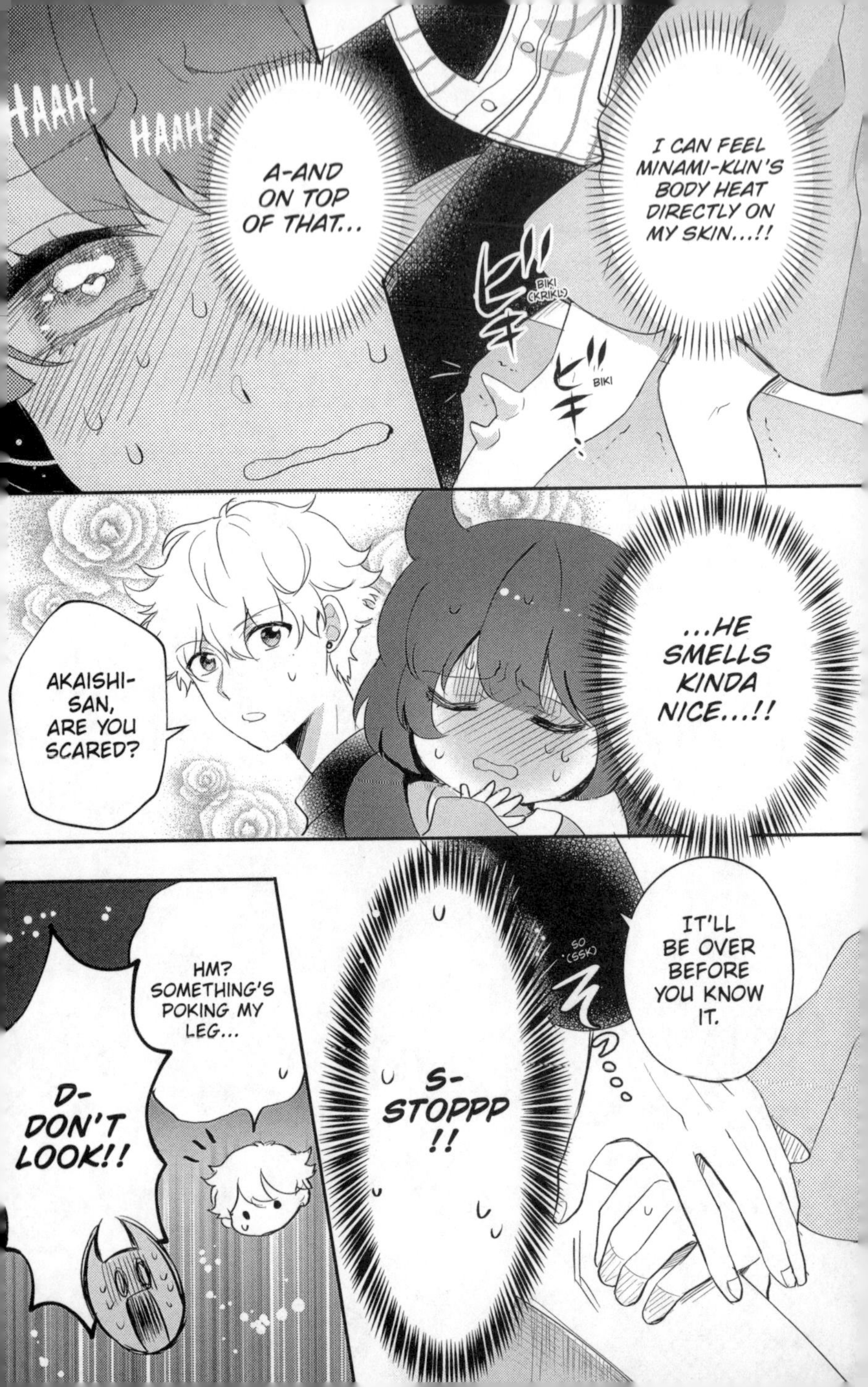
I CAN FEEL MINAMI-KUN'S BODY HEAT DIRECTLY ON MY SKIN...!!
BIKI (KRIKL)
BIKI
A-AND ON TOP OF THAT...
HAAH! HAAH!
...HE SMELLS KINDA NICE...!!
AKAISHI-SAN, ARE YOU SCARED?
IT'LL BE OVER BEFORE YOU KNOW IT.
SO (SSK)
S-STOPPP!!
HM? SOMETHING'S POKING MY LEG...
D-DON'T LOOK!!

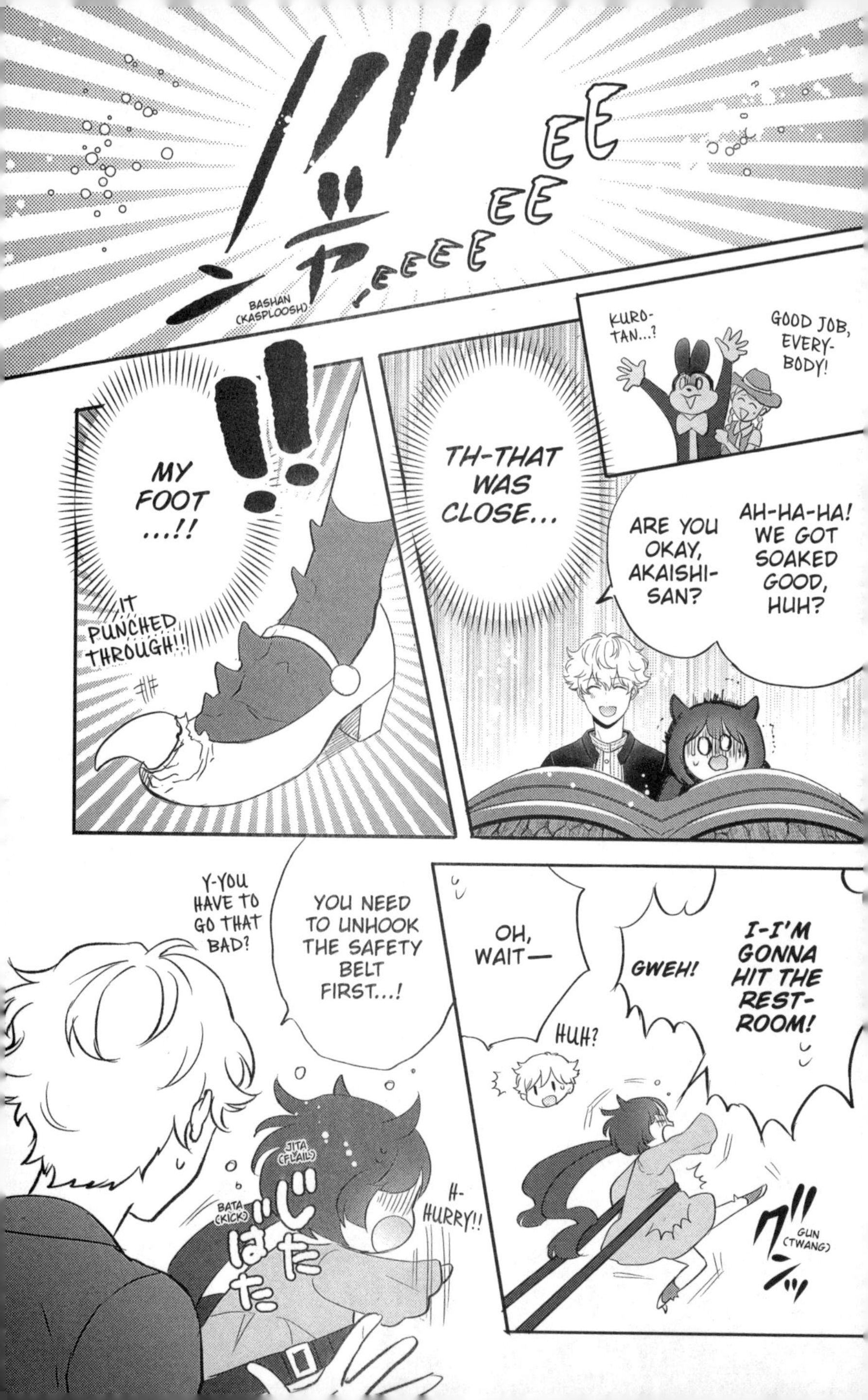
BASHAN (KASPLOOSH)
EEEEEEEEE
GOOD JOB, EVERYBODY!
KURO-TAN...?
AH-HA-HA! WE GOT SOAKED GOOD, HUH?
ARE YOU OKAY, AKAISHI-SAN?
TH-THAT WAS CLOSE...
MY FOOT ...!!
IT PUNCHED THROUGH!!
I-I'M GONNA HIT THE REST-ROOM!
GWEH!
OH, WAIT—
HUH?
GUN (TWANG)
YOU NEED TO UNHOOK THE SAFETY BELT FIRST...!
Y-YOU HAVE TO GO THAT BAD?
JITA (FLAIL)
BATA (KICK)
H-HURRY!!

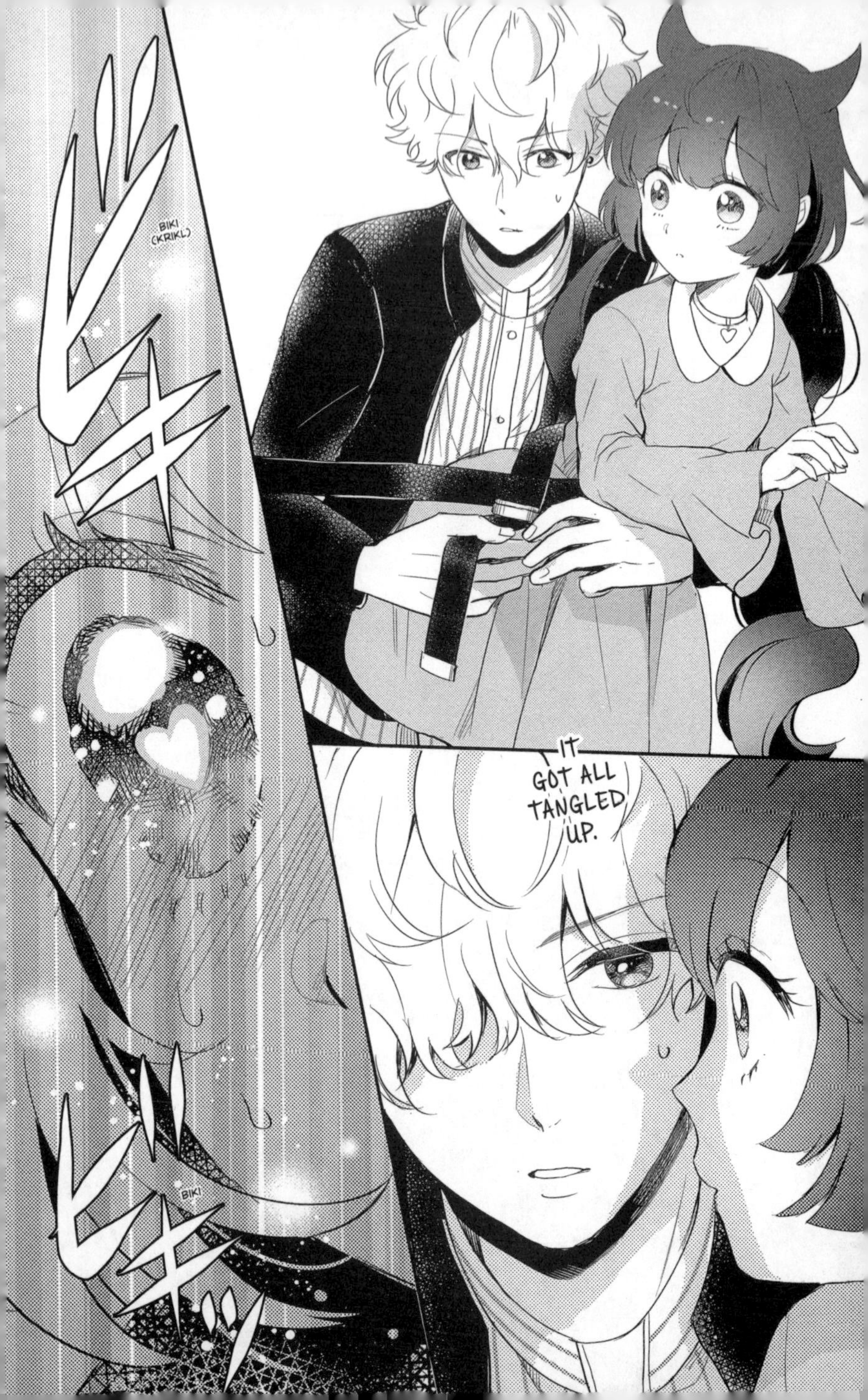
IT GOT ALL TANGLED UP.
BIKI (KRIKL)
BIKI

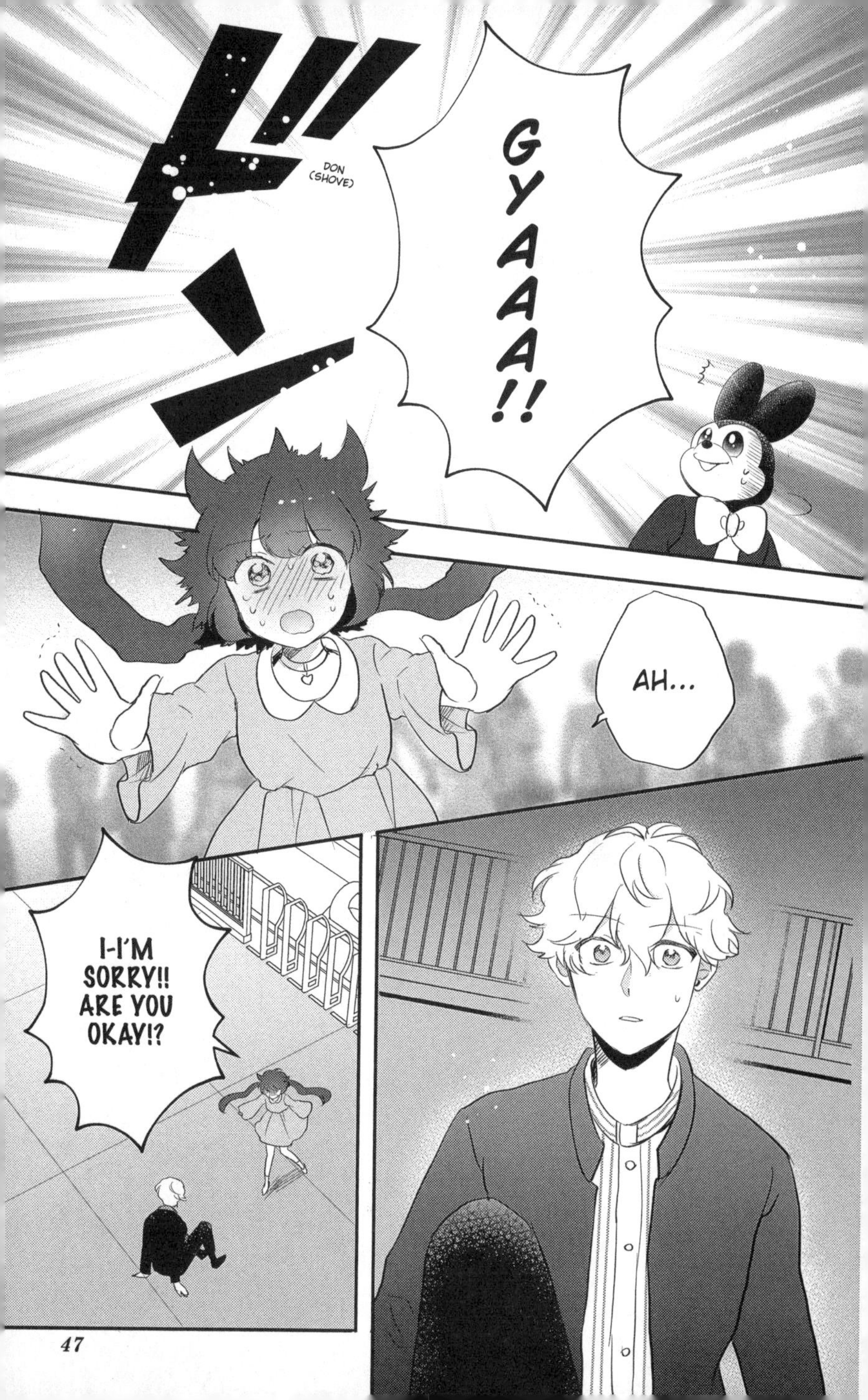
GYAAAA!!
DON (SHOVE)
AH...
I-I'M SORRY!! ARE YOU OKAY!?

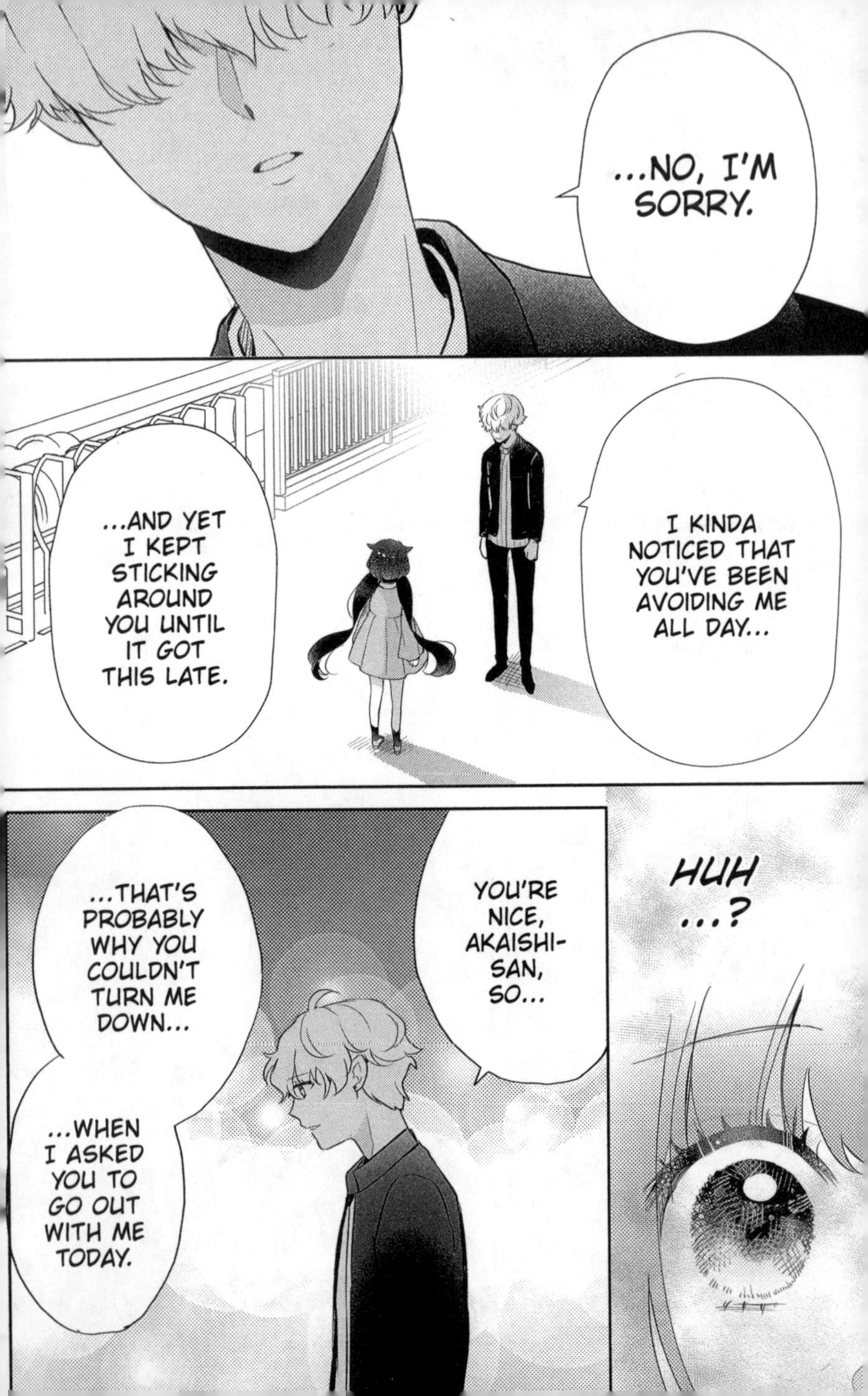
...NO, I'M SORRY.
I KINDA NOTICED THAT YOU'VE BEEN AVOIDING ME ALL DAY...
...AND YET I KEPT STICKING AROUND YOU UNTIL IT GOT THIS LATE.
HUH ...?
YOU'RE NICE, AKAISHI-SAN, SO...
...THAT'S PROBABLY WHY YOU COULDN'T TURN ME DOWN...
...WHEN I ASKED YOU TO GO OUT WITH ME TODAY.

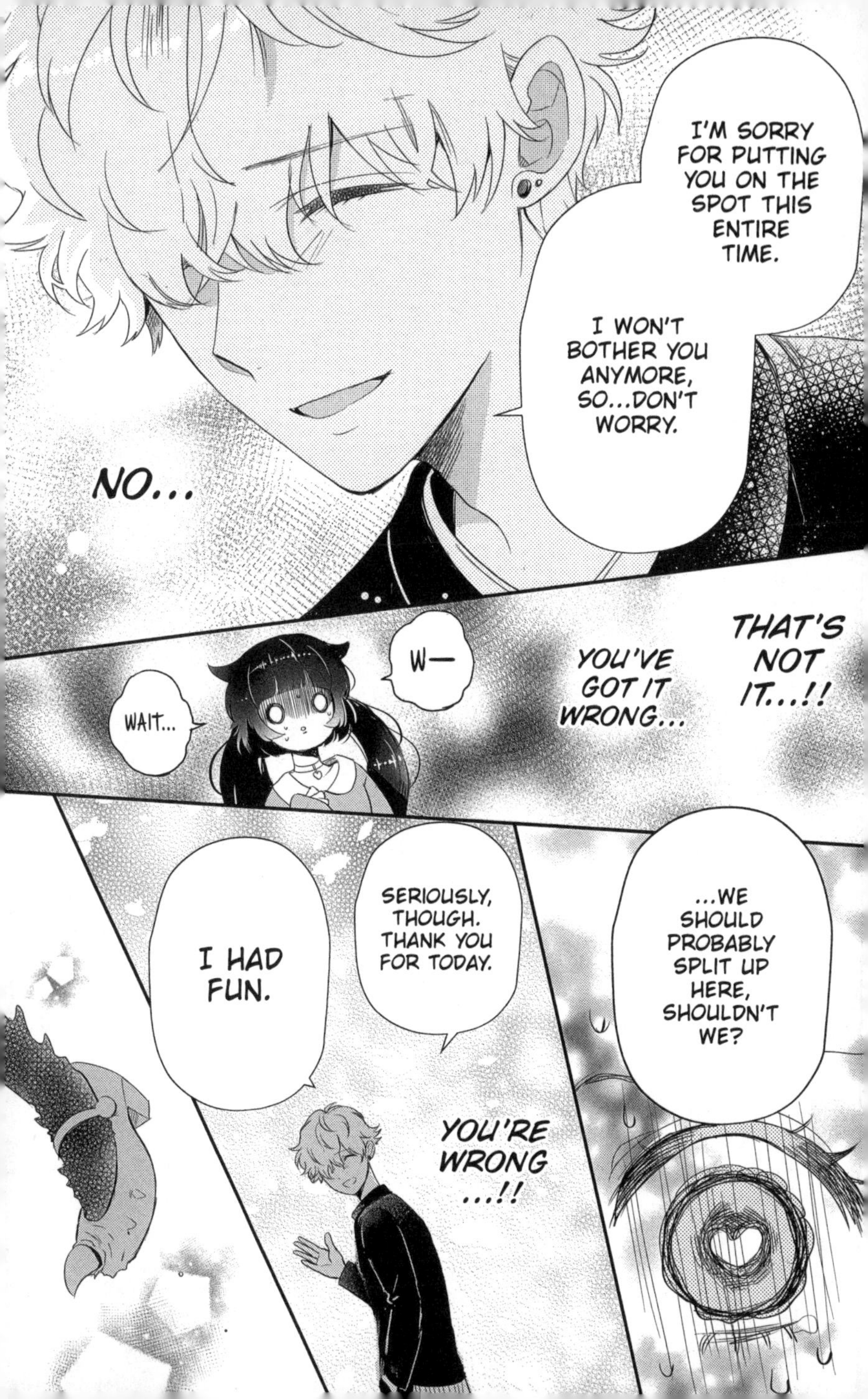
I'M SORRY FOR PUTTING YOU ON THE SPOT THIS ENTIRE TIME.
I WON'T BOTHER YOU ANYMORE, SO...DON'T WORRY.
NO...
THAT'S NOT IT...!!
YOU'VE GOT IT WRONG...
W—
WAIT...
...WE SHOULD PROBABLY SPLIT UP HERE, SHOULDN'T WE?
SERIOUSLY, THOUGH. THANK YOU FOR TODAY.
I HAD FUN.
YOU'RE WRONG...!!

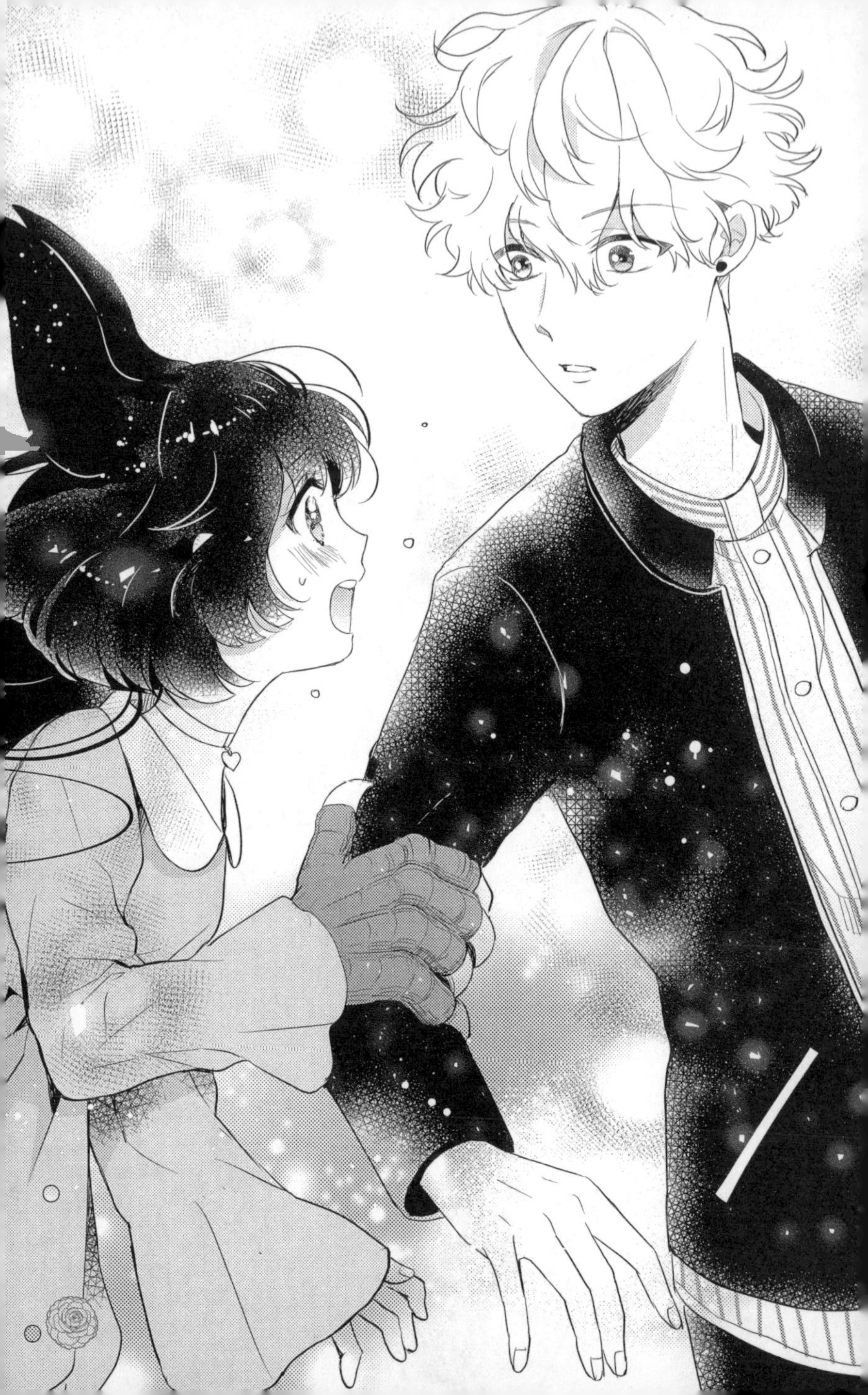

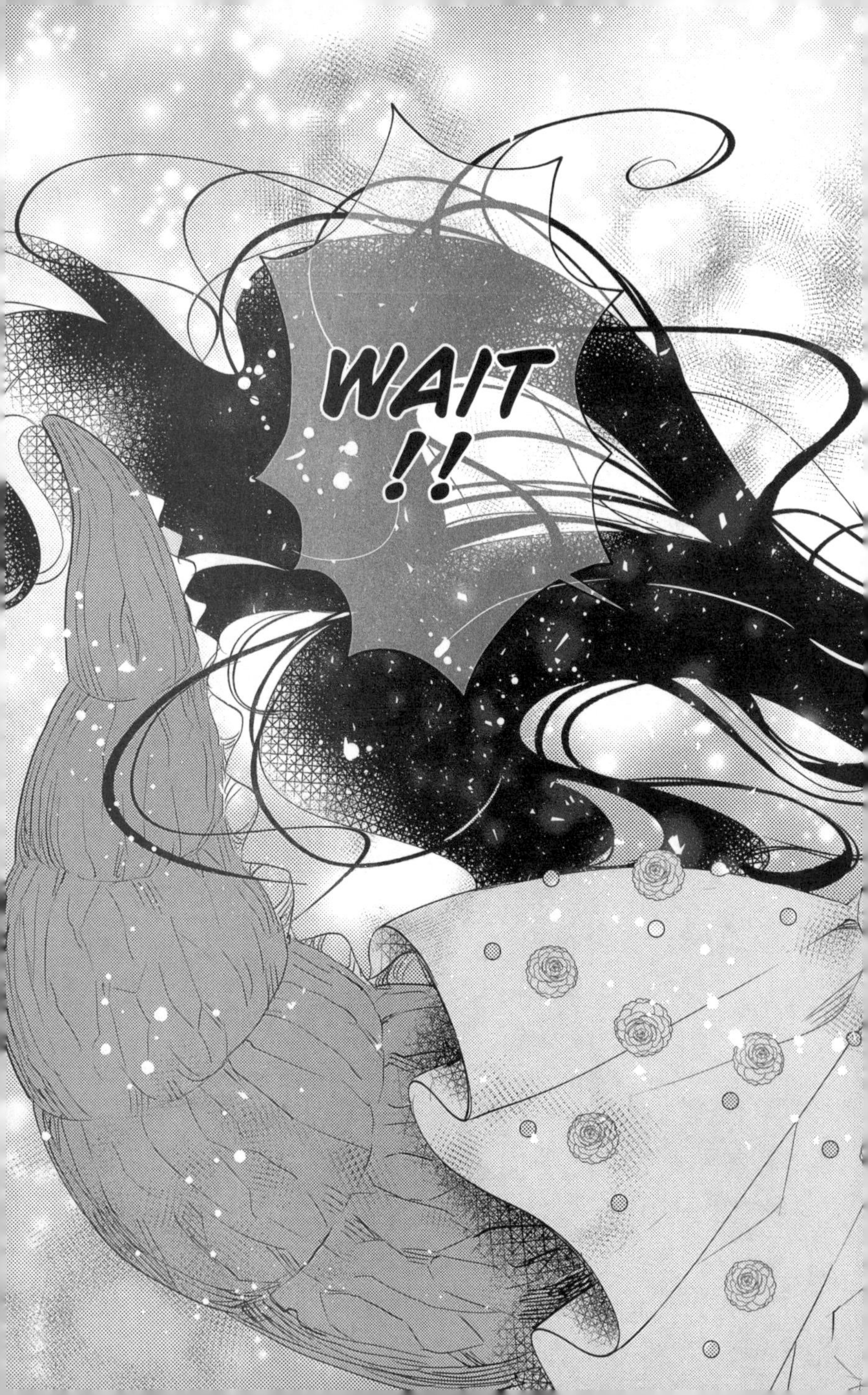
WAIT !!

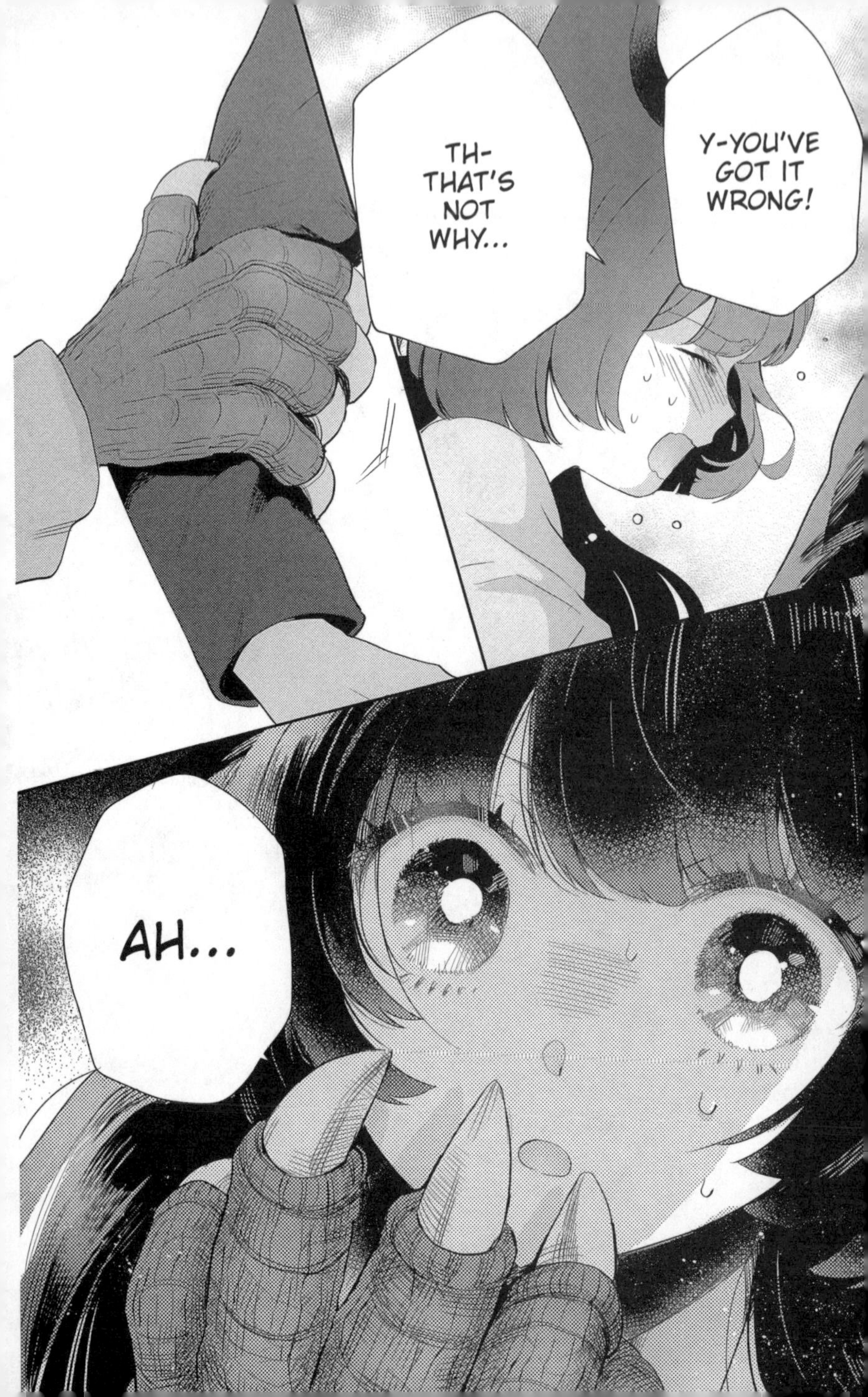
Y-YOU'VE GOT IT WRONG!
TH- THAT'S NOT WHY...
AH...

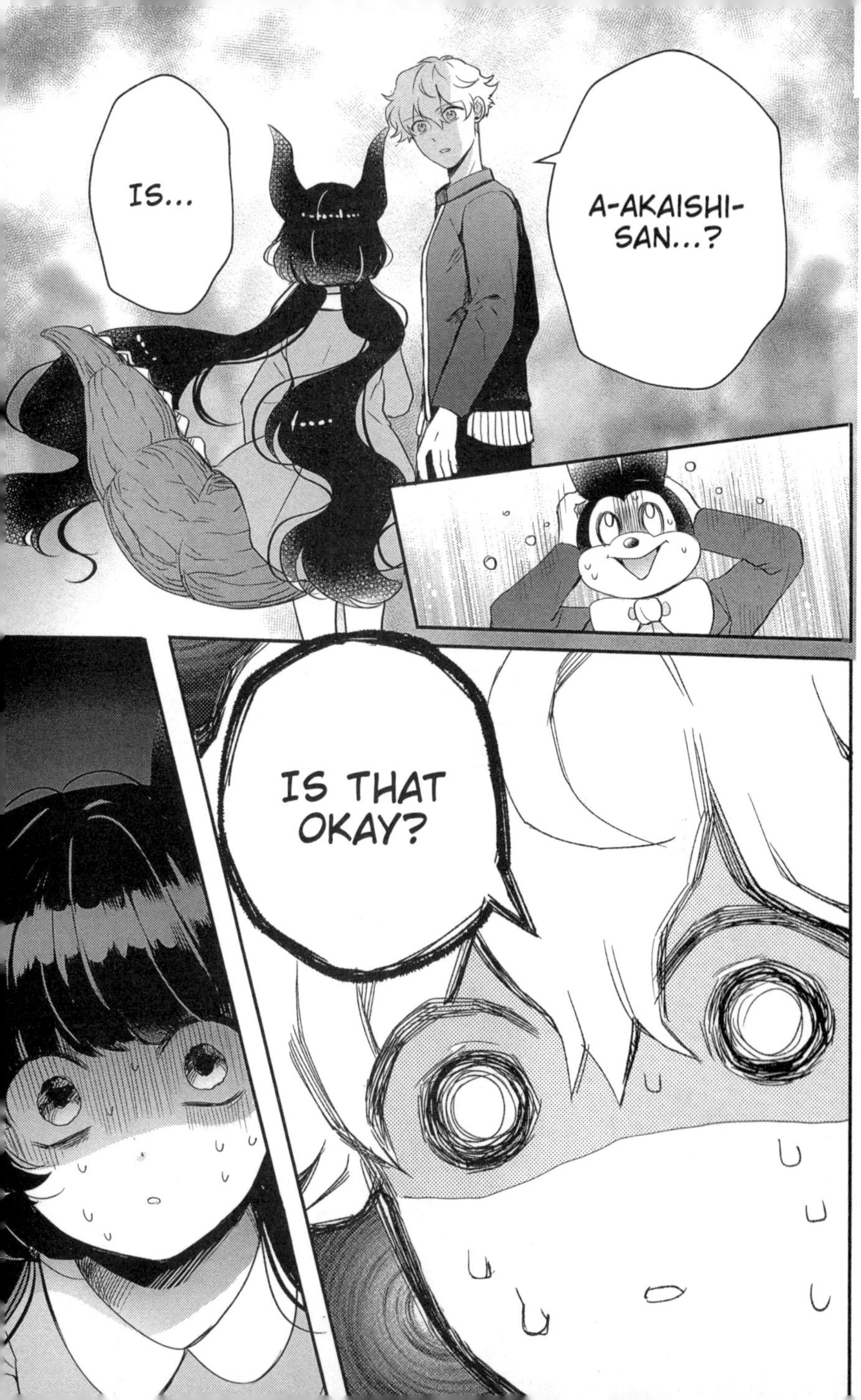
A-AKAISHI-SAN...?
IS...
IS THAT OKAY?

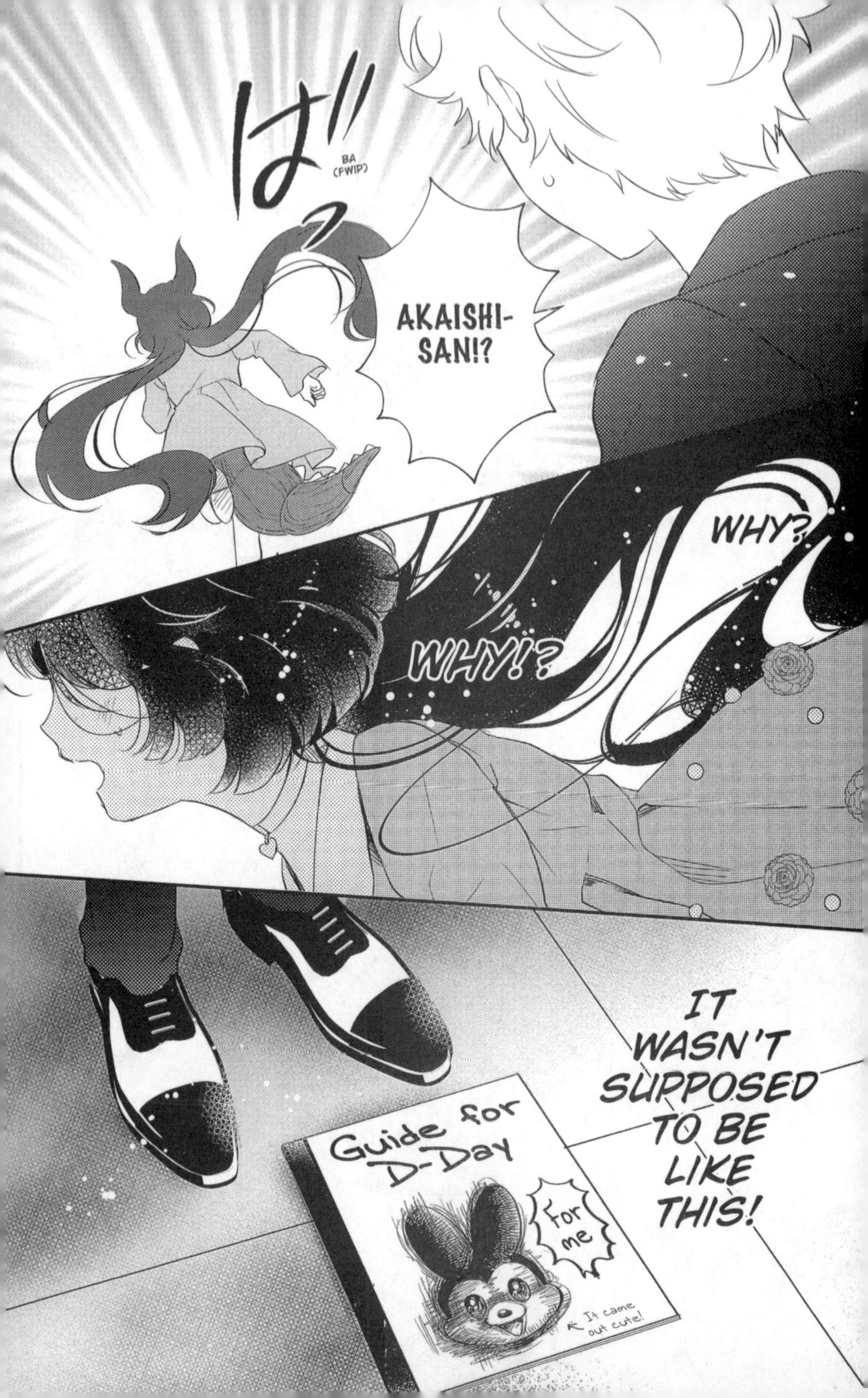
は
BA (FWIP)
AKAISHI-SAN!?
WHY?
WHY!?
IT WASN'T SUPPOSED TO BE LIKE THIS!
Guide for D-Day
for me
It came out cute!

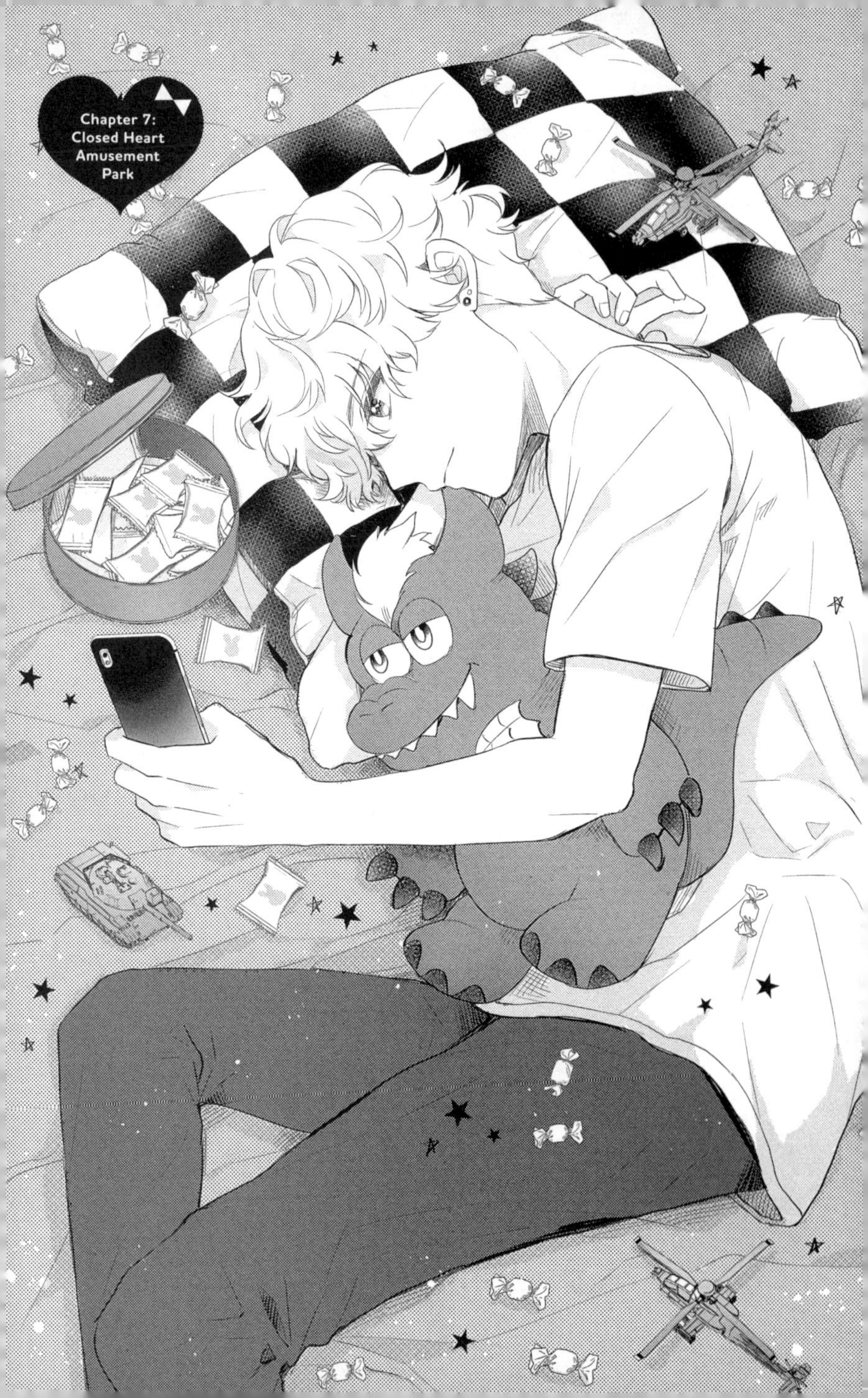
Chapter 7:
Closed Heart
Amusement
Park

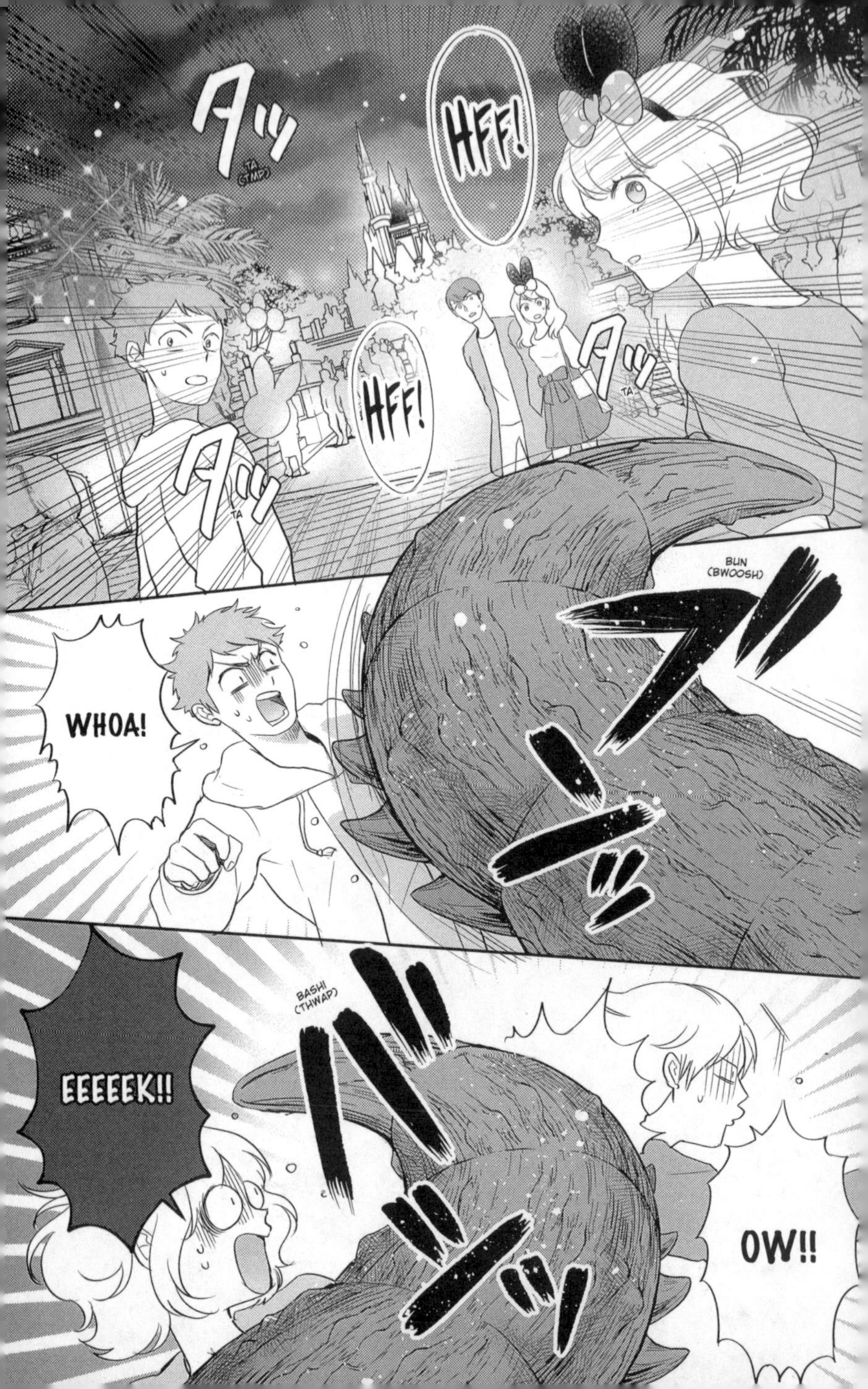
HFF!
タッ
TA
タッ
TA (STMP)
HFF!
タッ
TA
BUN (BWOOSH)
WHOA!
OW!!
BASHI (THWAP)
EEEEEK!!

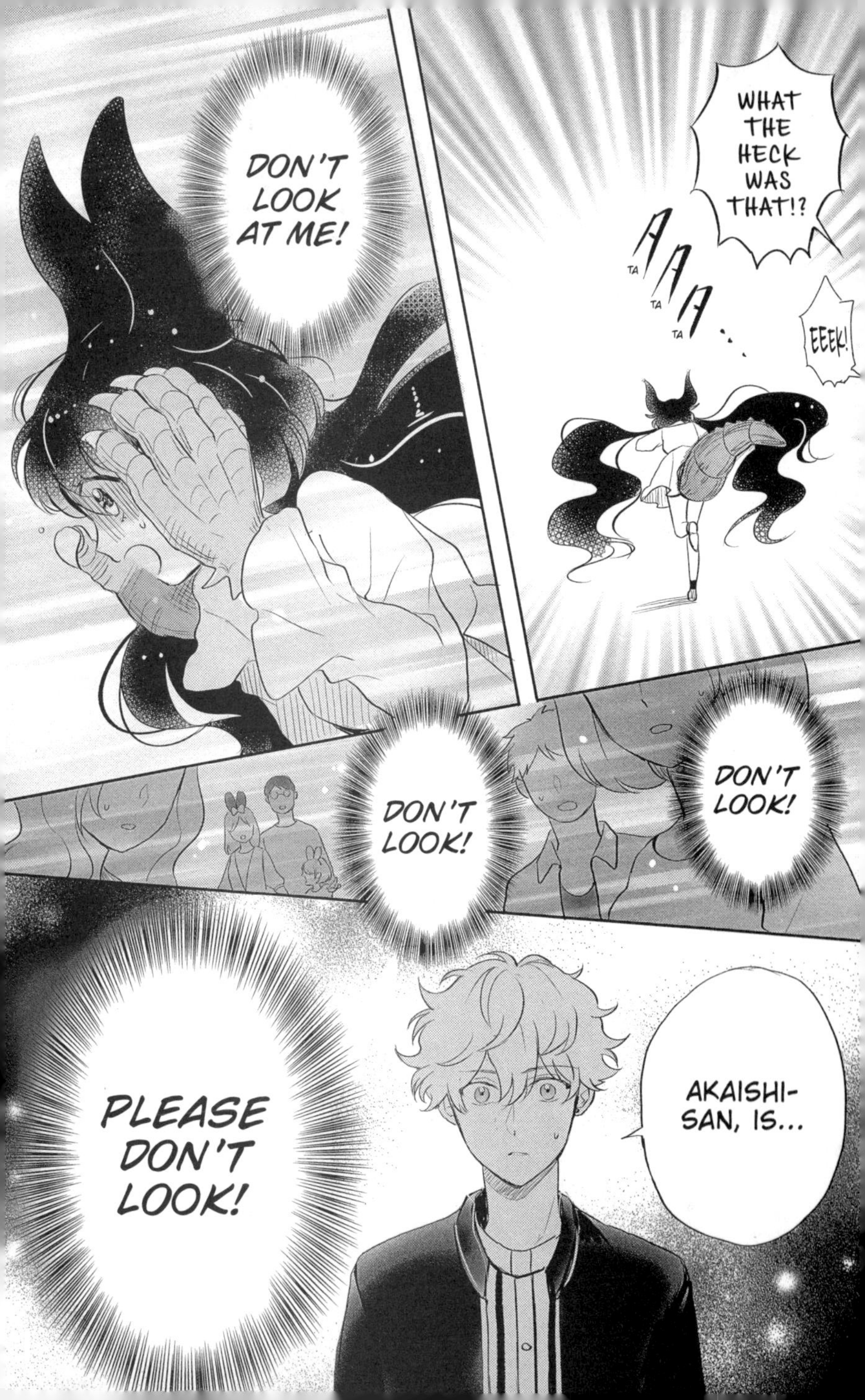
WHAT THE HECK WAS THAT!?
EEEK!
TA TA TA
DON'T LOOK AT ME!
DON'T LOOK!
DON'T LOOK!
AKAISHI-SAN, IS...
PLEASE DON'T LOOK!

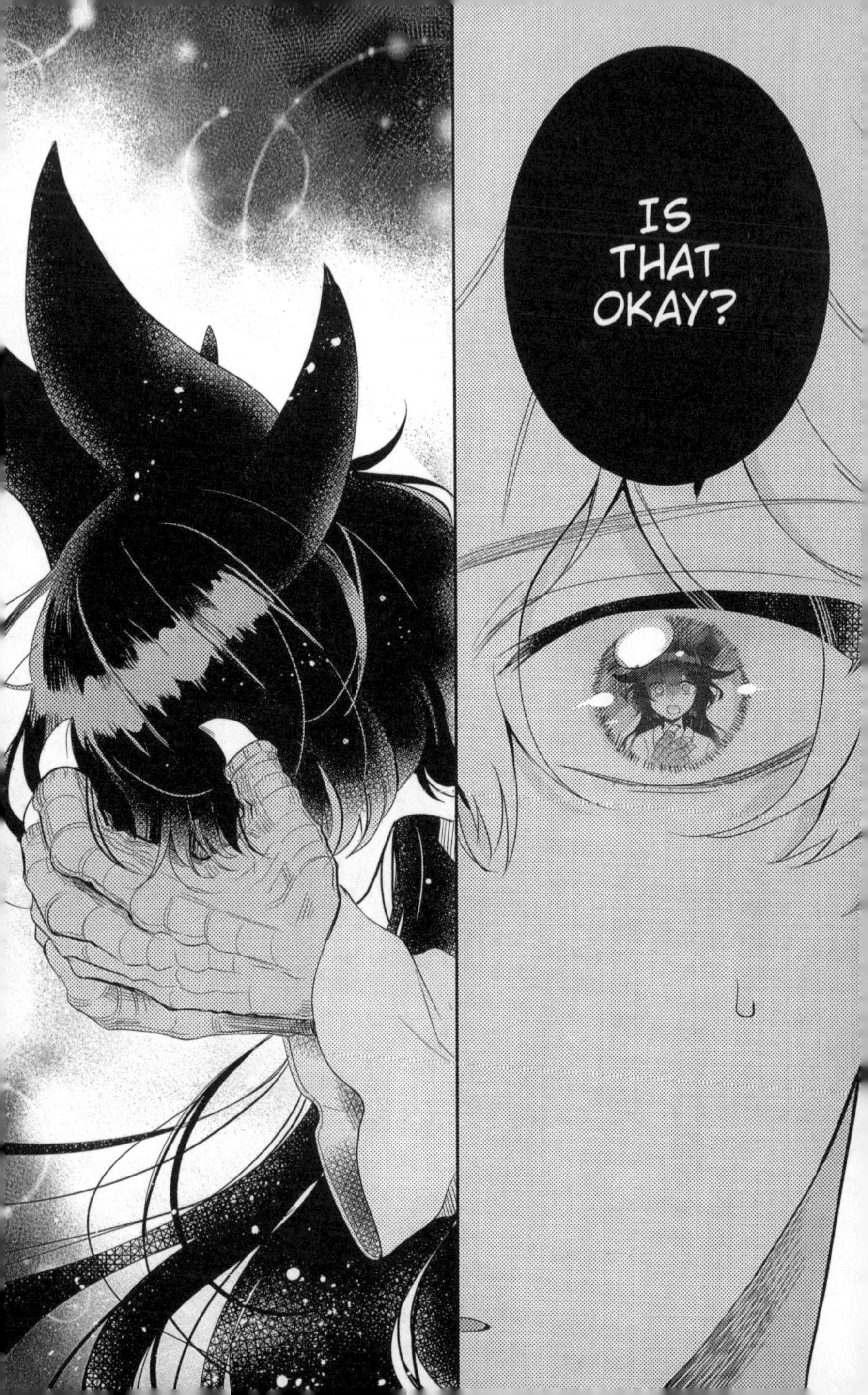
IS THAT OKAY?

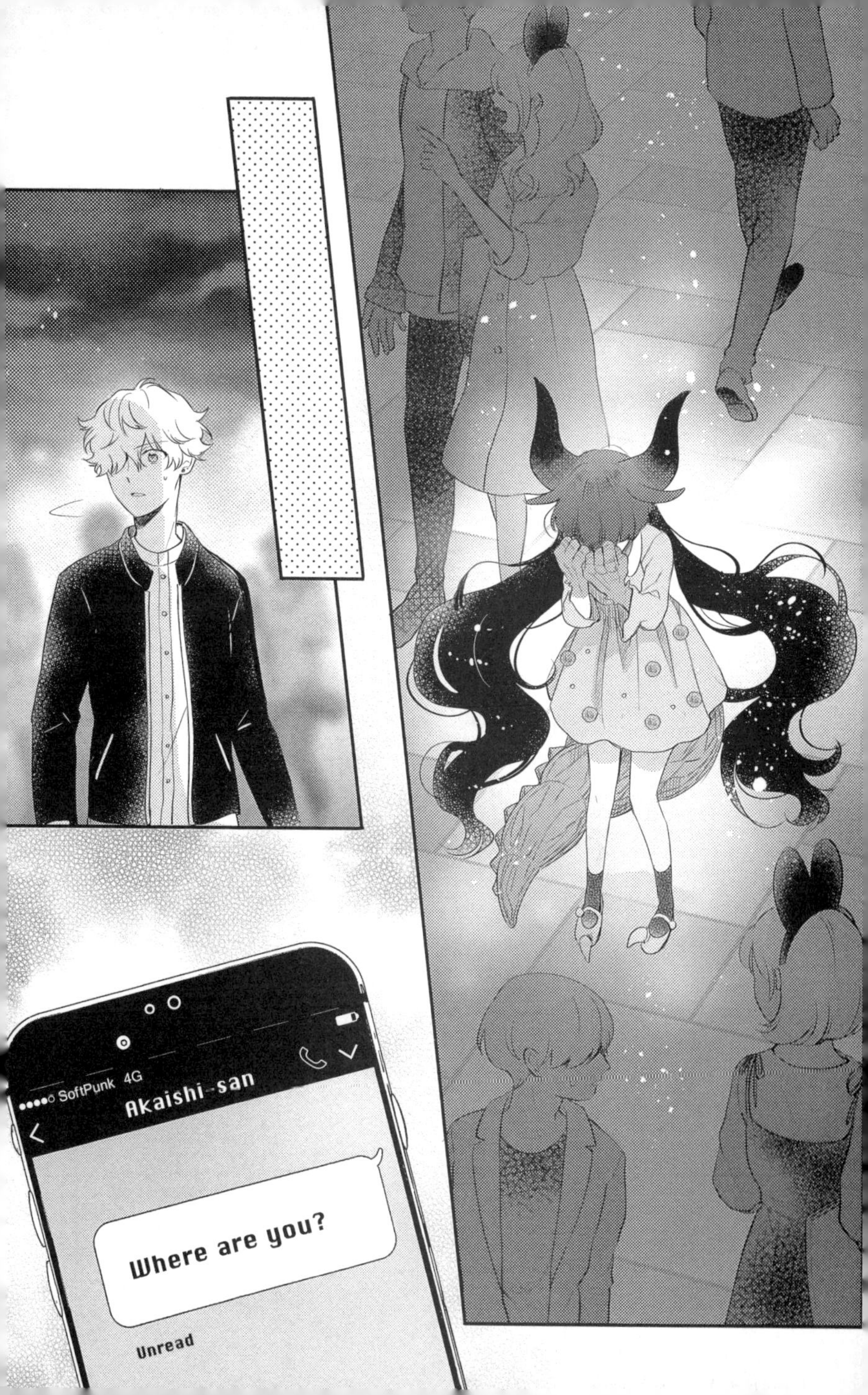
●●●●○ SoftPunk 4G
Akaishi-san
Where are you?
Unread

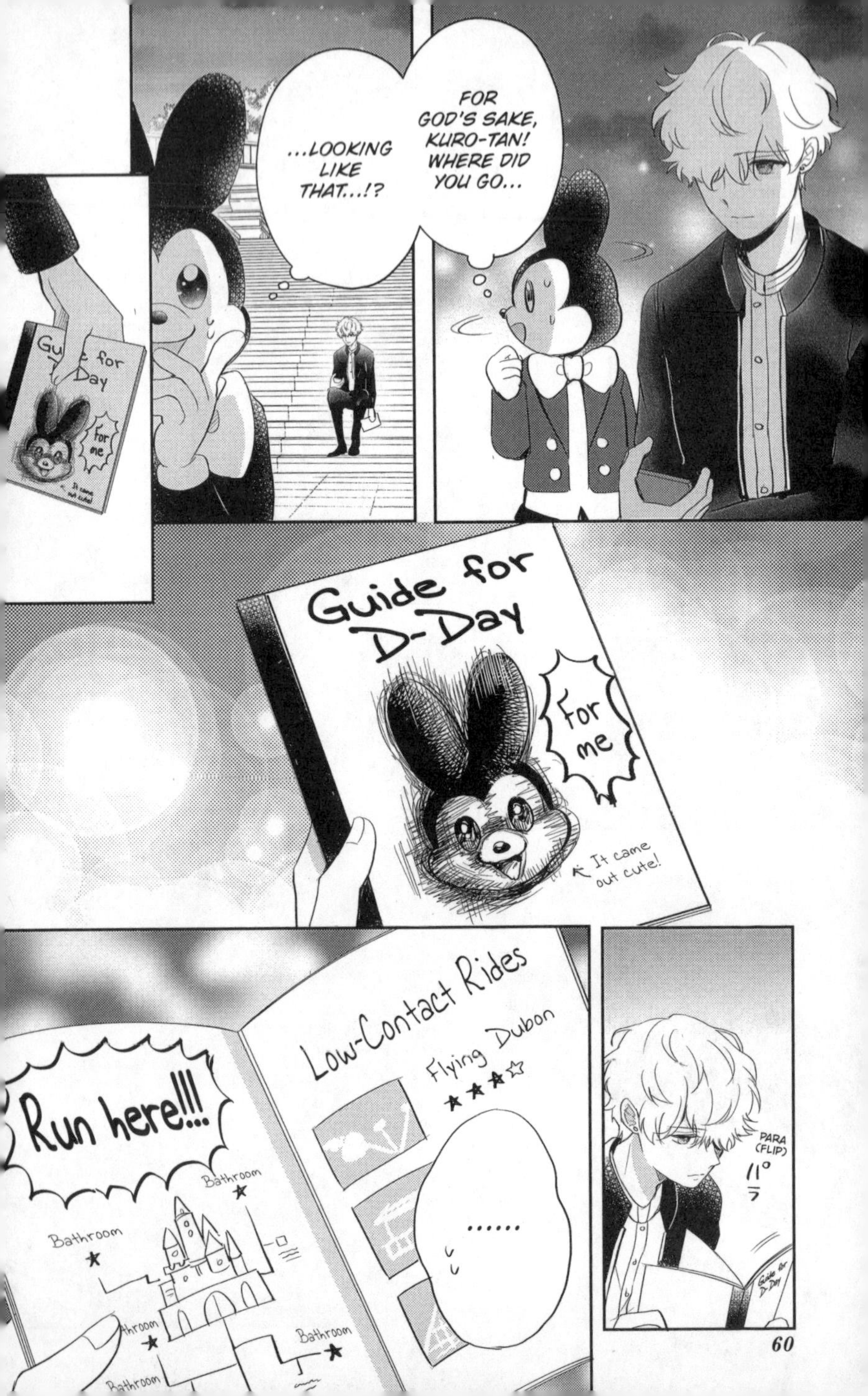
FOR GOD'S SAKE, KURO-TAN! WHERE DID YOU GO...
...LOOKING LIKE THAT...!?
Guide for D-Day
For me
It came out cute!
PARA (FLIP)
Low-Contact Rides
Flying Dubon
Run here!!!
Bathroom
Bathroom
Bathroom
Bathroom
......

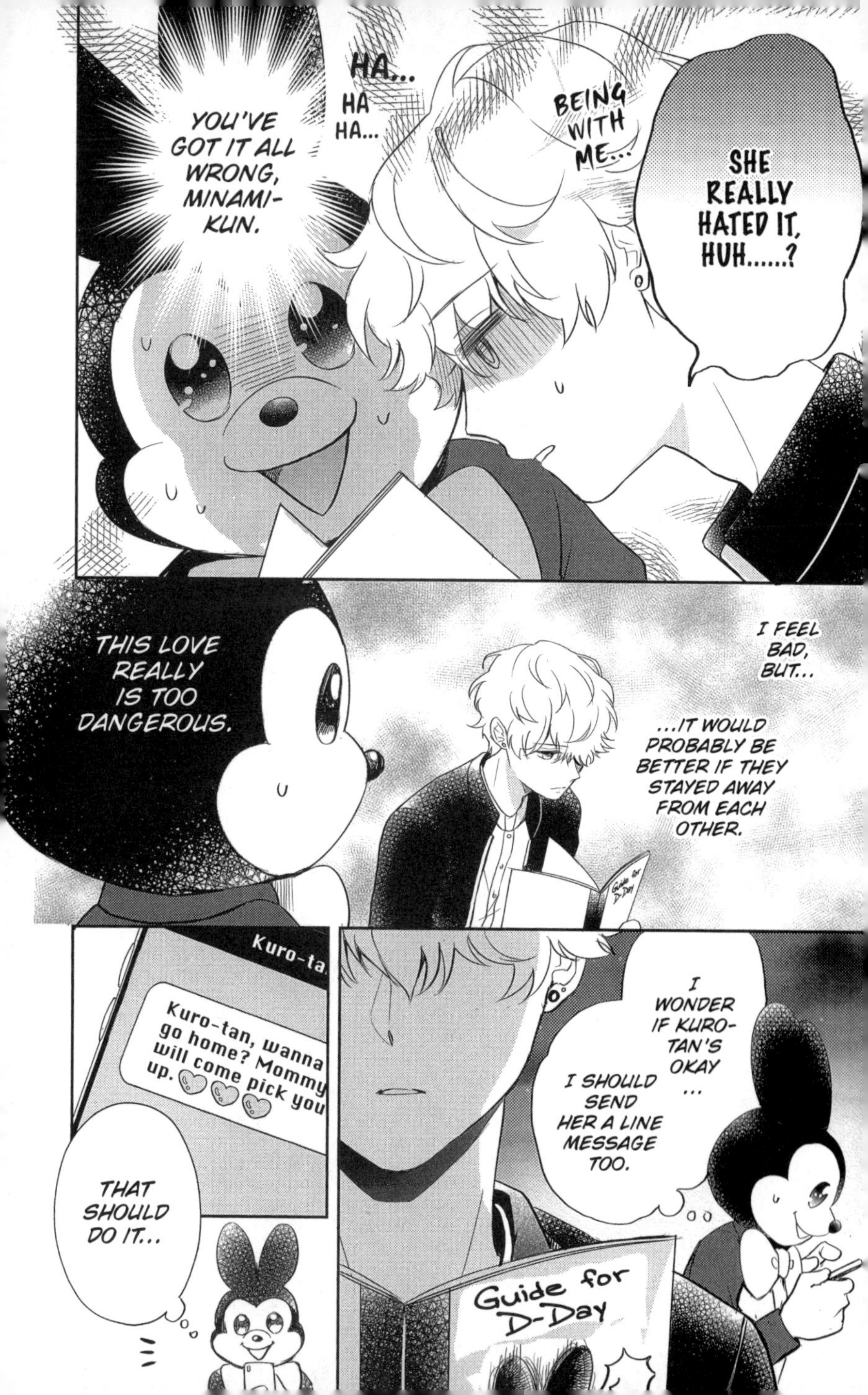
SHE REALLY HATED IT, HUH......?
BEING WITH ME...
HA...
HA HA...
YOU'VE GOT IT ALL WRONG, MINAMI-KUN.
I FEEL BAD, BUT...
...IT WOULD PROBABLY BE BETTER IF THEY STAYED AWAY FROM EACH OTHER.
Guide for D-Day
THIS LOVE REALLY IS TOO DANGEROUS.
I WONDER IF KURO-TAN'S OKAY ...
I SHOULD SEND HER A LINE MESSAGE TOO.
Guide for D-Day
Kuro-ta
Kuro-tan, wanna go home? Mommy will come pick you up.
THAT SHOULD DO IT...

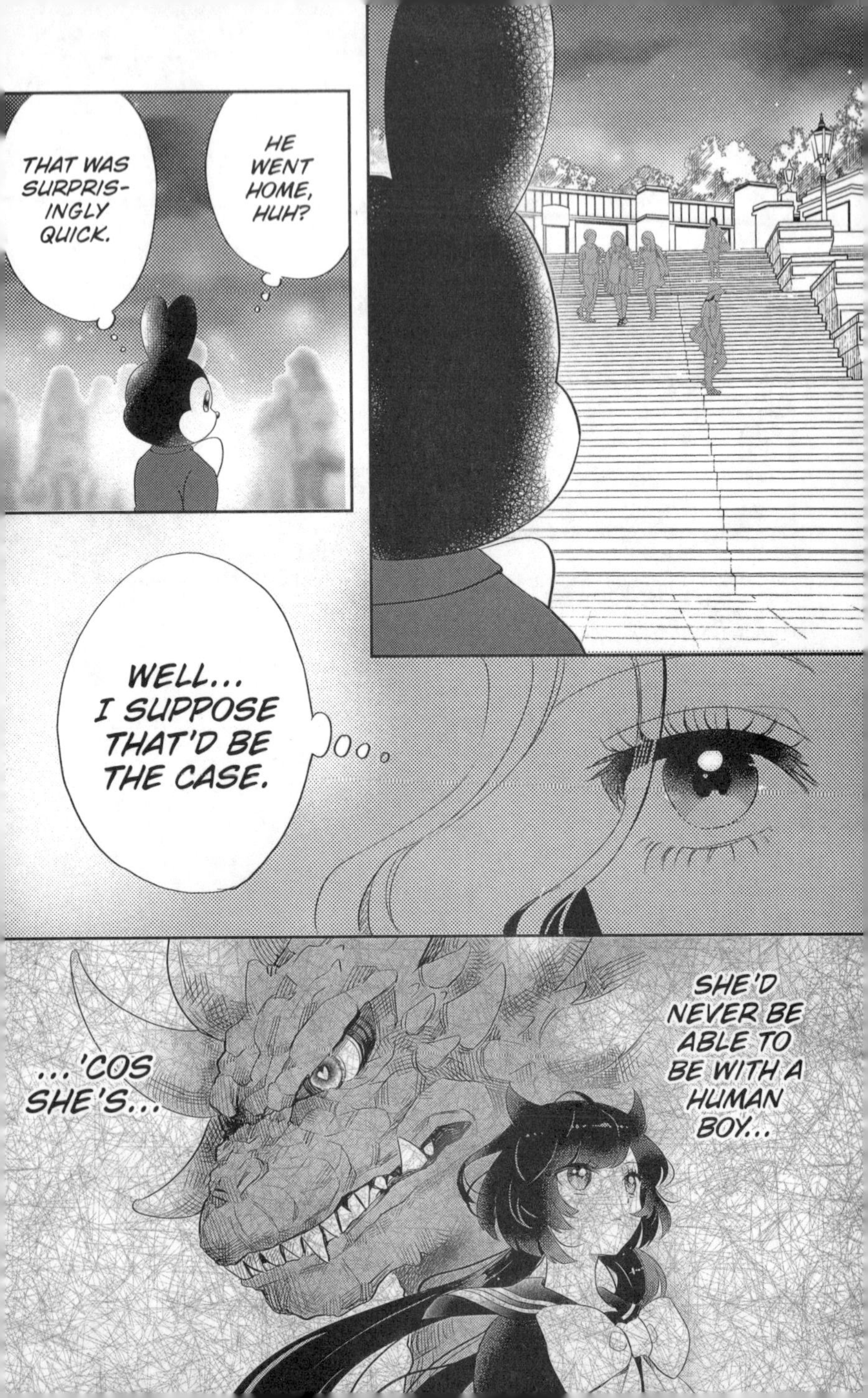
HE WENT HOME, HUH?
THAT WAS SURPRIS-INGLY QUICK.
WELL... I SUPPOSE THAT'D BE THE CASE.
SHE'D NEVER BE ABLE TO BE WITH A HUMAN BOY...
...'COS SHE'S...

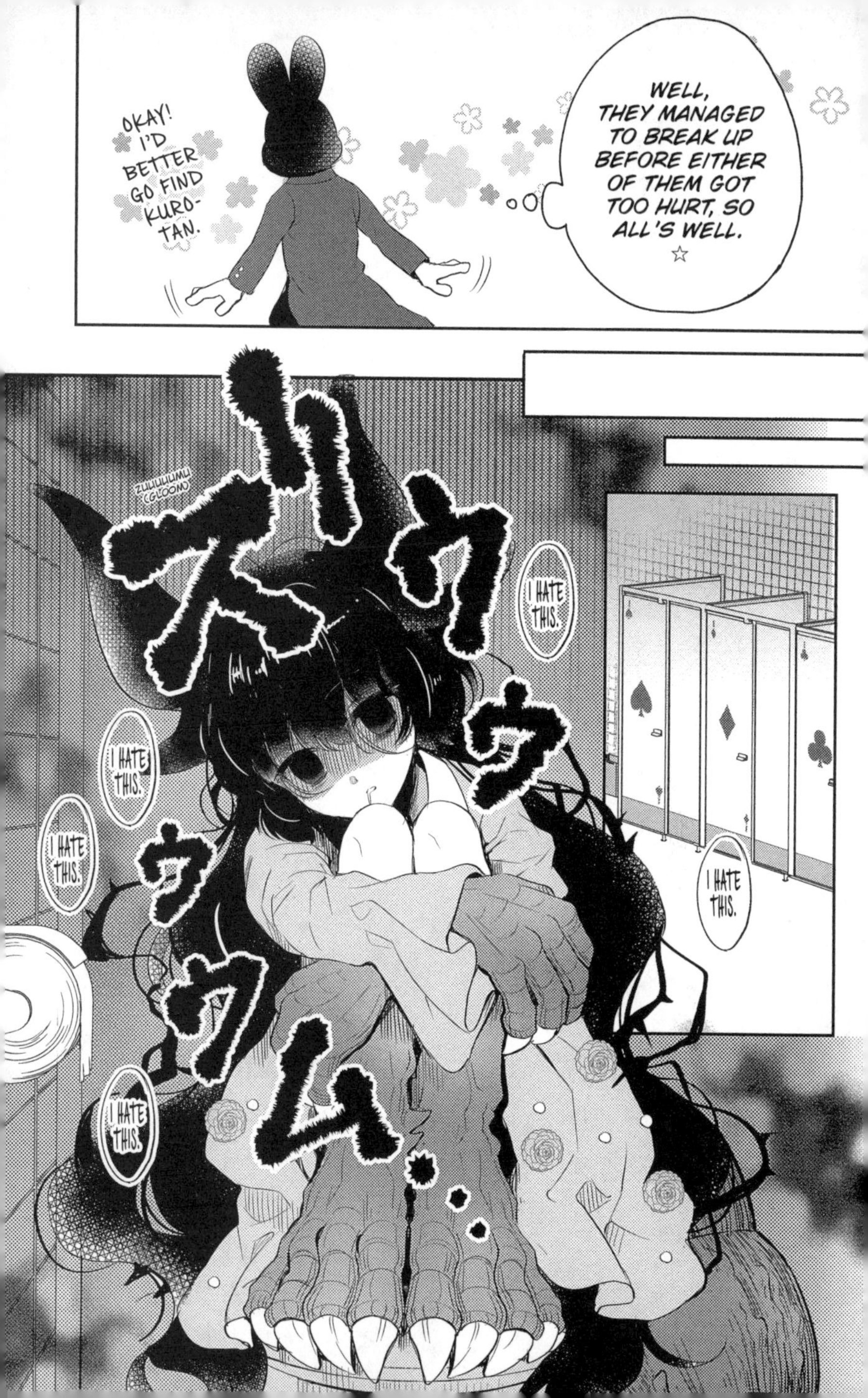
WELL, THEY MANAGED TO BREAK UP BEFORE EITHER OF THEM GOT TOO HURT, SO ALL'S WELL. ☆
OKAY! I'D BETTER GO FIND KURO-TAN.
I HATE THIS.
I HATE THIS.
ZUUUUUUMU (GLOOM)
ズウウウウム
I HATE THIS.
I HATE THIS.
I HATE THIS.

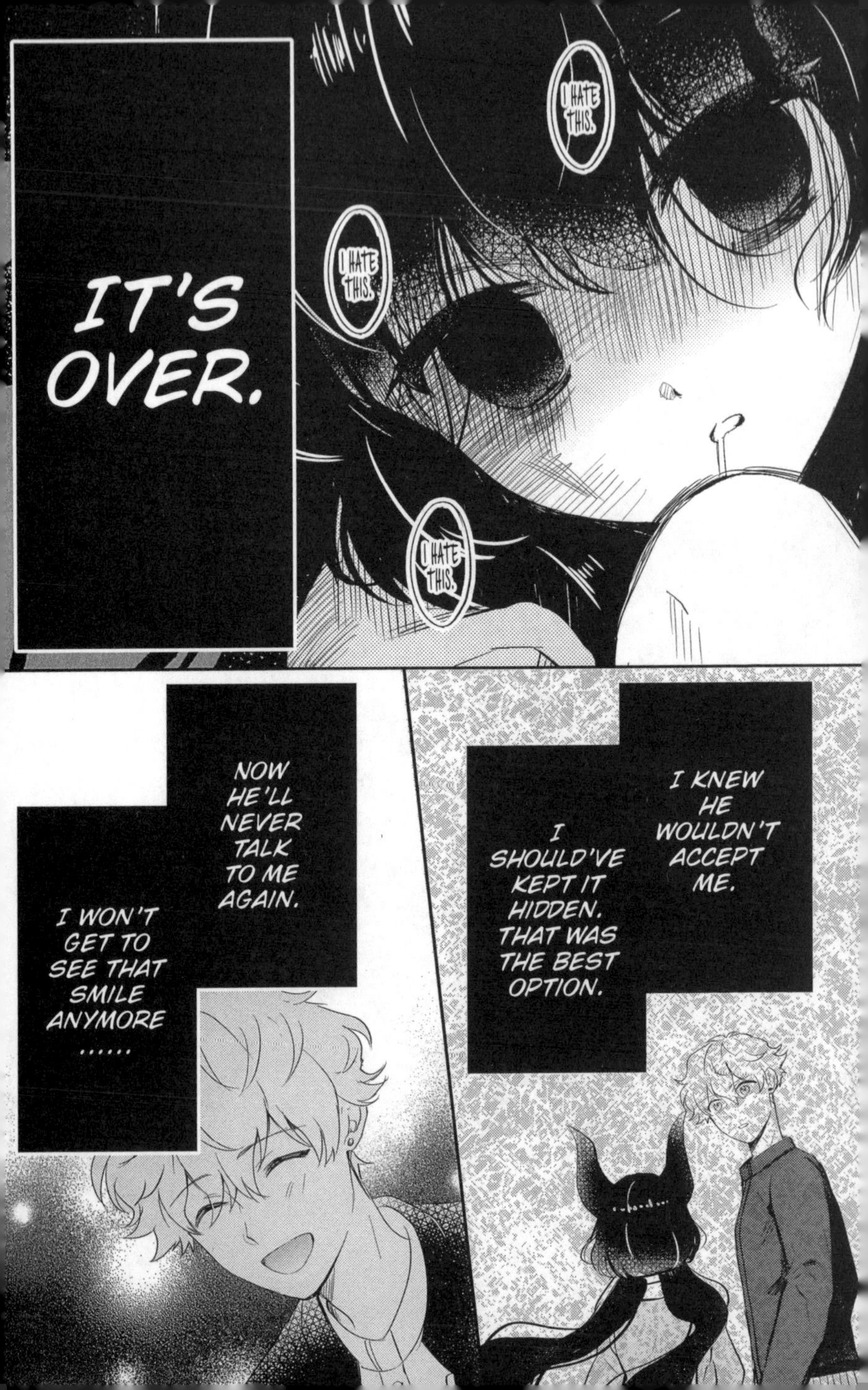
I HATE THIS.
I HATE THIS.
IT'S OVER.
I HATE THIS.
I KNEW HE WOULDN'T ACCEPT ME.
I SHOULD'VE KEPT IT HIDDEN. THAT WAS THE BEST OPTION.
NOW HE'LL NEVER TALK TO ME AGAIN.
I WON'T GET TO SEE THAT SMILE ANYMORE ......

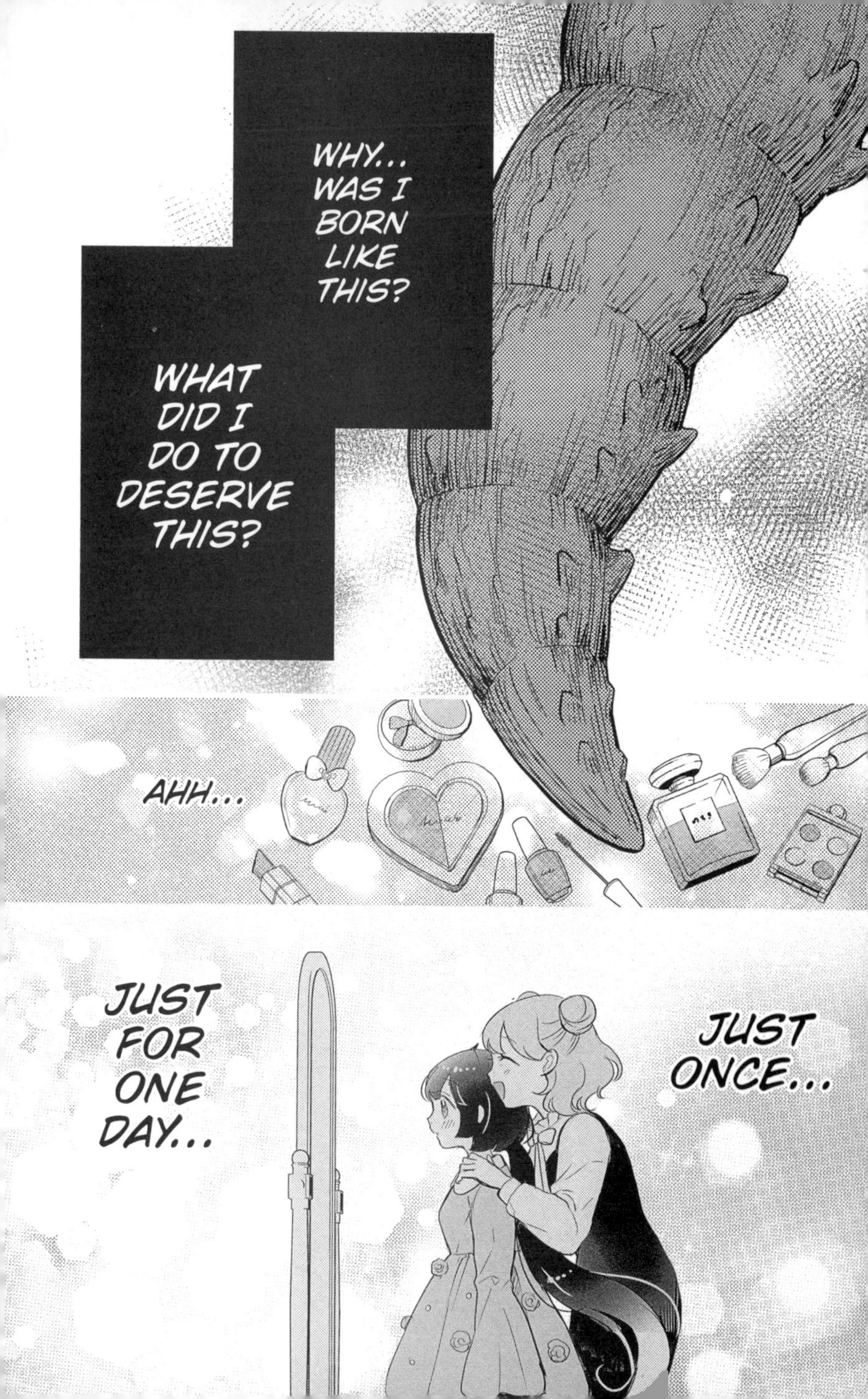
WHY... WAS I BORN LIKE THIS?
WHAT DID I DO TO DESERVE THIS?
AHH...
JUST ONCE...
JUST FOR ONE DAY...

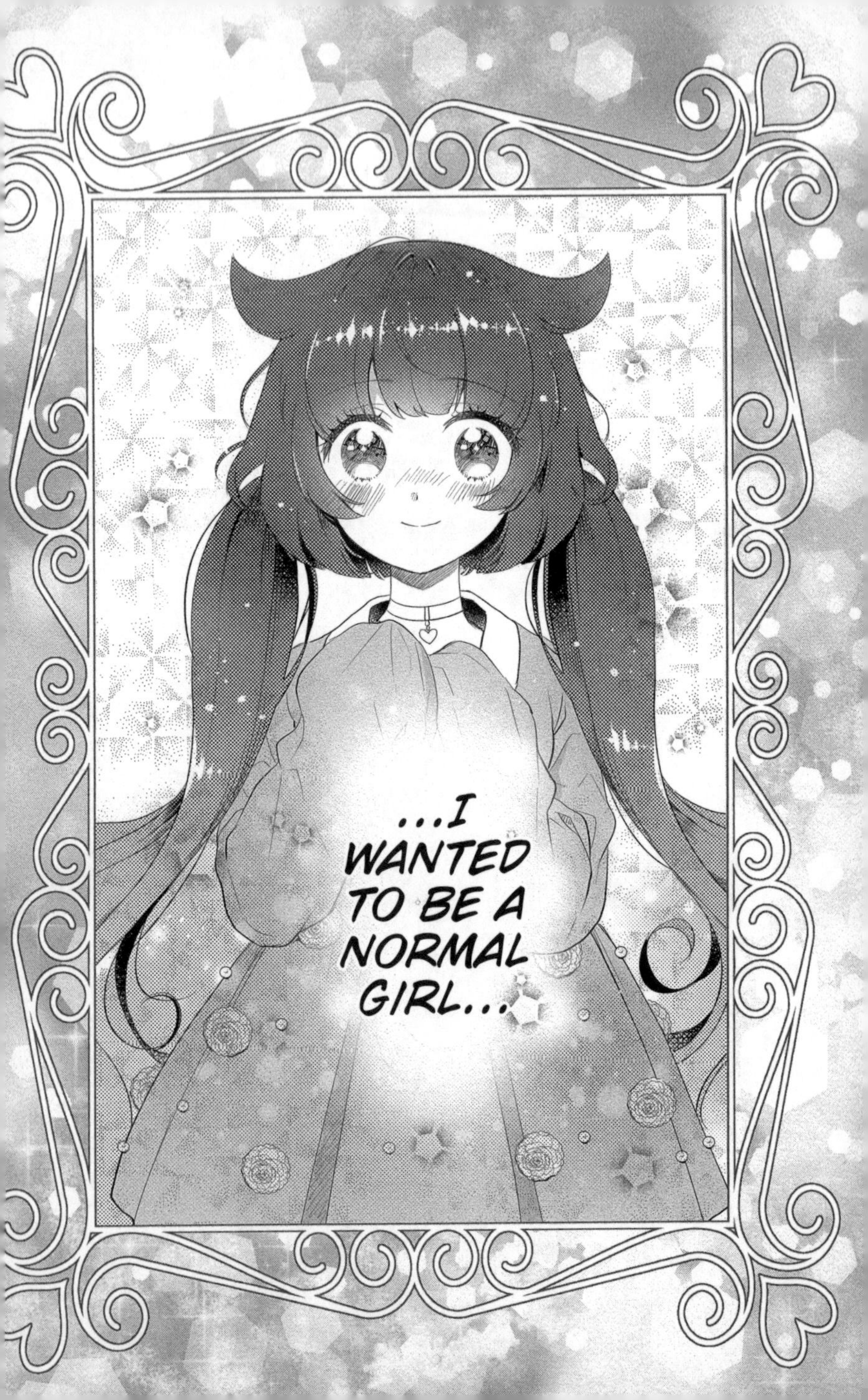
...I WANTED TO BE A NORMAL GIRL...

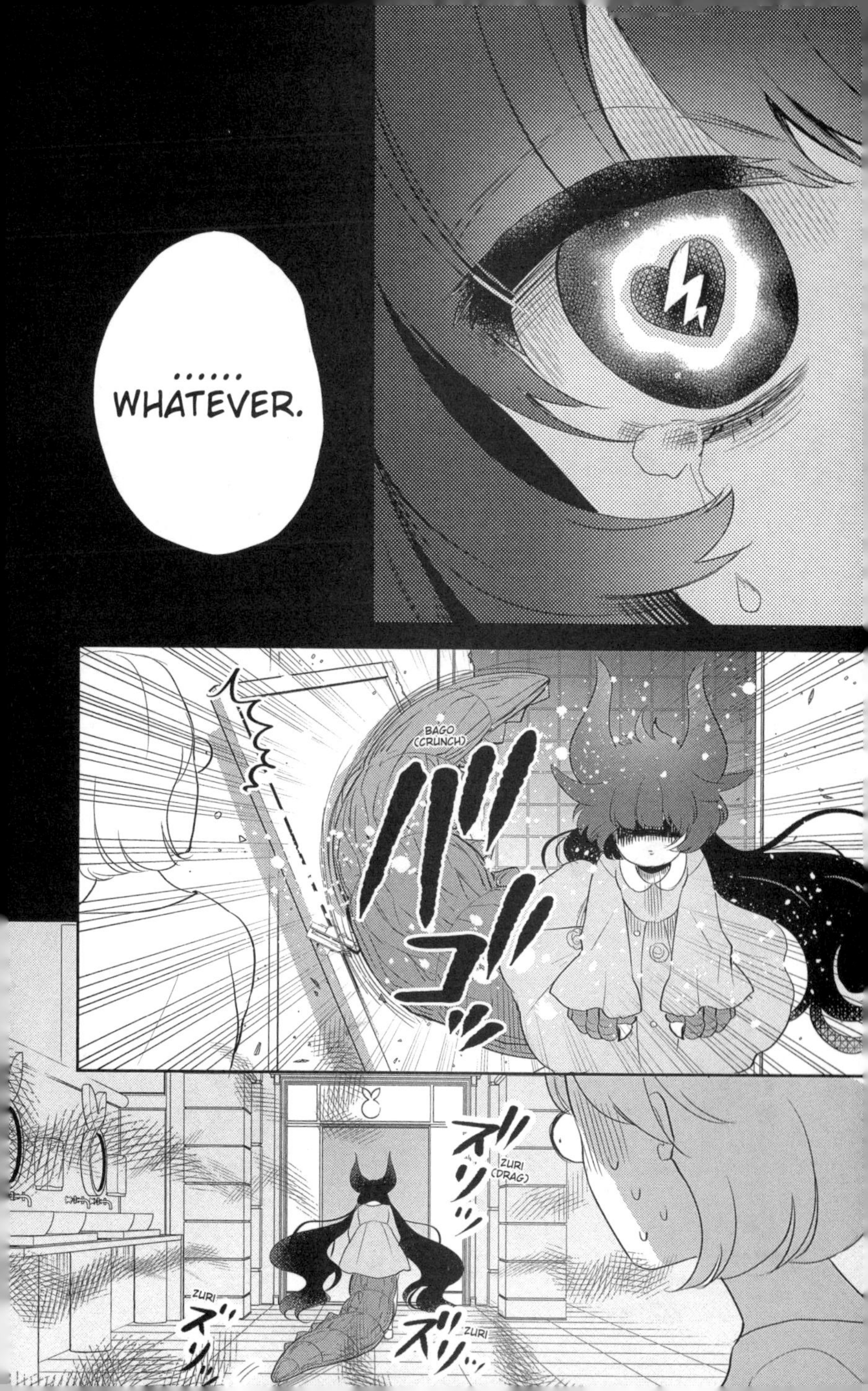

......
WHATEVER.
BAGO (CRUNCH)
バゴッ
ズリッ
ZURI (DRAG)
ZURI
ズリッ
ZURI
ズリッ

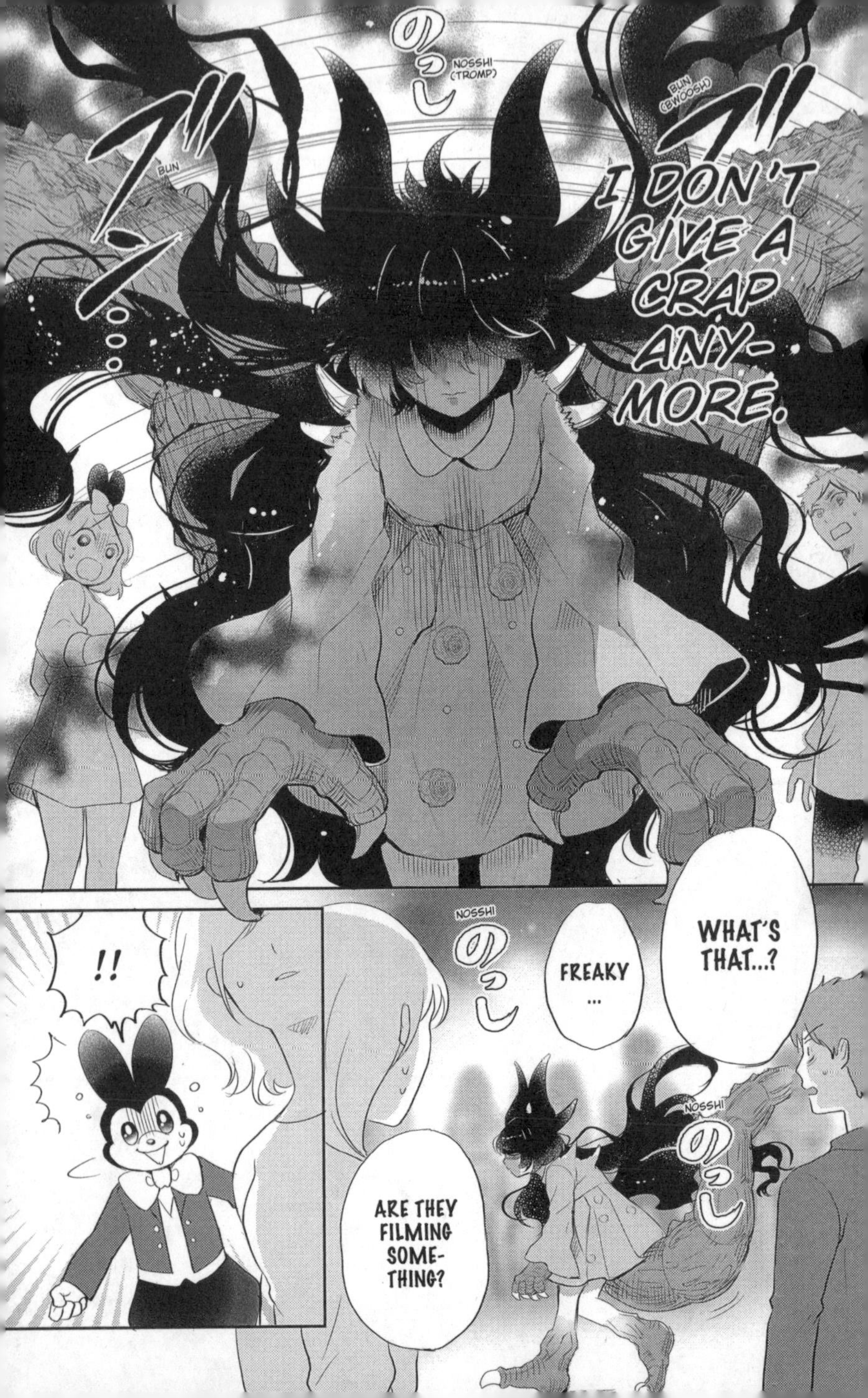

ブン
BUN (BWOOSH)
I DON'T GIVE A CRAP ANYMORE.
のっし
NOSSHI (TROMP)
ブン
BUN
......
WHAT'S THAT...?
FREAKY ...
のっし
NOSSHI
のっし
NOSSHI
ARE THEY FILMING SOMETHING?
!!

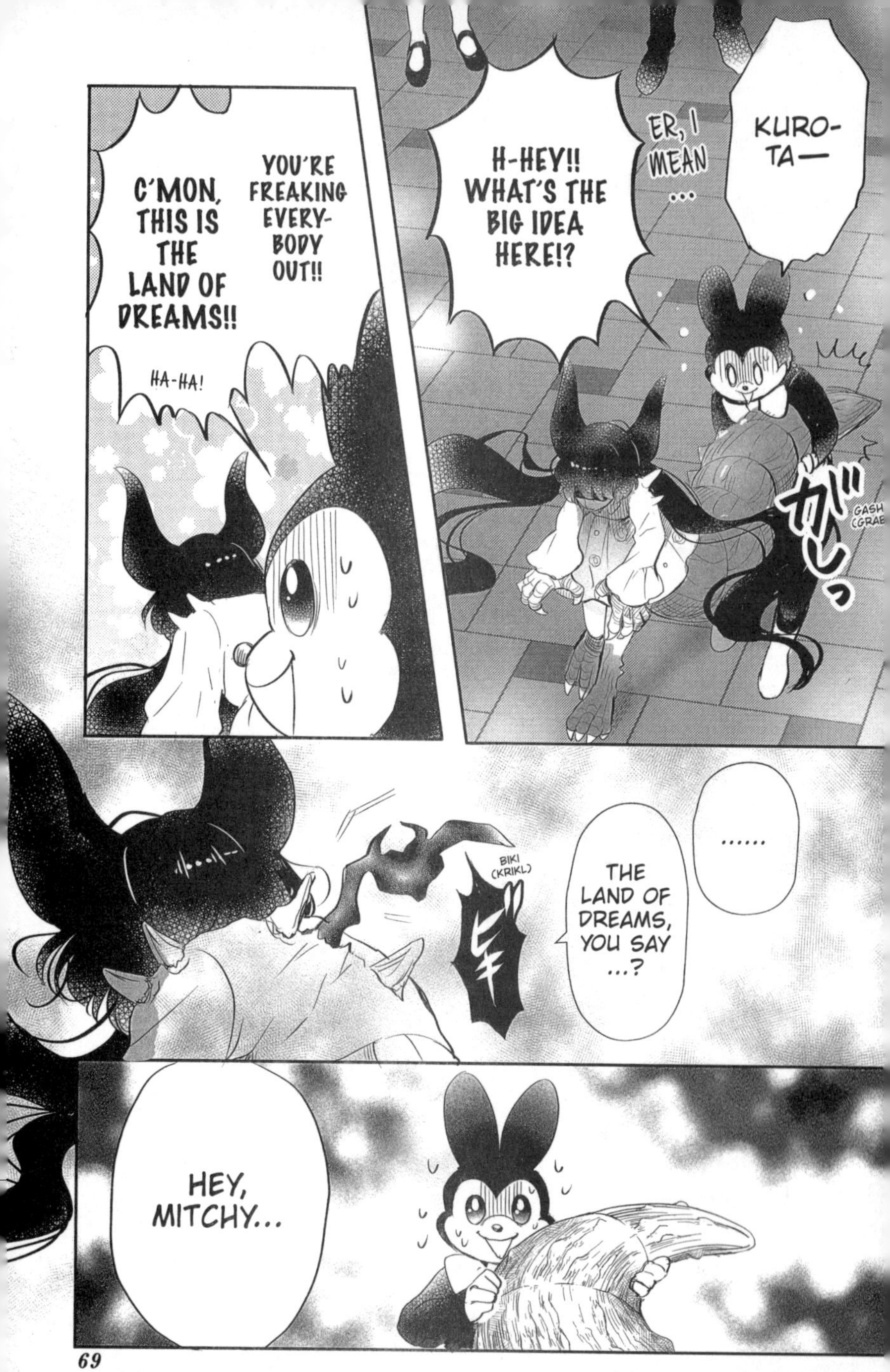
KURO-TA—
ER, I MEAN...
H-HEY!! WHAT'S THE BIG IDEA HERE!?
GASH (GRAB)
YOU'RE FREAKING EVERY-BODY OUT!!
C'MON, THIS IS THE LAND OF DREAMS!!
HA-HA!
......
THE LAND OF DREAMS, YOU SAY...?
BIKI (KRIKL)
HEY, MITCHY...

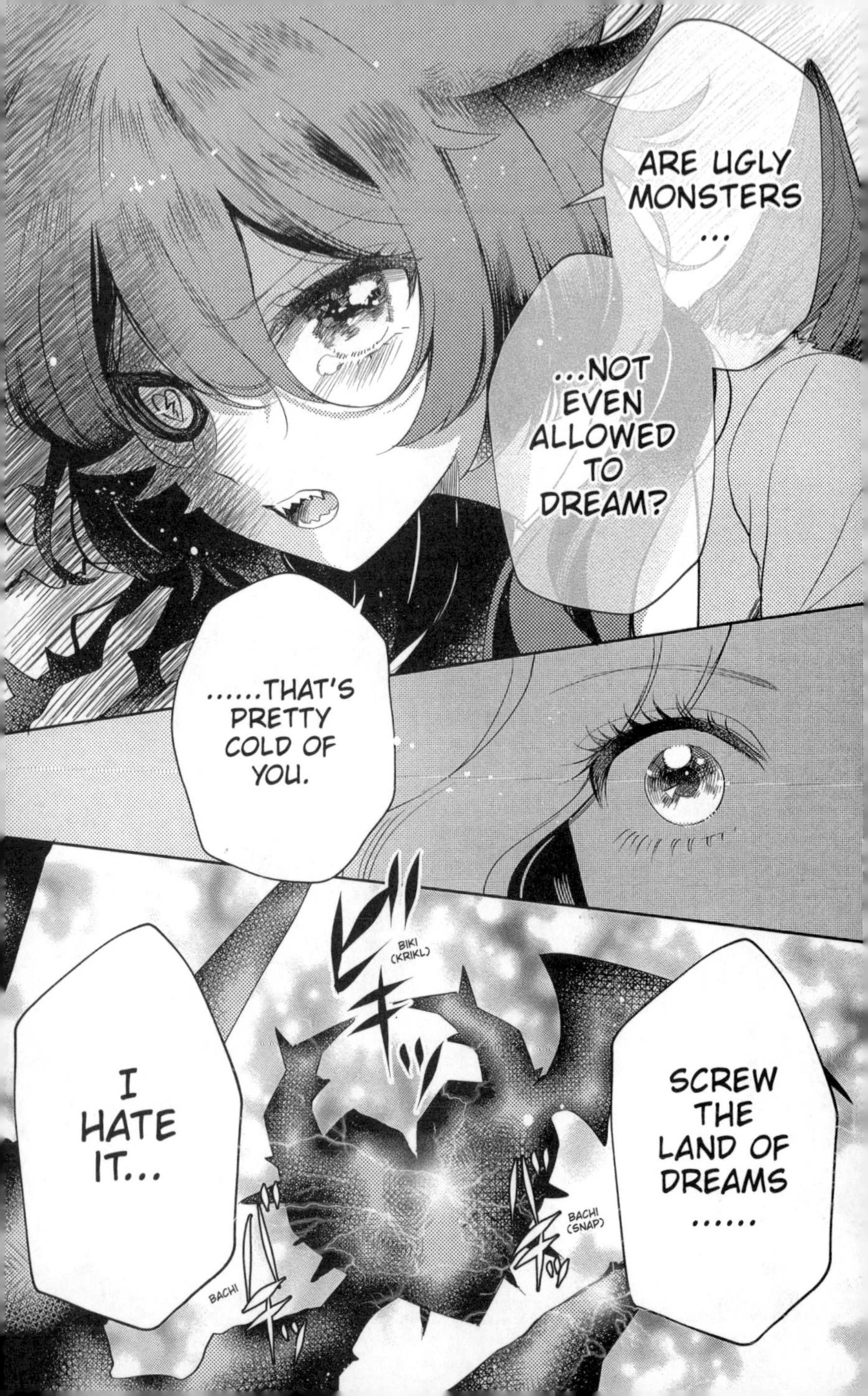
ARE UGLY MONSTERS ...
...NOT EVEN ALLOWED TO DREAM?
......THAT'S PRETTY COLD OF YOU.
SCREW THE LAND OF DREAMS ......
BIKI (KRIKL)
BACHI (SNAP)
I HATE IT...
BACHI

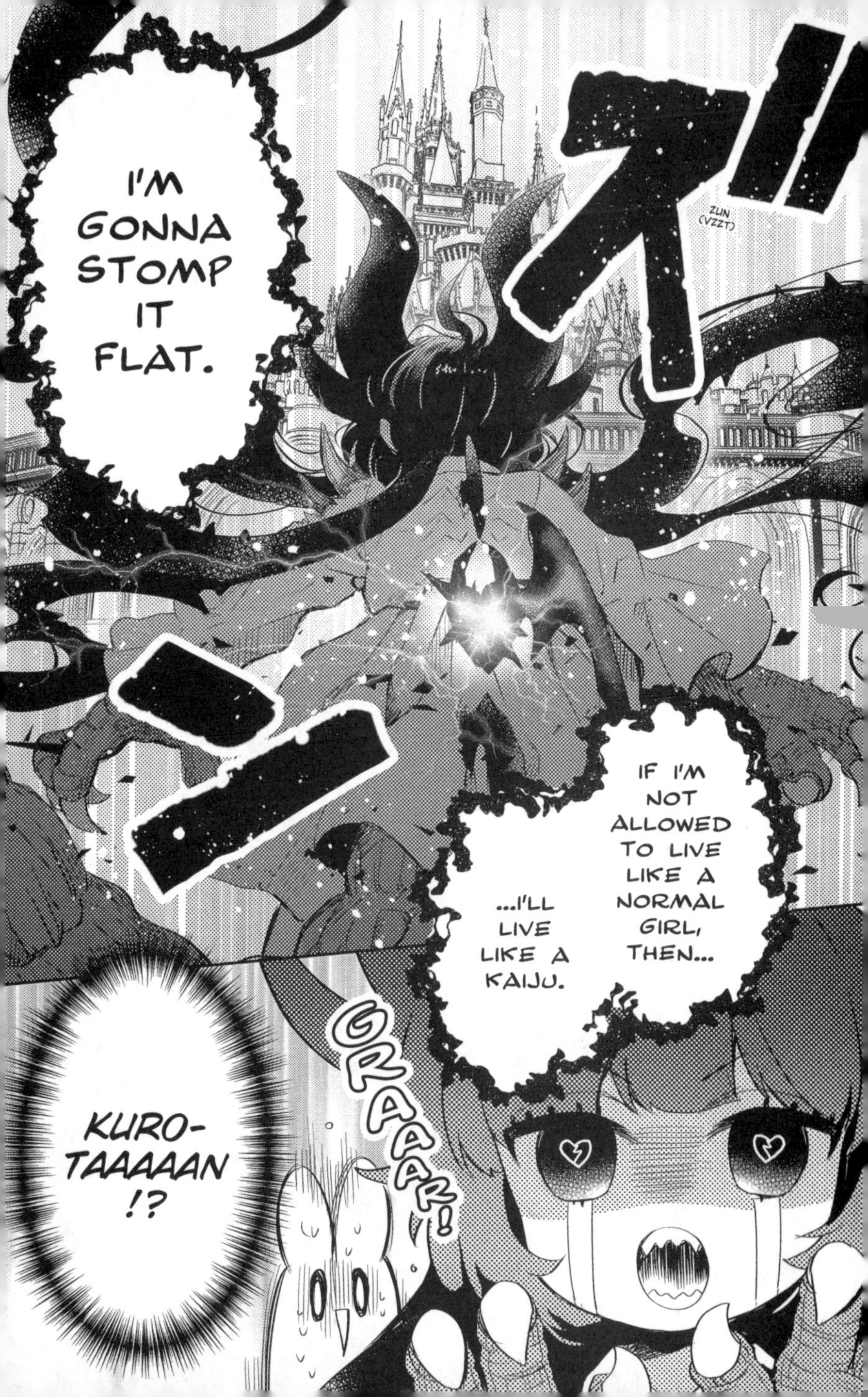
ZUN (VZZT)
I'M GONNA STOMP IT FLAT.
IF I'M NOT ALLOWED TO LIVE LIKE A NORMAL GIRL, THEN...
...I'LL LIVE LIKE A KAIJU.
GRAAAAR!
KURO-TAAAAAN!?

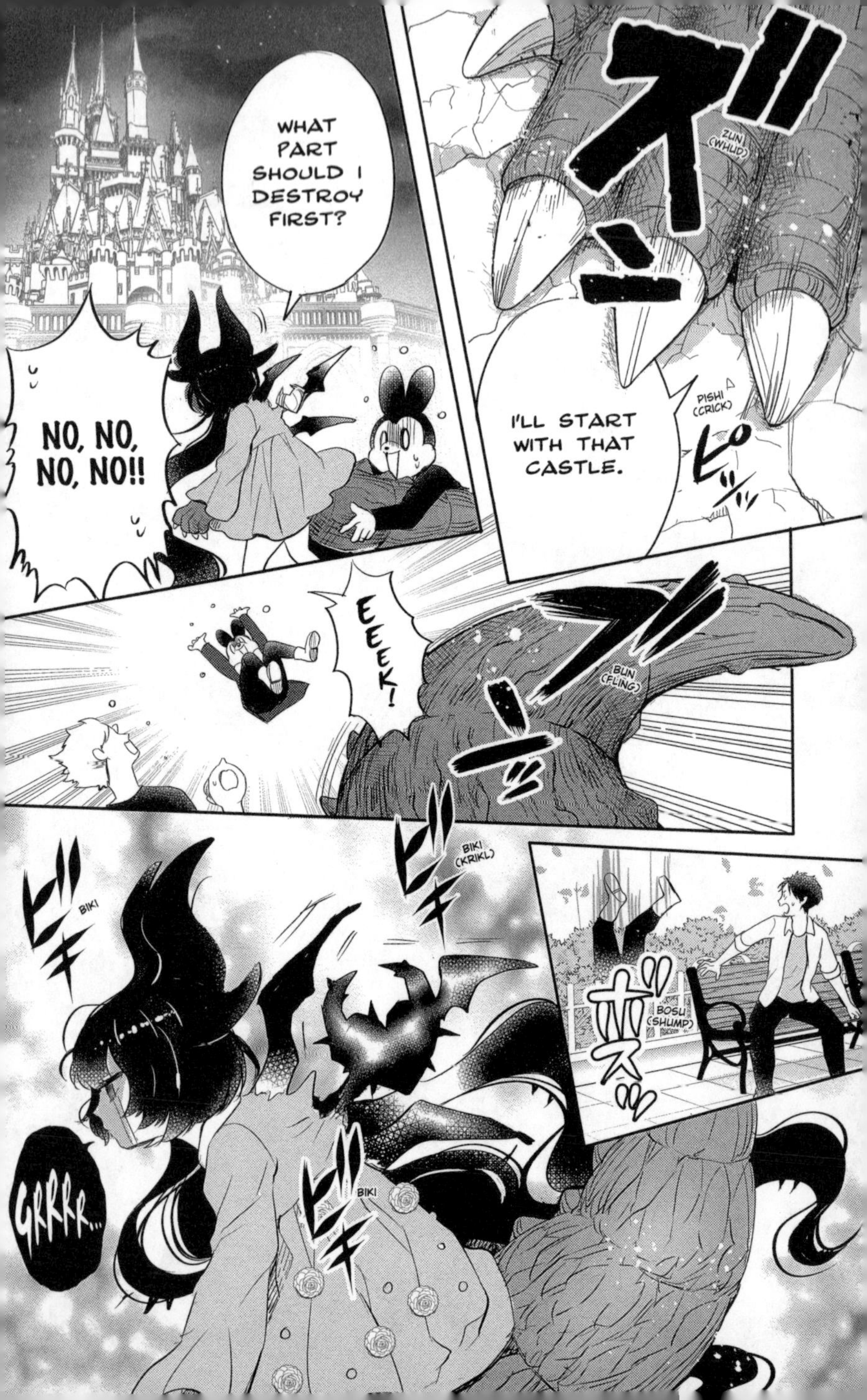
ZUN (WHUD)
I'LL START WITH THAT CASTLE.
PISHI (CRICK)
WHAT PART SHOULD I DESTROY FIRST?
NO, NO, NO, NO!!
BUN (FLING)
EEEK!
BOSU (SHUMP)
BIKI (KRIKL)
BIKI
BIKI
GRRRR...

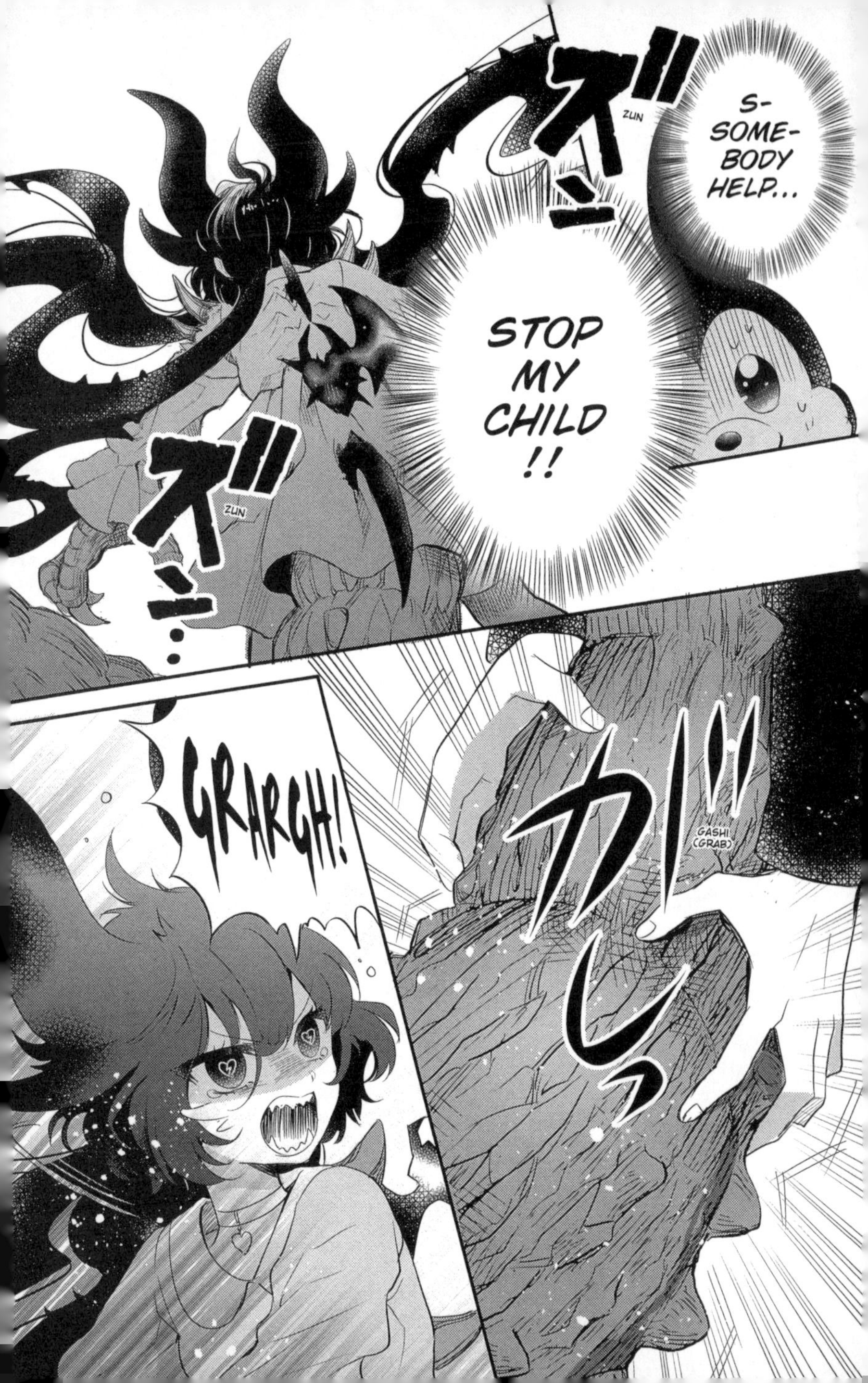
S-SOMEBODY HELP...
ZUN
STOP MY CHILD!!
ZUN
GASHI (GRAB)
GRARGH!

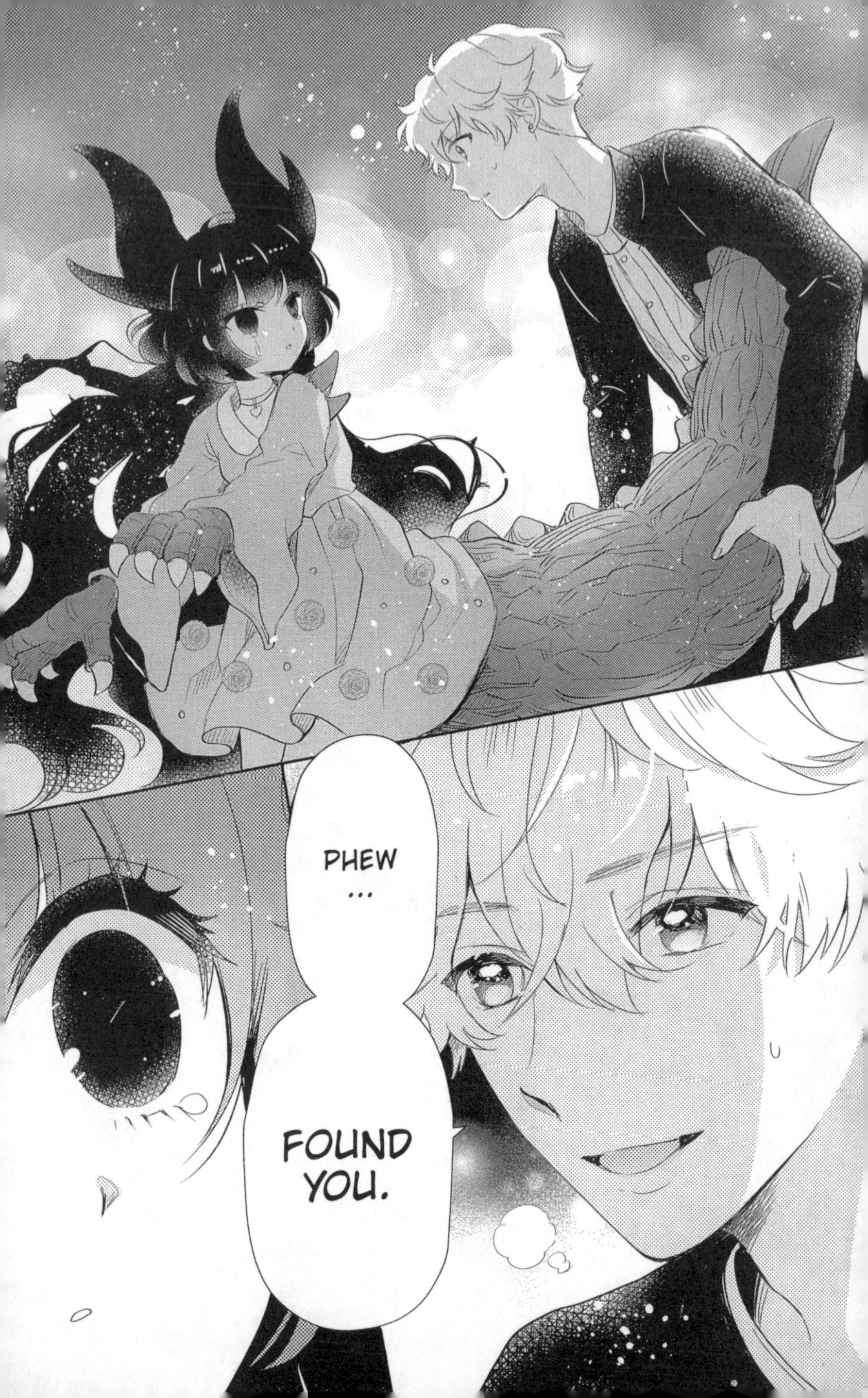
PHEW ...
FOUND YOU.

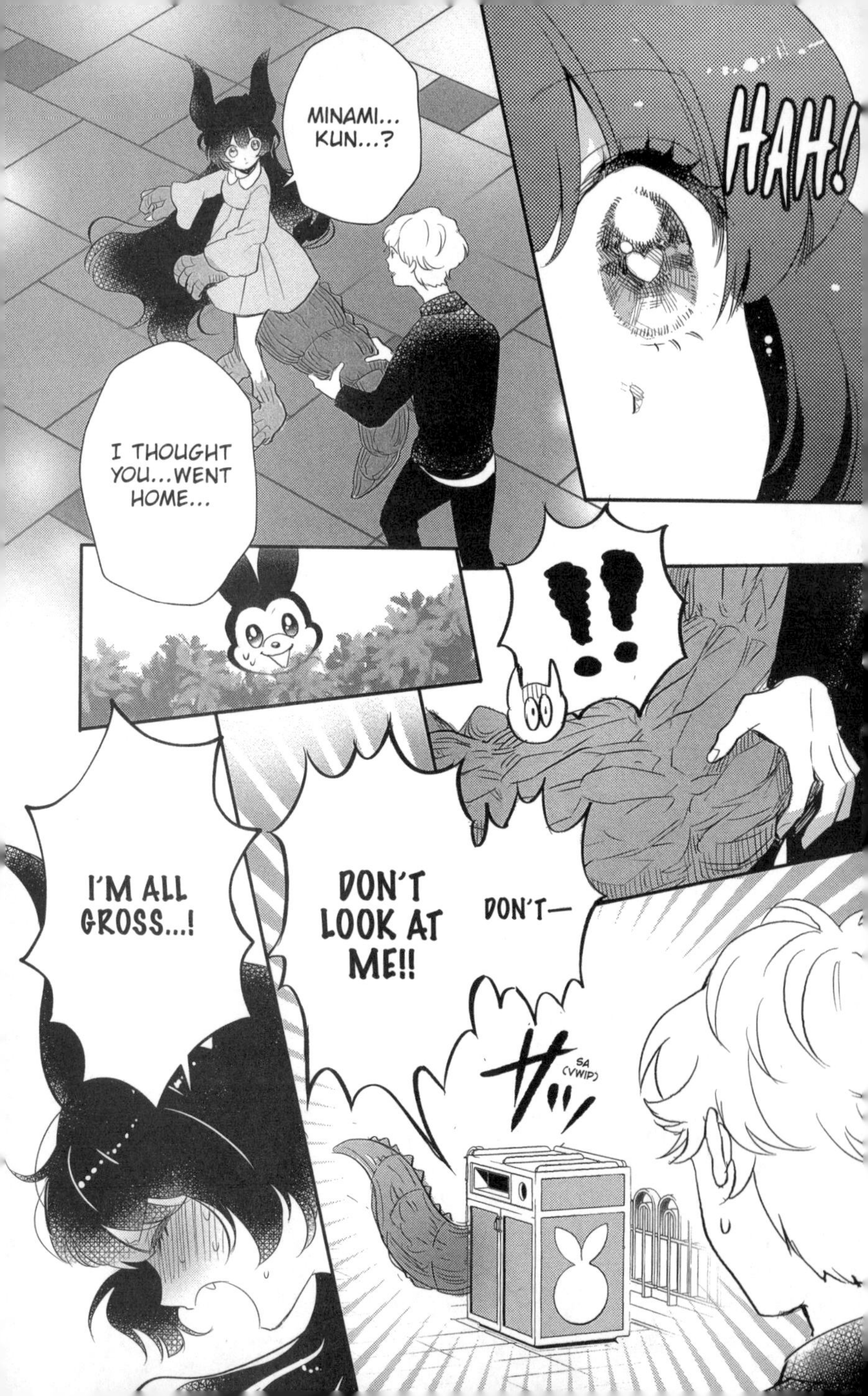
HAH!
MINAMI... KUN...?
I THOUGHT YOU...WENT HOME...
!!
DON'T—
DON'T LOOK AT ME!!
I'M ALL GROSS...!
SA (VWIP)

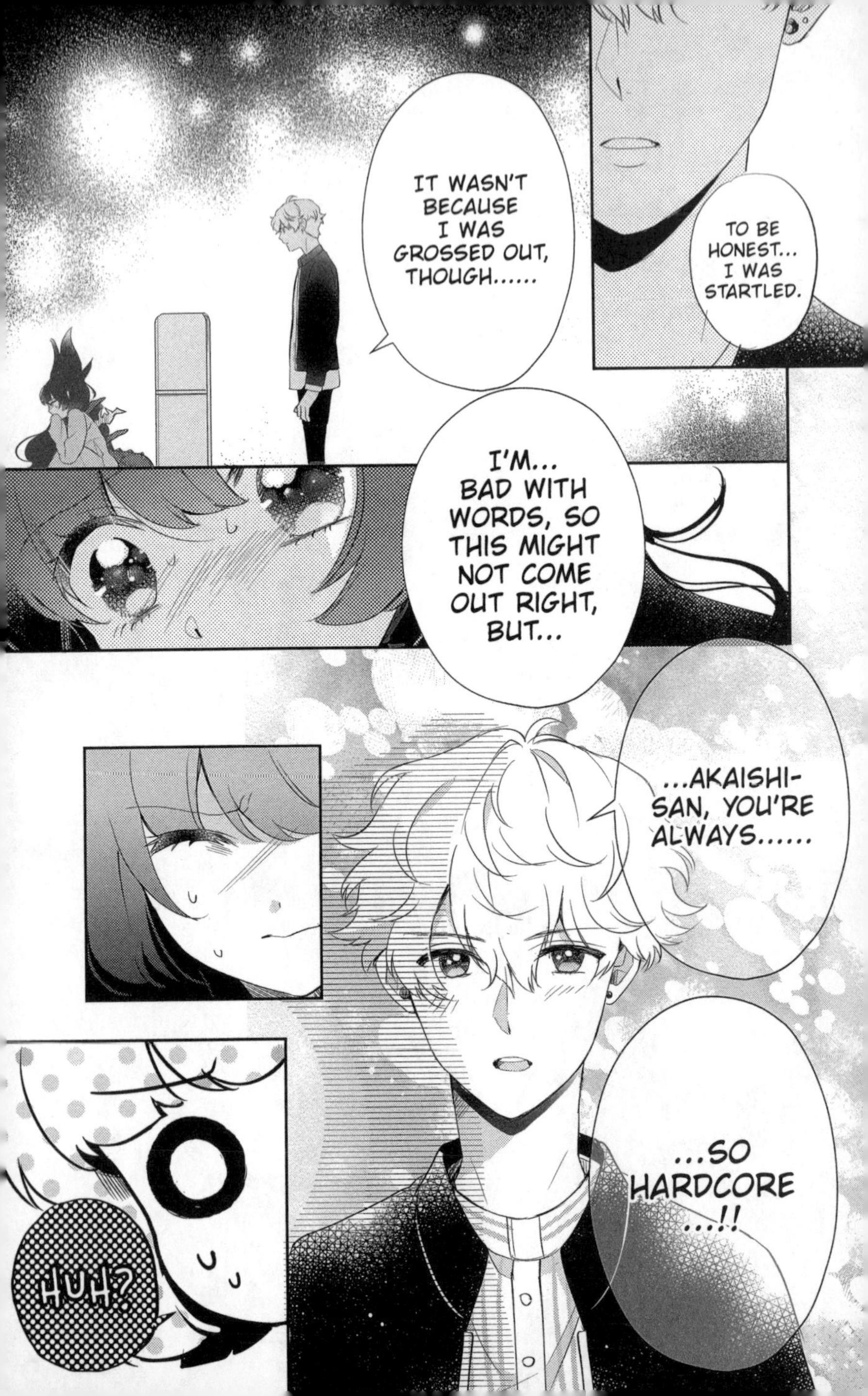
TO BE HONEST... I WAS STARTLED.
IT WASN'T BECAUSE I WAS GROSSED OUT, THOUGH......
I'M... BAD WITH WORDS, SO THIS MIGHT NOT COME OUT RIGHT, BUT...
...AKAISHI-SAN, YOU'RE ALWAYS......
...SO HARDCORE ...!!
HUH?

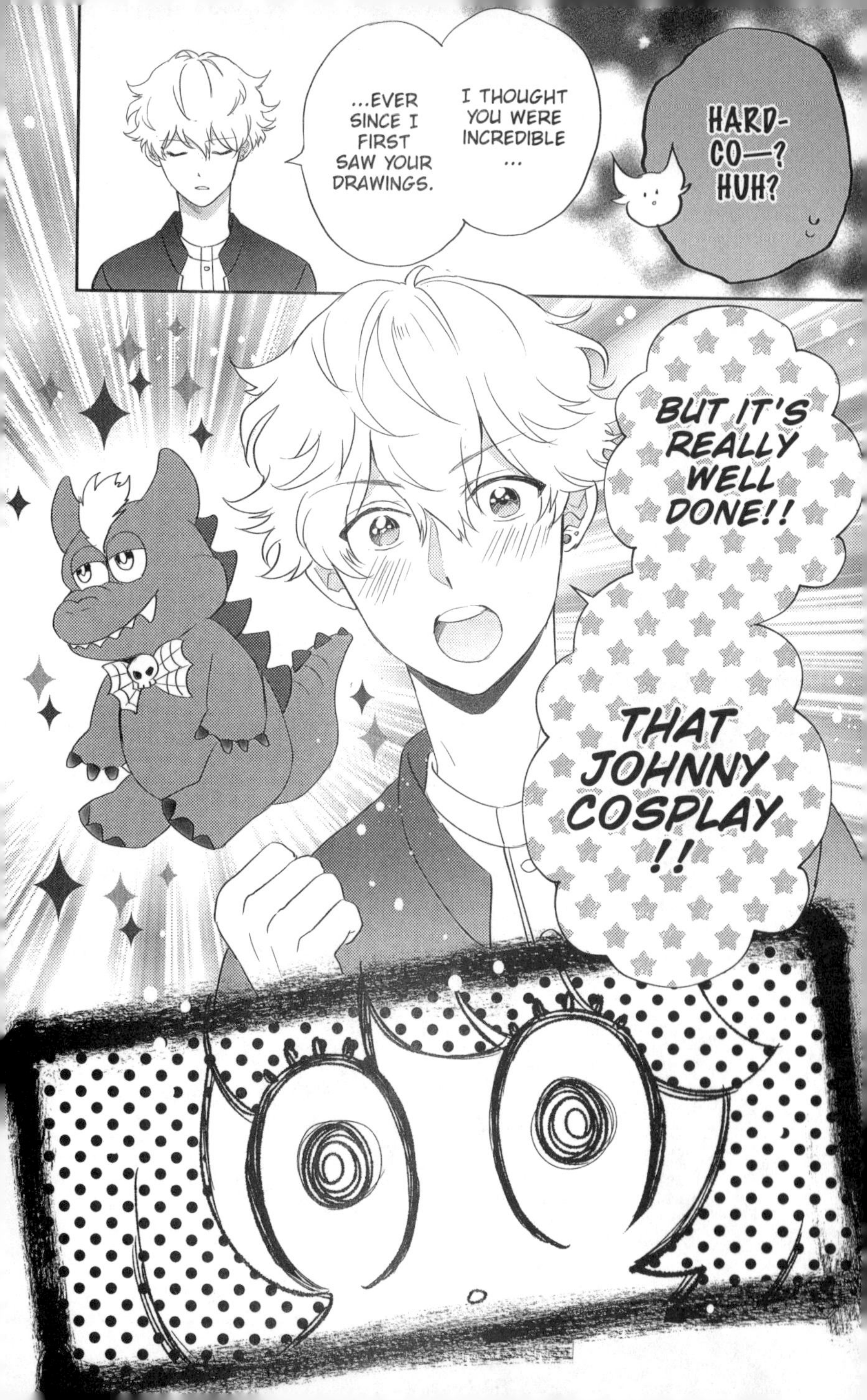
HARD-CO—? HUH?
I THOUGHT YOU WERE INCREDIBLE...
...EVER SINCE I FIRST SAW YOUR DRAWINGS.
BUT IT'S REALLY WELL DONE!!
THAT JOHNNY COSPLAY!!

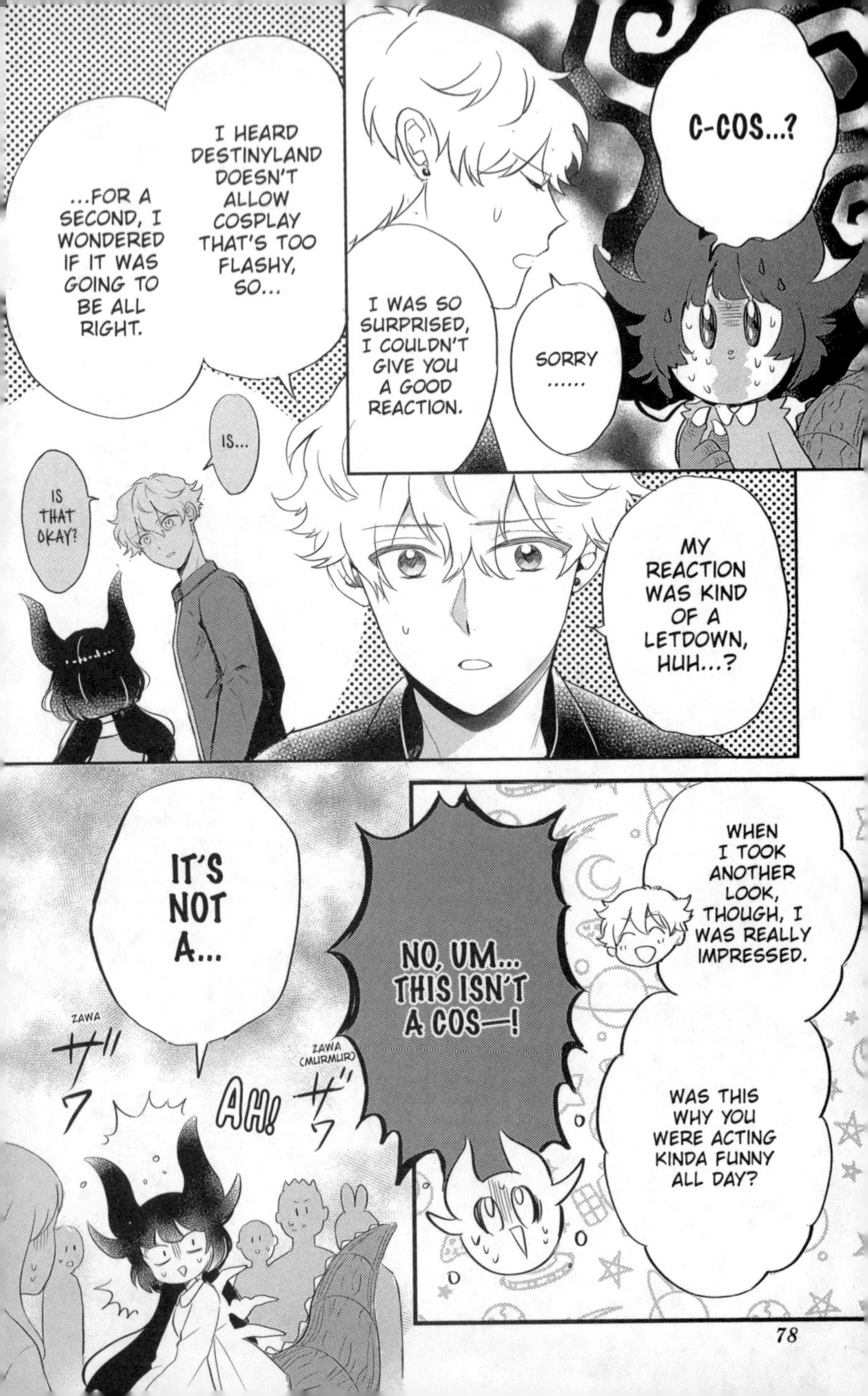
C-COS...?
SORRY......
I WAS SO SURPRISED, I COULDN'T GIVE YOU A GOOD REACTION.
I HEARD DESTINYLAND DOESN'T ALLOW COSPLAY THAT'S TOO FLASHY, SO...
...FOR A SECOND, I WONDERED IF IT WAS GOING TO BE ALL RIGHT.
MY REACTION WAS KIND OF A LETDOWN, HUH...?
IS...
IS THAT OKAY?
WHEN I TOOK ANOTHER LOOK, THOUGH, I WAS REALLY IMPRESSED.
WAS THIS WHY YOU WERE ACTING KINDA FUNNY ALL DAY?
NO, UM... THIS ISN'T A COS—!
ZAWA (MURMUR)
AH!
IT'S NOT A...
ZAWA

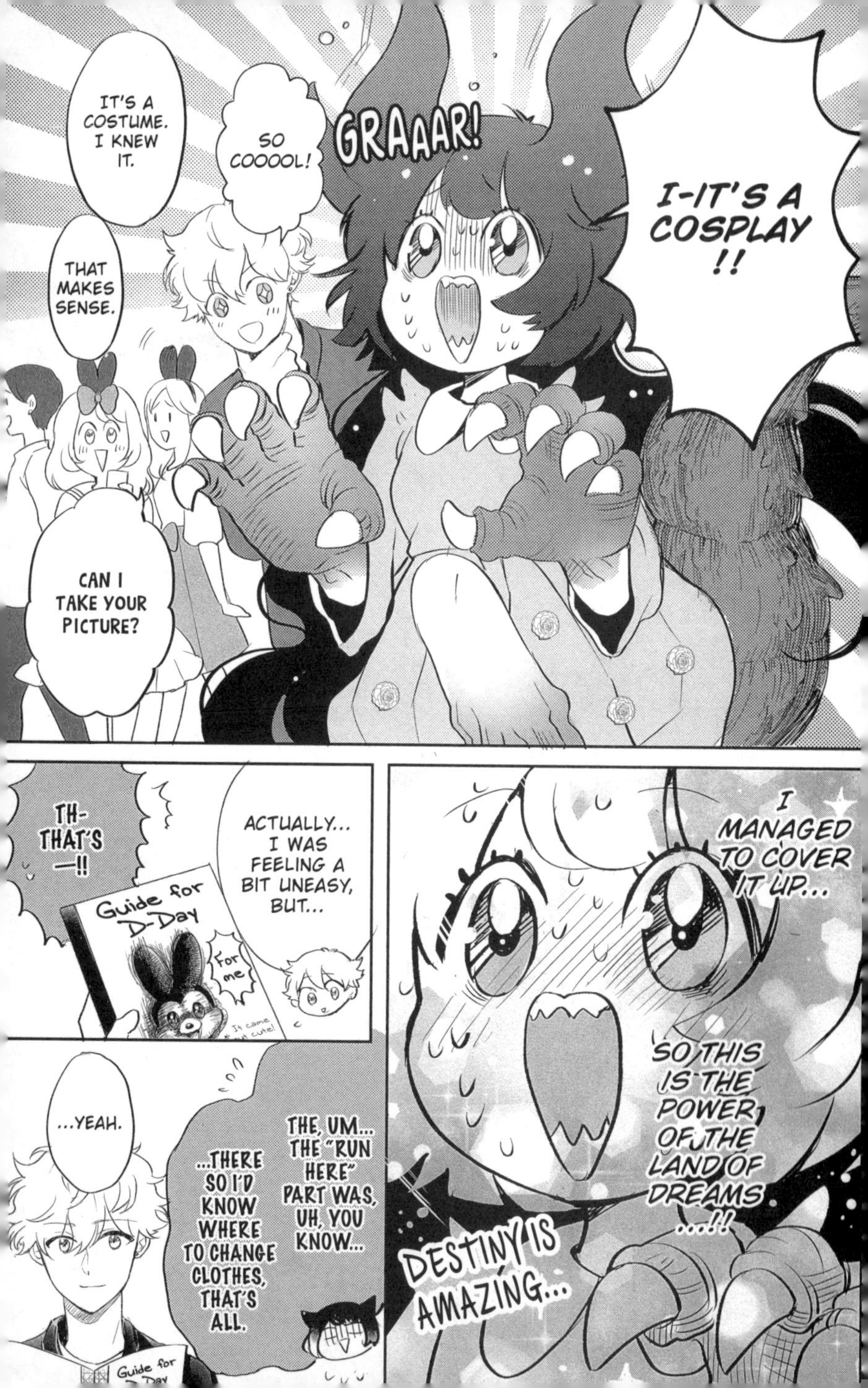
I-IT'S A COSPLAY!!
GRAAAR!
SO COOOOL!
IT'S A COSTUME. I KNEW IT.
THAT MAKES SENSE.
CAN I TAKE YOUR PICTURE?
I MANAGED TO COVER IT UP...
SO THIS IS THE POWER OF THE LAND OF DREAMS...!!
DESTINY IS AMAZING...
ACTUALLY... I WAS FEELING A BIT UNEASY, BUT...
TH-THAT'S—!!
Guide for D-Day
For me
THE, UM... THE "RUN HERE" PART WAS, UH, YOU KNOW...
...THERE SO I'D KNOW WHERE TO CHANGE CLOTHES, THAT'S ALL.
...YEAH.

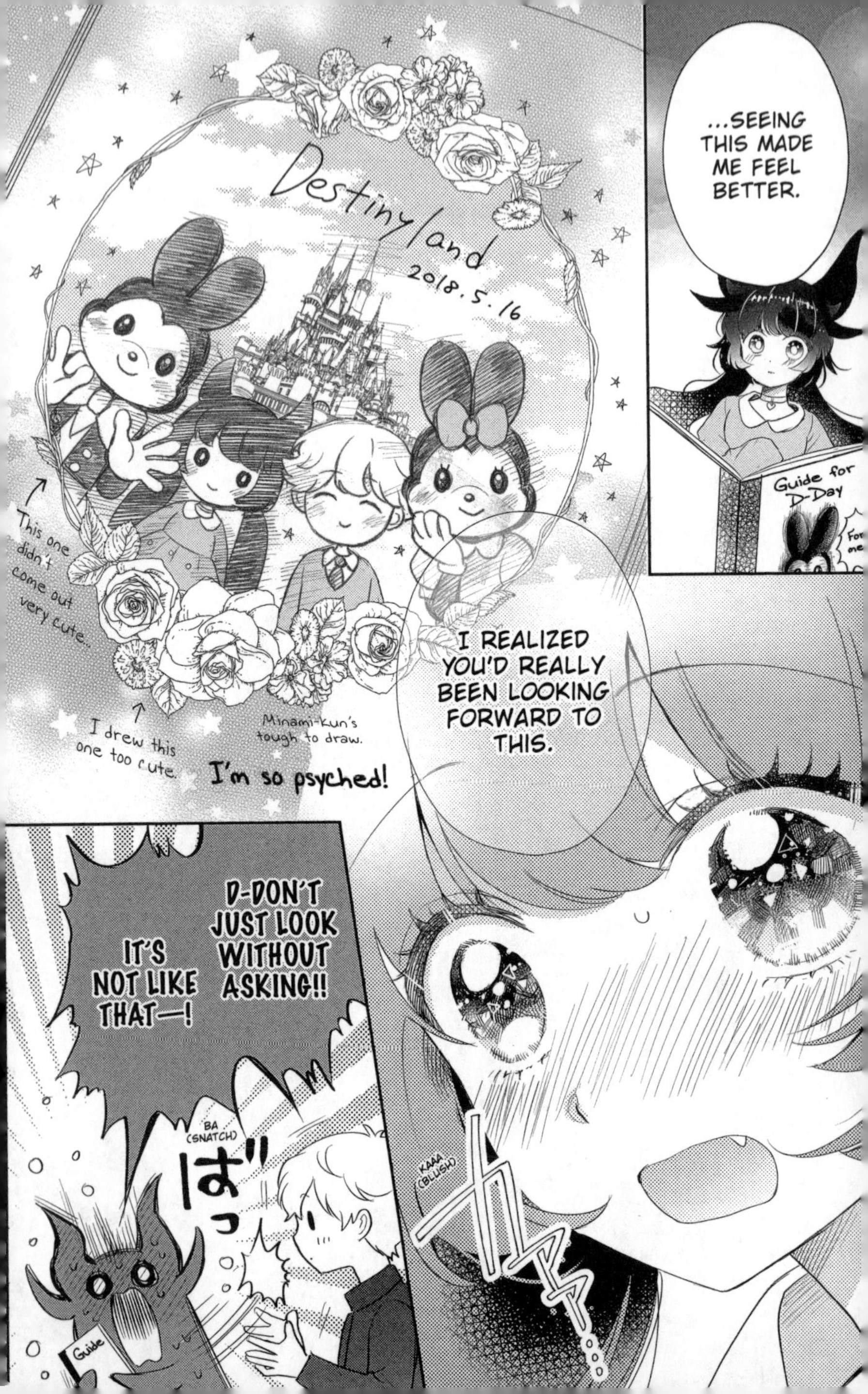
...SEEING THIS MADE ME FEEL BETTER.
Guide for D-Day
Destinyland
2018.5.16
This one didn't come out very cute...
I drew this one too cute.
Minami-kun's tough to draw.
I'm so psyched!
I REALIZED YOU'D REALLY BEEN LOOKING FORWARD TO THIS.
KAAA (BLUSH)
D-DON'T JUST LOOK WITHOUT ASKING!!
IT'S NOT LIKE THAT—!
BA (SNATCH)
Guide

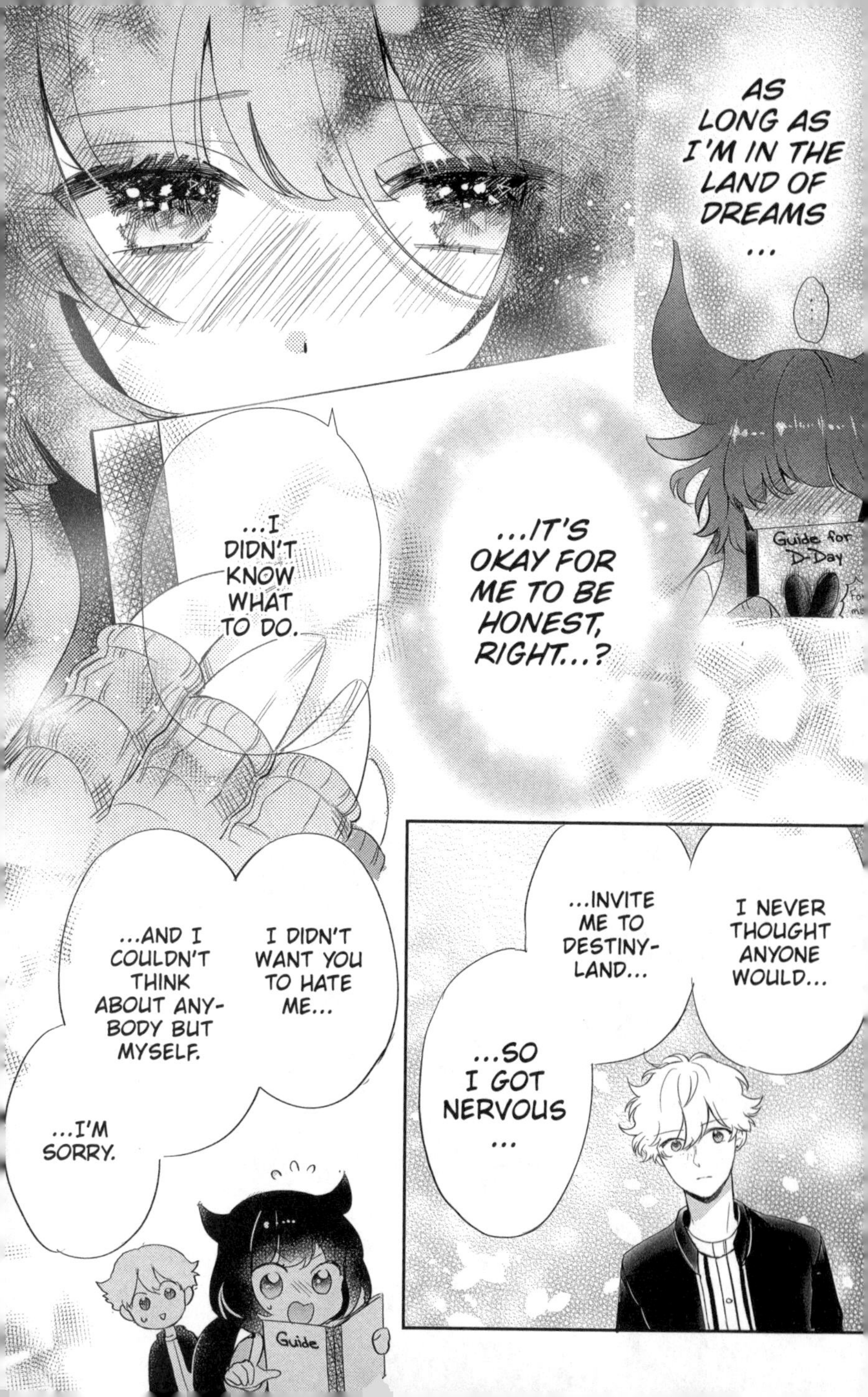
AS LONG AS I'M IN THE LAND OF DREAMS...
Guide for D-Day
...IT'S OKAY FOR ME TO BE HONEST, RIGHT...?
...I DIDN'T KNOW WHAT TO DO.
I NEVER THOUGHT ANYONE WOULD...
...INVITE ME TO DESTINY-LAND...
...SO I GOT NERVOUS...
I DIDN'T WANT YOU TO HATE ME...
...AND I COULDN'T THINK ABOUT ANY-BODY BUT MYSELF.
...I'M SORRY.
Guide

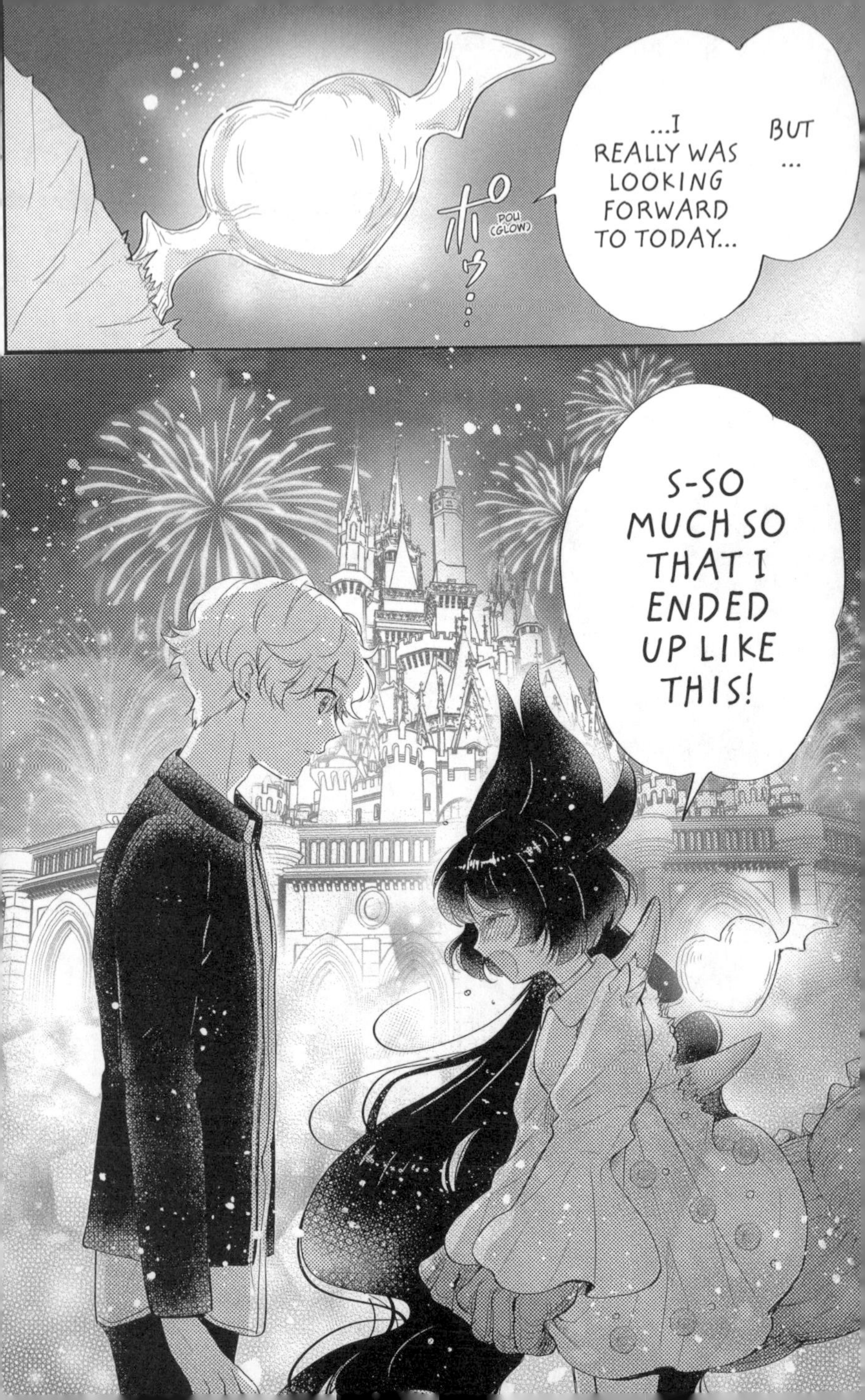
BUT ...
...I REALLY WAS LOOKING FORWARD TO TODAY...
POU (GLOW)
S-SO MUCH SO THAT I ENDED UP LIKE THIS!

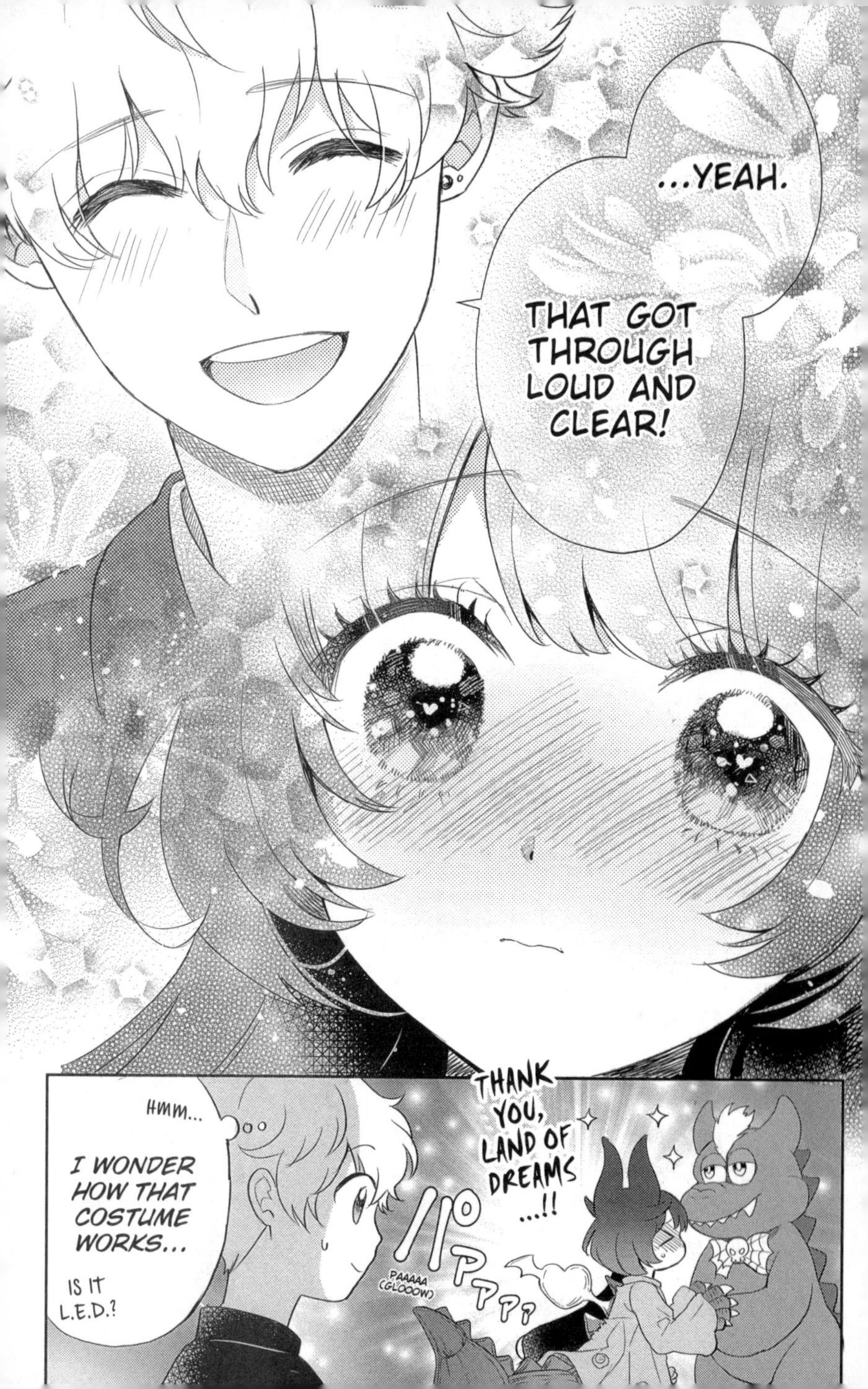
...YEAH.
THAT GOT THROUGH LOUD AND CLEAR!
THANK YOU, LAND OF DREAMS ...!!
PAAAAA (GLOOOW)
HMM...
I WONDER HOW THAT COSTUME WORKS...
IS IT L.E.D.?

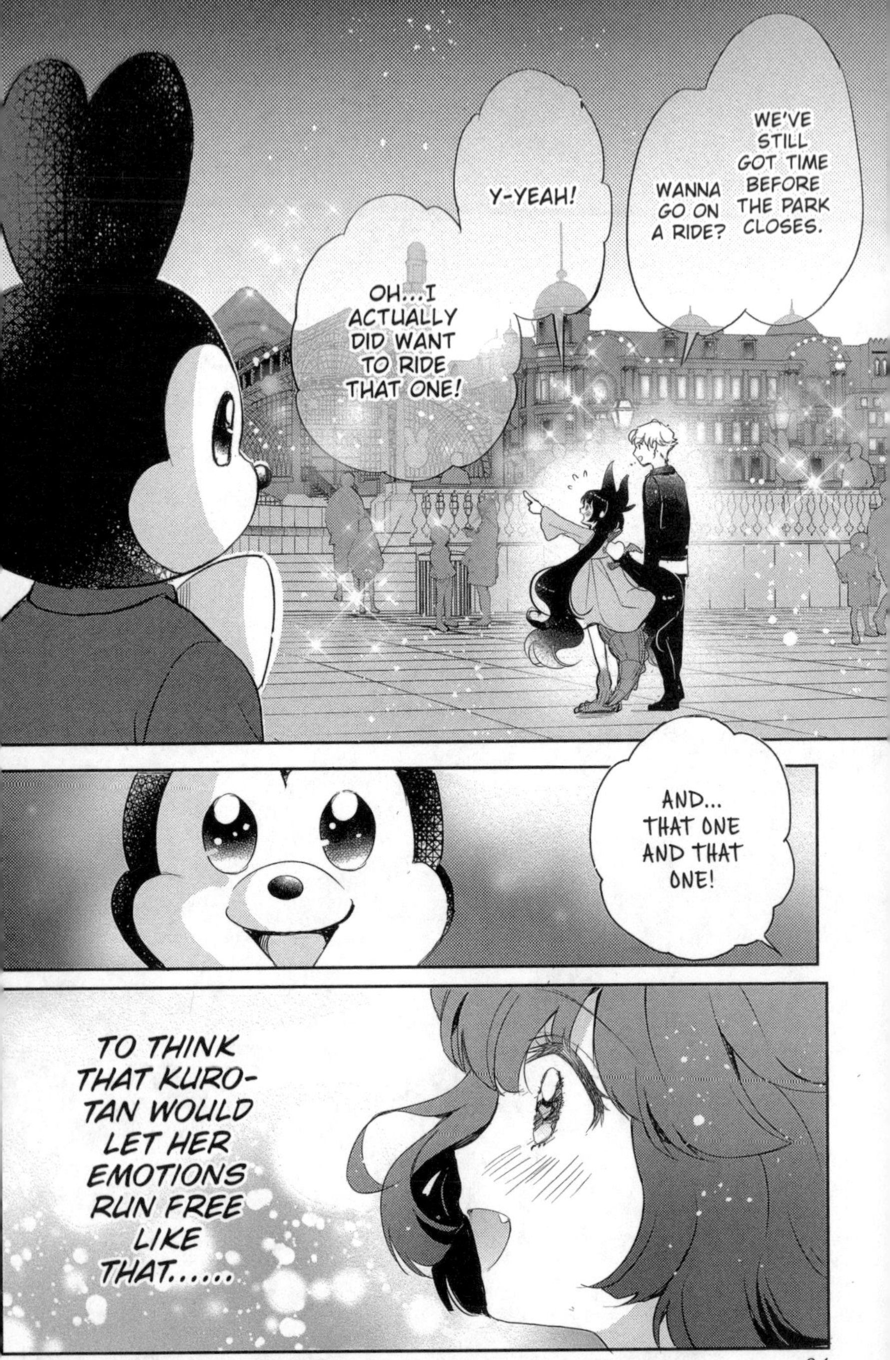
WE'VE STILL GOT TIME BEFORE THE PARK CLOSES.
WANNA GO ON A RIDE?
Y-YEAH!
OH...I ACTUALLY DID WANT TO RIDE THAT ONE!
AND... THAT ONE AND THAT ONE!
TO THINK THAT KURO-TAN WOULD LET HER EMOTIONS RUN FREE LIKE THAT......

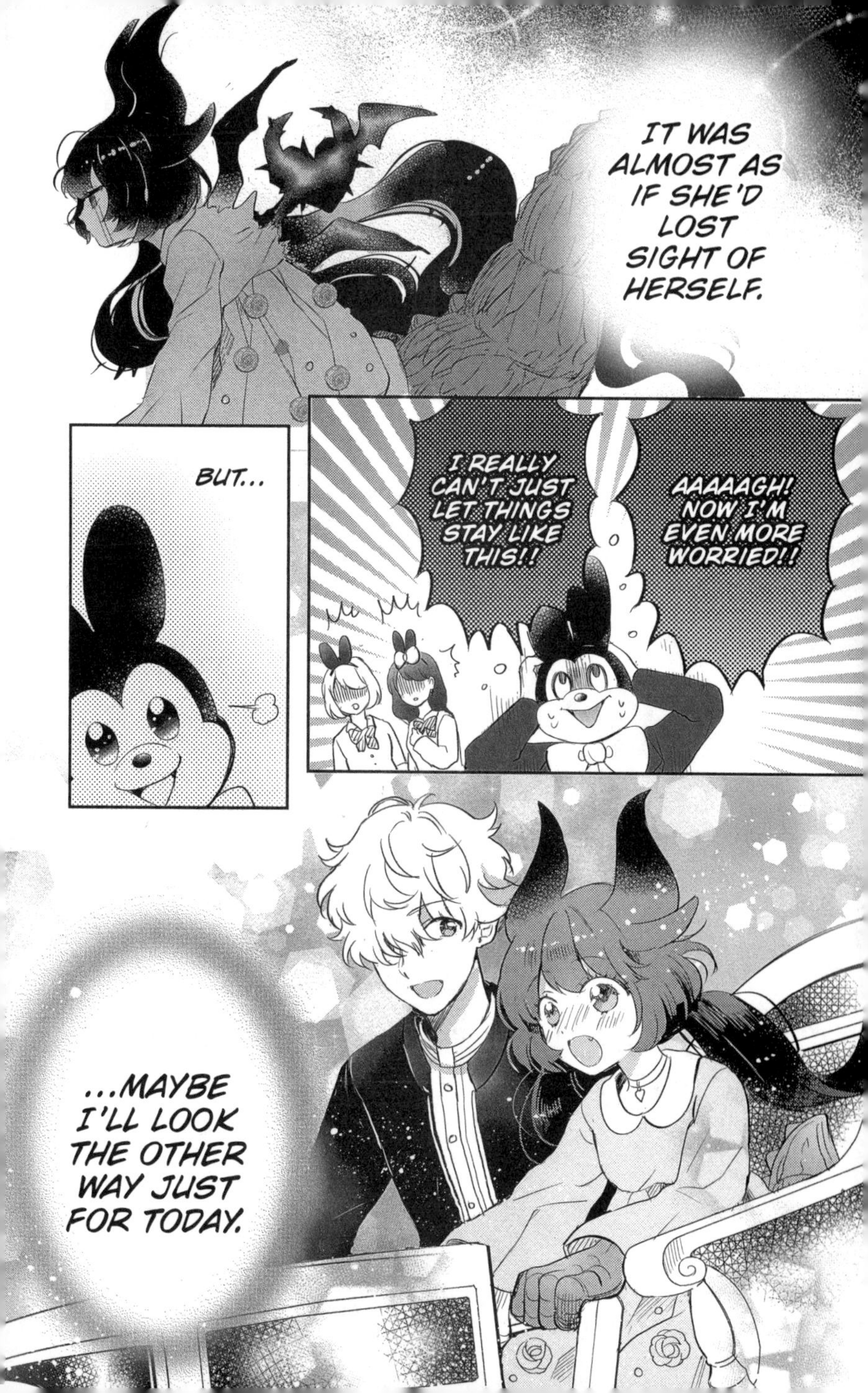
IT WAS ALMOST AS IF SHE'D LOST SIGHT OF HERSELF.
AAAAAGH! NOW I'M EVEN MORE WORRIED!!
I REALLY CAN'T JUST LET THINGS STAY LIKE THIS!!
BUT...
...MAYBE I'LL LOOK THE OTHER WAY JUST FOR TODAY.

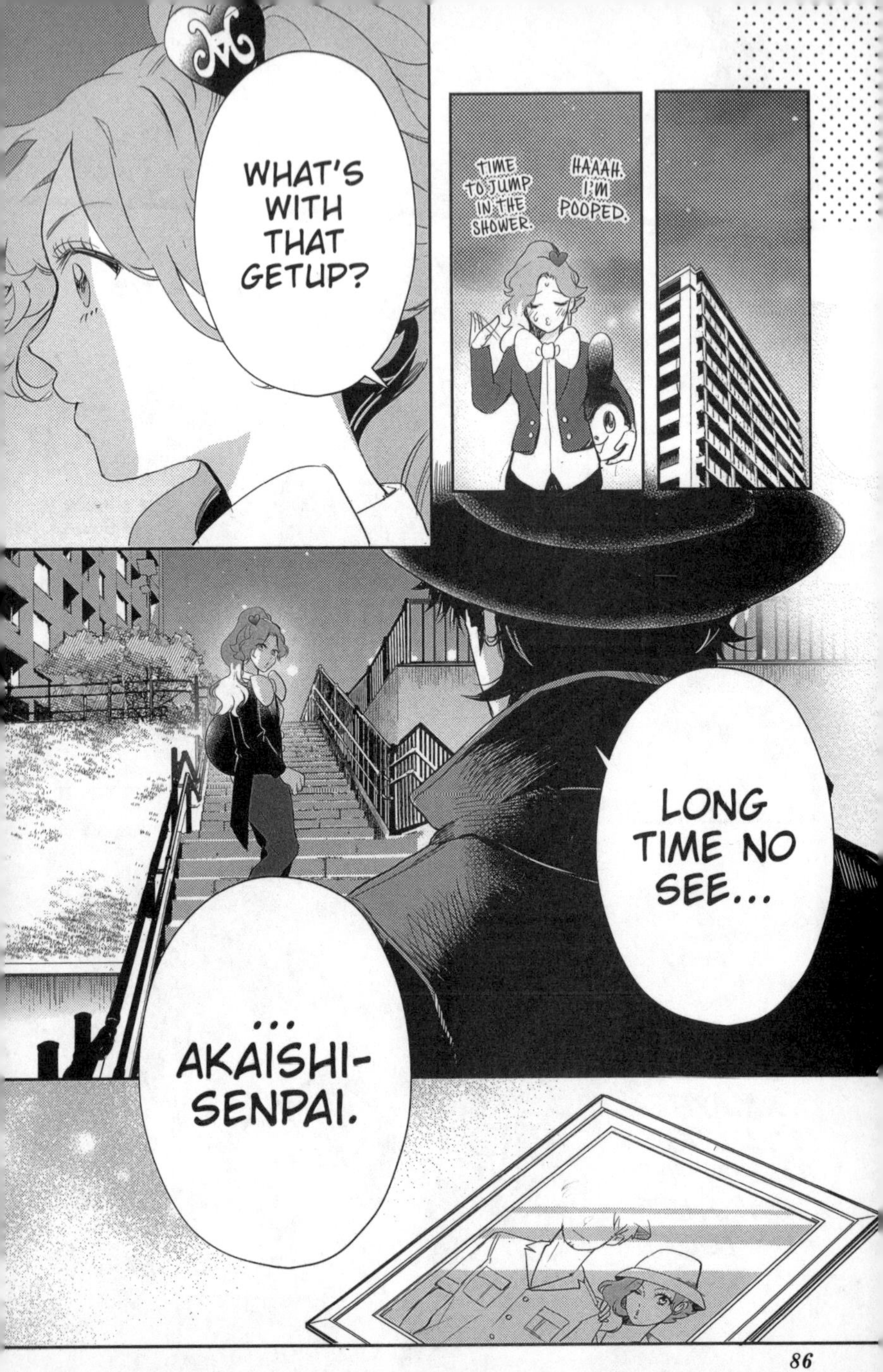
HAAAH. I'M POOPED.
TIME TO JUMP IN THE SHOWER.
WHAT'S WITH THAT GETUP?
LONG TIME NO SEE...
... AKAISHI-SENPAI.

KAIJU♥GIRL
CARAMELISE

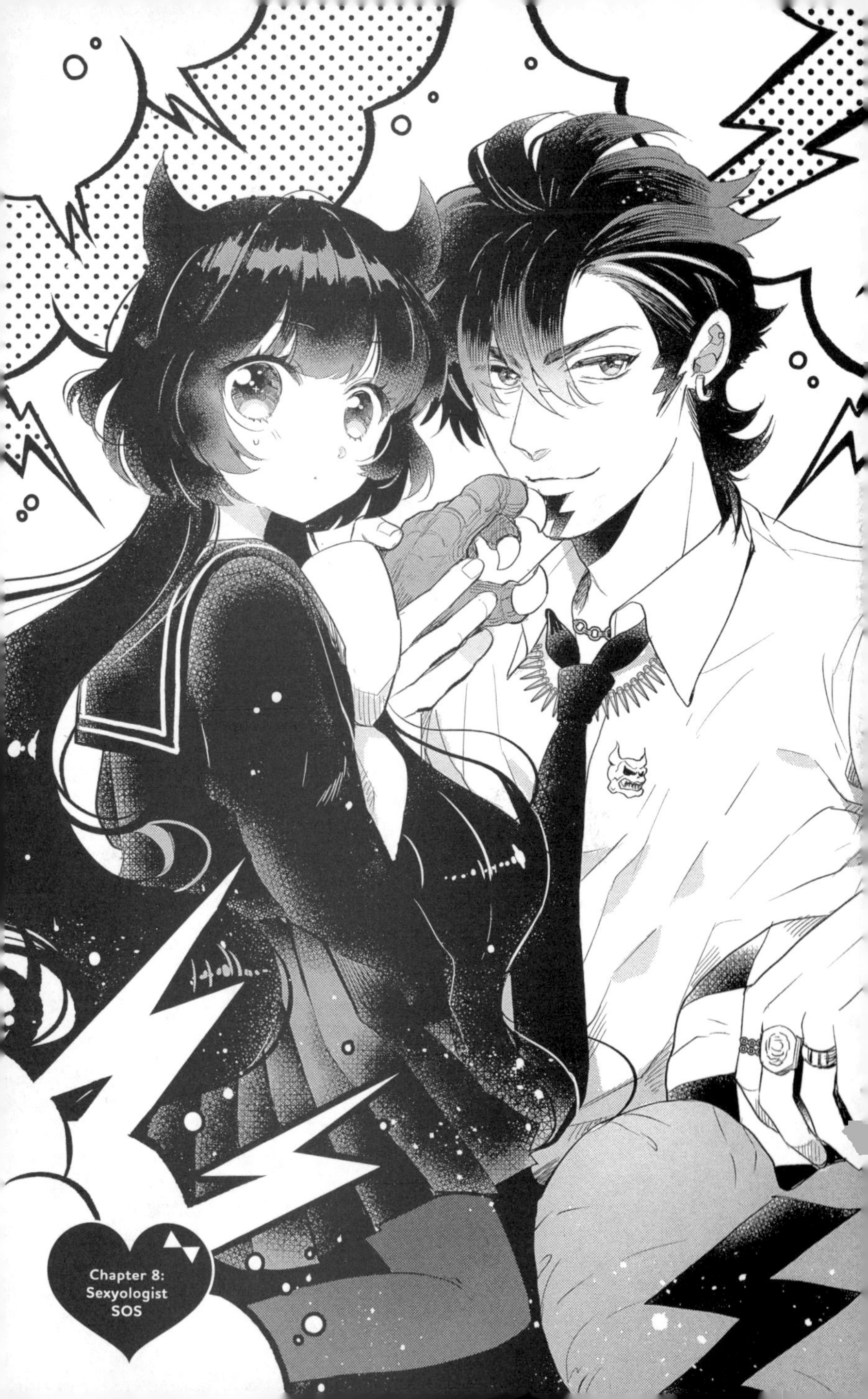
Chapter 8:
Sexyologist
SOS

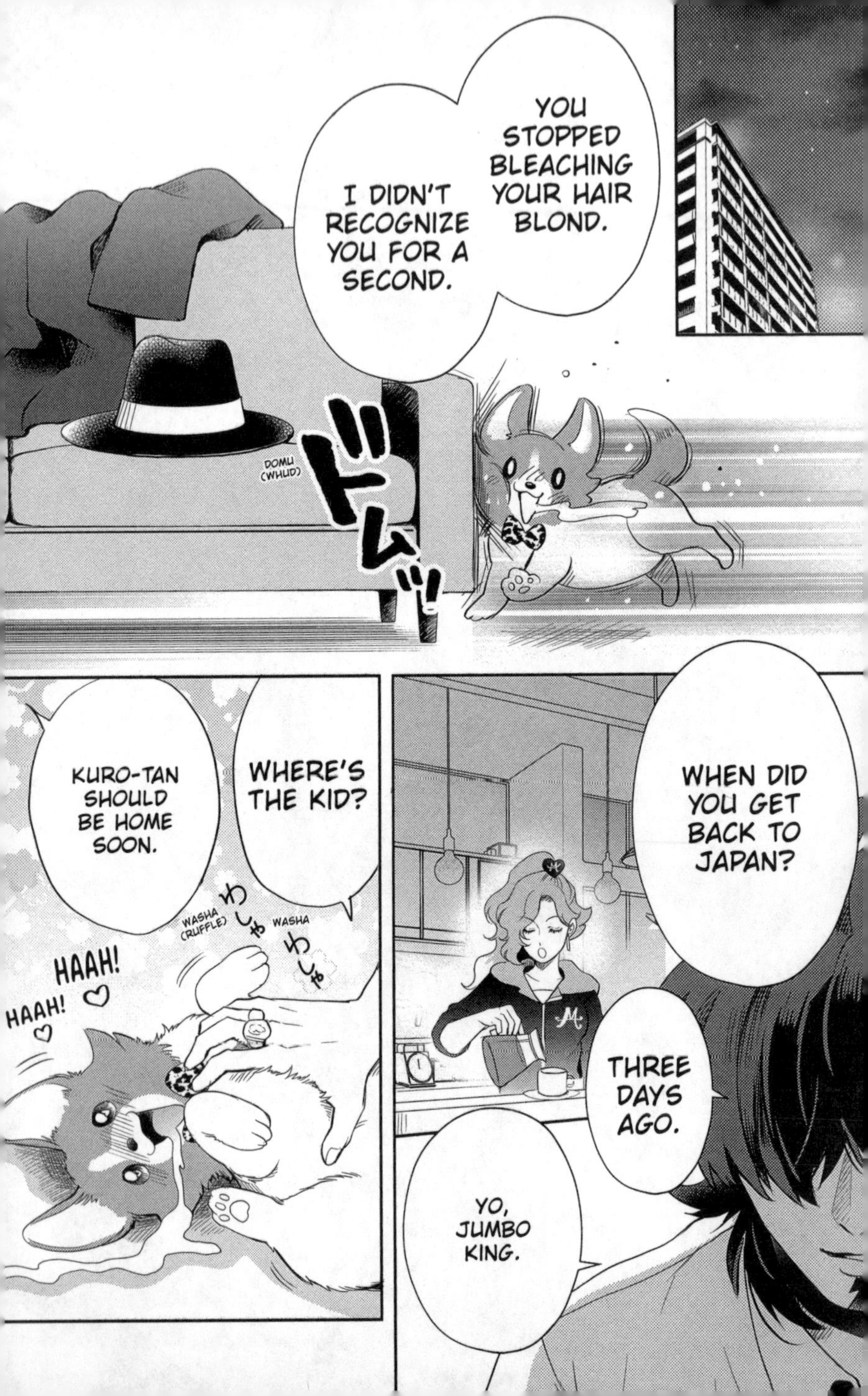
YOU STOPPED BLEACHING YOUR HAIR BLOND.
I DIDN'T RECOGNIZE YOU FOR A SECOND.
ドムッ
DOMU (WHUD)
WHEN DID YOU GET BACK TO JAPAN?
THREE DAYS AGO.
YO, JUMBO KING.
WHERE'S THE KID?
KURO-TAN SHOULD BE HOME SOON.
わしゃ
WASHA (RUFFLE)
わしゃ
WASHA
HAAH!
HAAH!

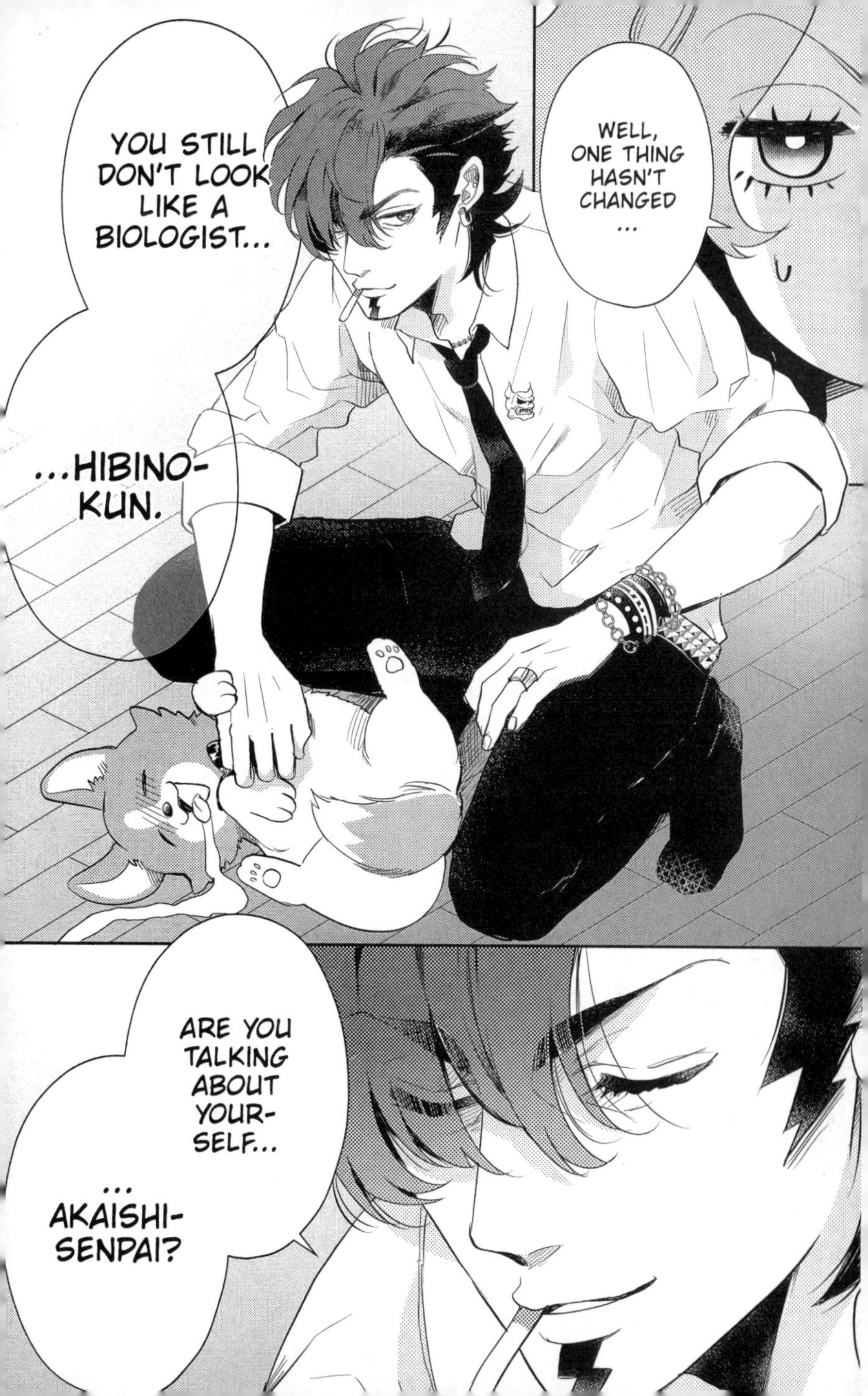
WELL, ONE THING HASN'T CHANGED...
YOU STILL DON'T LOOK LIKE A BIOLOGIST...
...HIBINO-KUN.
ARE YOU TALKING ABOUT YOUR-SELF...
...AKAISHI-SENPAI?

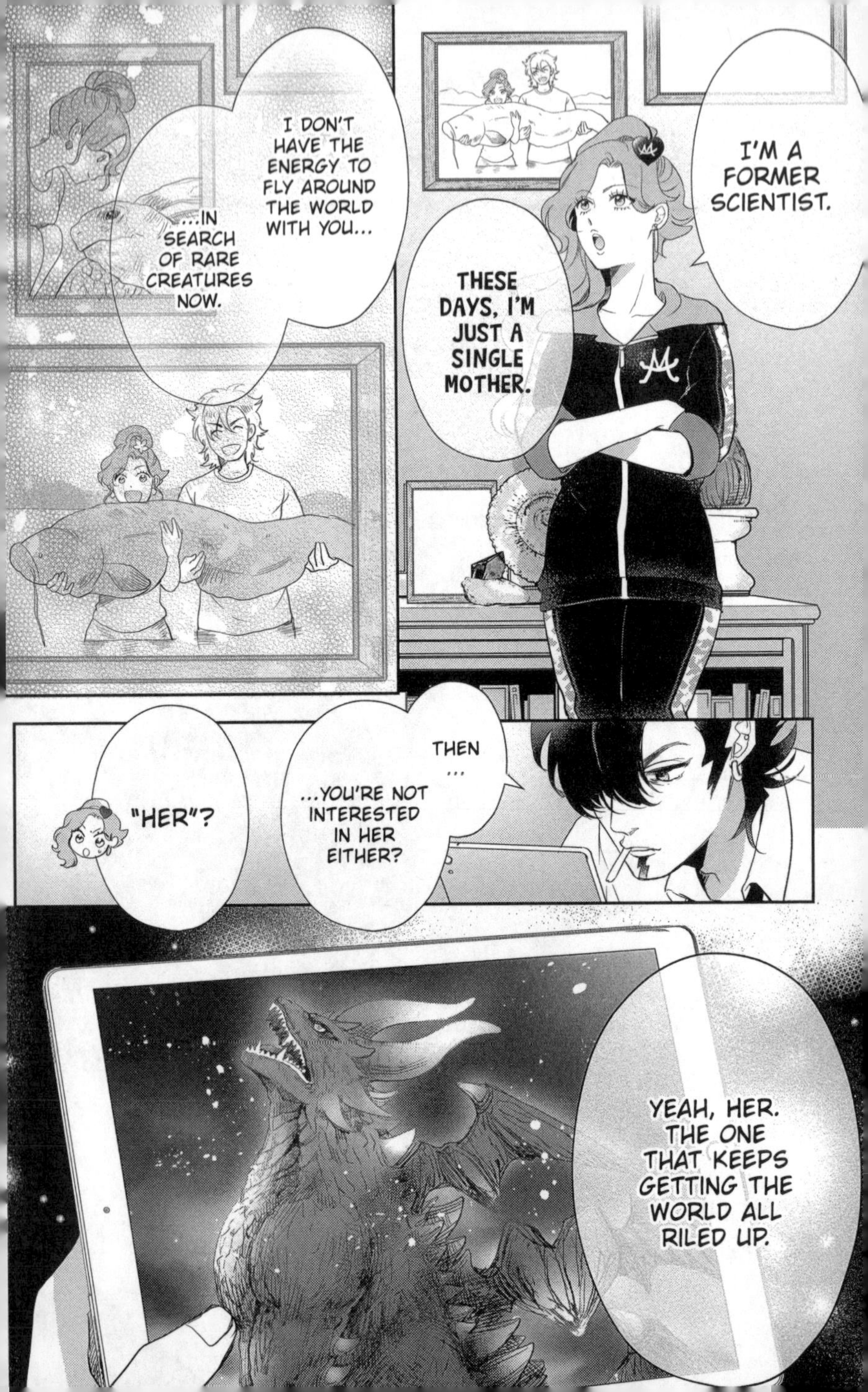
I'M A FORMER SCIENTIST.
THESE DAYS, I'M JUST A SINGLE MOTHER.
I DON'T HAVE THE ENERGY TO FLY AROUND THE WORLD WITH YOU...
...IN SEARCH OF RARE CREATURES NOW.
THEN ...
...YOU'RE NOT INTERESTED IN HER EITHER?
"HER"?
YEAH, HER. THE ONE THAT KEEPS GETTING THE WORLD ALL RILED UP.

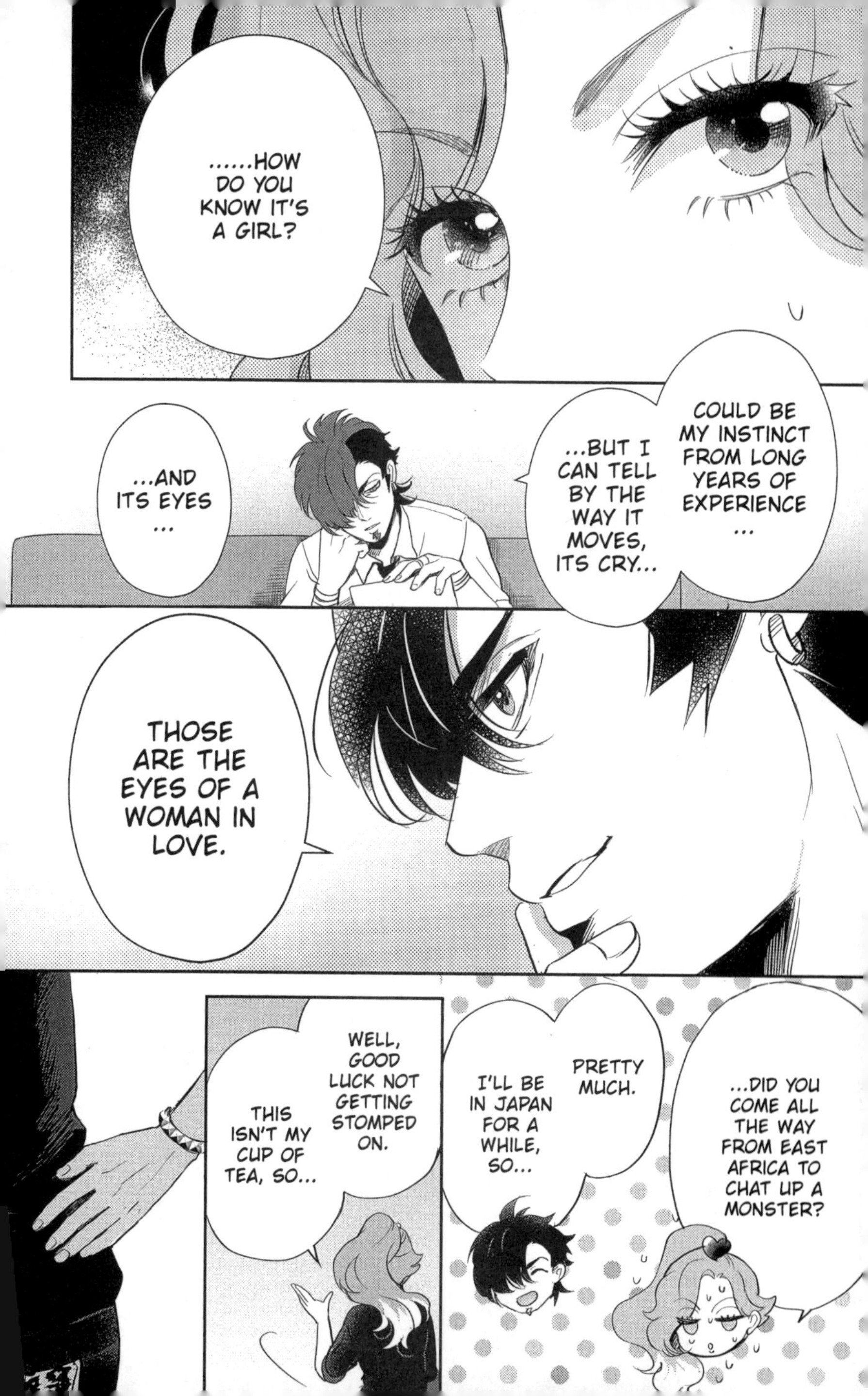
......HOW DO YOU KNOW IT'S A GIRL?
COULD BE MY INSTINCT FROM LONG YEARS OF EXPERIENCE ...
...BUT I CAN TELL BY THE WAY IT MOVES, ITS CRY...
...AND ITS EYES ...
THOSE ARE THE EYES OF A WOMAN IN LOVE.
...DID YOU COME ALL THE WAY FROM EAST AFRICA TO CHAT UP A MONSTER?
PRETTY MUCH.
I'LL BE IN JAPAN FOR A WHILE, SO...
WELL, GOOD LUCK NOT GETTING STOMPED ON.
THIS ISN'T MY CUP OF TEA, SO...

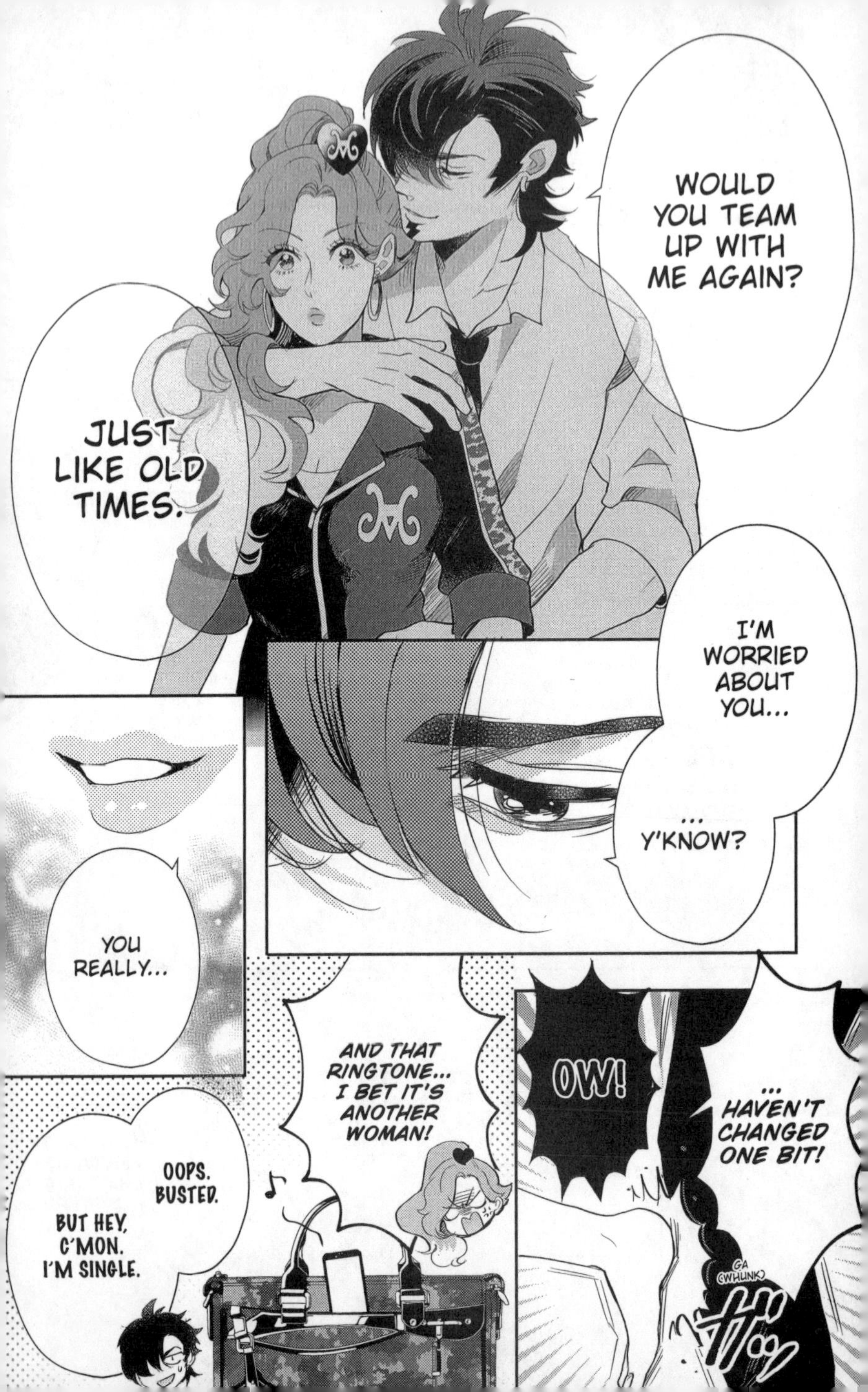
WOULD YOU TEAM UP WITH ME AGAIN?
JUST LIKE OLD TIMES.
I'M WORRIED ABOUT YOU...
...Y'KNOW?
YOU REALLY...
...HAVEN'T CHANGED ONE BIT!
OW!
GA (WHUNK)
AND THAT RINGTONE... I BET IT'S ANOTHER WOMAN!
OOPS. BUSTED.
BUT HEY, C'MON. I'M SINGLE.

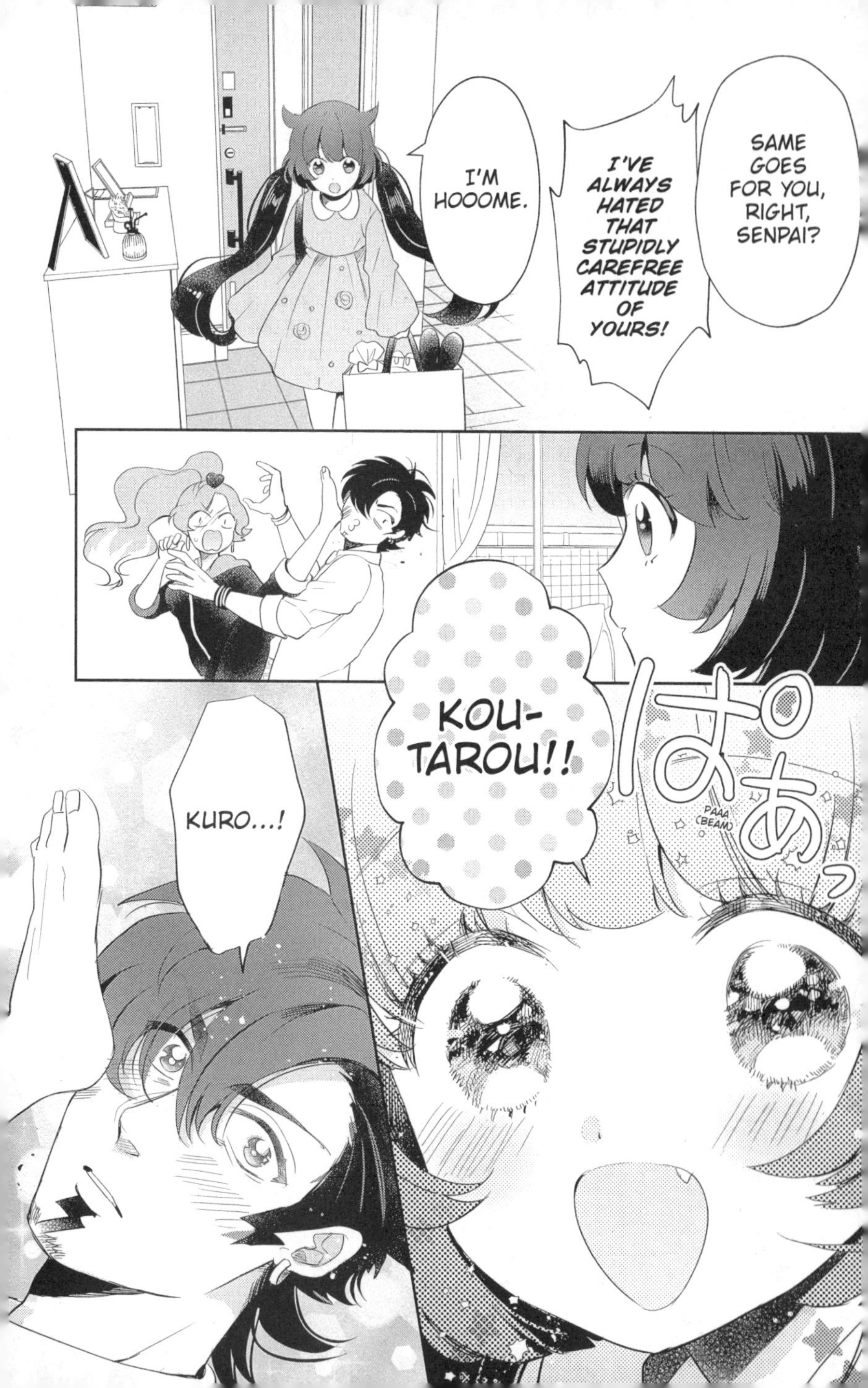

SAME GOES FOR YOU, RIGHT, SENPAI?
I'VE ALWAYS HATED THAT STUPIDLY CAREFREE ATTITUDE OF YOURS!
I'M HOOOME.
KOU-TAROU!!
ぱあっ
PAAA (BEAM)
KURO...!

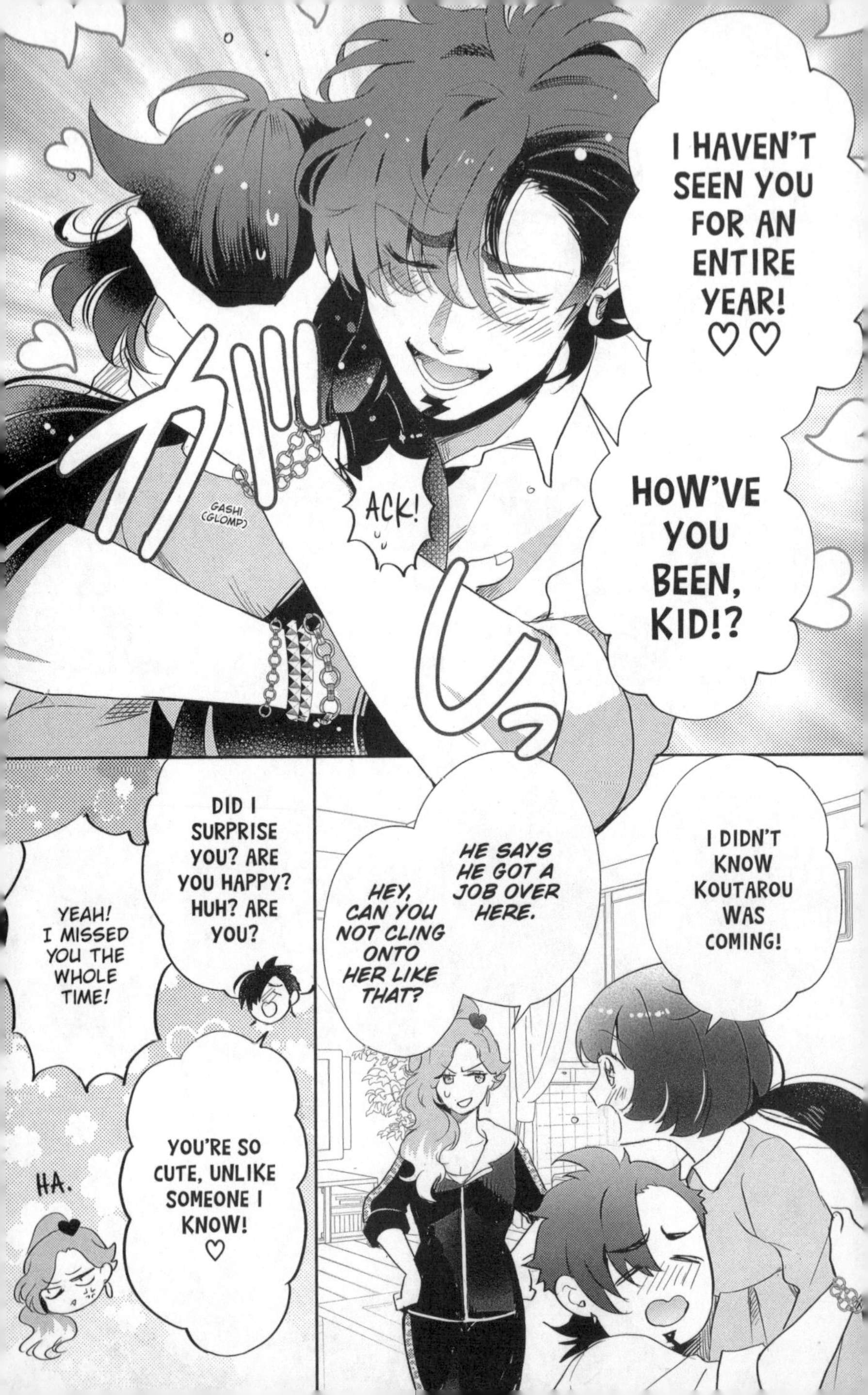
I HAVEN'T SEEN YOU FOR AN ENTIRE YEAR! ♡♡
HOW'VE YOU BEEN, KID!?
ACK!
GASHI (GLOMP)
I DIDN'T KNOW KOUTAROU WAS COMING!
HE SAYS HE GOT A JOB OVER HERE.
HEY, CAN YOU NOT CLING ONTO HER LIKE THAT?
DID I SURPRISE YOU? ARE YOU HAPPY? HUH? ARE YOU?
YEAH! I MISSED YOU THE WHOLE TIME!
YOU'RE SO CUTE, UNLIKE SOMEONE I KNOW! ♡
HA.

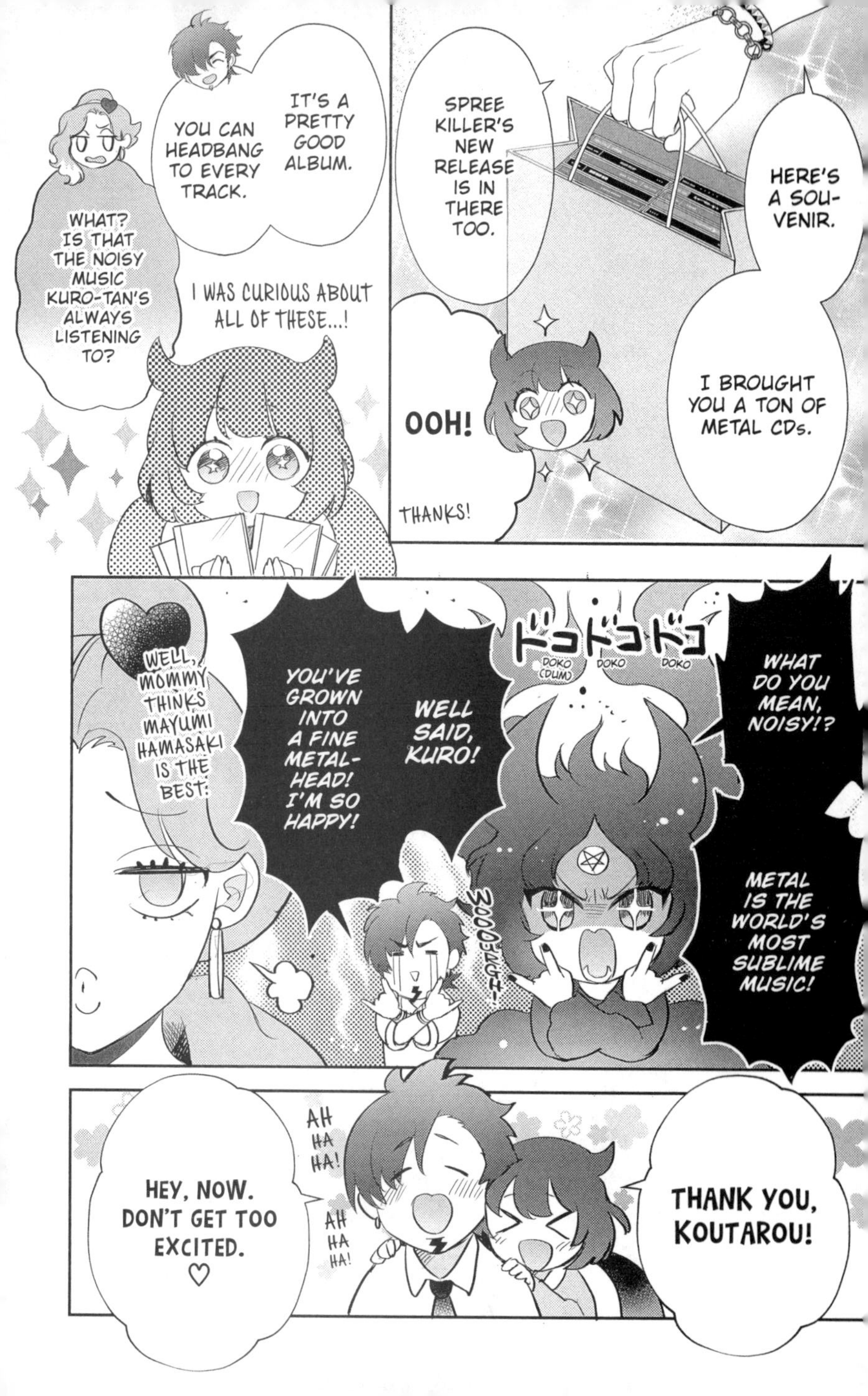
HERE'S A SOU-VENIR.
SPREE KILLER'S NEW RELEASE IS IN THERE TOO.
I BROUGHT YOU A TON OF METAL CDs.
OOH!
THANKS!
IT'S A PRETTY GOOD ALBUM.
YOU CAN HEADBANG TO EVERY TRACK.
WHAT? IS THAT THE NOISY MUSIC KURO-TAN'S ALWAYS LISTENING TO?
I WAS CURIOUS ABOUT ALL OF THESE...!
WHAT DO YOU MEAN, NOISY!?
METAL IS THE WORLD'S MOST SUBLIME MUSIC!
ドコドコドコ
DOKO (DUM) DOKO DOKO
WOOOURGH!
WELL SAID, KURO!
YOU'VE GROWN INTO A FINE METAL-HEAD! I'M SO HAPPY!
WELL, MOMMY THINKS MAYUMI HAMASAKI IS THE BEST.
THANK YOU, KOUTAROU!
AH HA HA!
AH HA HA!
HEY, NOW. DON'T GET TOO EXCITED. ♡

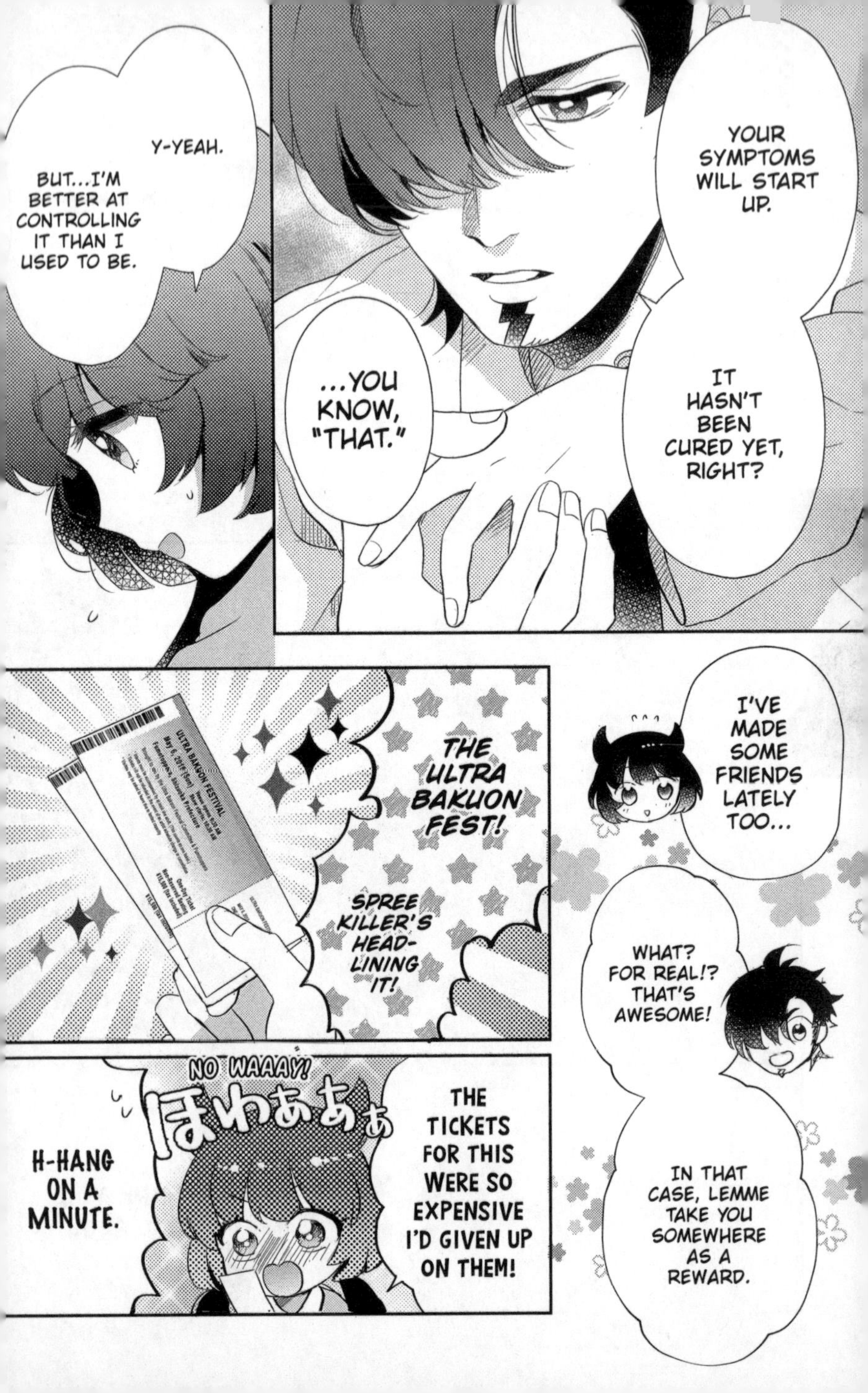
YOUR SYMPTOMS WILL START UP.
IT HASN'T BEEN CURED YET, RIGHT?
...YOU KNOW, "THAT."
Y-YEAH.
BUT...I'M BETTER AT CONTROLLING IT THAN I USED TO BE.
I'VE MADE SOME FRIENDS LATELY TOO...
WHAT? FOR REAL!? THAT'S AWESOME!
IN THAT CASE, LEMME TAKE YOU SOMEWHERE AS A REWARD.
ULTRA BAKUON FESTIVAL
THE ULTRA BAKUON FEST!
SPREE KILLER'S HEAD-LINING IT!
NO WAAAY!
ほわああぁ
THE TICKETS FOR THIS WERE SO EXPENSIVE I'D GIVEN UP ON THEM!
H-HANG ON A MINUTE.

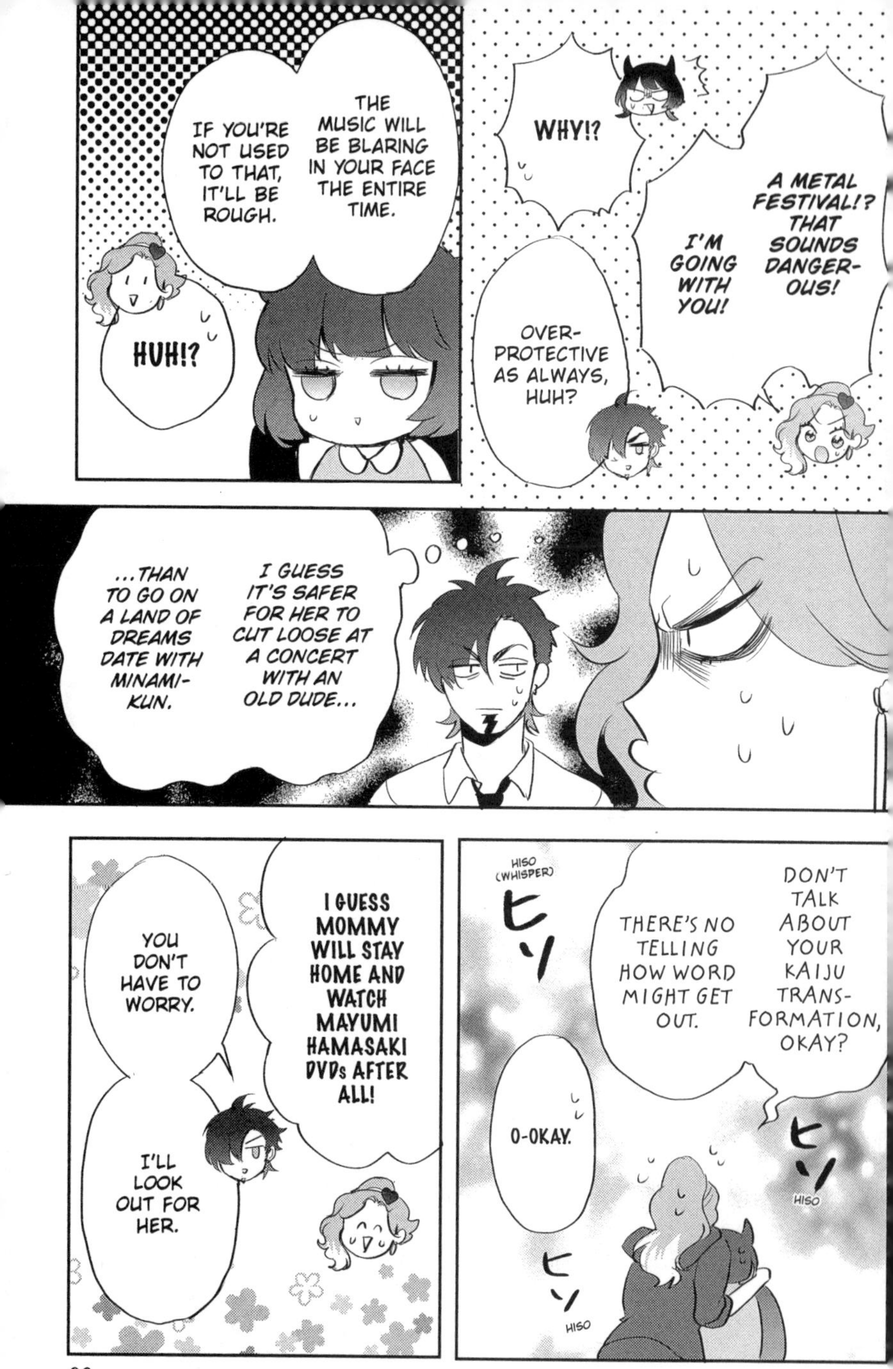
WHY!?
A METAL FESTIVAL!? THAT SOUNDS DANGER-OUS!
I'M GOING WITH YOU!
OVER-PROTECTIVE AS ALWAYS, HUH?
THE MUSIC WILL BE BLARING IN YOUR FACE THE ENTIRE TIME.
IF YOU'RE NOT USED TO THAT, IT'LL BE ROUGH.
HUH!?
I GUESS IT'S SAFER FOR HER TO CUT LOOSE AT A CONCERT WITH AN OLD DUDE...
...THAN TO GO ON A LAND OF DREAMS DATE WITH MINAMI-KUN.
DON'T TALK ABOUT YOUR KAIJU TRANS-FORMATION, OKAY?
THERE'S NO TELLING HOW WORD MIGHT GET OUT.
ヒソ HISO (WHISPER)
ヒソ HISO
O-OKAY.
ヒソ HISO
I GUESS MOMMY WILL STAY HOME AND WATCH MAYUMI HAMASAKI DVDs AFTER ALL!
YOU DON'T HAVE TO WORRY.
I'LL LOOK OUT FOR HER.

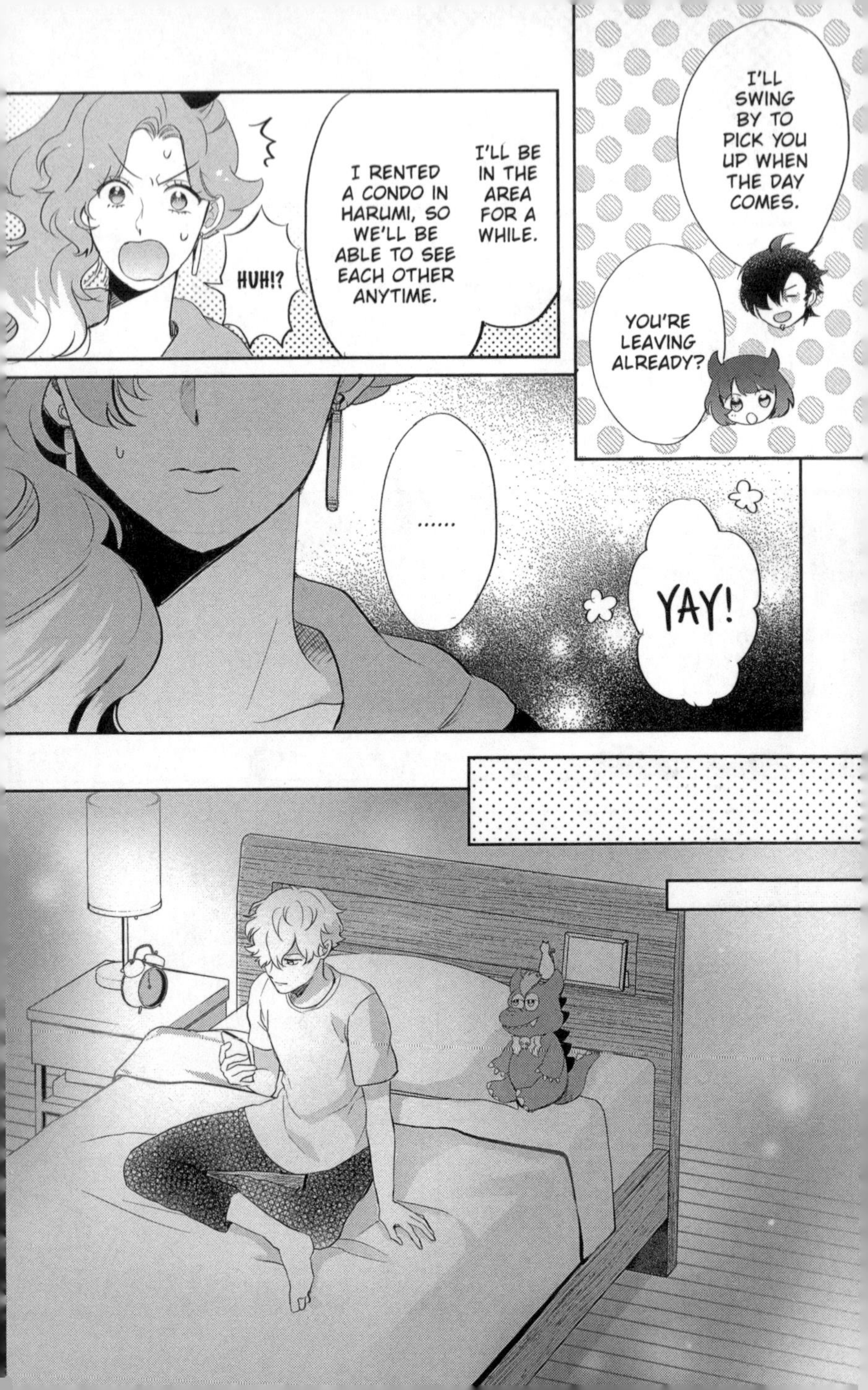
I'LL SWING BY TO PICK YOU UP WHEN THE DAY COMES.
YOU'RE LEAVING ALREADY?
I'LL BE IN THE AREA FOR A WHILE.
I RENTED A CONDO IN HARUMI, SO WE'LL BE ABLE TO SEE EACH OTHER ANYTIME.
HUH!?
YAY!
......

MINAMI Arata Minami

Thanks for today. Destiny was fun!

Unread

Since it's spring break, do you want to go somewhere aga|

ABC | DEF | GHI

JKL | MNO | PQRS

I NEED TO GET A PART-TIME JOB...

ピコン♪
PIKON
(BING)

......

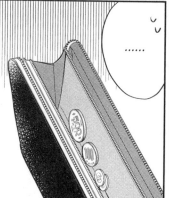

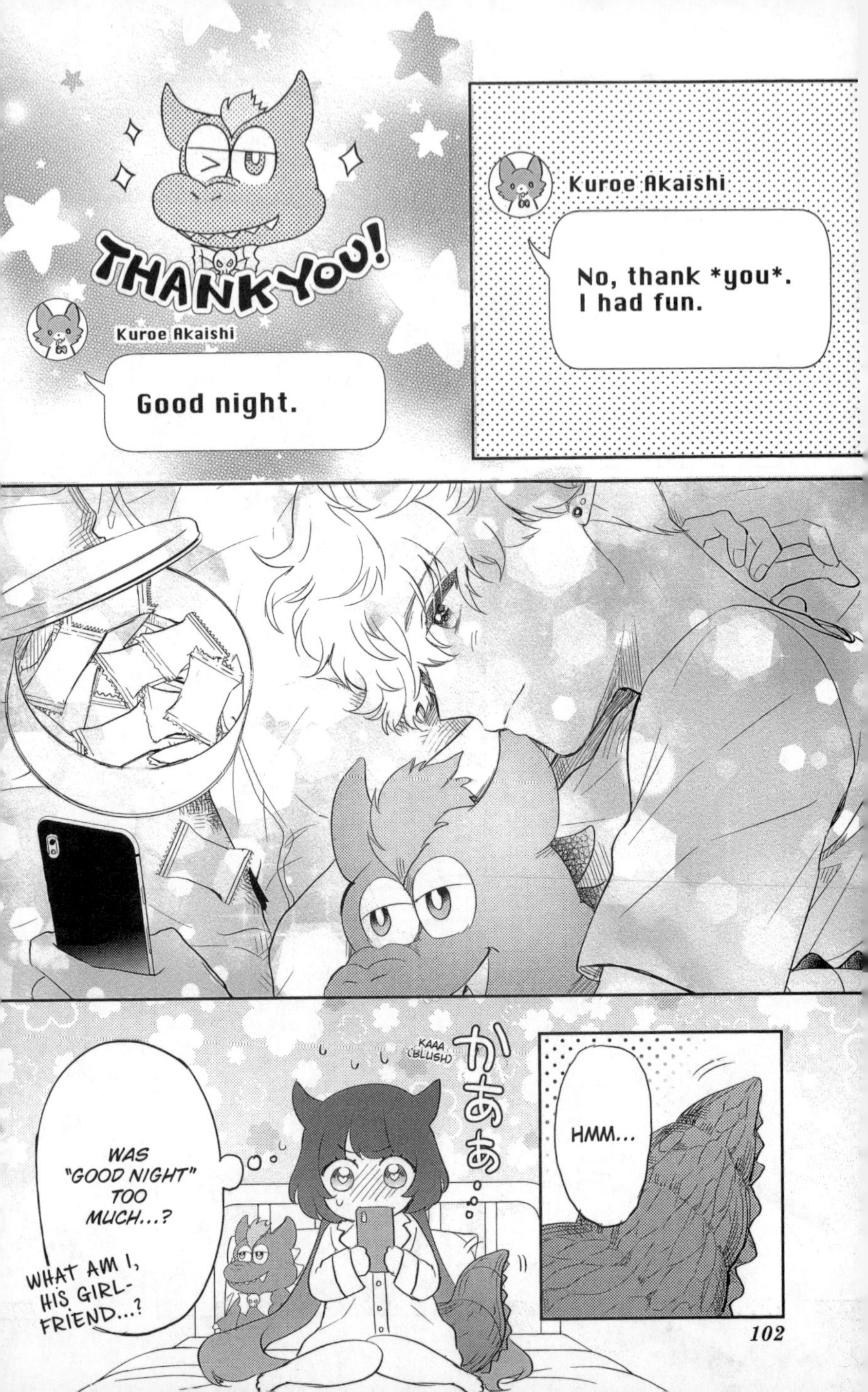
Kuroe Akaishi
No, thank *you*. I had fun.
THANK YOU!
Kuroe Akaishi
Good night.
HMM...
KAAA (BLUSH)
かあぁ
WAS "GOOD NIGHT" TOO MUCH...?
WHAT AM I, HIS GIRLFRIEND...?

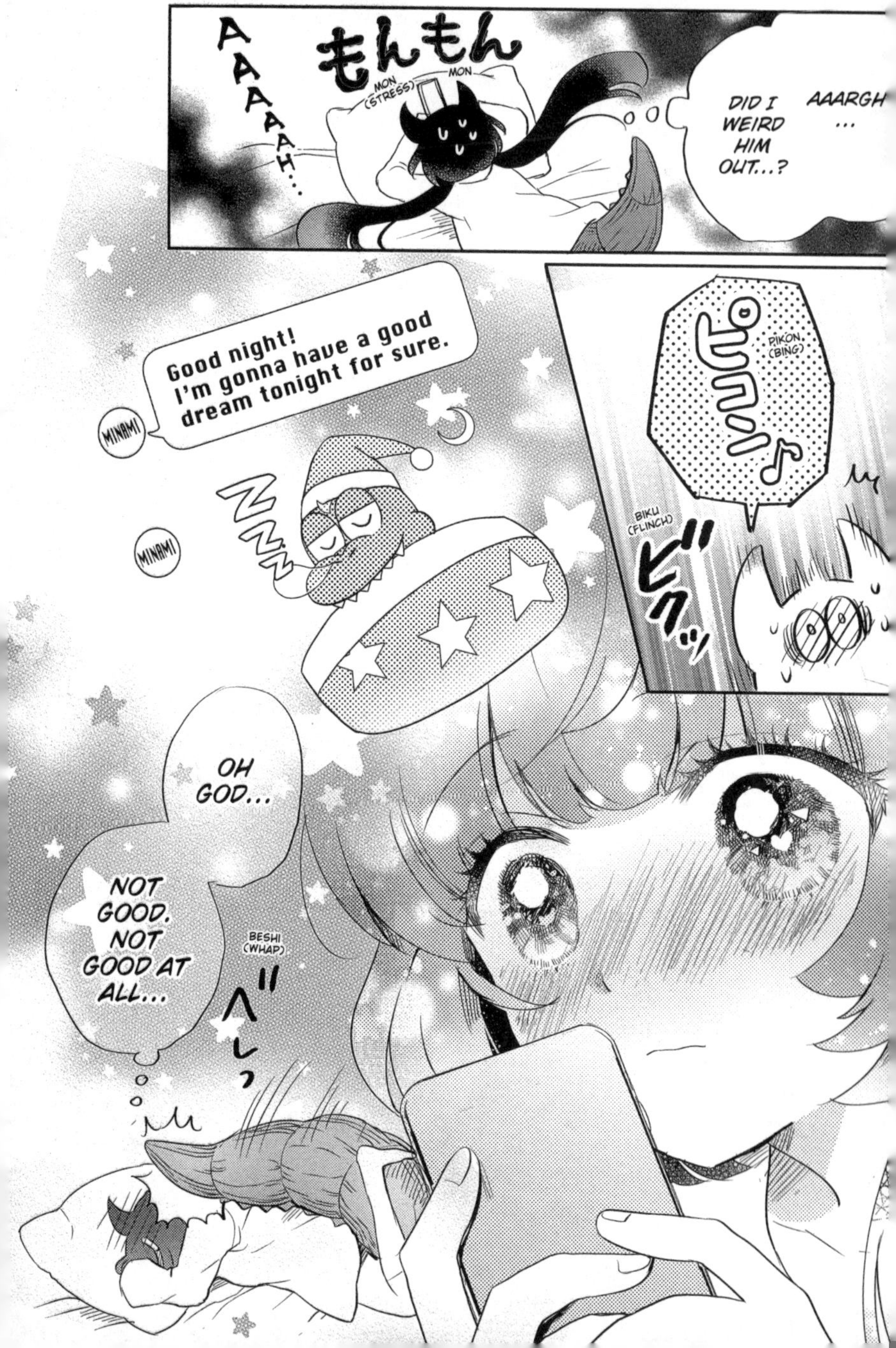
AAARGH...
DID I WEIRD HIM OUT...?
もんもん
MON (STRESS) MON
AAAAAH...
ピコン♪
PIKON (BING)
ビクッ
BIKU (FLINCH)
MINAMI
Good night! I'm gonna have a good dream tonight for sure.
MINAMI
OH GOD...
NOT GOOD. NOT GOOD AT ALL...
BESHI (WHAP)
べしっ

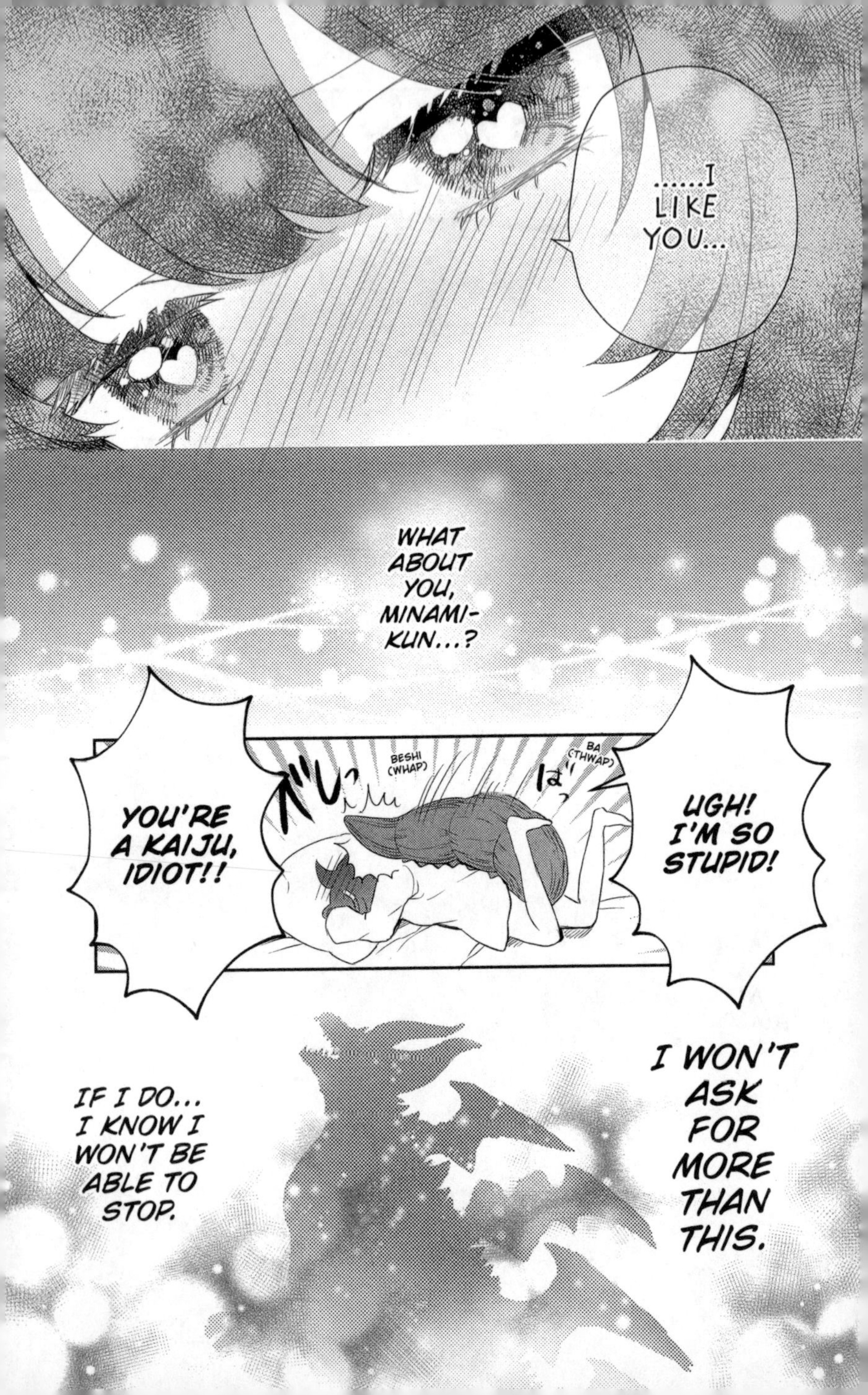
......I LIKE YOU...
WHAT ABOUT YOU, MINAMI-KUN...?
UGH! I'M SO STUPID!
BA (THWAP)
BESHI (WHAP)
YOU'RE A KAIJU, IDIOT!!
I WON'T ASK FOR MORE THAN THIS.
IF I DO... I KNOW I WON'T BE ABLE TO STOP.

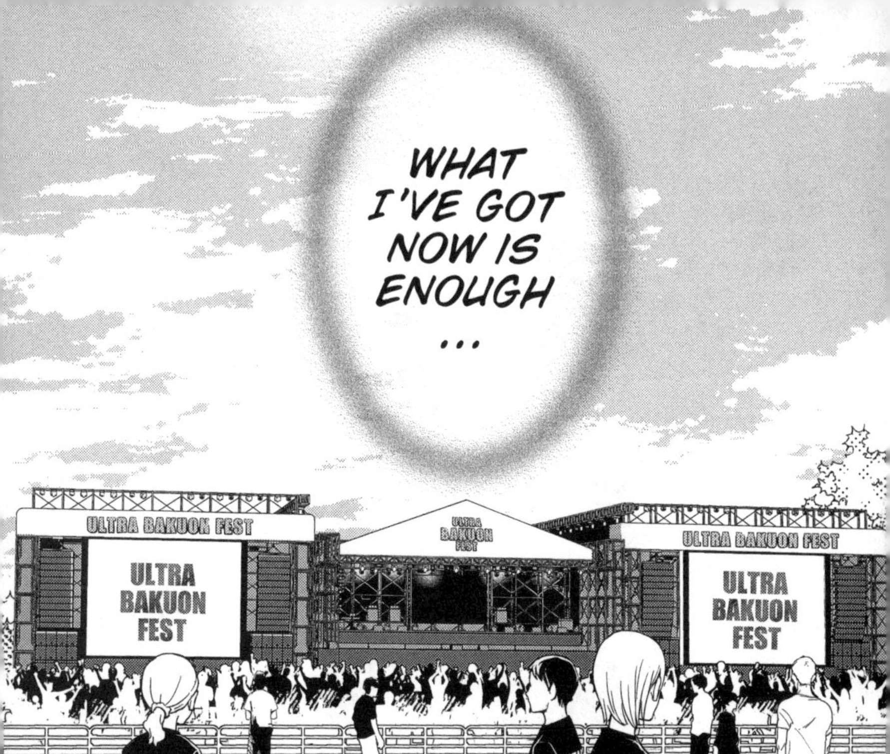
WHAT I'VE GOT NOW IS ENOUGH ...
ULTRA BAKUON FEST
ULTRA BAKUON FEST
ULTRA BAKUON FEST
ULTRA BAKUON FEST
ULTRA BAKUON FEST
STAFF
STAFF

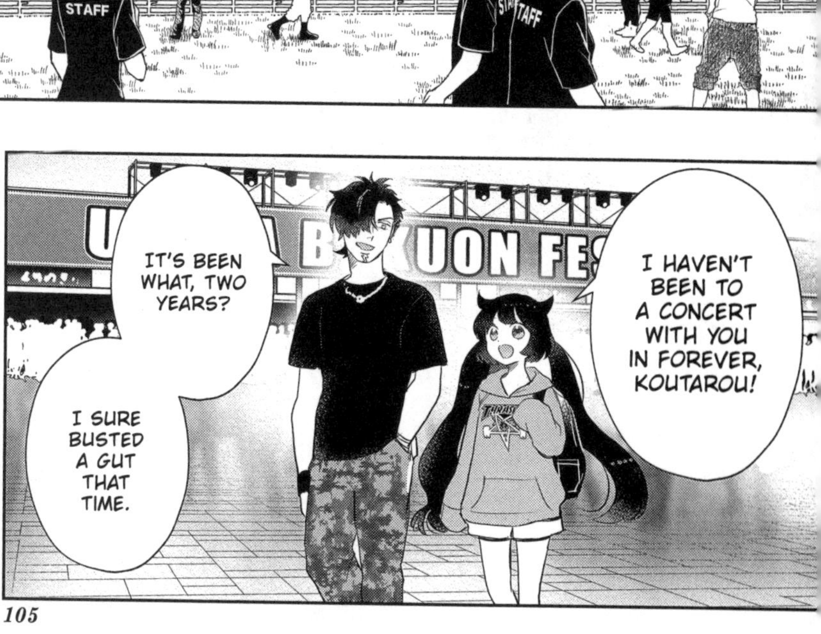
I HAVEN'T BEEN TO A CONCERT WITH YOU IN FOREVER, KOUTAROU!
IT'S BEEN WHAT, TWO YEARS?
I SURE BUSTED A GUT THAT TIME.

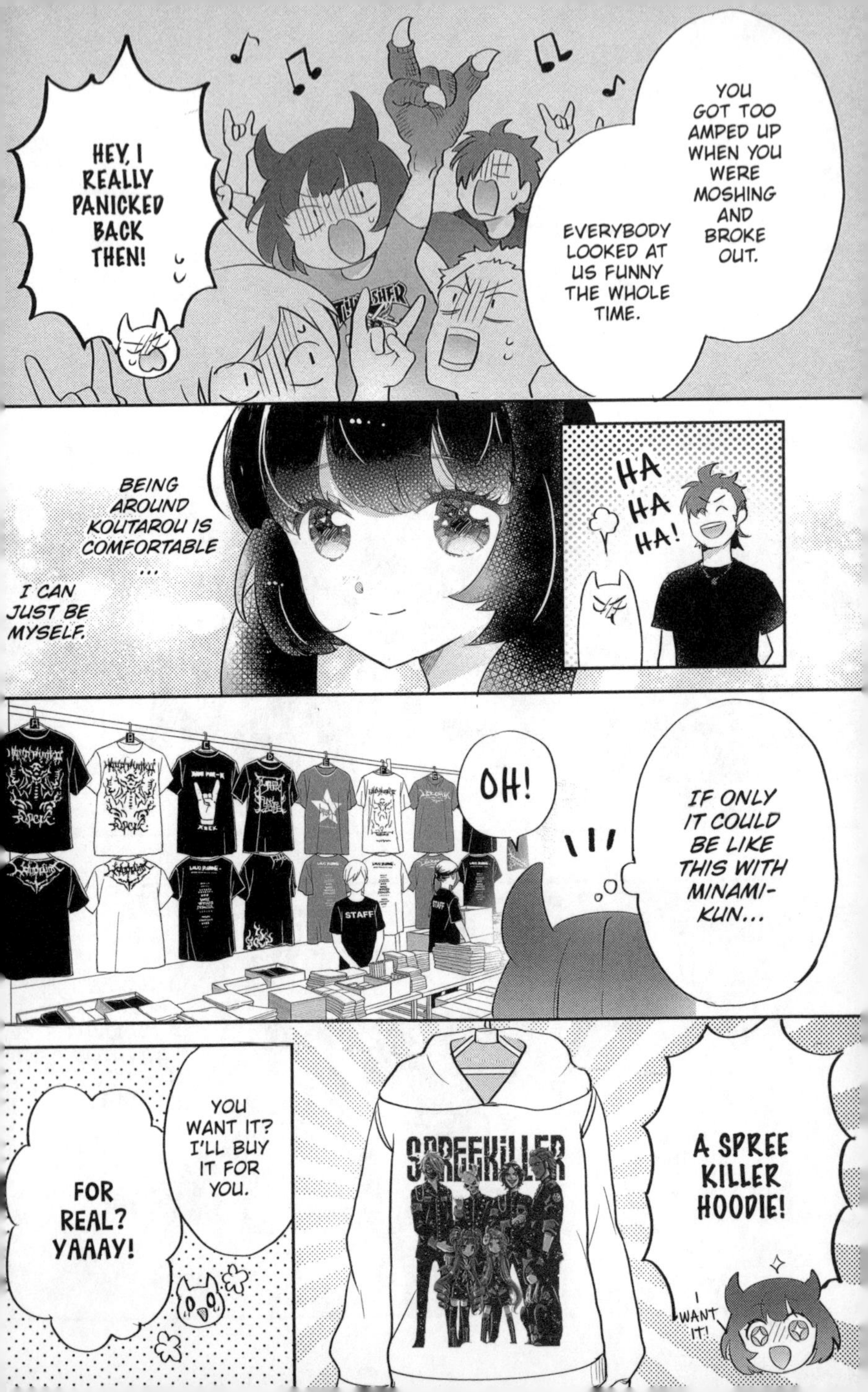
YOU GOT TOO AMPED UP WHEN YOU WERE MOSHING AND BROKE OUT.
EVERYBODY LOOKED AT US FUNNY THE WHOLE TIME.
HEY, I REALLY PANICKED BACK THEN!
HA HA HA!
BEING AROUND KOUTAROU IS COMFORTABLE...
I CAN JUST BE MYSELF.
IF ONLY IT COULD BE LIKE THIS WITH MINAMI-KUN...
OH!
STAFF
STAFF
A SPREE KILLER HOODIE!
I WANT IT!
SPREEKILLER
YOU WANT IT? I'LL BUY IT FOR YOU.
FOR REAL? YAAAY!

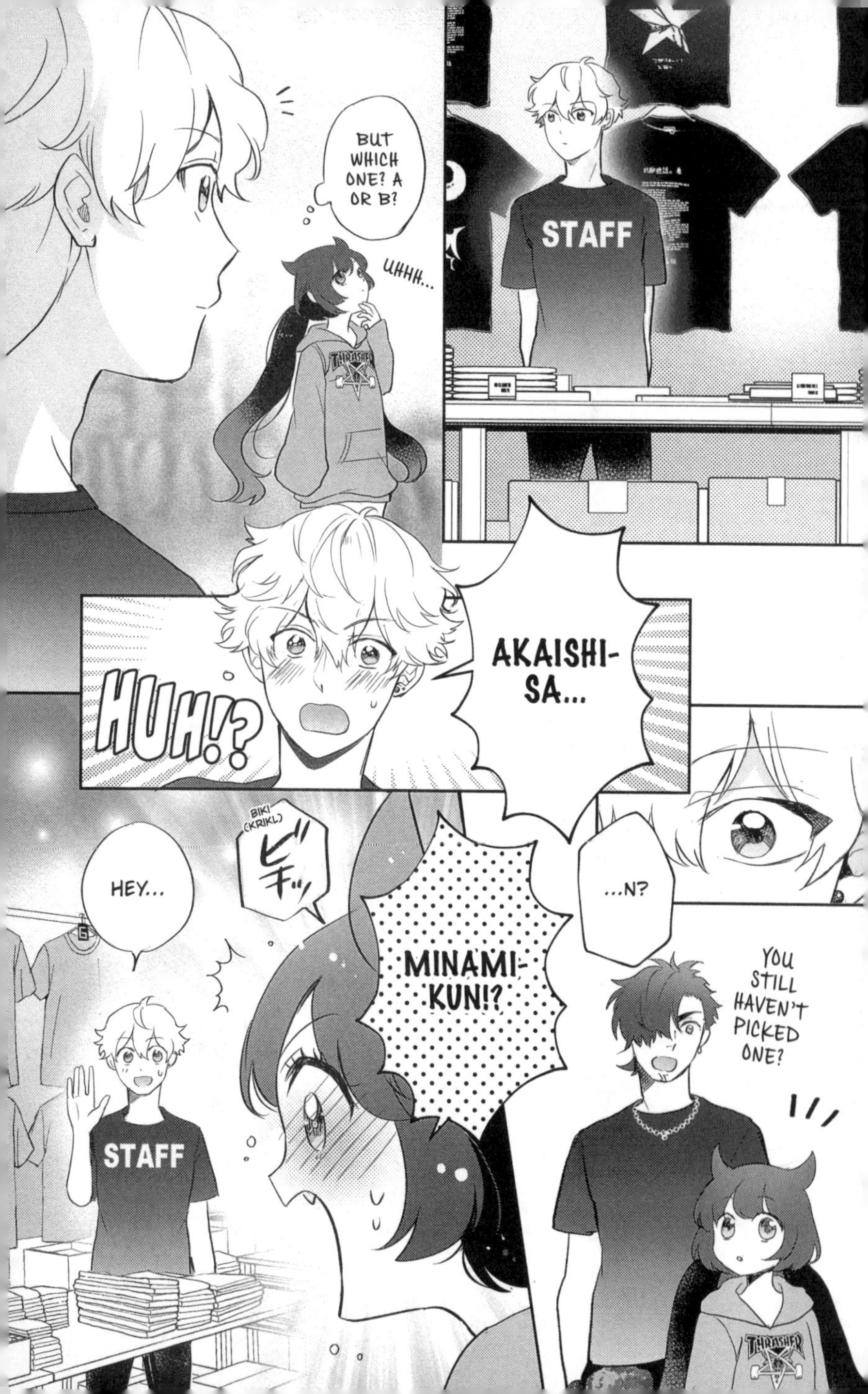
BUT WHICH ONE? A OR B?
UHHH...
STAFF
AKAISHI-SA...
HUH!?
...N?
YOU STILL HAVEN'T PICKED ONE?
MINAMI-KUN!?
BIKI (KRIKL)
HEY...
STAFF

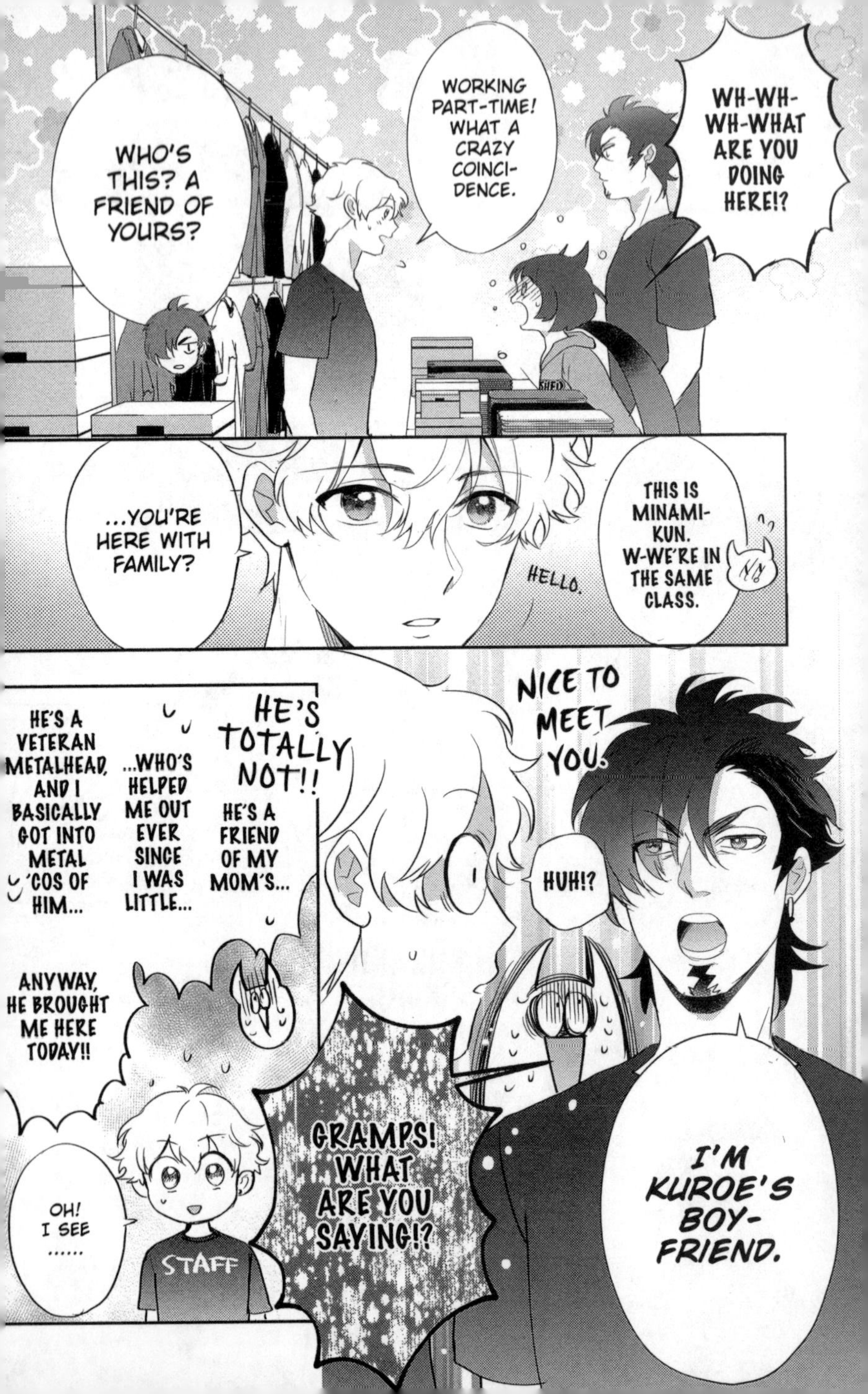
WH-WH-WH-WHAT ARE YOU DOING HERE!?
WORKING PART-TIME! WHAT A CRAZY COINCIDENCE.
WHO'S THIS? A FRIEND OF YOURS?
THIS IS MINAMI-KUN. W-WE'RE IN THE SAME CLASS.
HELLO.
...YOU'RE HERE WITH FAMILY?
NICE TO MEET YOU.
HUH!?
I'M KUROE'S BOYFRIEND.
GRAMPS! WHAT ARE YOU SAYING!?
HE'S TOTALLY NOT!!
HE'S A FRIEND OF MY MOM'S...
...WHO'S HELPED ME OUT EVER SINCE I WAS LITTLE...
HE'S A VETERAN METALHEAD, AND I BASICALLY GOT INTO METAL 'COS OF HIM...
ANYWAY, HE BROUGHT ME HERE TODAY!!
OH! I SEE ......
STAFF

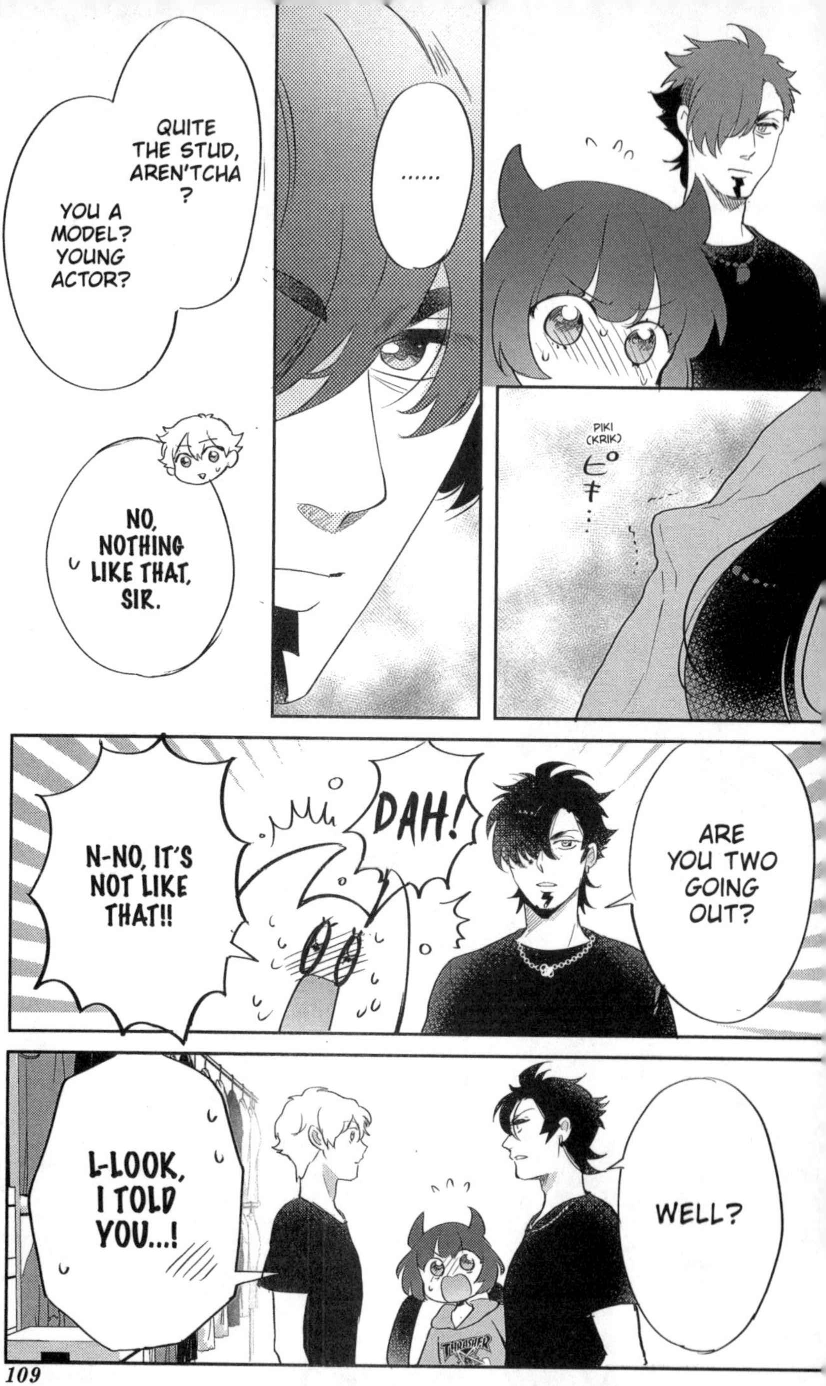
QUITE THE STUD, AREN'TCHA? YOU A MODEL? YOUNG ACTOR?
......
NO, NOTHING LIKE THAT, SIR.
PIKI (KRIK)
ピキ…
ARE YOU TWO GOING OUT?
DAH!
N-NO, IT'S NOT LIKE THAT!!
WELL?
L-LOOK, I TOLD YOU...!
THRASHER

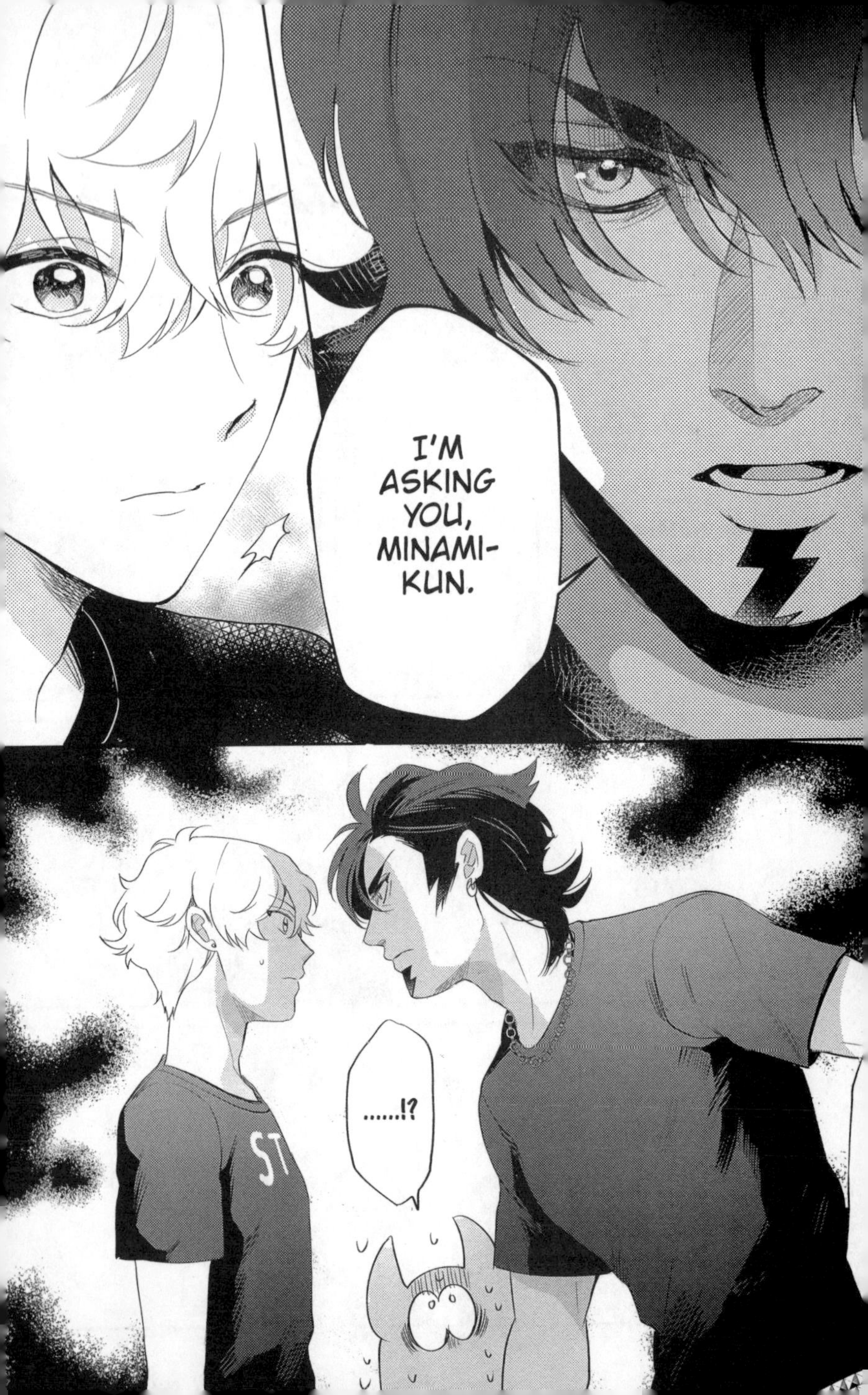
I'M ASKING YOU, MINAMI-KUN.
......!?

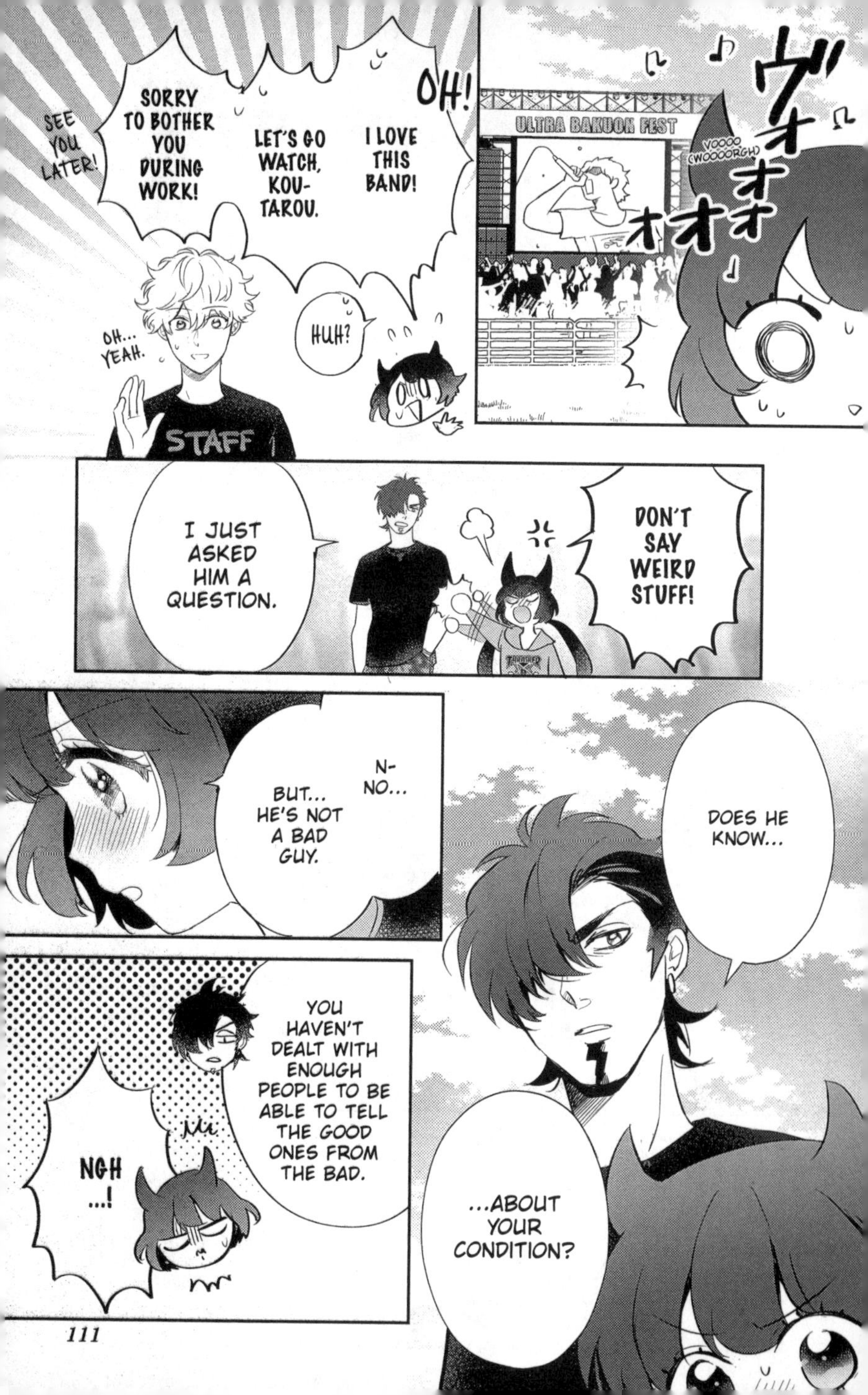
ヴォオォオオ
VOOOO (WOOOORGH)
ULTRA BAKUOK FEST
OH!
I LOVE THIS BAND!
LET'S GO WATCH, KOU-TAROU.
SORRY TO BOTHER YOU DURING WORK!
SEE YOU LATER!
HUH?
OH... YEAH.
STAFF
DON'T SAY WEIRD STUFF!
I JUST ASKED HIM A QUESTION.
DOES HE KNOW...
...ABOUT YOUR CONDITION?
N-NO...
BUT... HE'S NOT A BAD GUY.
YOU HAVEN'T DEALT WITH ENOUGH PEOPLE TO BE ABLE TO TELL THE GOOD ONES FROM THE BAD.
NGH ...!

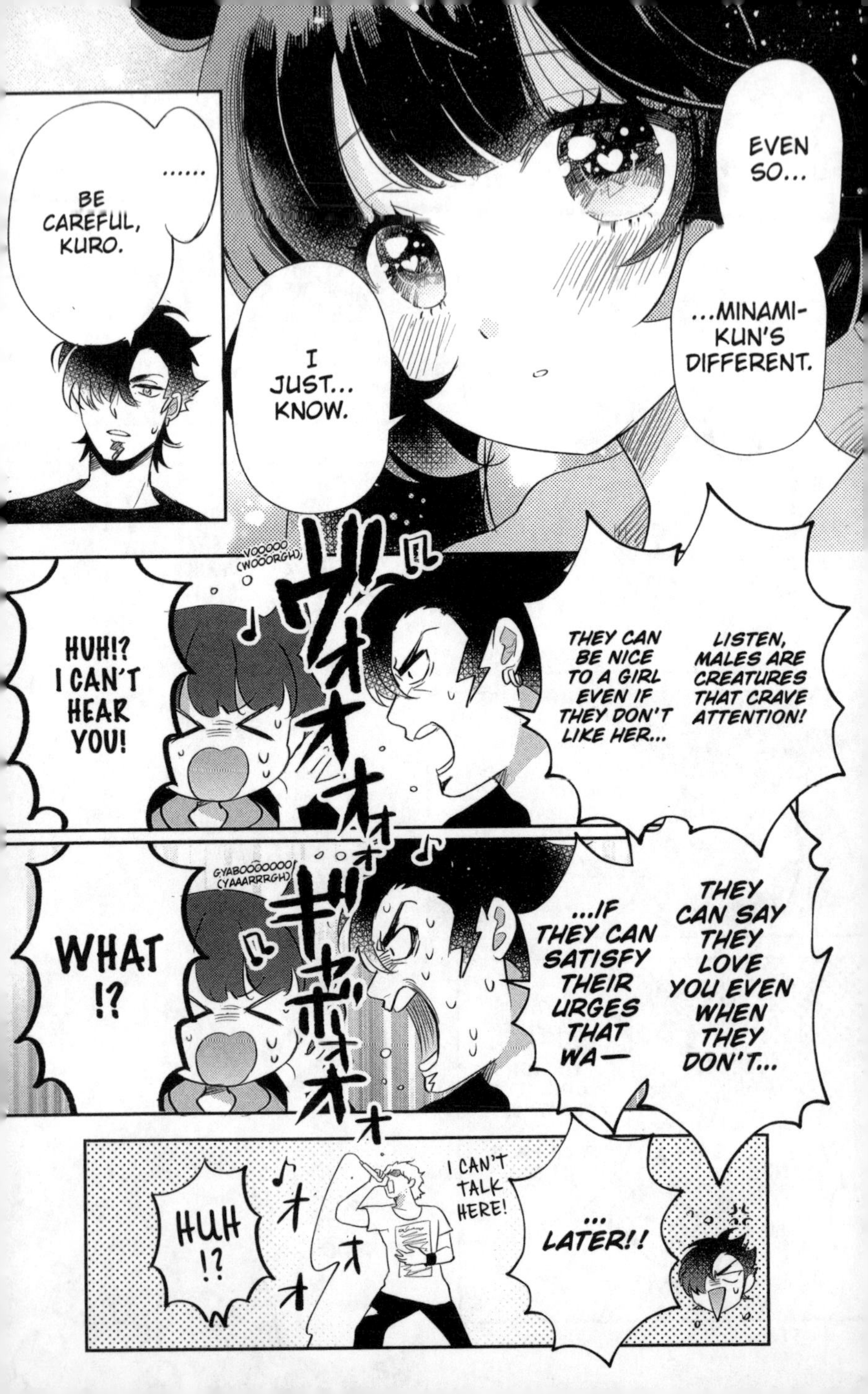
EVEN SO...
...MINAMI-KUN'S DIFFERENT.
I JUST... KNOW.
......
BE CAREFUL, KURO.
LISTEN, MALES ARE CREATURES THAT CRAVE ATTENTION!
THEY CAN BE NICE TO A GIRL EVEN IF THEY DON'T LIKE HER...
VOOOOO (WOOORGH)
HUH!? I CAN'T HEAR YOU!
THEY CAN SAY THEY LOVE YOU EVEN WHEN THEY DON'T...
...IF THEY CAN SATISFY THEIR URGES THAT WA—
GYABOOOOOOOO! (YAAARRRGH)
WHAT!?
...LATER!!
I CAN'T TALK HERE!
HUH!?

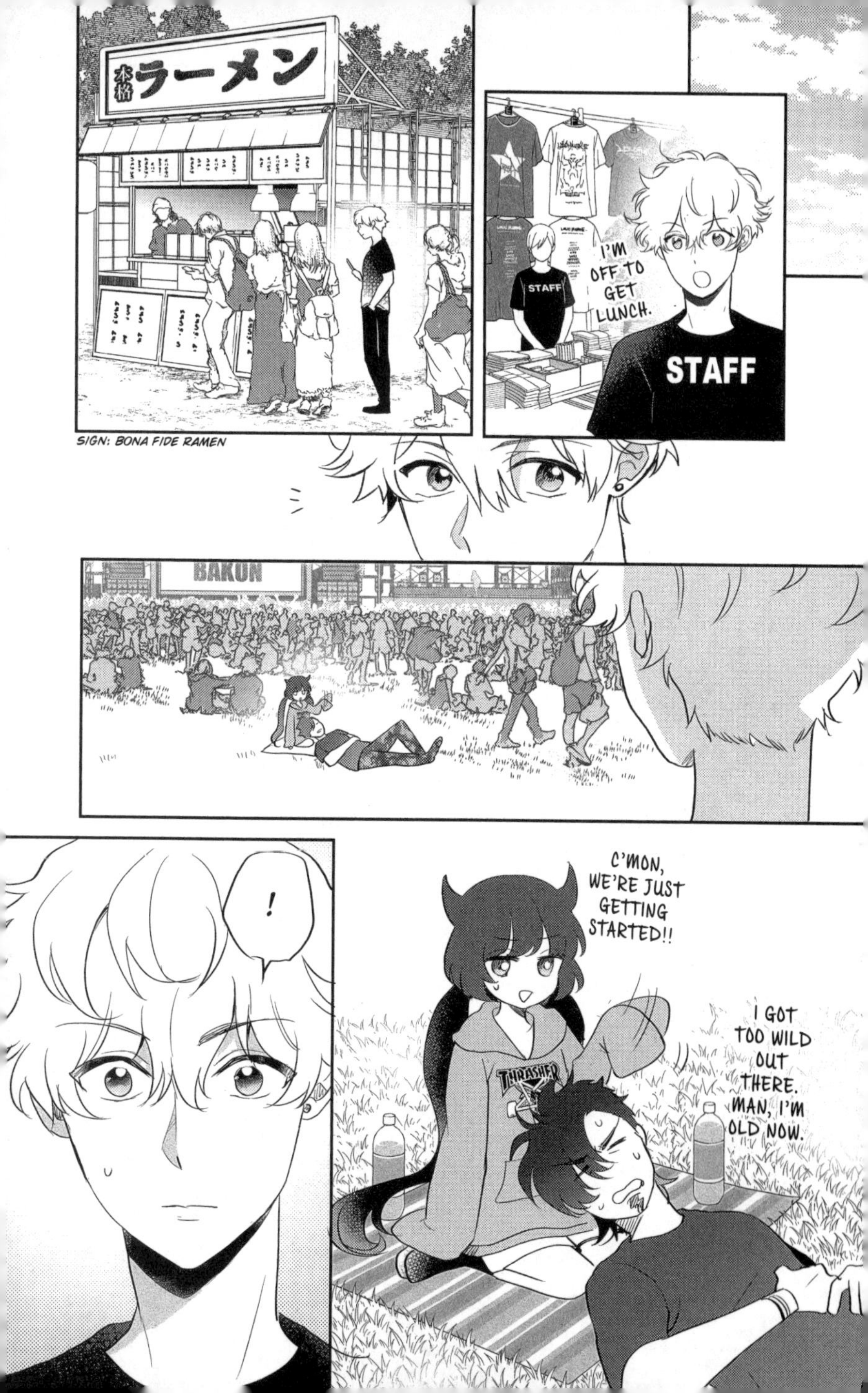

STAFF
I'M OFF TO GET LUNCH.
STAFF
本格ラーメン
SIGN: BONA FIDE RAMEN
BAKON
C'MON, WE'RE JUST GETTING STARTED!!
I GOT TOO WILD OUT THERE. MAN, I'M OLD NOW.
!

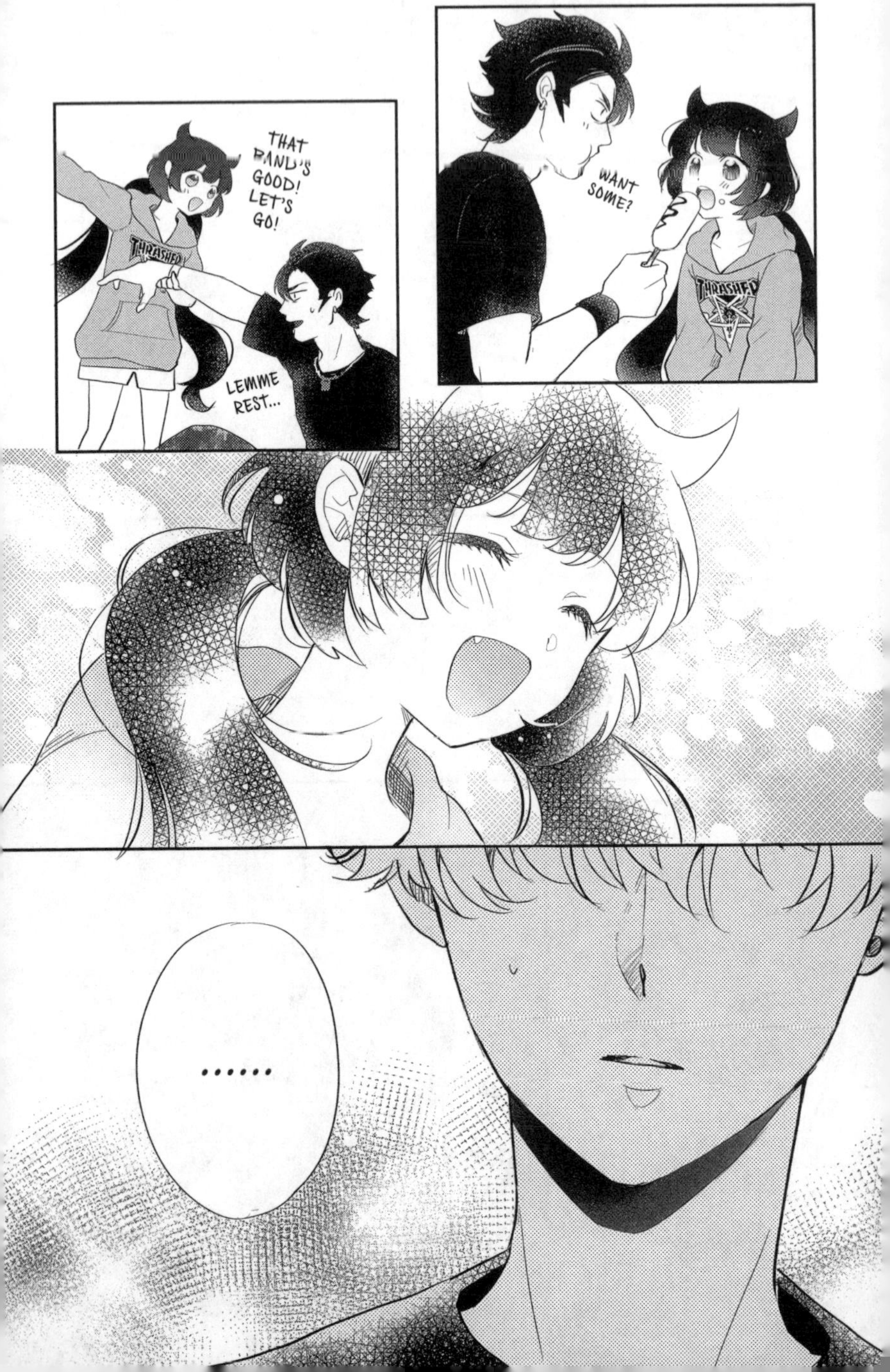

WANT SOME?
THAT BAND'S GOOD! LET'S GO!
LEMME REST...
......

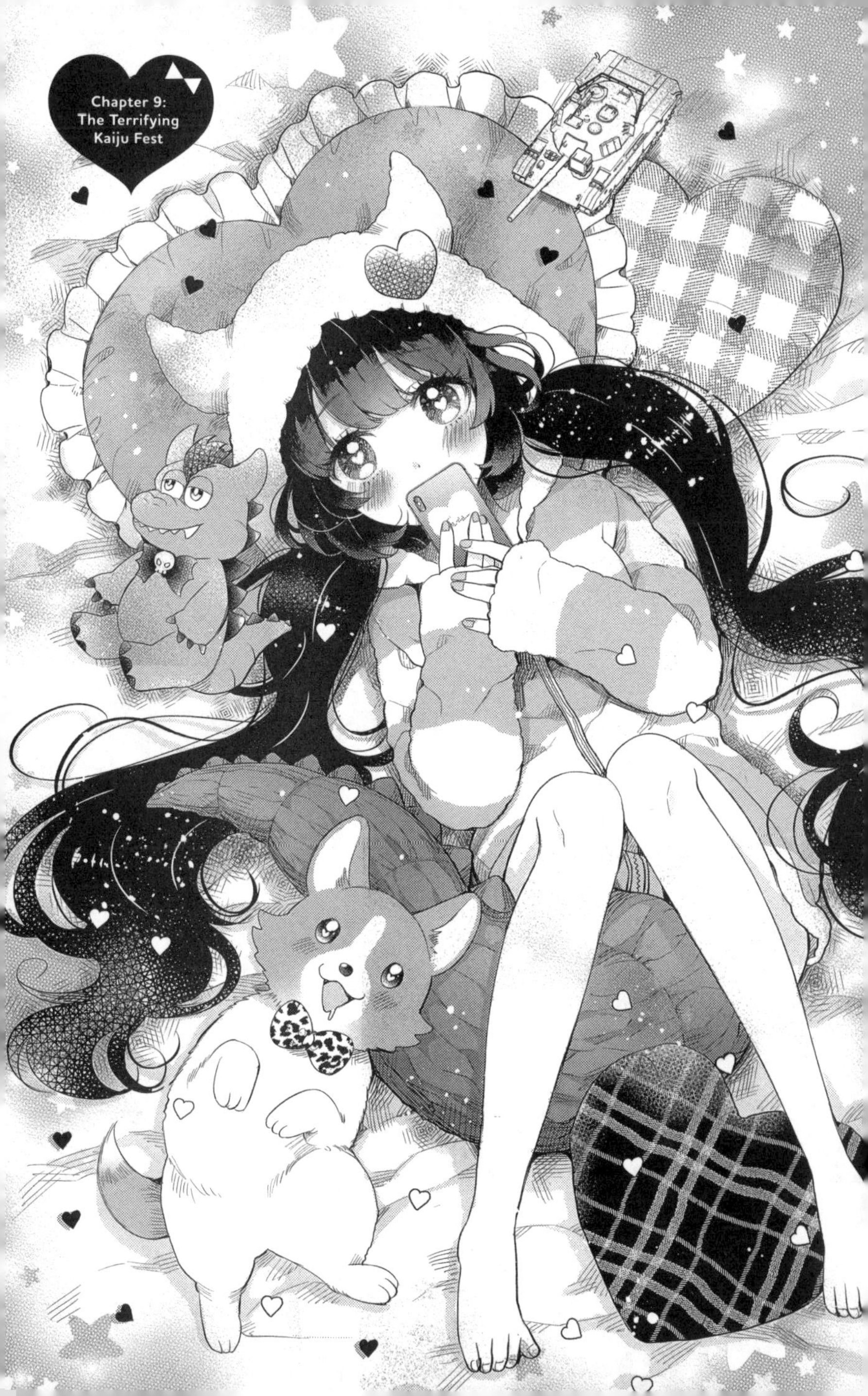
Chapter 9:
The Terrifying
Kaiju Fest

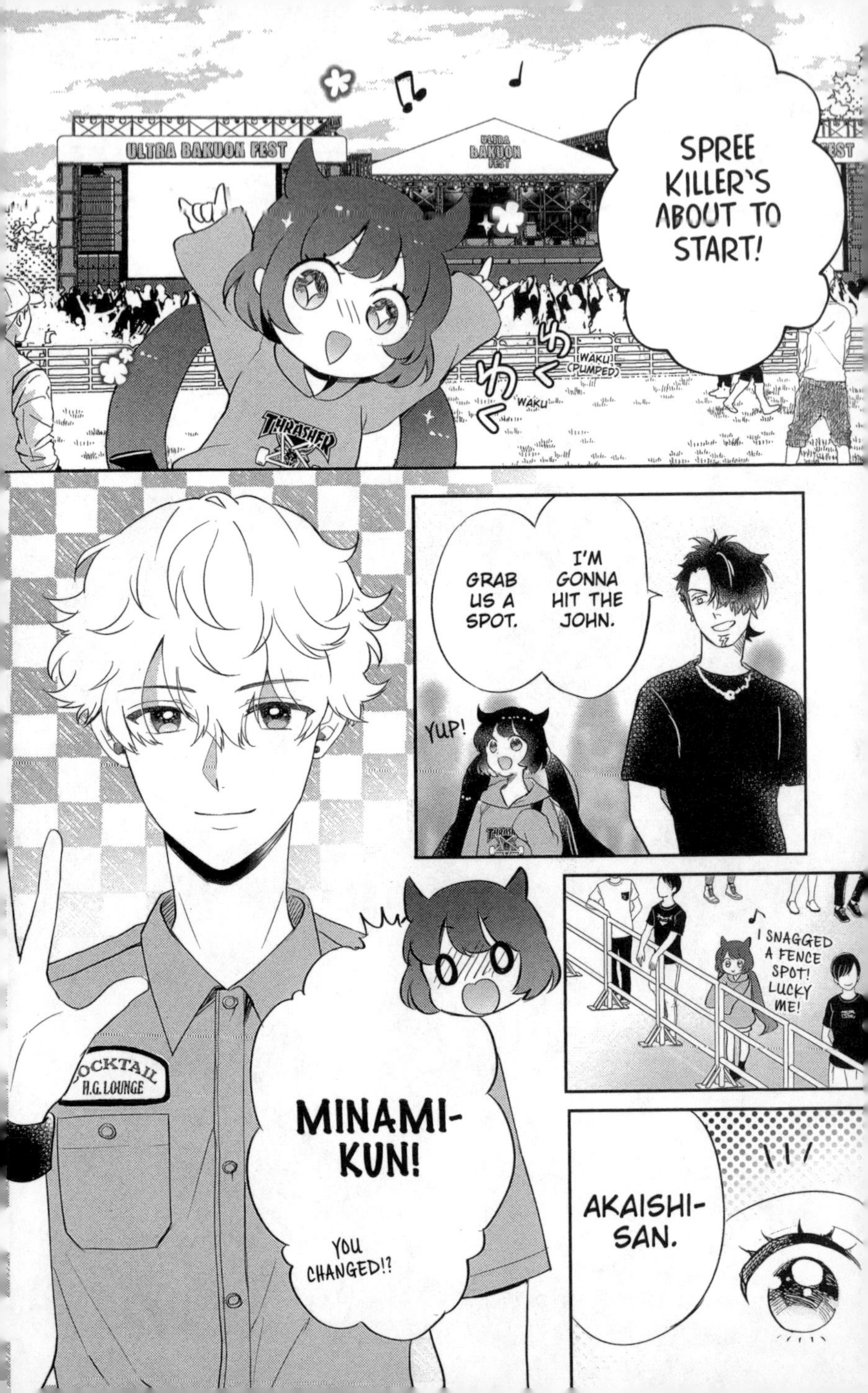

SPREE KILLER'S ABOUT TO START!
WAKU (PUMPED)
WAKU
I'M GONNA HIT THE JOHN.
GRAB US A SPOT.
YUP!
I SNAGGED A FENCE SPOT! LUCKY ME!
AKAISHI-SAN.
MINAMI-KUN!
YOU CHANGED!?

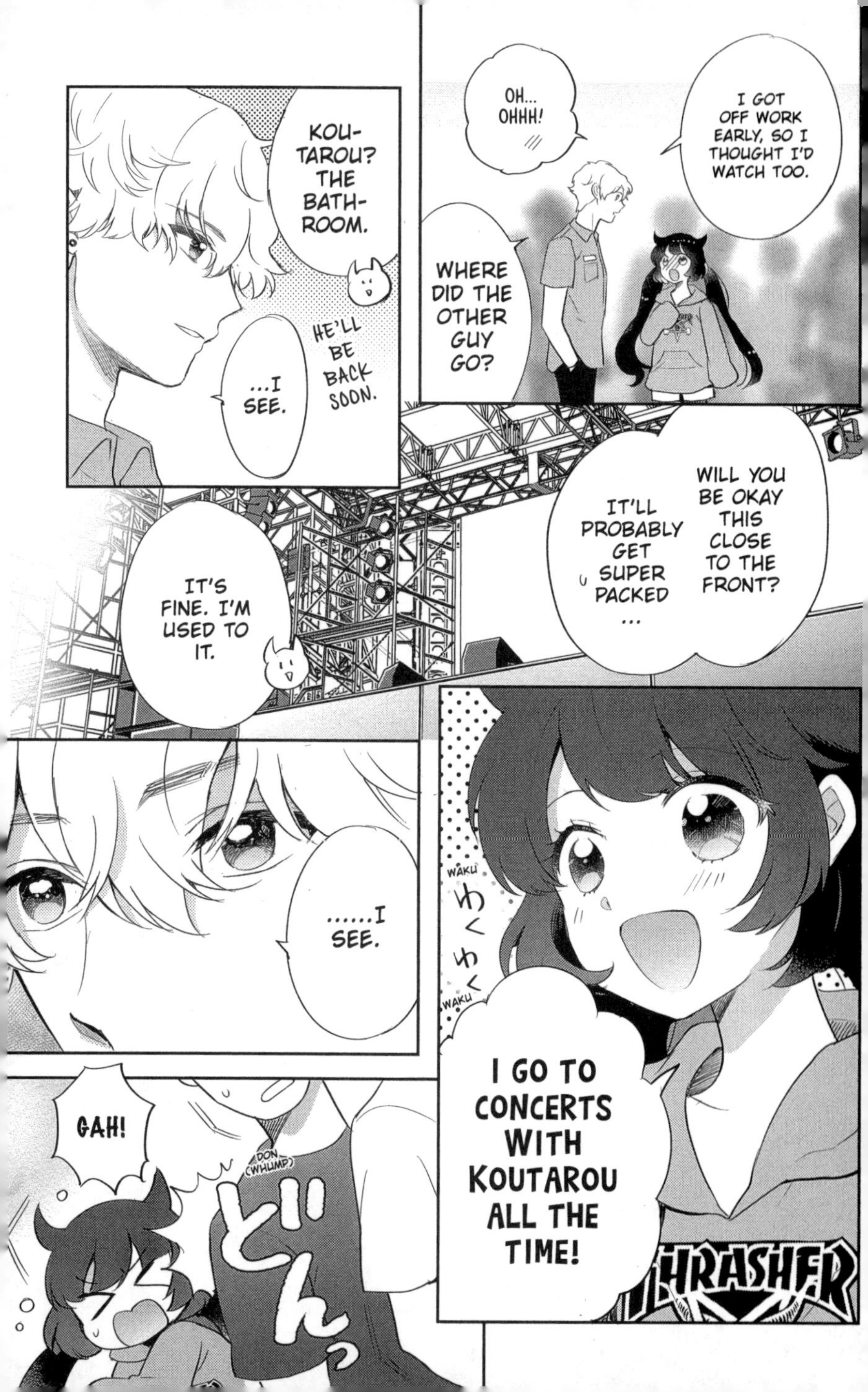
I GOT OFF WORK EARLY, SO I THOUGHT I'D WATCH TOO.
OH... OHHH!
WHERE DID THE OTHER GUY GO?
KOU-TAROU? THE BATH-ROOM.
HE'LL BE BACK SOON.
...I SEE.
WILL YOU BE OKAY THIS CLOSE TO THE FRONT?
IT'LL PROBABLY GET SUPER PACKED...
IT'S FINE. I'M USED TO IT.
WAKU WAKU
I GO TO CONCERTS WITH KOUTAROU ALL THE TIME!
THRASHER
......I SEE.
GAH!
DON (WHUMP)

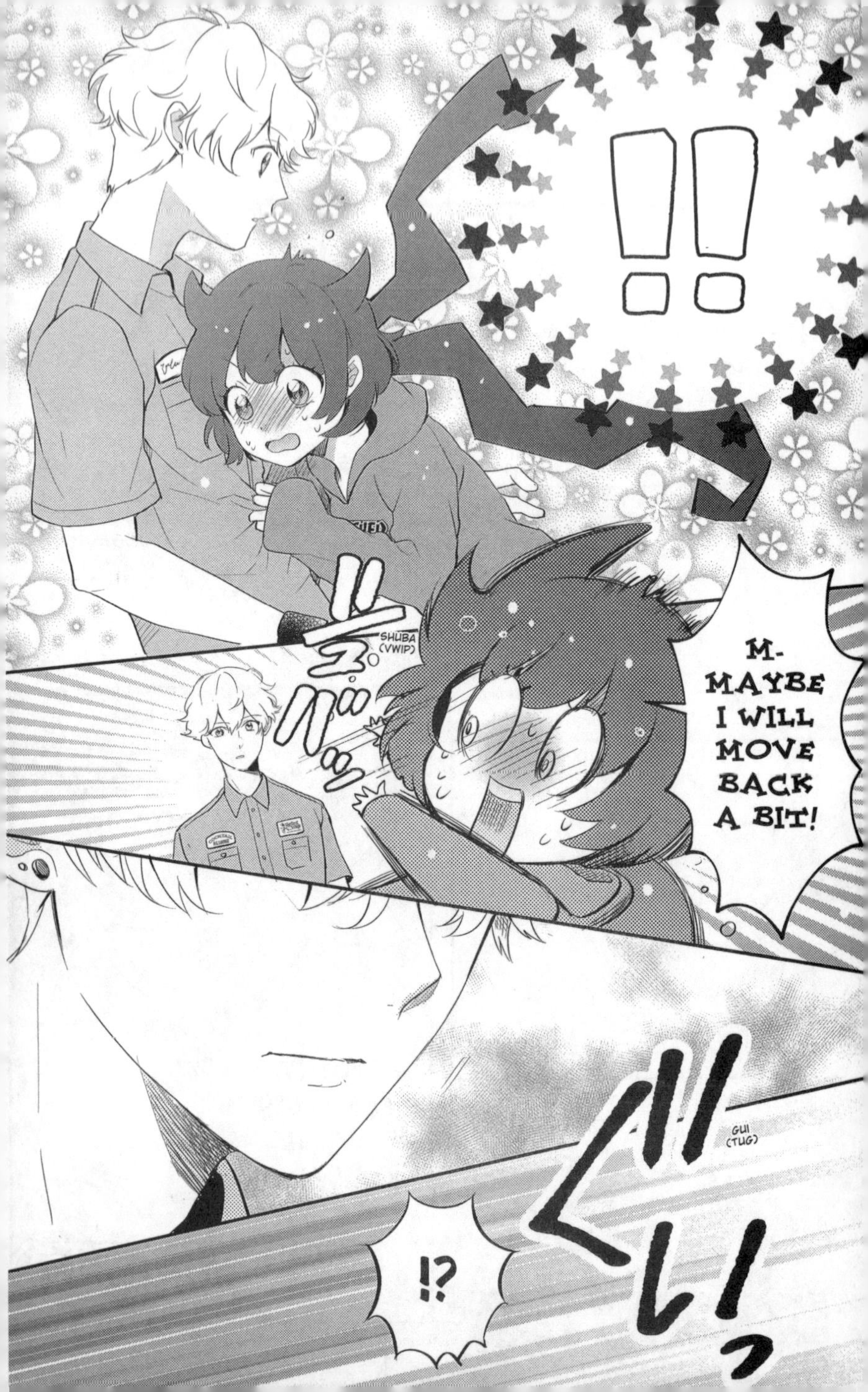
!!
M-MAYBE I WILL MOVE BACK A BIT!
SHUBA (VWIP)
GUI (TUG)
!?

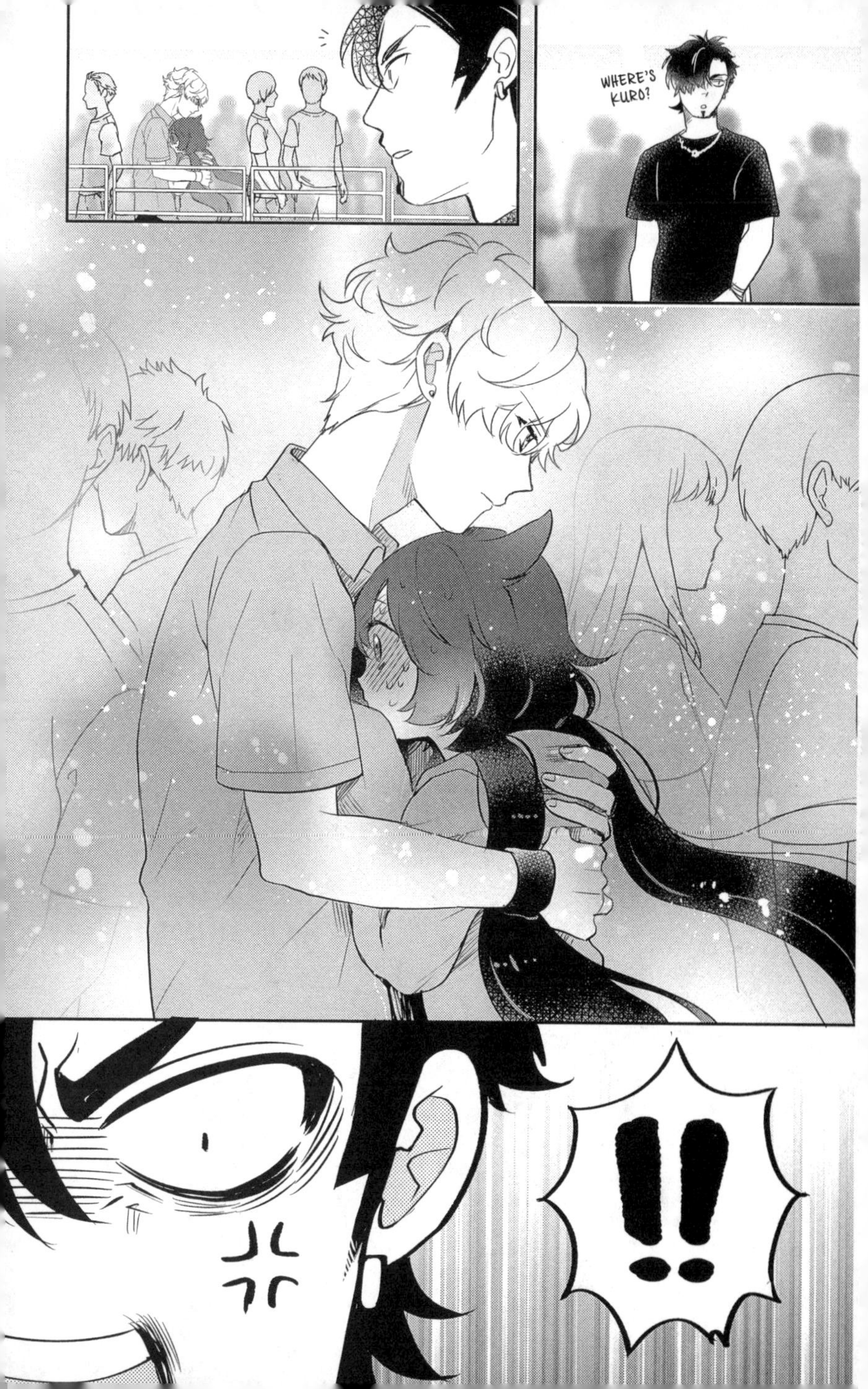
WHERE'S KURO?
!!

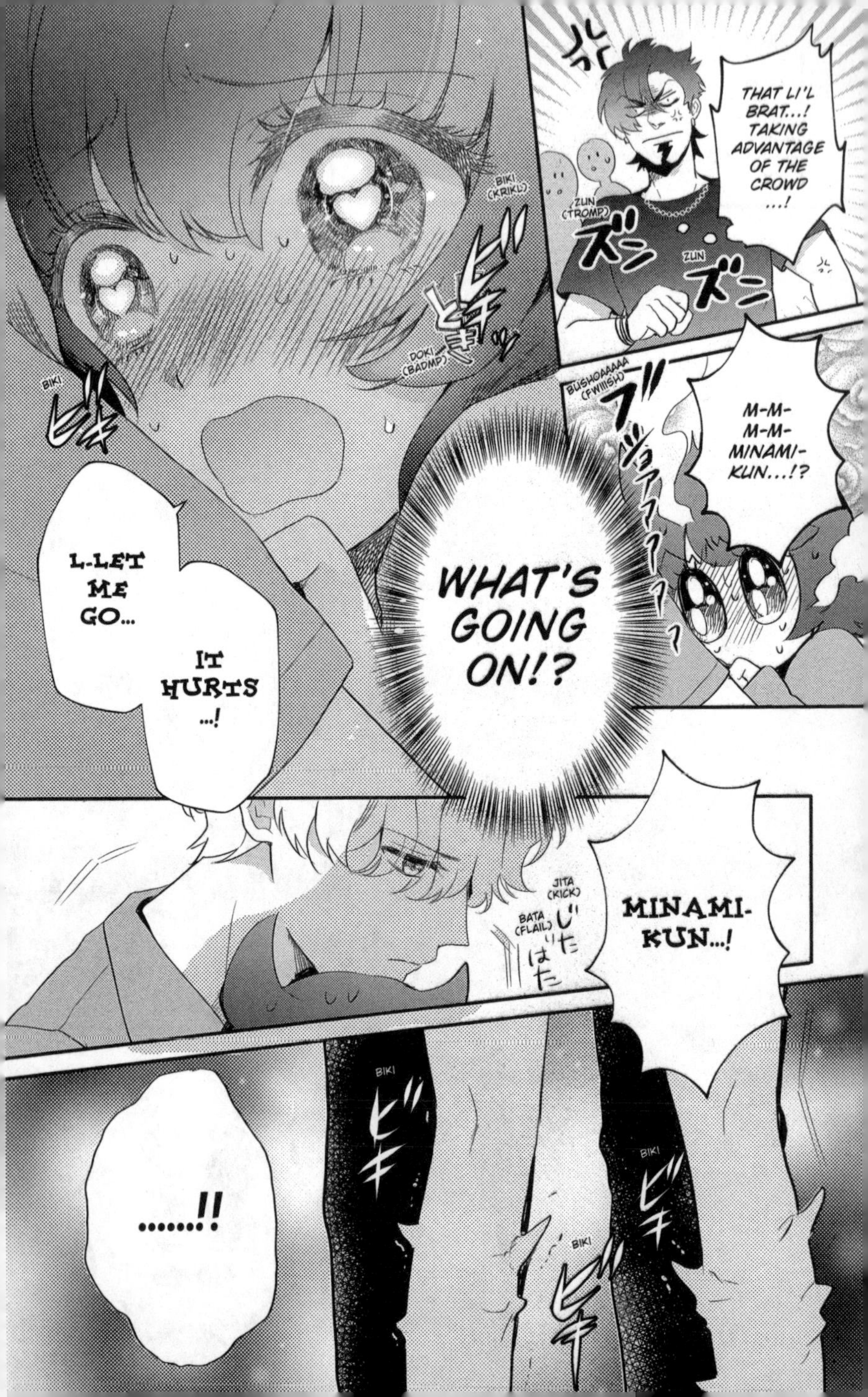
ZUN (TROMP)
ZUN
THAT LI'L BRAT...! TAKING ADVANTAGE OF THE CROWD...!
BUSHOAAAAA (FWIIISH)
M-M-M-M-MINAMI-KUN...!?
WHAT'S GOING ON!?
BIKI (KRIKL)
DOKI (BADMP)
BIKI
L-LET ME GO...
IT HURTS...!
MINAMI-KUN...!
JITA (KICK)
BATA (FLAIL)
......!!
BIKI
BIKI
BIKI

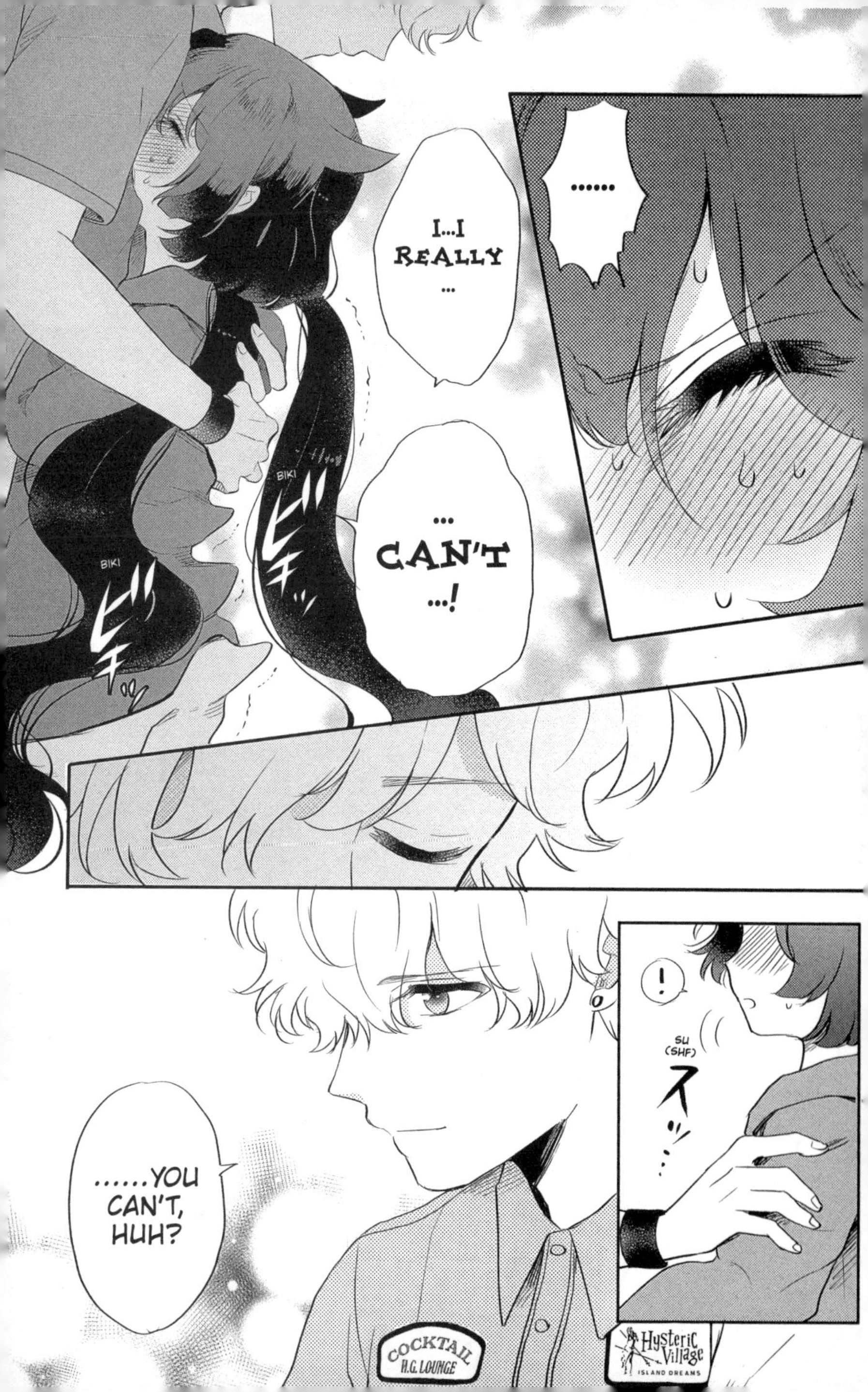
....
I...I REALLY ...
... CAN'T ...!
BIKI
BIKI
!
SU (SHF)
......YOU CAN'T, HUH?
COCKTAIL H.G. LOUNGE
Hysteric Village ISLAND DREAMS

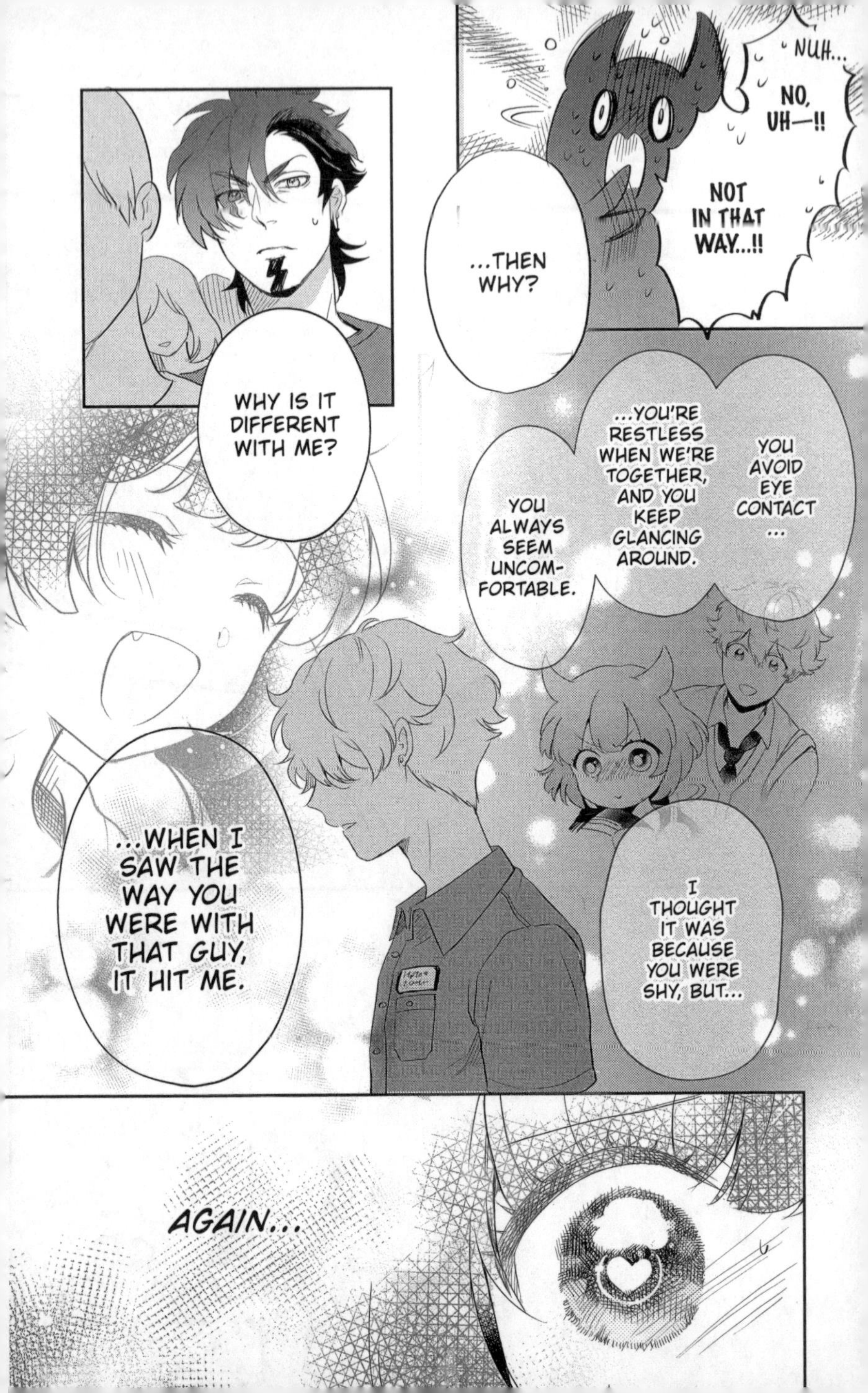
NUH...
NO, UH—!!
NOT IN THAT WAY...!!
...THEN WHY?
WHY IS IT DIFFERENT WITH ME?
YOU AVOID EYE CONTACT...
...YOU'RE RESTLESS WHEN WE'RE TOGETHER, AND YOU KEEP GLANCING AROUND.
YOU ALWAYS SEEM UNCOM-FORTABLE.
I THOUGHT IT WAS BECAUSE YOU WERE SHY, BUT...
...WHEN I SAW THE WAY YOU WERE WITH THAT GUY, IT HIT ME.
AGAIN...

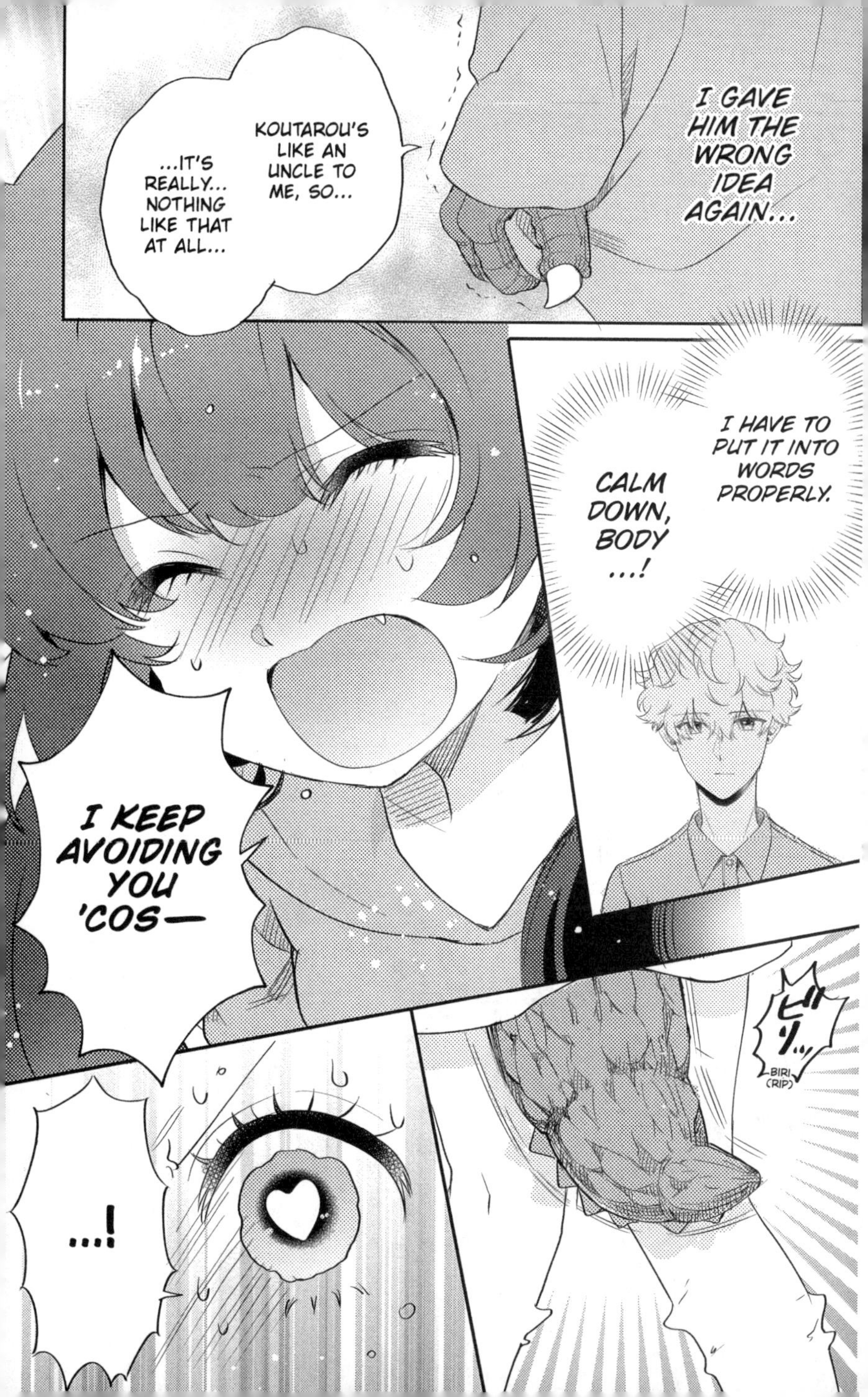
I GAVE HIM THE WRONG IDEA AGAIN...
KOUTAROU'S LIKE AN UNCLE TO ME, SO...
...IT'S REALLY... NOTHING LIKE THAT AT ALL...
I HAVE TO PUT IT INTO WORDS PROPERLY.
CALM DOWN, BODY ...!
I KEEP AVOIDING YOU 'COS—
ビリッ
BIRI (RIP)
...!

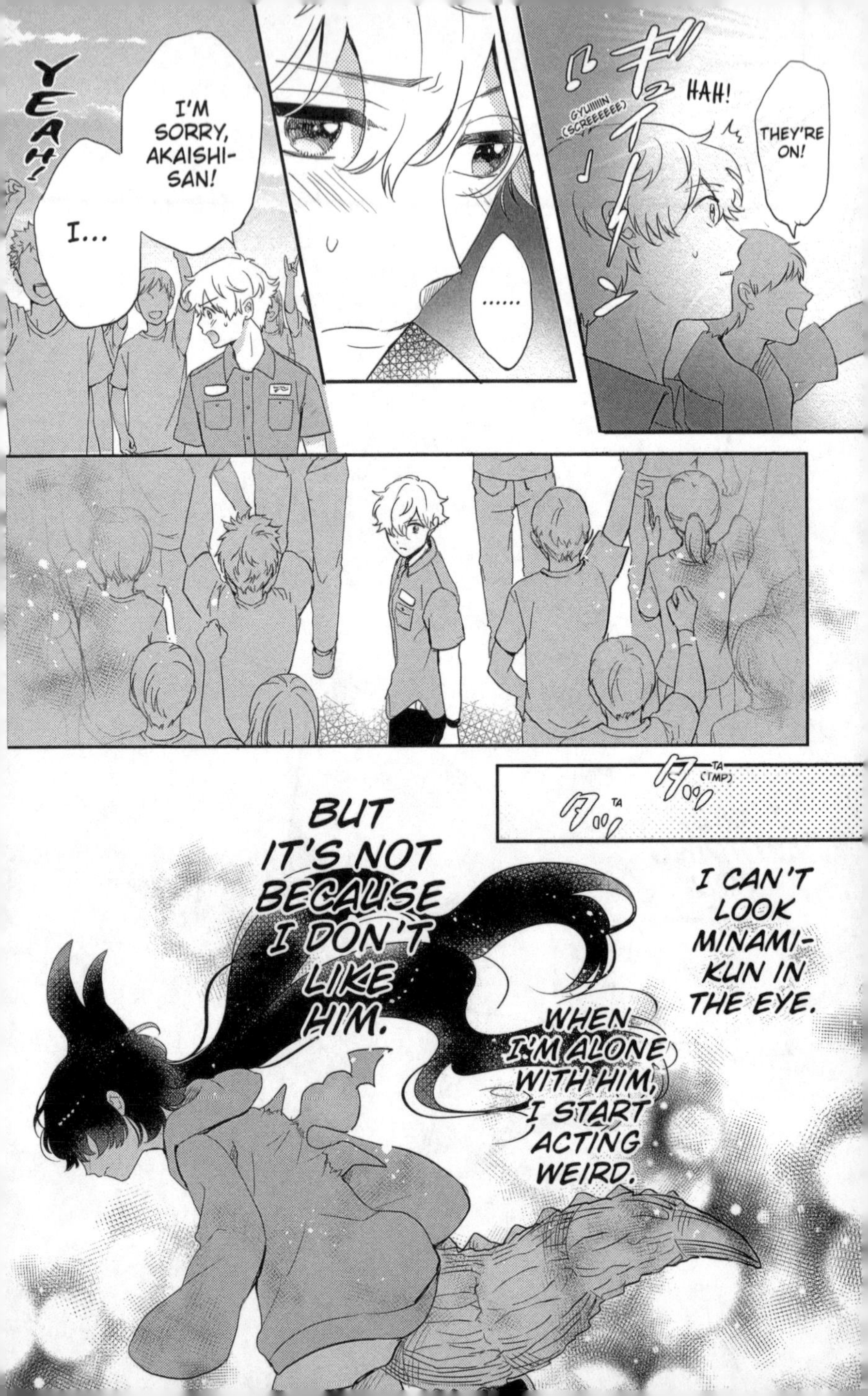
THEY'RE ON!
HAH!
GYUIIIIIN (SCREEEEEEE)
......
YEAH!
I'M SORRY, AKAISHI-SAN!
I...
TA (TMP)
TA
I CAN'T LOOK MINAMI-KUN IN THE EYE.
WHEN I'M ALONE WITH HIM, I START ACTING WEIRD.
BUT IT'S NOT BECAUSE I DON'T LIKE HIM.

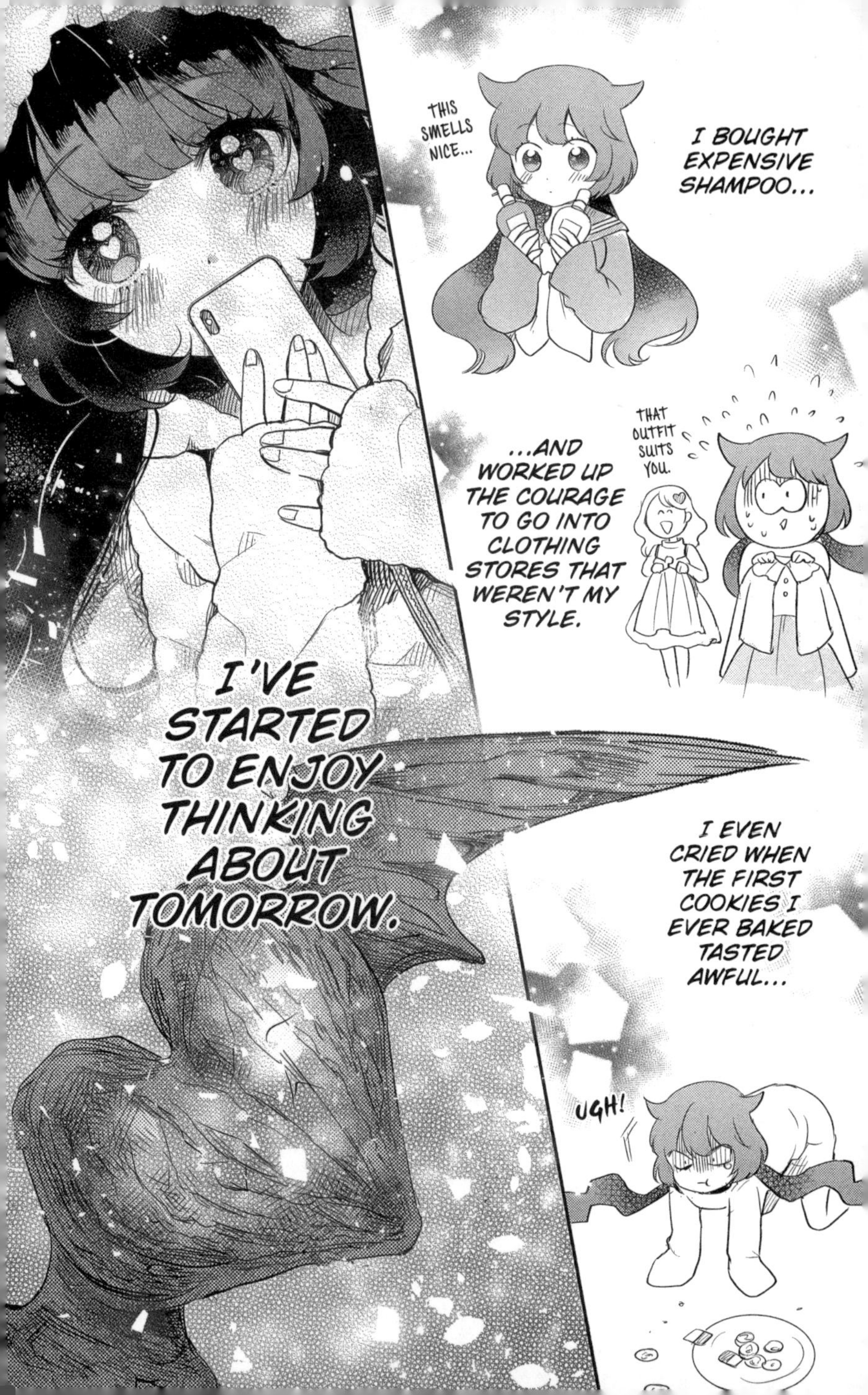
I BOUGHT EXPENSIVE SHAMPOO...
THIS SMELLS NICE...
THAT OUTFIT SUITS YOU.
...AND WORKED UP THE COURAGE TO GO INTO CLOTHING STORES THAT WEREN'T MY STYLE.
I EVEN CRIED WHEN THE FIRST COOKIES I EVER BAKED TASTED AWFUL...
UGH!
I'VE STARTED TO ENJOY THINKING ABOUT TOMORROW.

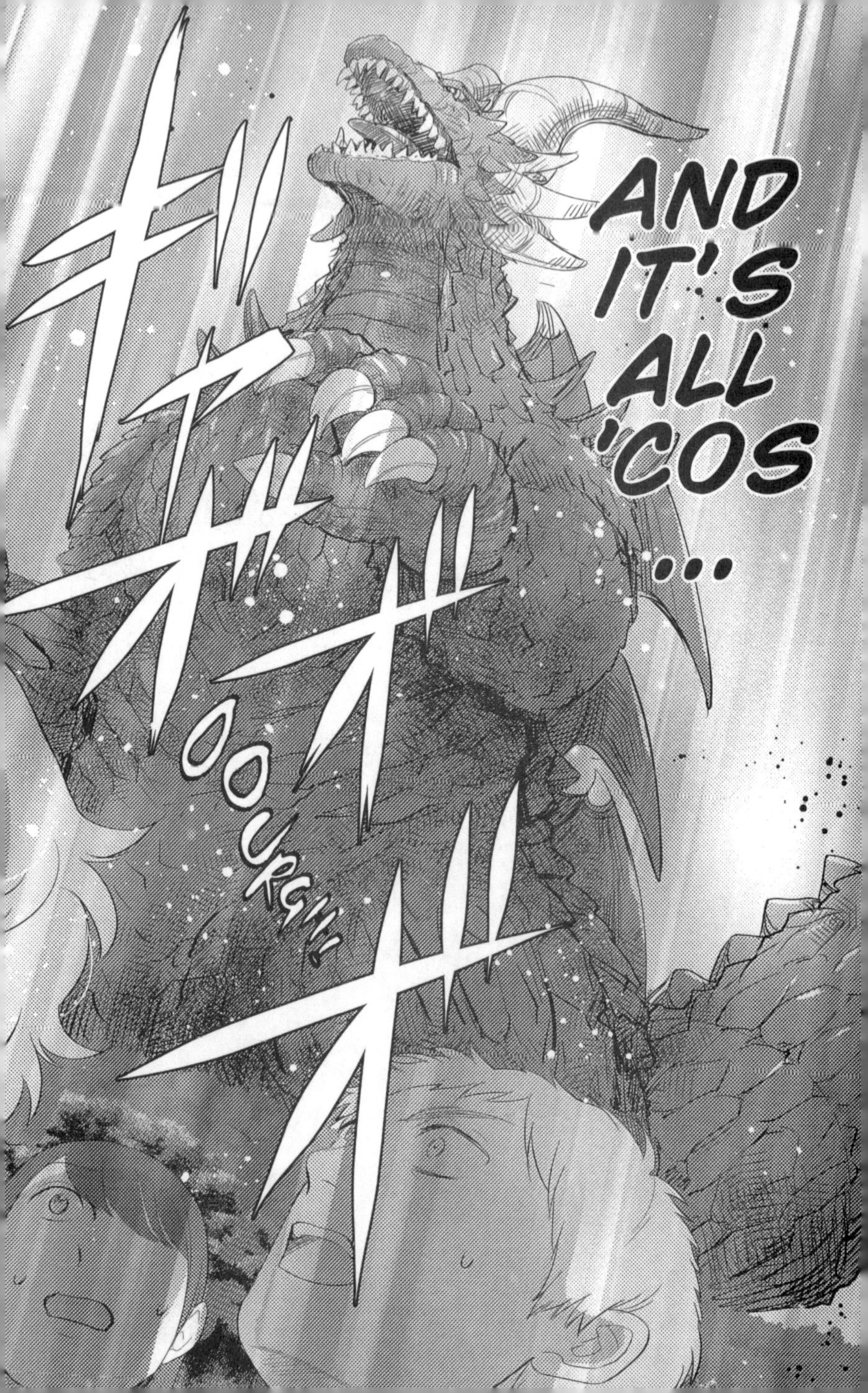
AND IT'S ALL 'COS...
OOURGH!!

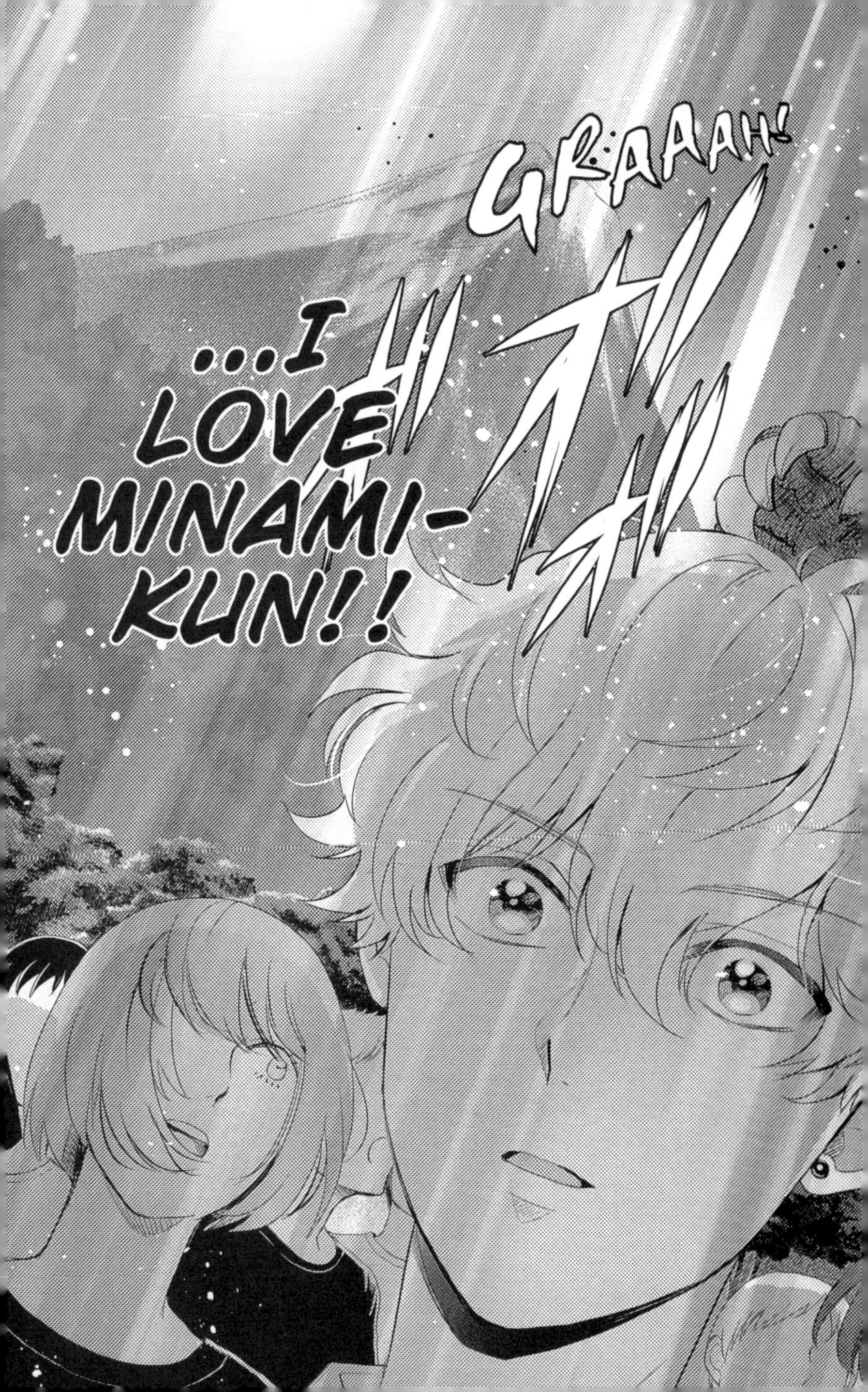
GRAAAH!
...I LOVE MINAMI-KUN!!

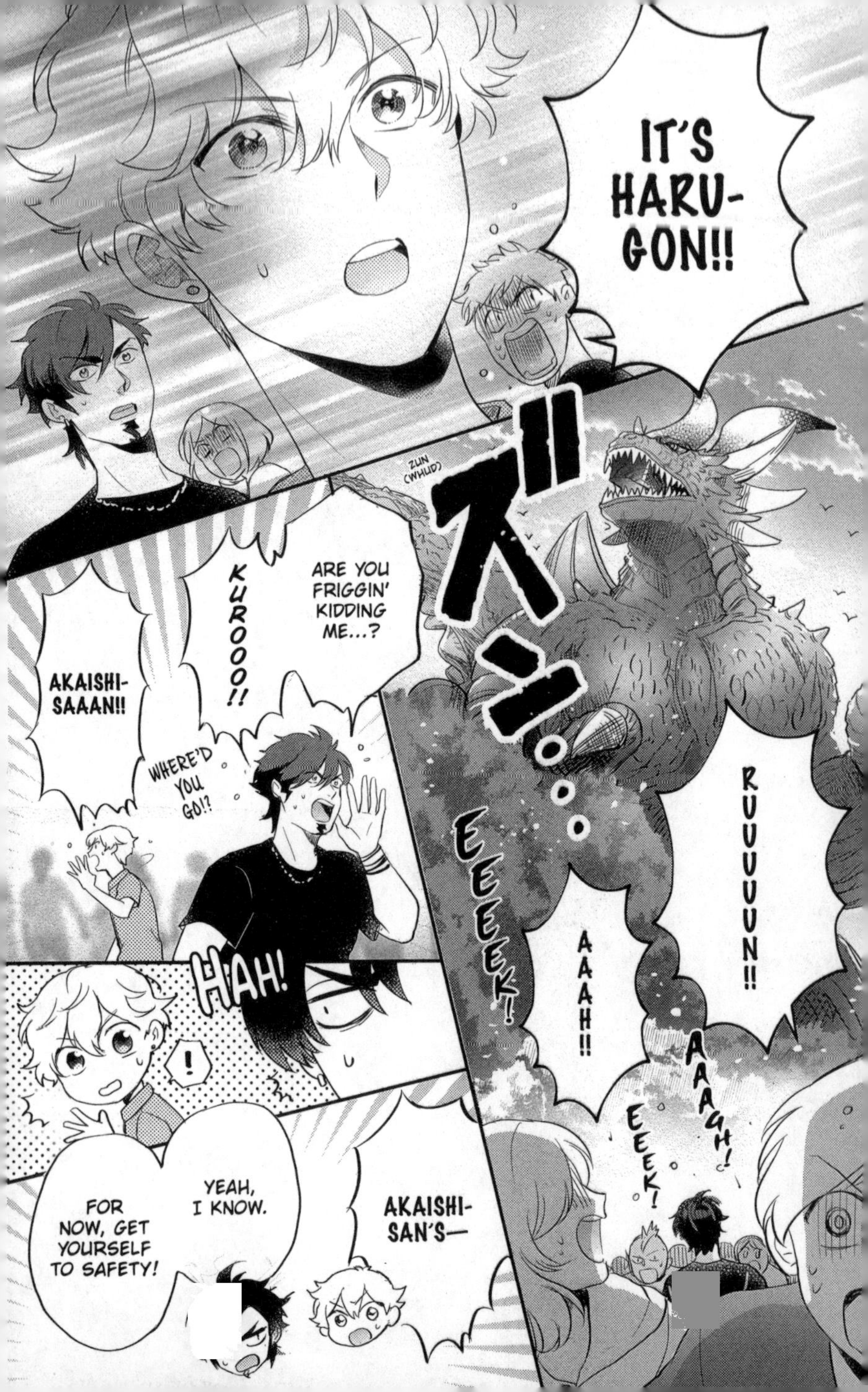
IT'S HARU-GON!!
ズン
ZUN (WHUD)
RUUUUUN!!
AAAAH!!
EEEEEK!
AAAAGH!
EEEEK!
ARE YOU FRIGGIN' KIDDING ME...?
KUROOOO!!
AKAISHI-SAAAN!!
WHERE'D YOU GO!?
HAH!
!
AKAISHI-SAN'S—
YEAH, I KNOW.
FOR NOW, GET YOURSELF TO SAFETY!

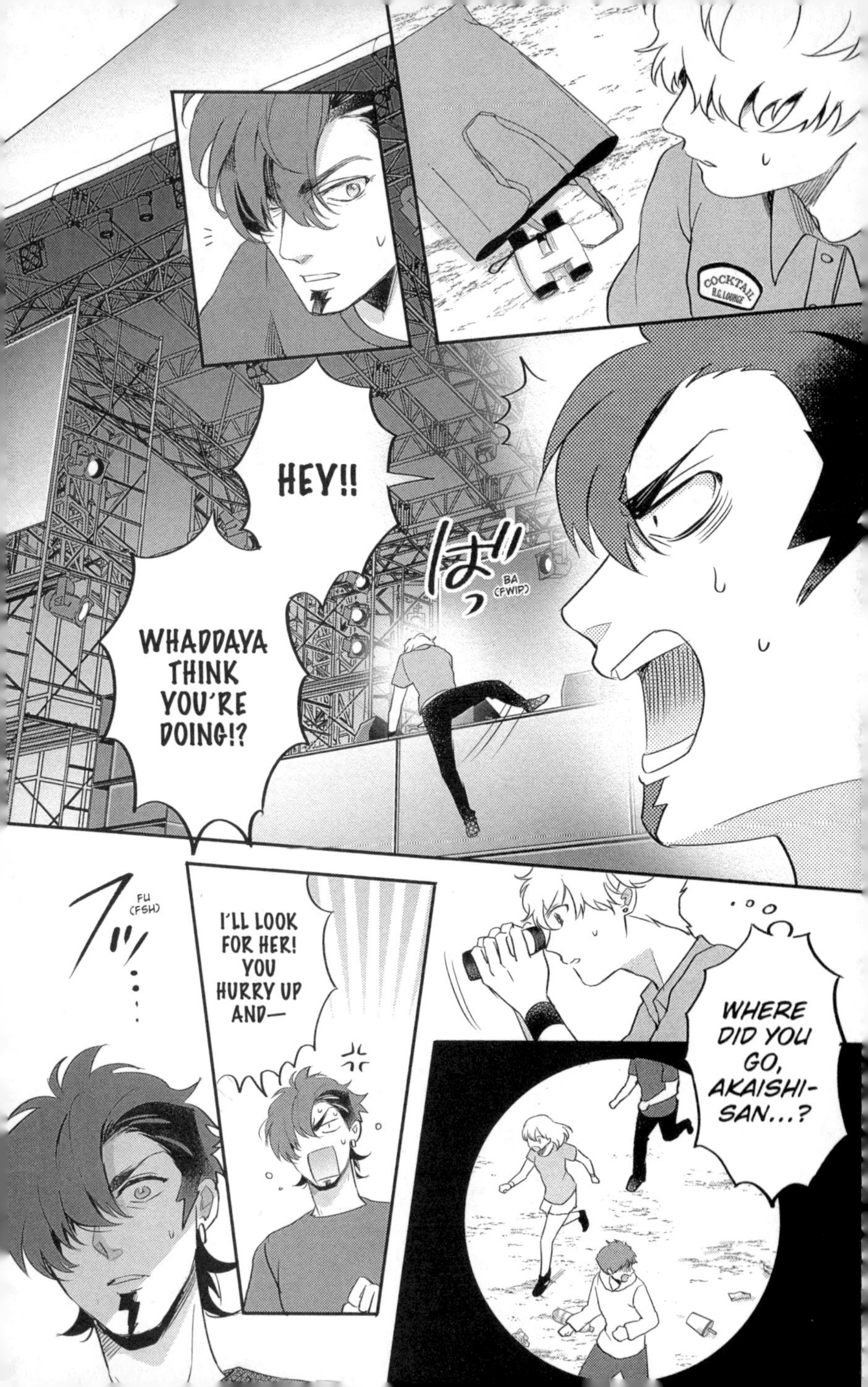
COCKTAIL H.G. LOUNGE
HEY!!
ばっ
BA (FWIP)
WHADDAYA THINK YOU'RE DOING!?
WHERE DID YOU GO, AKAISHI-SAN...?
I'LL LOOK FOR HER! YOU HURRY UP AND—
フッ
FU (FSH)
...

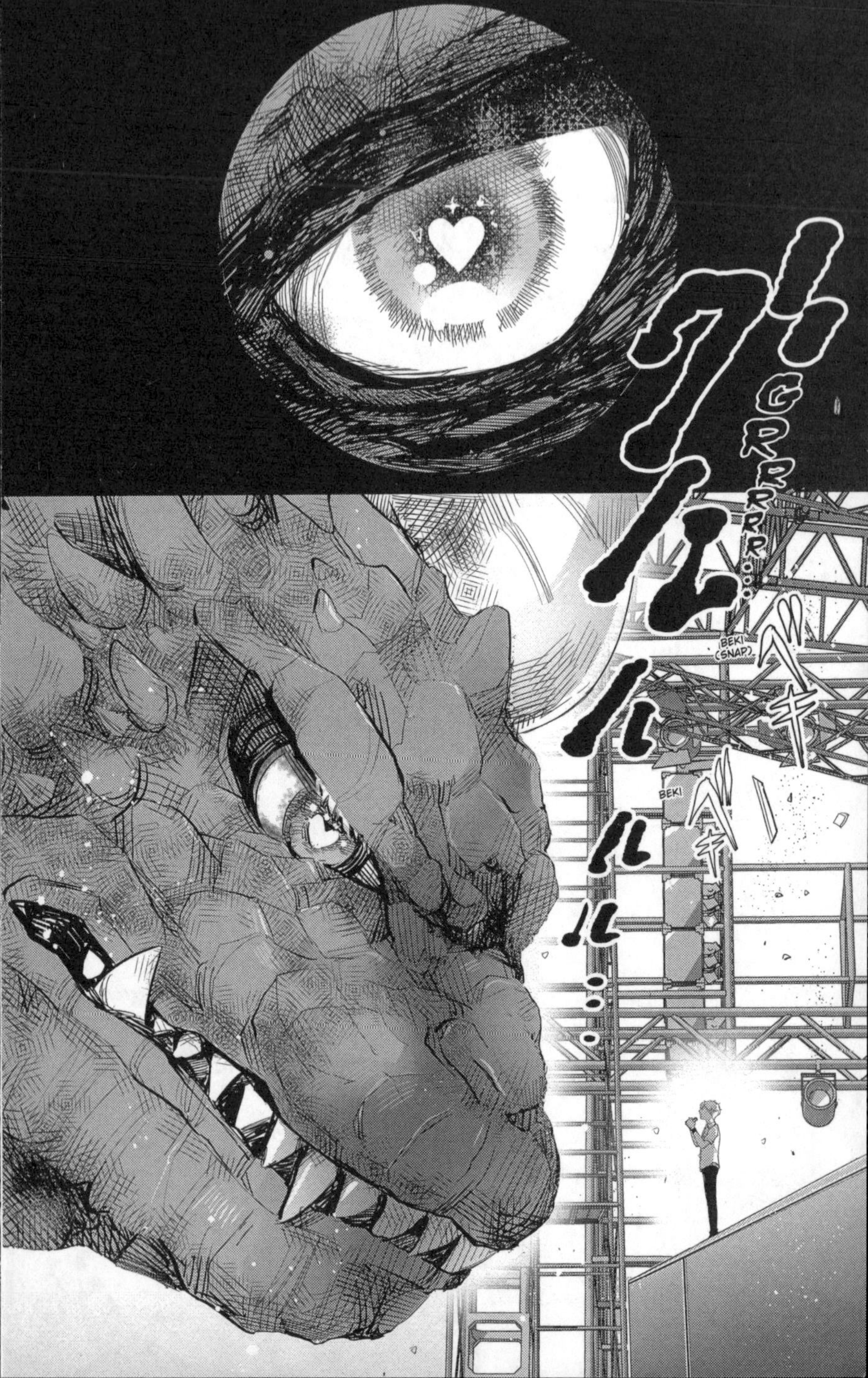
グルルル…
GRRRRR...
ベキ
BEKI (SNAP)
ベキ
BEKI

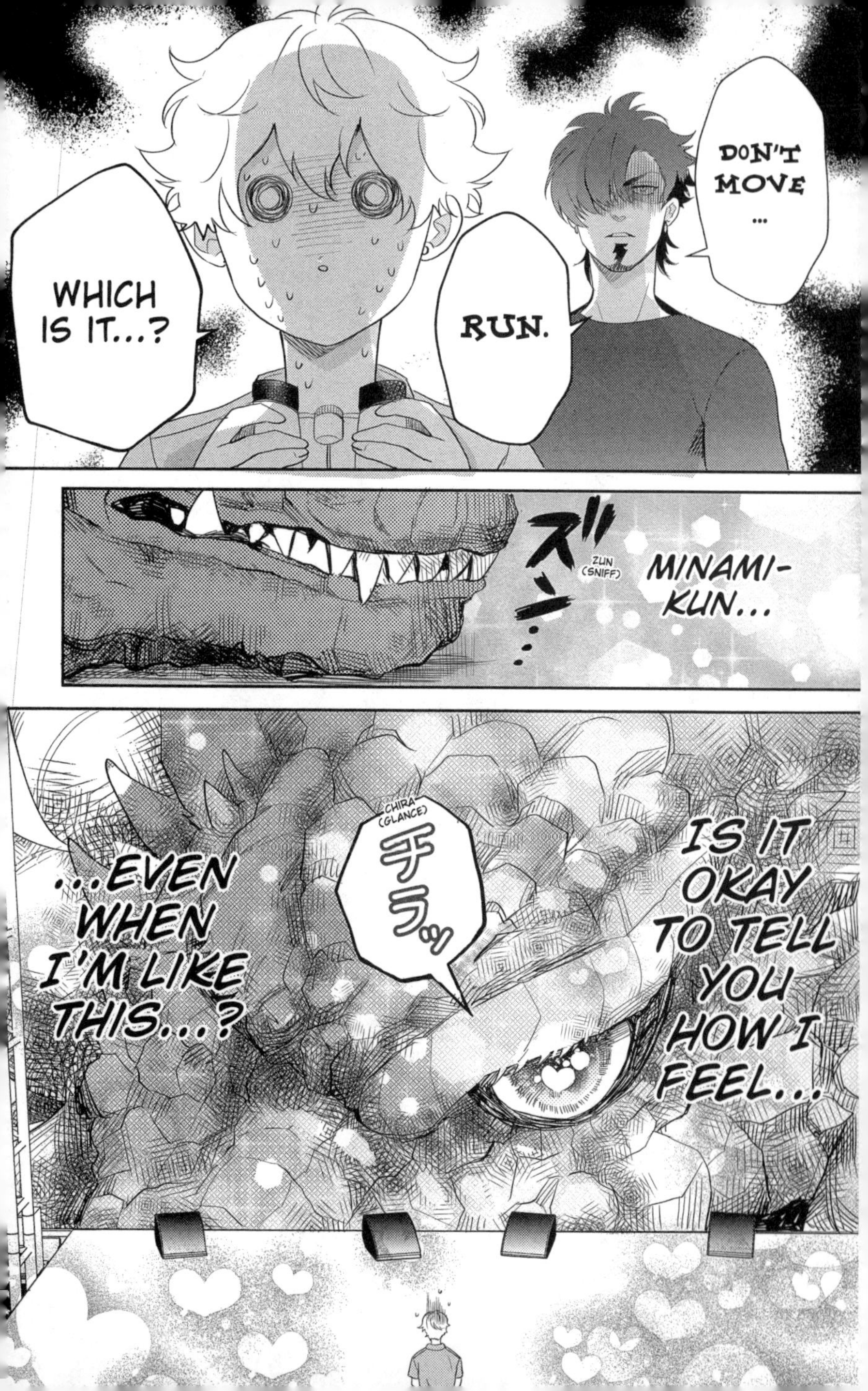
DON'T MOVE ...
RUN.
WHICH IS IT...?
ズン
ZUN (SNIFF)
MINAMI-KUN...
IS IT OKAY TO TELL YOU HOW I FEEL...
チラッ
CHIRA (GLANCE)
...EVEN WHEN I'M LIKE THIS...?

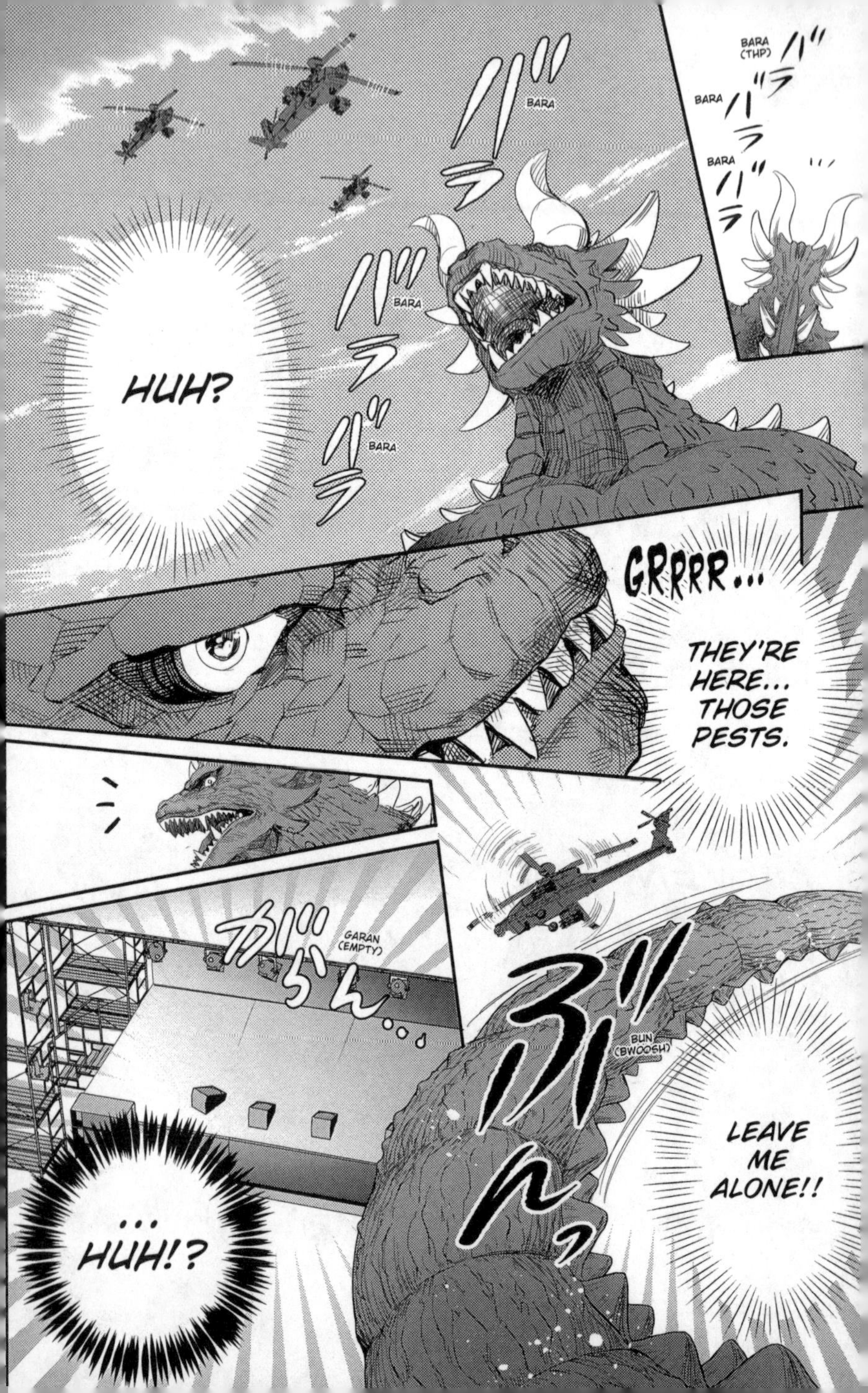

バラ
BARA (THP)
バラ
BARA
バラ
BARA
バラ
BARA
バラ
BARA
バラ
BARA
HUH?
GRRRR...
THEY'RE HERE... THOSE PESTS.
ぶんっ
BUN (BWOOSH)
LEAVE ME ALONE!!
がらん...
GARAN (EMPTY)
... HUH!?

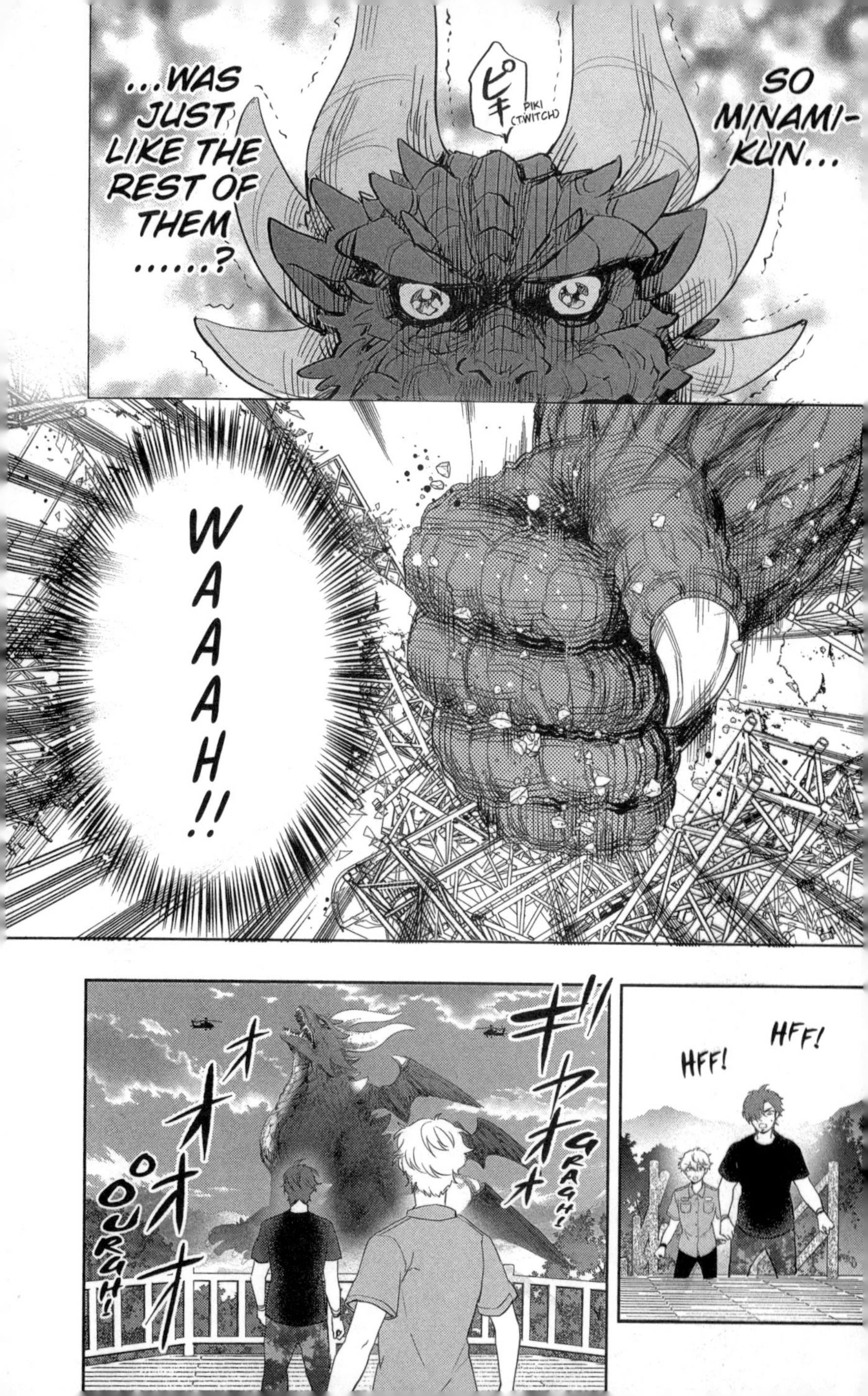
SO MINAMI-KUN...
ピキ
PIKI (TWITCH)
...WAS JUST LIKE THE REST OF THEM ......?
WAAAAH!!
HFF!
HFF!
ギャオオ
GRAGH!
オオオ
OURAGH!

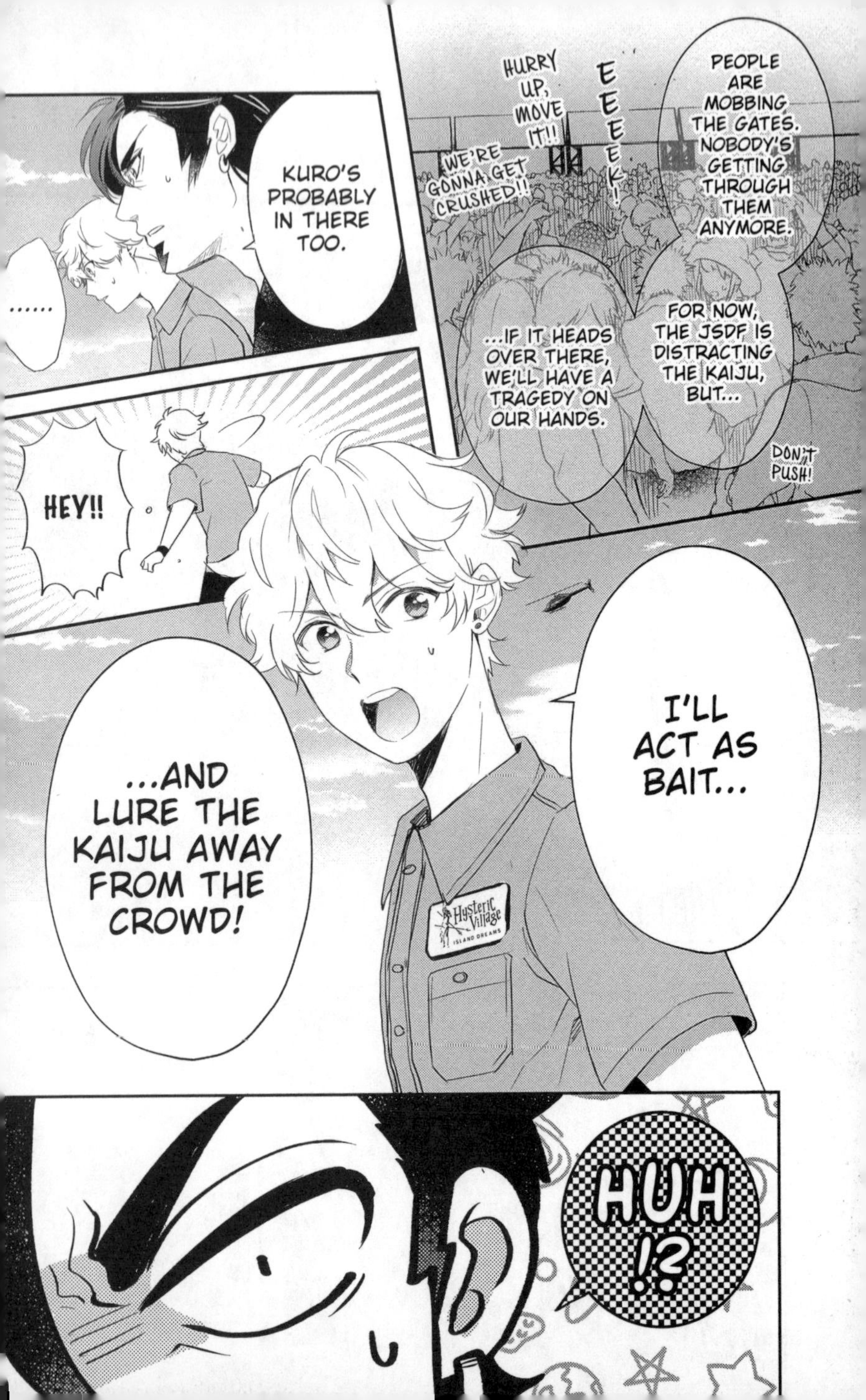
PEOPLE ARE MOBBING THE GATES. NOBODY'S GETTING THROUGH THEM ANYMORE.
EEEEEK!
HURRY UP, MOVE IT!!
WE'RE GONNA GET CRUSHED!!
FOR NOW, THE JSDF IS DISTRACTING THE KAIJU, BUT...
...IF IT HEADS OVER THERE, WE'LL HAVE A TRAGEDY ON OUR HANDS.
DON'T PUSH!
KURO'S PROBABLY IN THERE TOO.
......
HEY!!
I'LL ACT AS BAIT...
...AND LURE THE KAIJU AWAY FROM THE CROWD!
Hysteric Village
ISLAND DREAMS
HUH!?

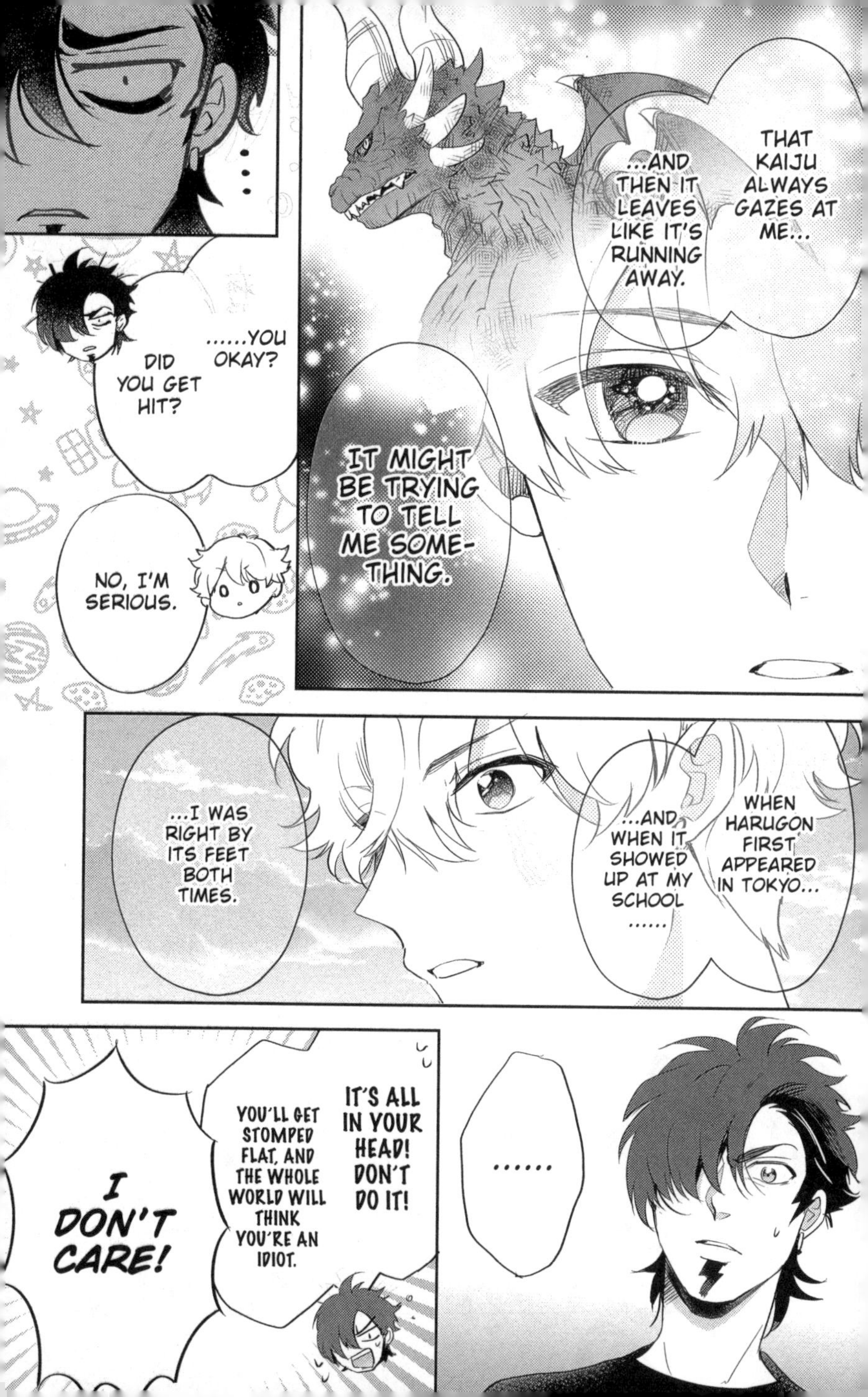
THAT KAIJU ALWAYS GAZES AT ME...
...AND THEN IT LEAVES LIKE IT'S RUNNING AWAY.
IT MIGHT BE TRYING TO TELL ME SOME-THING.
...
......YOU OKAY?
DID YOU GET HIT?
NO, I'M SERIOUS.
WHEN HARUGON FIRST APPEARED IN TOKYO...
...AND WHEN IT SHOWED UP AT MY SCHOOL ......
...I WAS RIGHT BY ITS FEET BOTH TIMES.
......
IT'S ALL IN YOUR HEAD! DON'T DO IT!
YOU'LL GET STOMPED FLAT, AND THE WHOLE WORLD WILL THINK YOU'RE AN IDIOT.
I DON'T CARE!

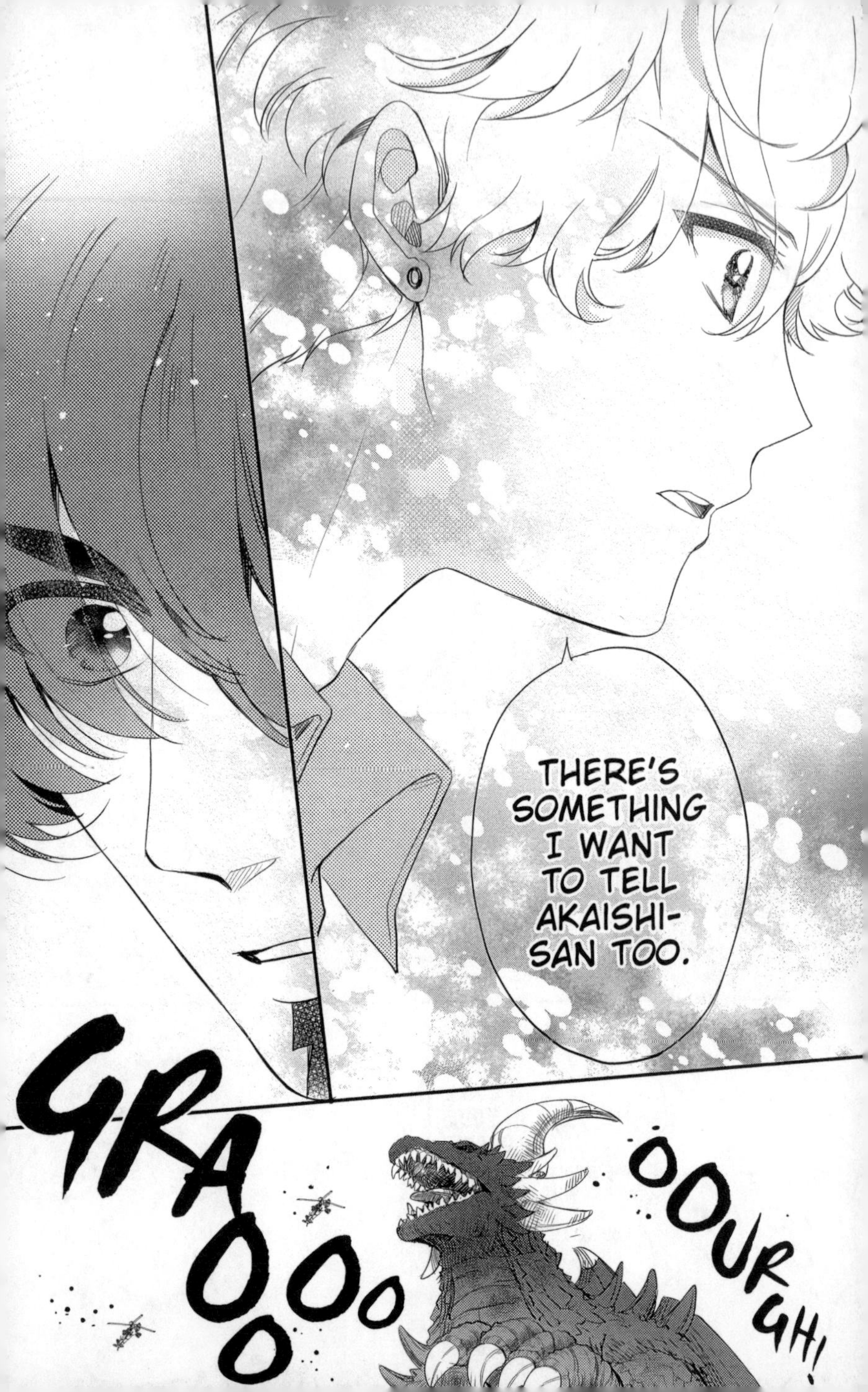
THERE'S SOMETHING I WANT TO TELL AKAISHI-SAN TOO.
GRAOOOOOOOURGH!

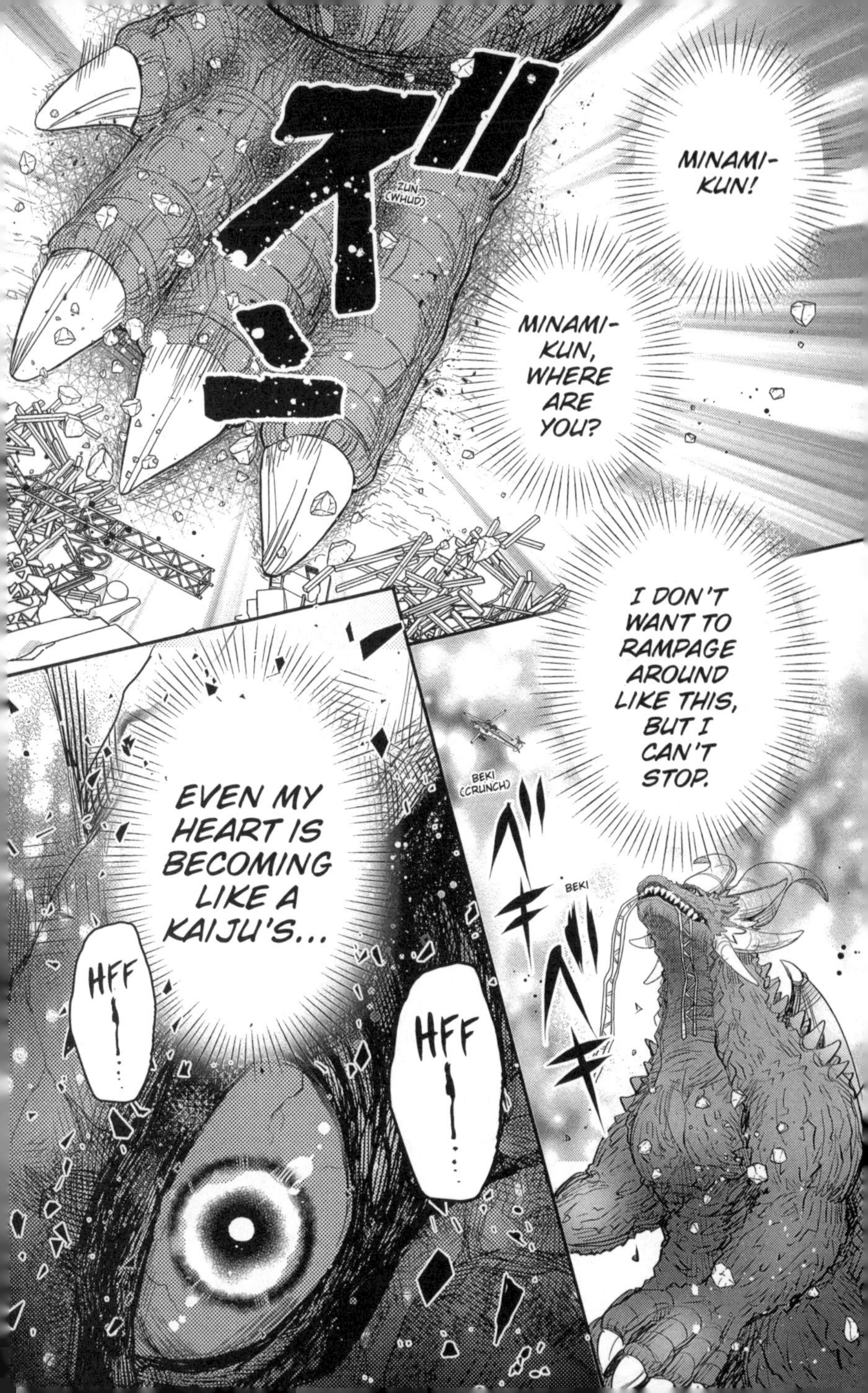
MINAMI-KUN!
ZUN (WHUD)
MINAMI-KUN, WHERE ARE YOU?
I DON'T WANT TO RAMPAGE AROUND LIKE THIS, BUT I CAN'T STOP.
BEKI (CRUNCH)
BEKI
EVEN MY HEART IS BECOMING LIKE A KAIJU'S...
HFF ...
HFF ...

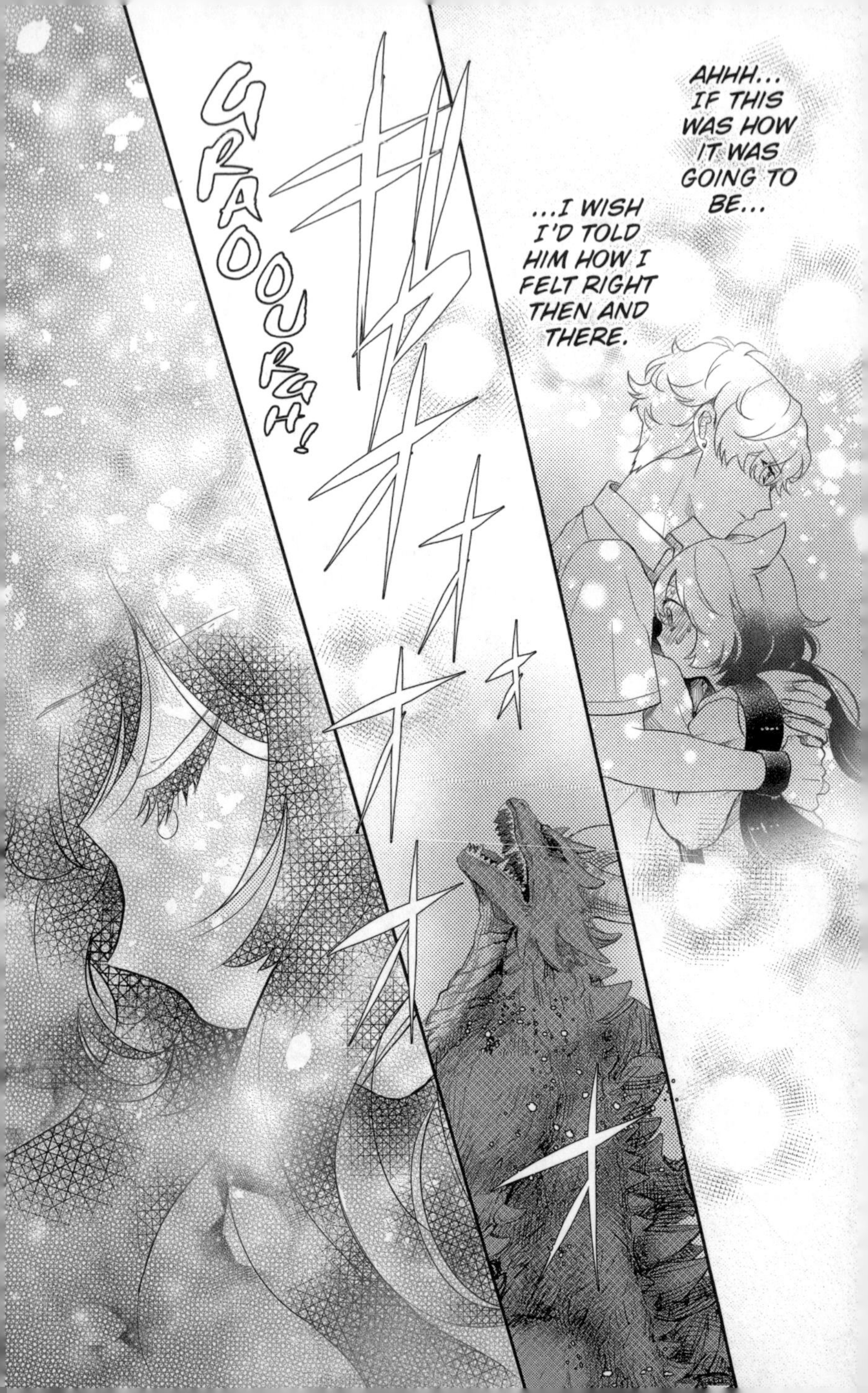
AHHH... IF THIS WAS HOW IT WAS GOING TO BE...
...I WISH I'D TOLD HIM HOW I FELT RIGHT THEN AND THERE.
URAOOURUH!

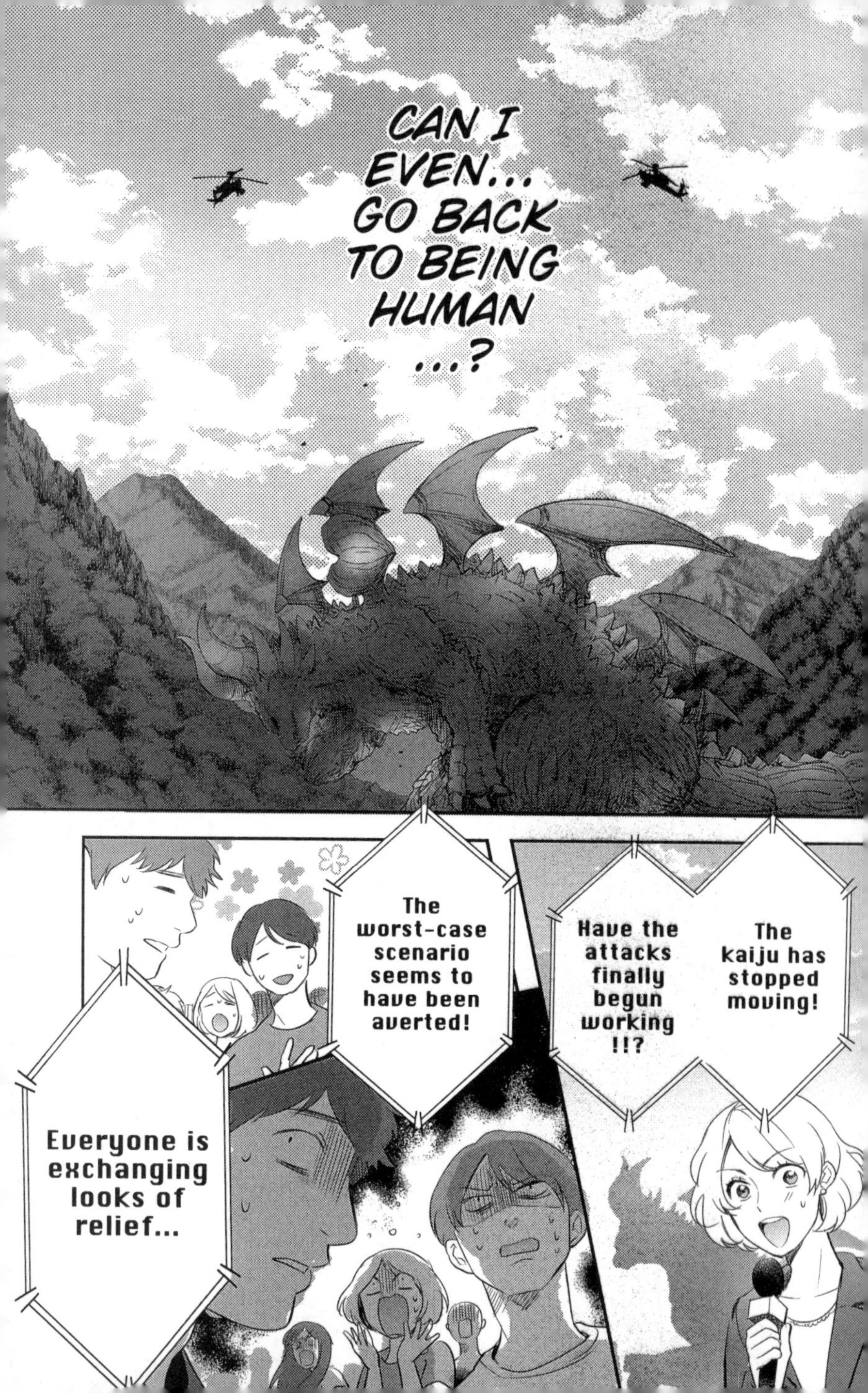
CAN I EVEN... GO BACK TO BEING HUMAN ...?
The kaiju has stopped moving!
Have the attacks finally begun working !!?
The worst-case scenario seems to have been averted!
Everyone is exchanging looks of relief...

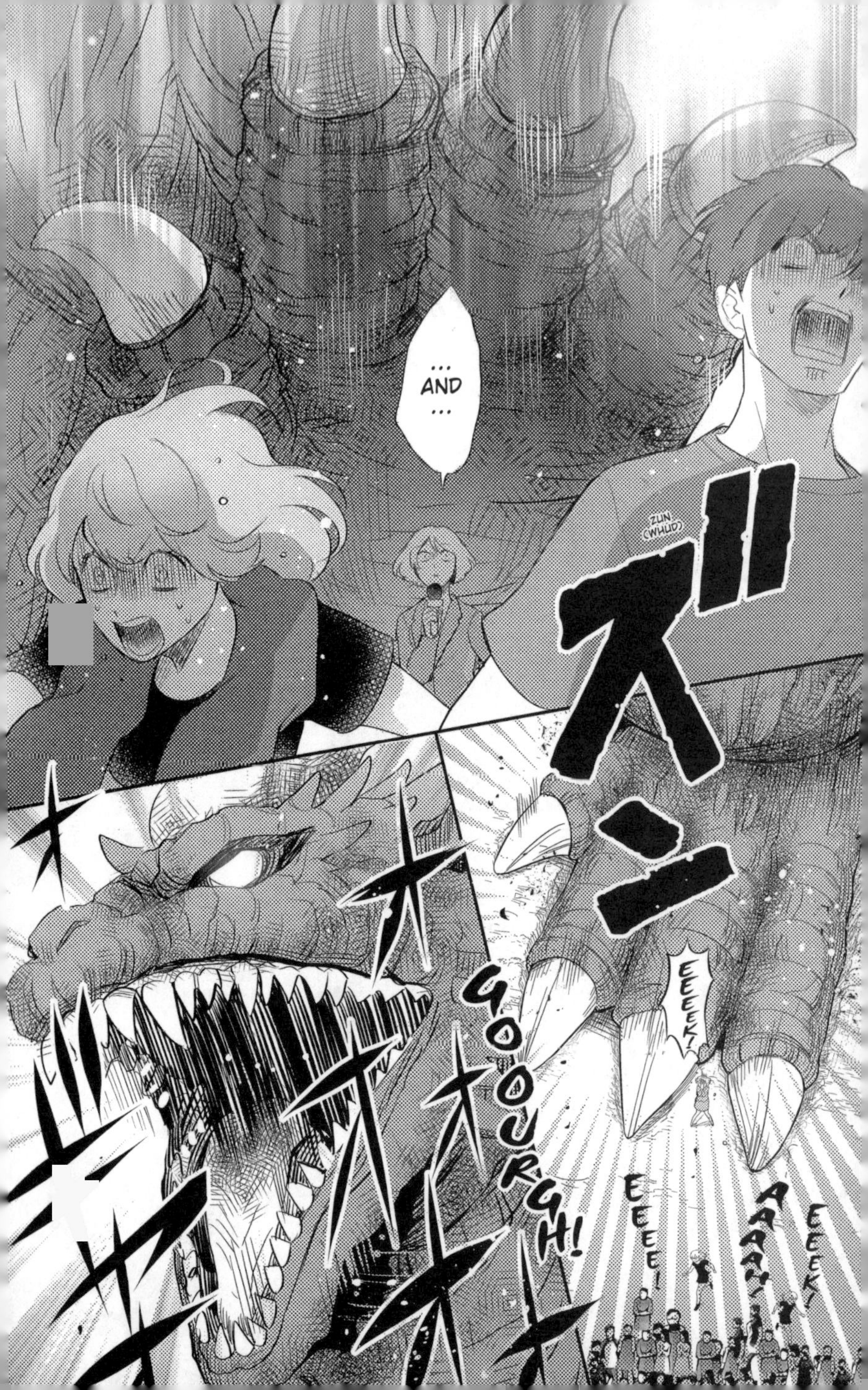
...AND...
ズン
ZUN (WHUD)
EEEEK!
GOOOURGH!
EEEEK!
AAAAH!
EEEEE!

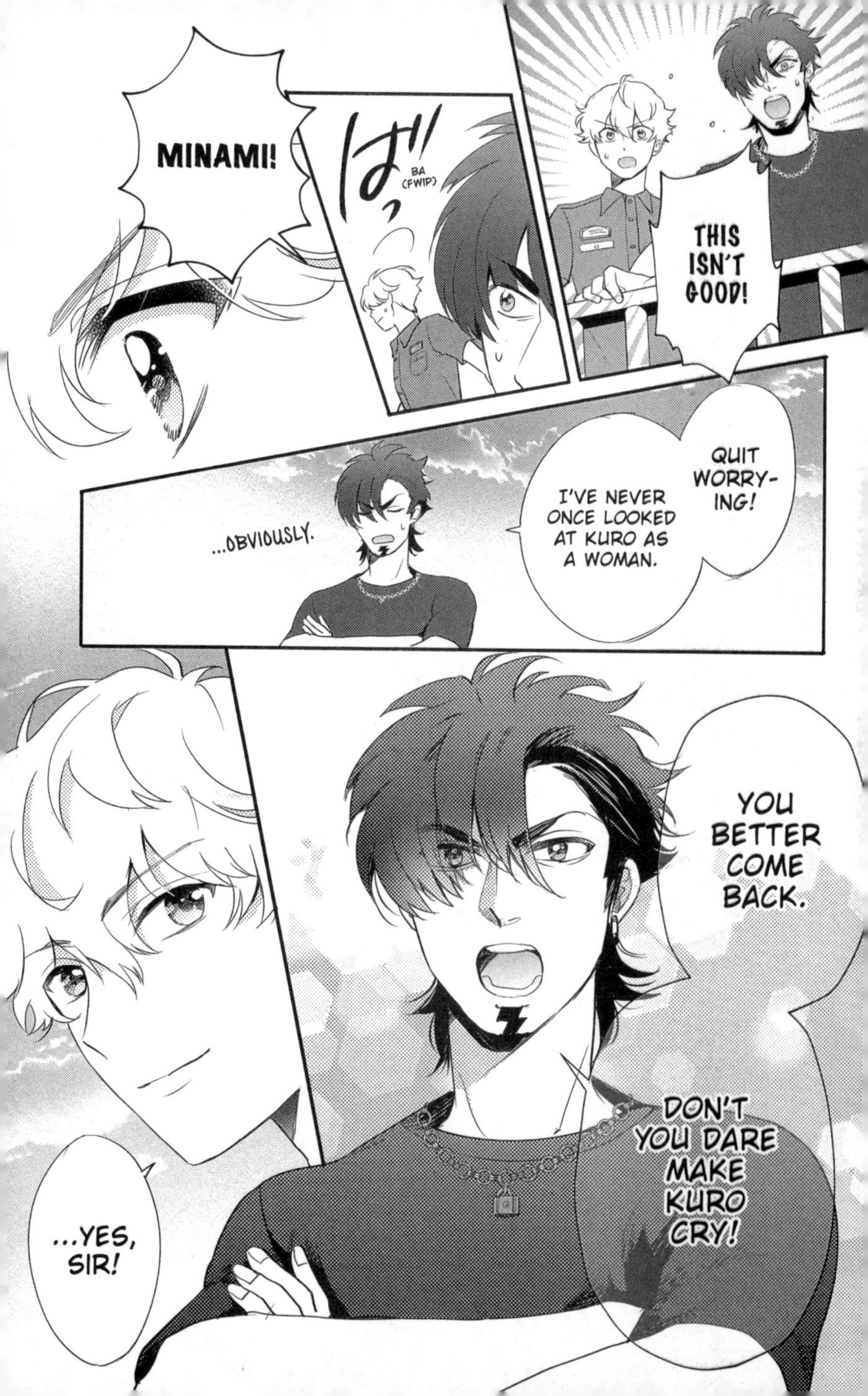

THIS ISN'T GOOD!
BA (FWIP)
MINAMI!
QUIT WORRYING!
I'VE NEVER ONCE LOOKED AT KURO AS A WOMAN.
...OBVIOUSLY.
YOU BETTER COME BACK.
DON'T YOU DARE MAKE KURO CRY!
...YES, SIR!

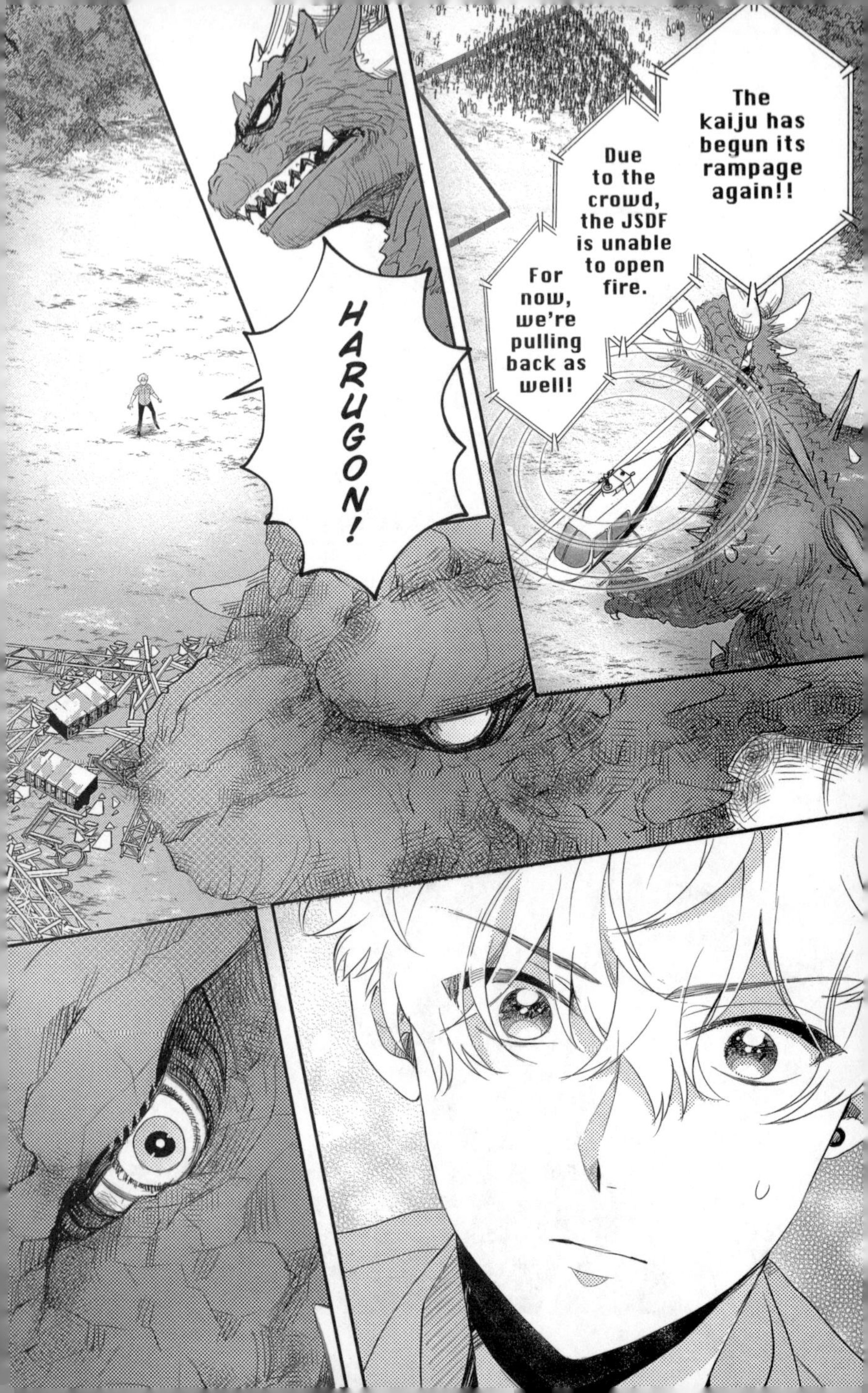
The kaiju has begun its rampage again!!
Due to the crowd, the JSDF is unable to open fire.
For now, we're pulling back as well!
HARUGON!

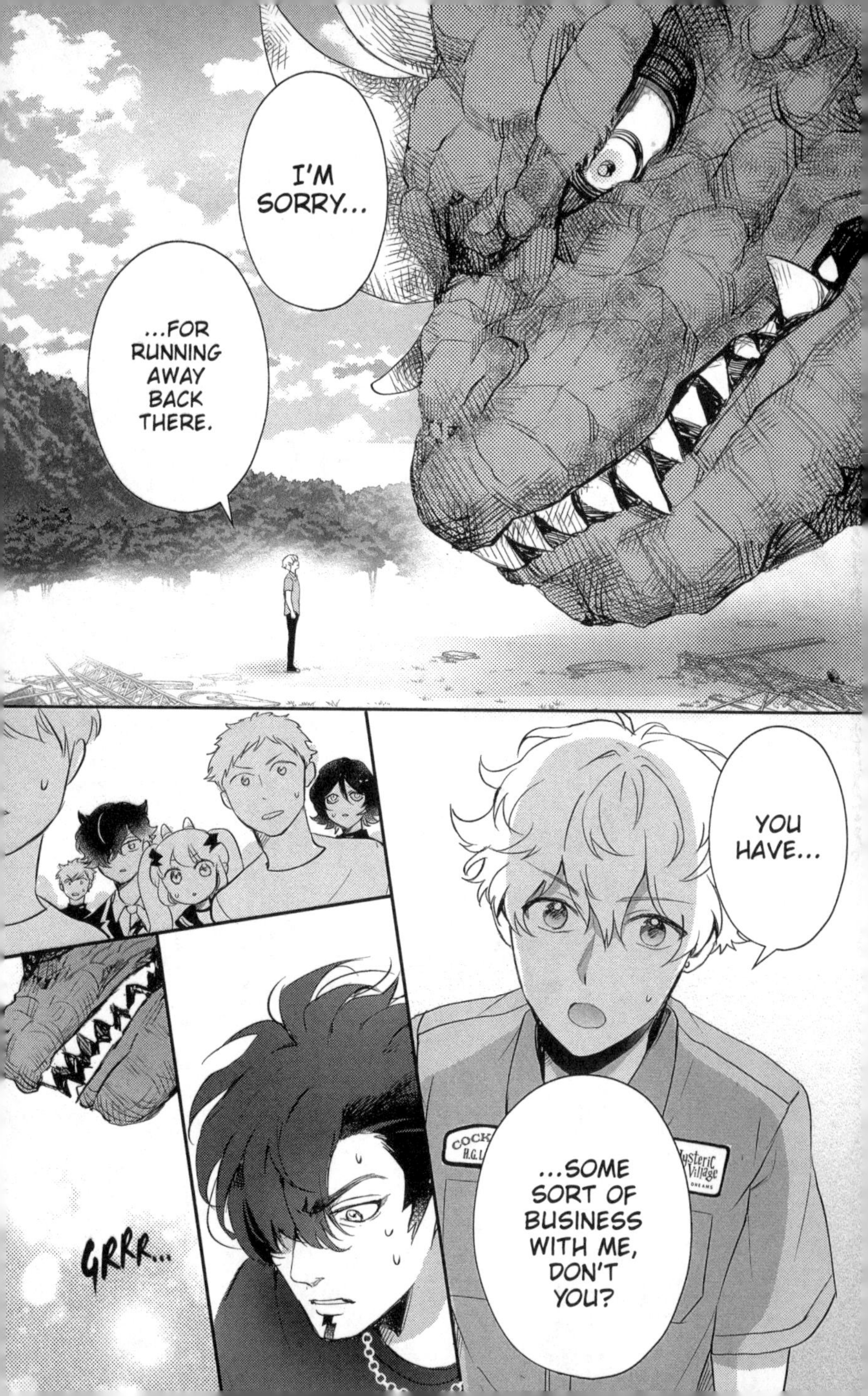
I'M SORRY...
...FOR RUNNING AWAY BACK THERE.
YOU HAVE...
...SOME SORT OF BUSINESS WITH ME, DON'T YOU?
GRRR...

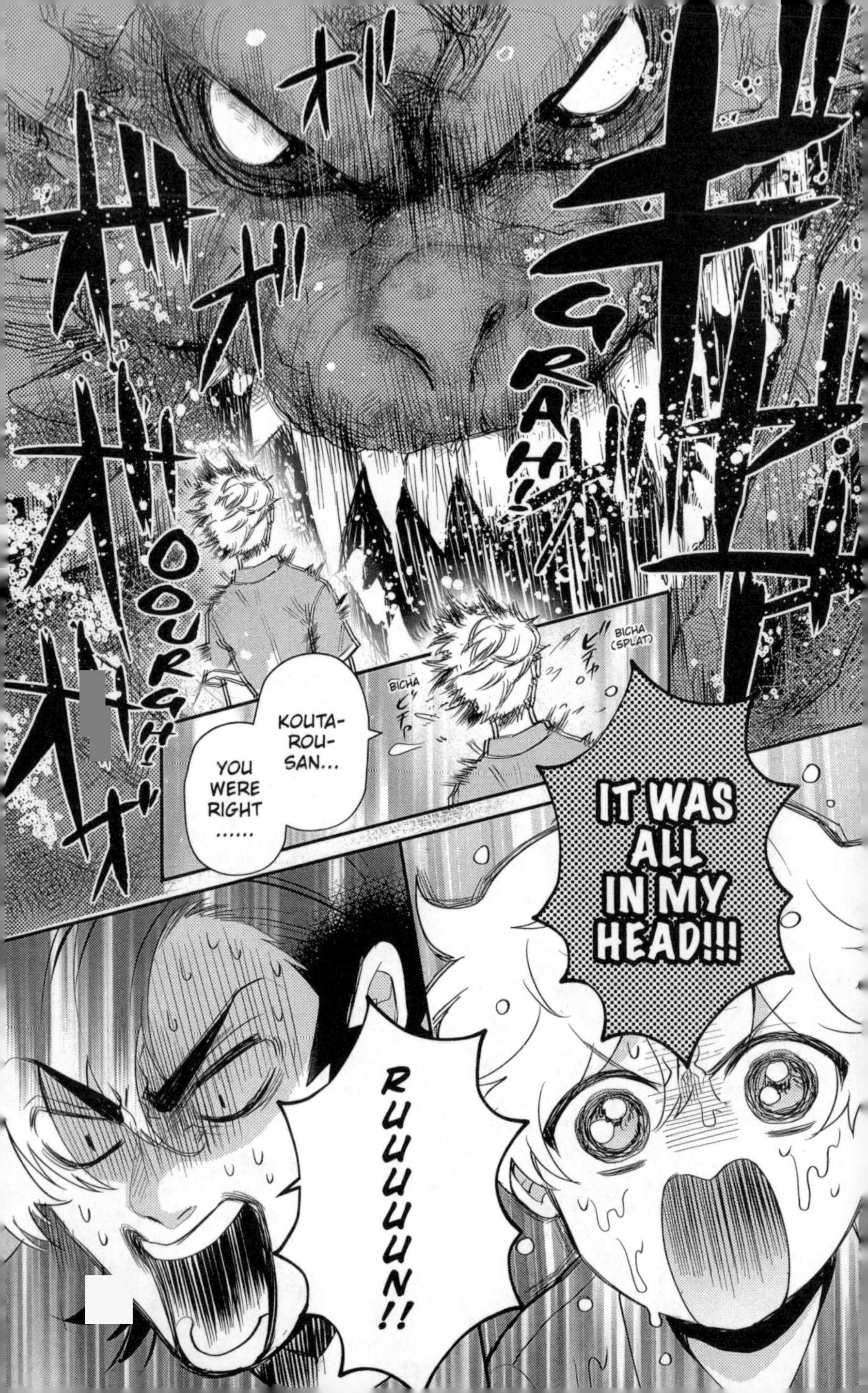
GRAHH!!
OOURGH!!
BICHA (SPLAT)
BICHA
KOUTA-ROU-SAN... YOU WERE RIGHT ......
IT WAS ALL IN MY HEAD!!!
RUUUUUUN!!

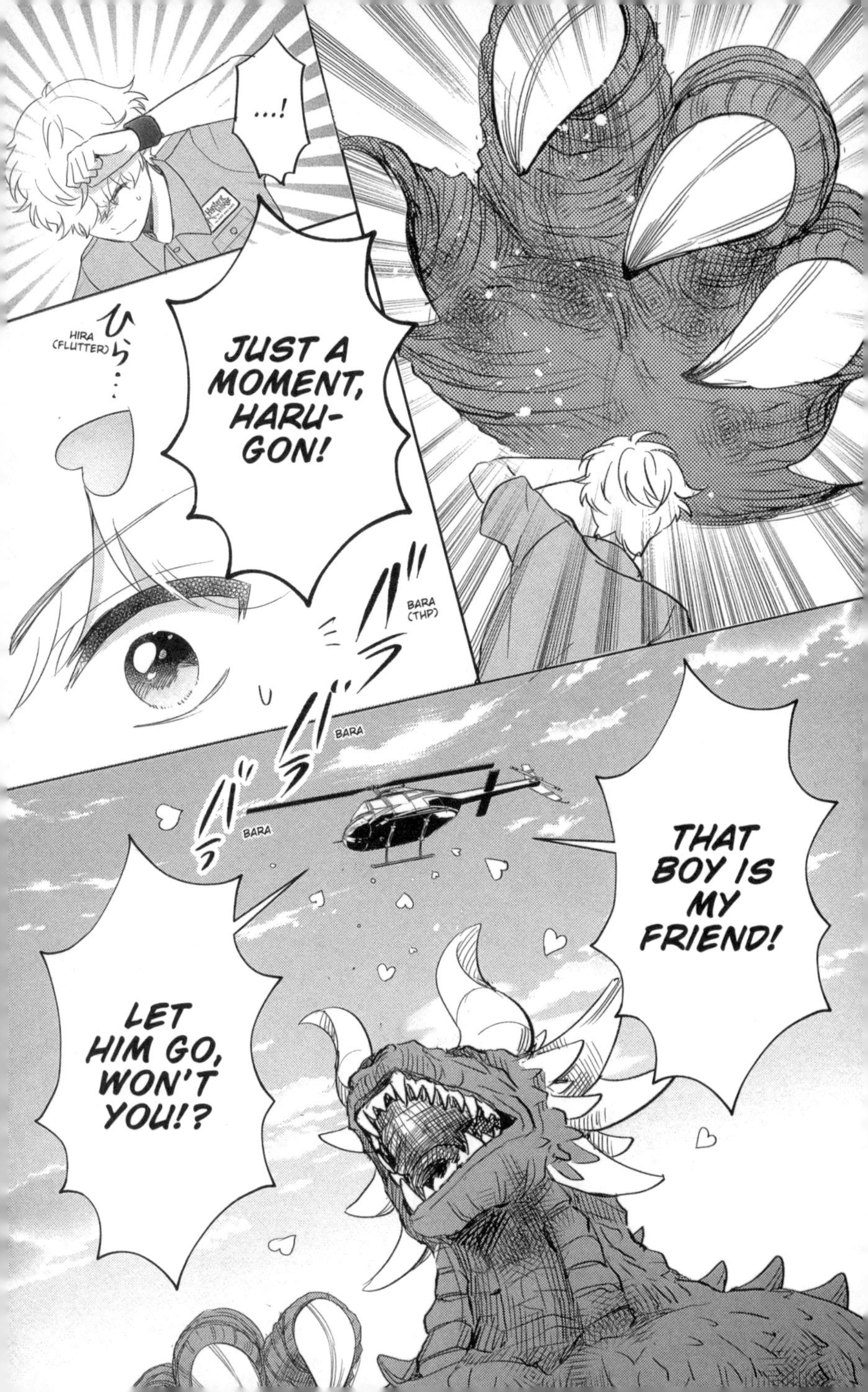
...!
ひら…
HIRA (FLUTTER)
JUST A MOMENT, HARU-GON!
BARA (THP)
BARA
BARA
THAT BOY IS MY FRIEND!
LET HIM GO, WON'T YOU!?

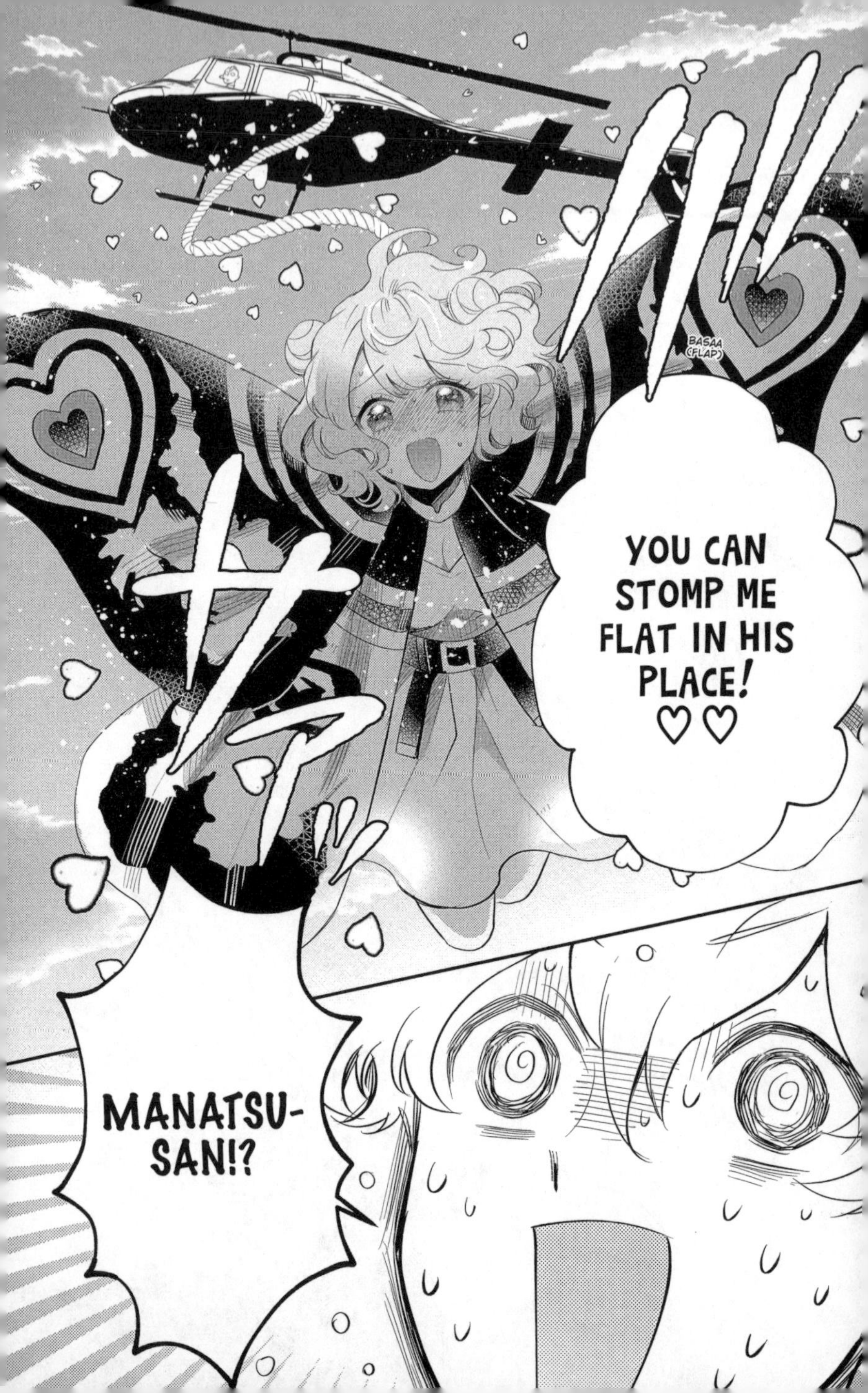
BASAA (FLAP)
YOU CAN STOMP ME FLAT IN HIS PLACE! ♡♡
MANATSU-SAN!?

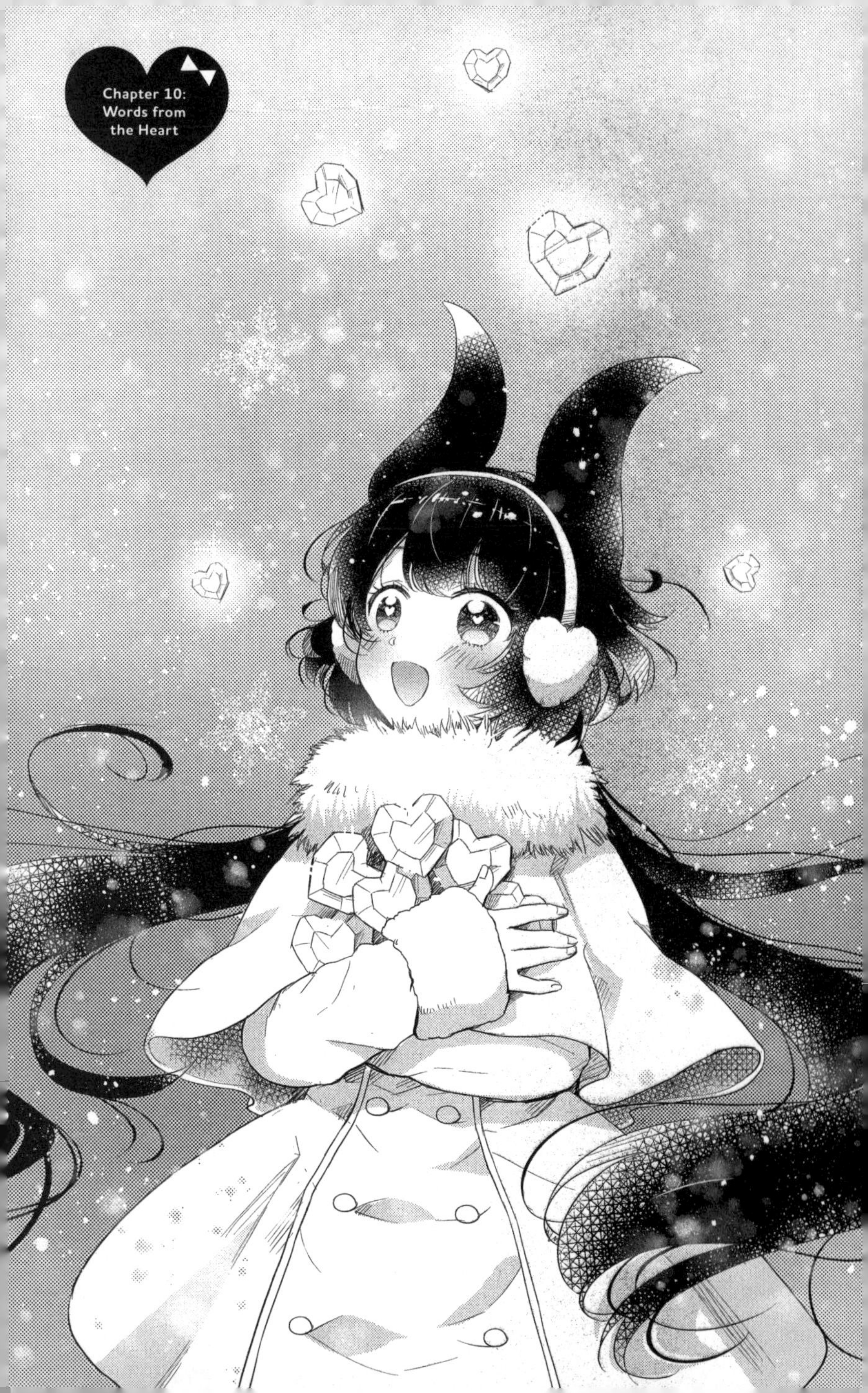
Chapter 10:
Words from
the Heart

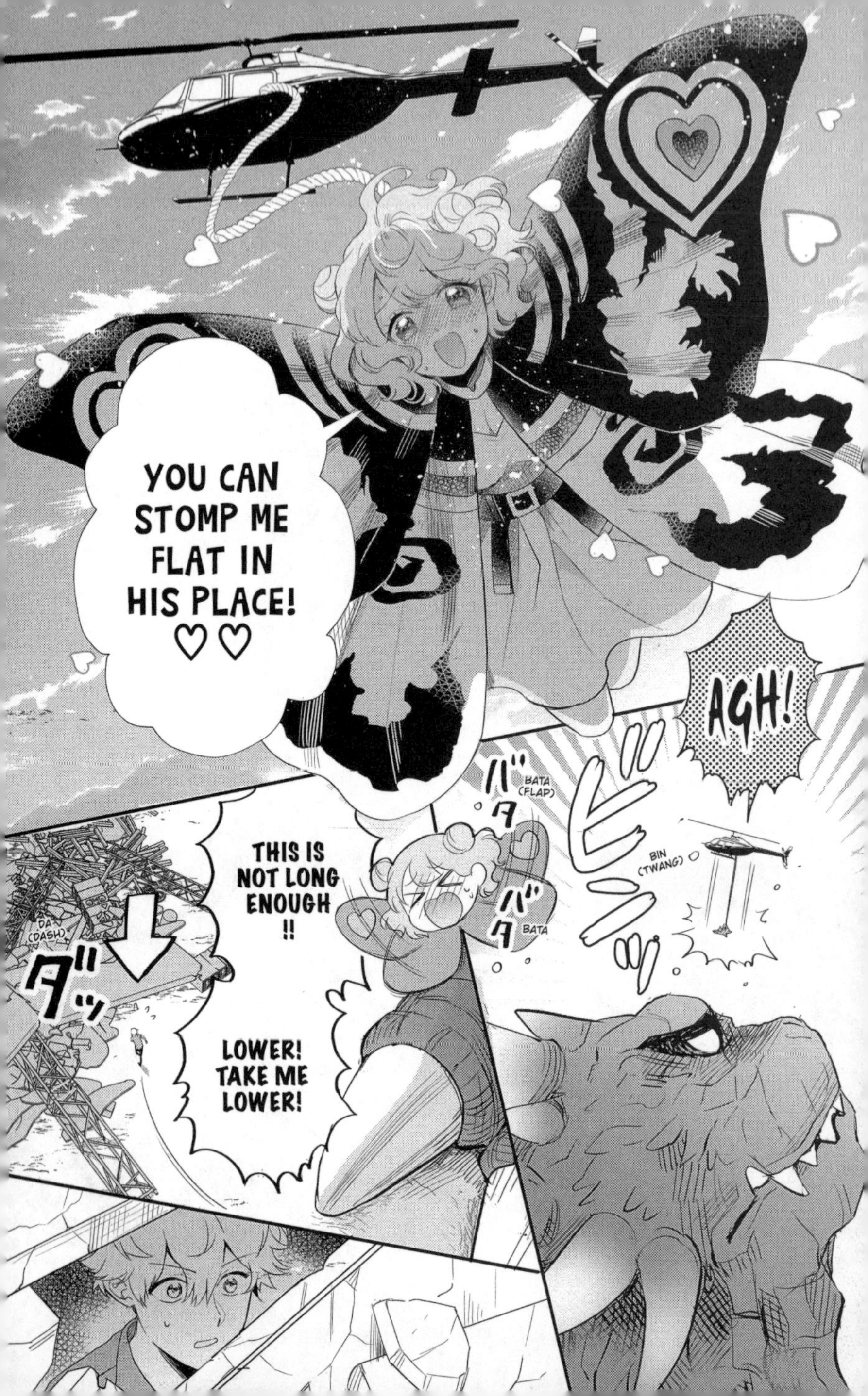
YOU CAN STOMP ME FLAT IN HIS PLACE! ♡♡
AGH!
BIN (TWANG)
BATA (FLAP)
THIS IS NOT LONG ENOUGH !!
BATA
LOWER! TAKE ME LOWER!
DA (DASH)

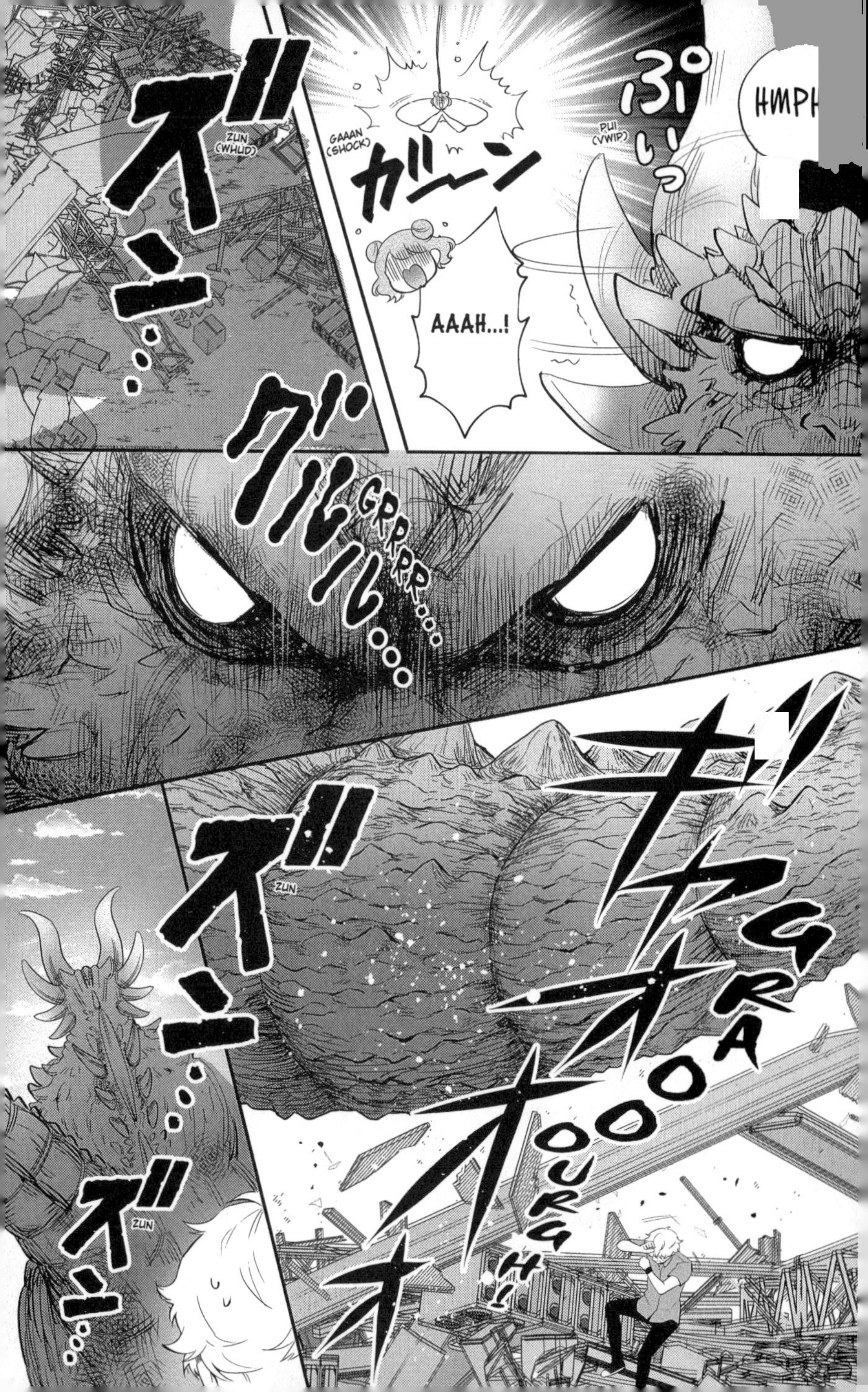
HMPH
ぷいっ
PUI (VWIP)
ガーン
GAAAN (SHOCK)
AAAH...!
ズン…
ZUN (WHUD)
グルルル…
GRRRRR...
ギャオオオオ
GRAOOOOURUGH!
ズン…
ZUN
ズン…
ZUN

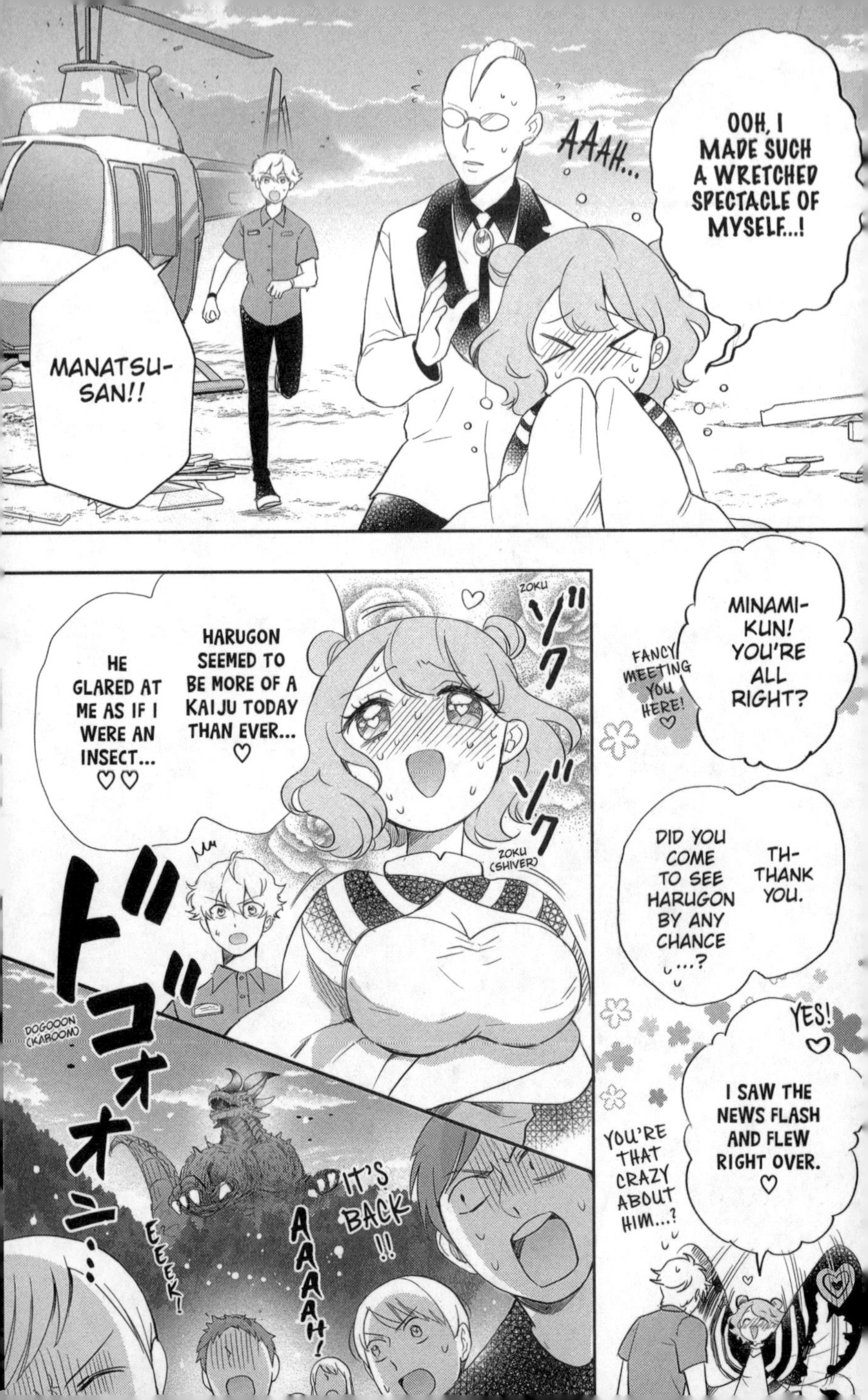
OOH, I MADE SUCH A WRETCHED SPECTACLE OF MYSELF...!
AAAH...
MANATSU-SAN!!
MINAMI-KUN! YOU'RE ALL RIGHT?
FANCY MEETING YOU HERE! ♡
TH-THANK YOU.
DID YOU COME TO SEE HARUGON BY ANY CHANCE...?
YES! ♡
I SAW THE NEWS FLASH AND FLEW RIGHT OVER. ♡
YOU'RE THAT CRAZY ABOUT HIM...?
ZOKU
ZOKU (SHIVER)
HARUGON SEEMED TO BE MORE OF A KAIJU TODAY THAN EVER... ♡
HE GLARED AT ME AS IF I WERE AN INSECT... ♡♡
MU
DOGOOON (KABOOM)
IT'S BACK!!
AAAAH!
EEEK!

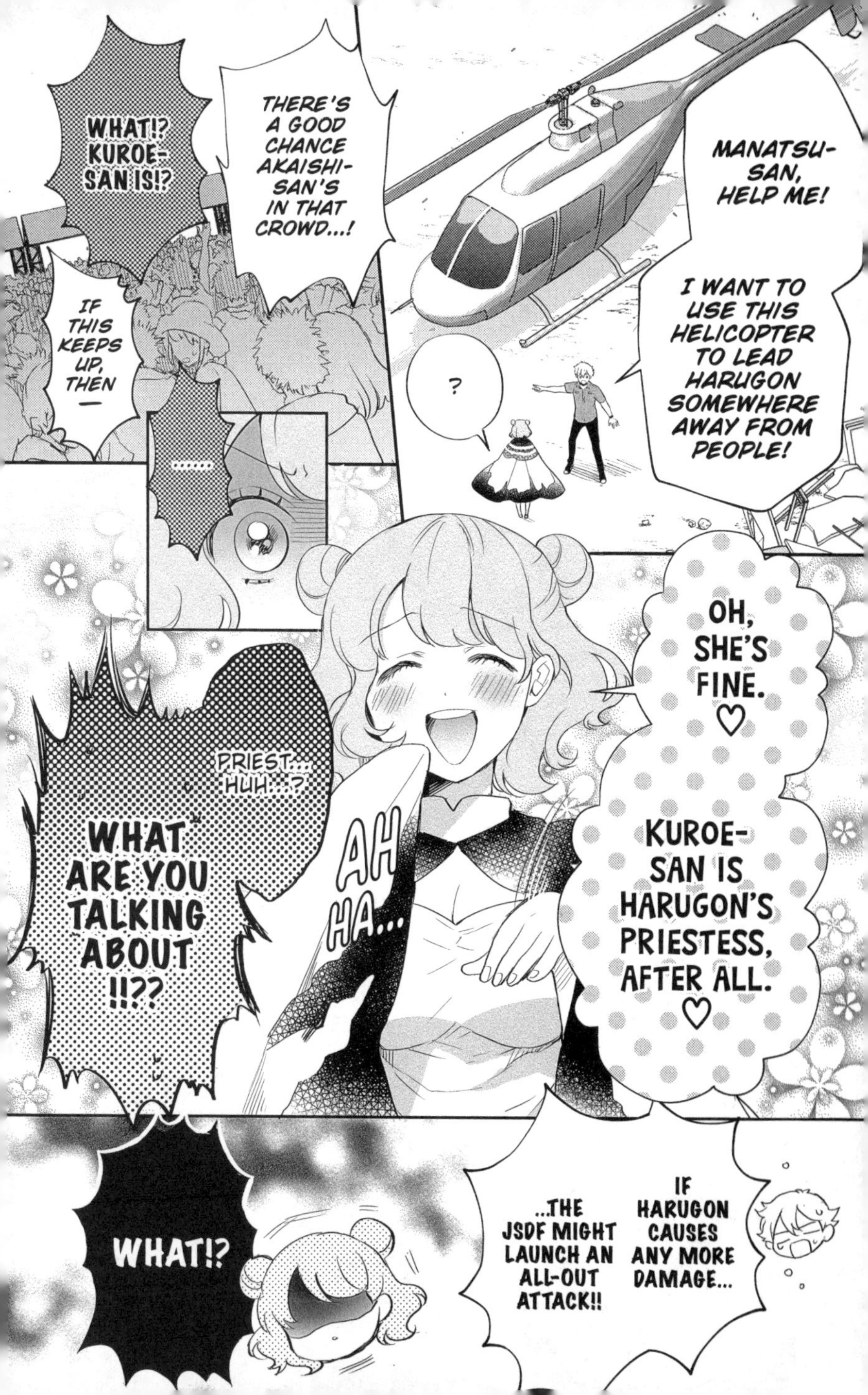
MANATSU-SAN, HELP ME!
I WANT TO USE THIS HELICOPTER TO LEAD HARUGON SOMEWHERE AWAY FROM PEOPLE!
?
THERE'S A GOOD CHANCE AKAISHI-SAN'S IN THAT CROWD...!
WHAT!? KUROE-SAN IS!?
IF THIS KEEPS UP, THEN —
......
OH, SHE'S FINE. ♡
KUROE-SAN IS HARUGON'S PRIESTESS, AFTER ALL. ♡
AH HA...
PRIEST... HUH...?
WHAT ARE YOU TALKING ABOUT!!??
IF HARUGON CAUSES ANY MORE DAMAGE...
...THE JSDF MIGHT LAUNCH AN ALL-OUT ATTACK!!
WHAT!?

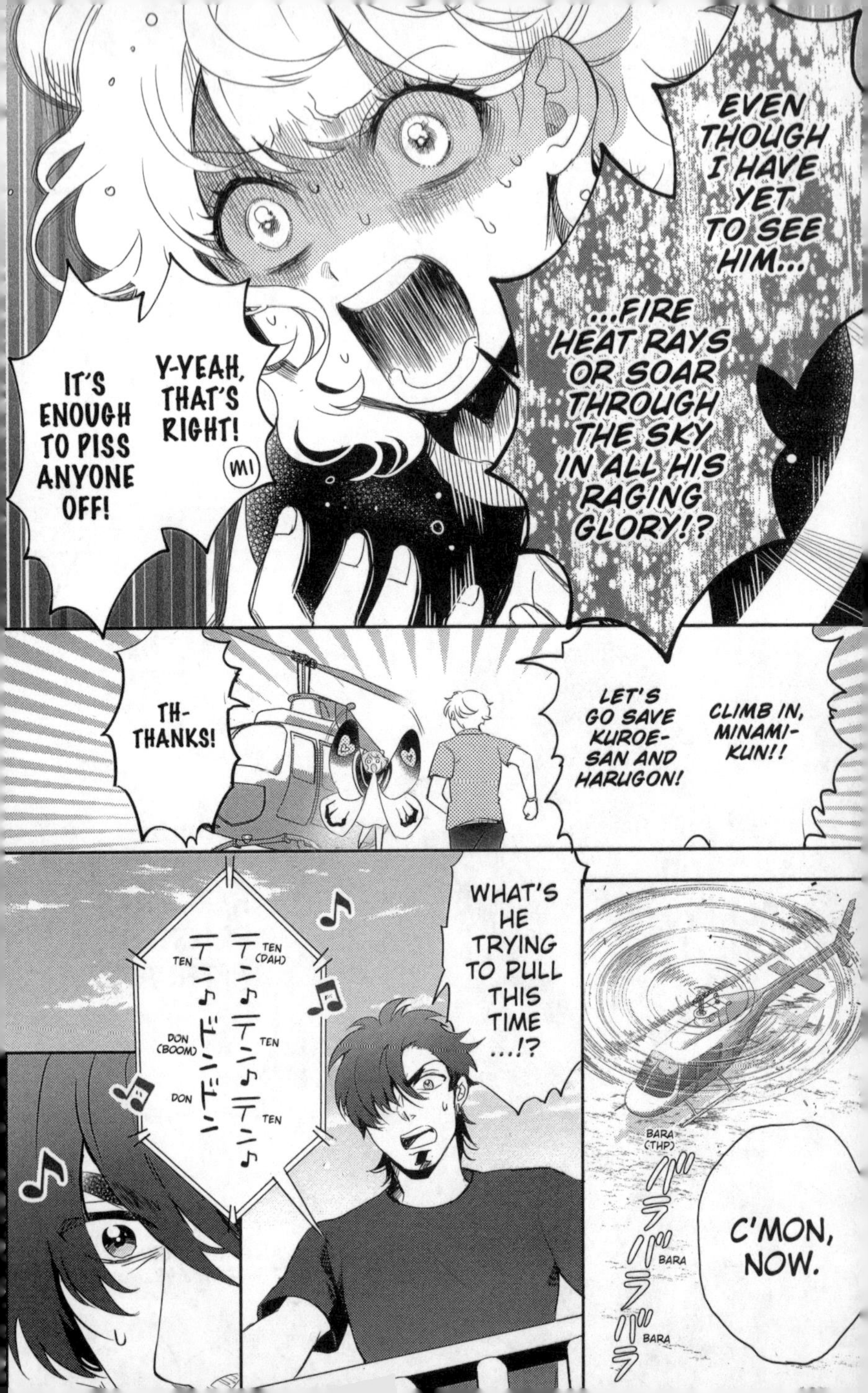
EVEN THOUGH I HAVE YET TO SEE HIM...
...FIRE HEAT RAYS OR SOAR THROUGH THE SKY IN ALL HIS RAGING GLORY!?
Y-YEAH, THAT'S RIGHT!
MI
IT'S ENOUGH TO PISS ANYONE OFF!
CLIMB IN, MINAMI-KUN!!
LET'S GO SAVE KUROE-SAN AND HARUGON!
TH-THANKS!
BARA (THP)
BARA
BARA
C'MON, NOW.
WHAT'S HE TRYING TO PULL THIS TIME...!?
TEN (DAH)
TEN
TEN
TEN
DON (BOOM)
DON

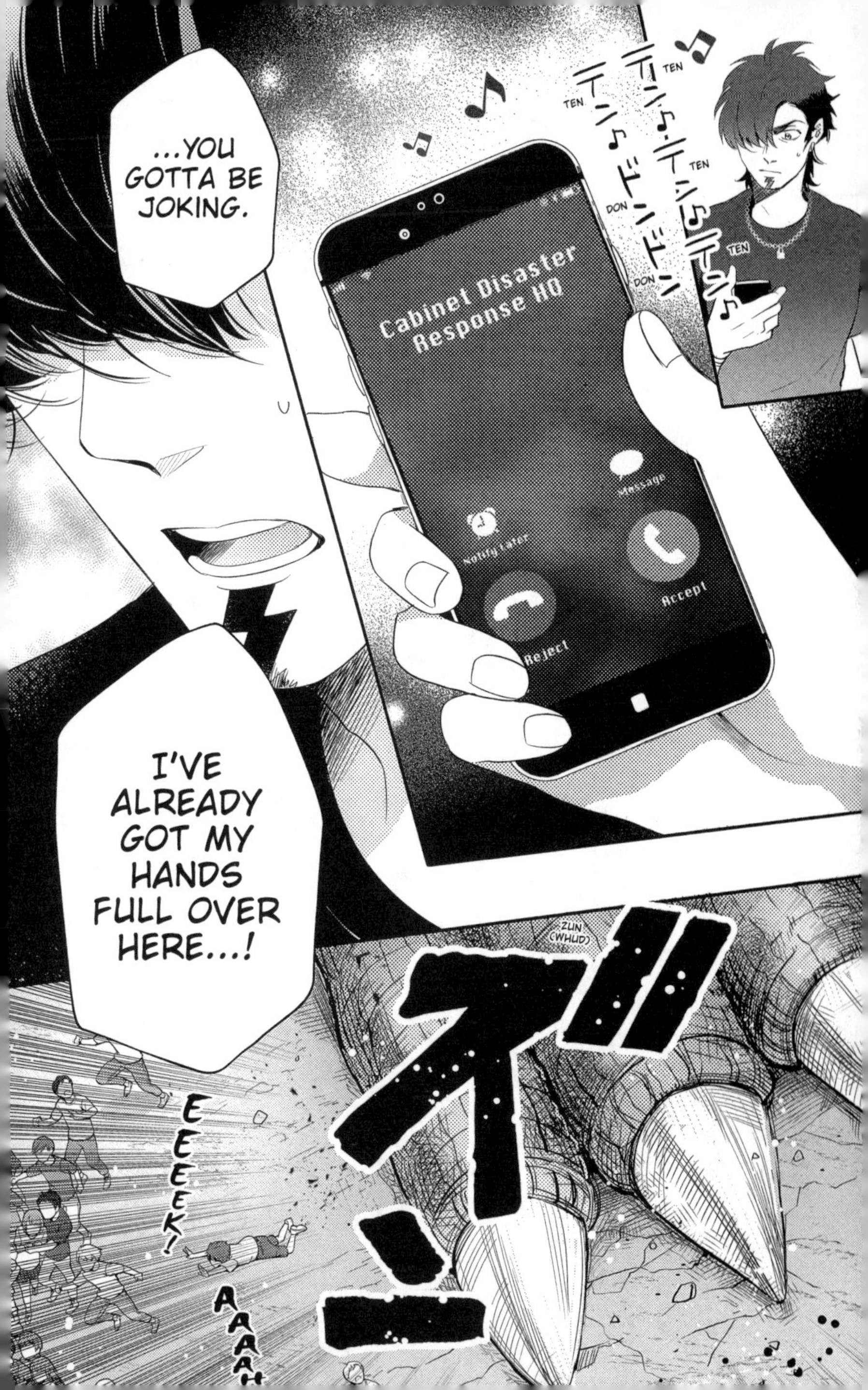
テン♪テン♪テン♪
TEN TEN TEN
テン♪ドンドン
TEN DON DON
Cabinet Disaster Response HQ
Message
Notify Later
Accept
Reject
...YOU GOTTA BE JOKING.
I'VE ALREADY GOT MY HANDS FULL OVER HERE...!
ZUN (WHUD)
EEEEEK!
AAAAH

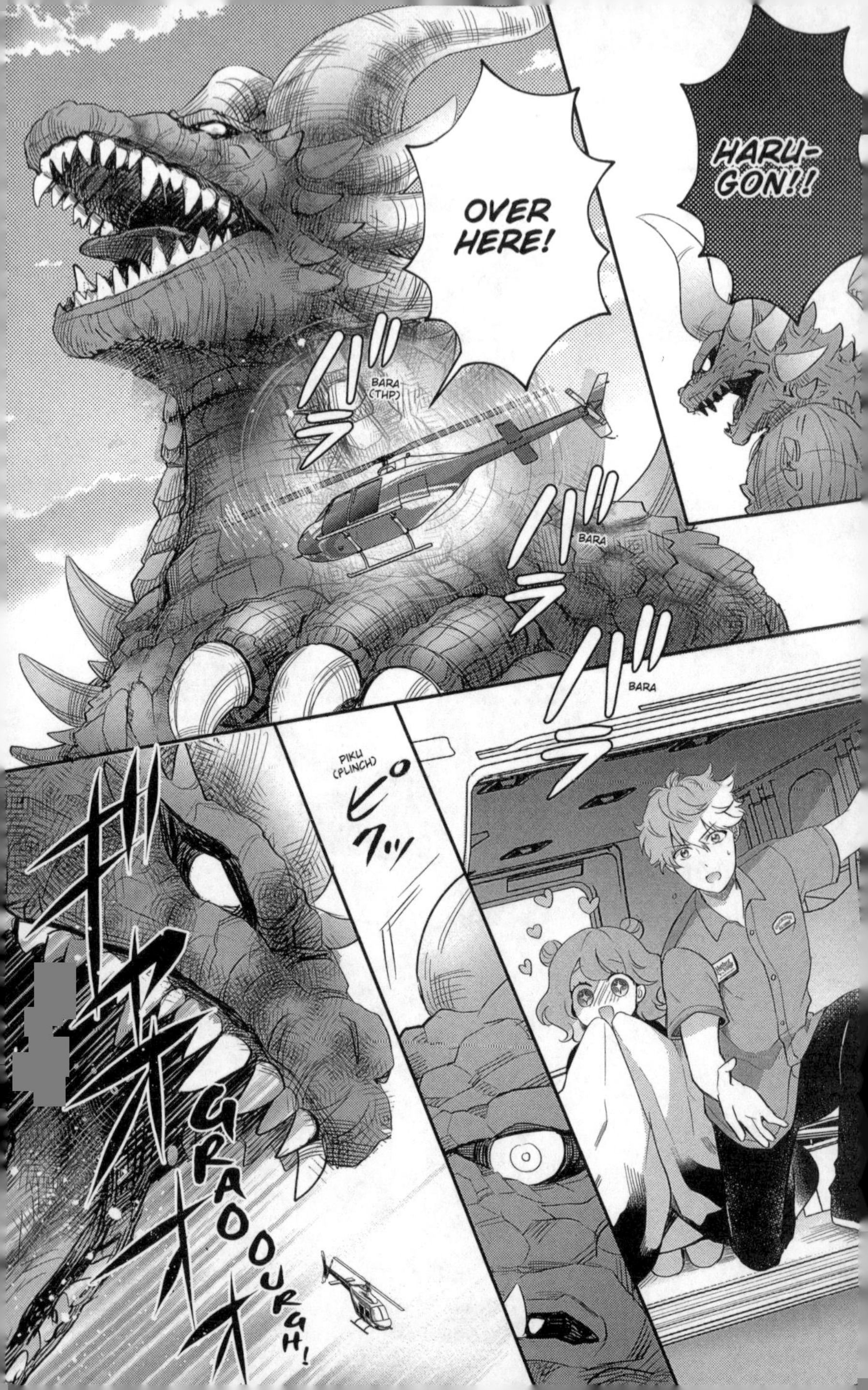
HARU-GON!!
OVER HERE!
BARA (THP)
BARA
BARA
PIKU (PLINCH)
GRAOOURGH!

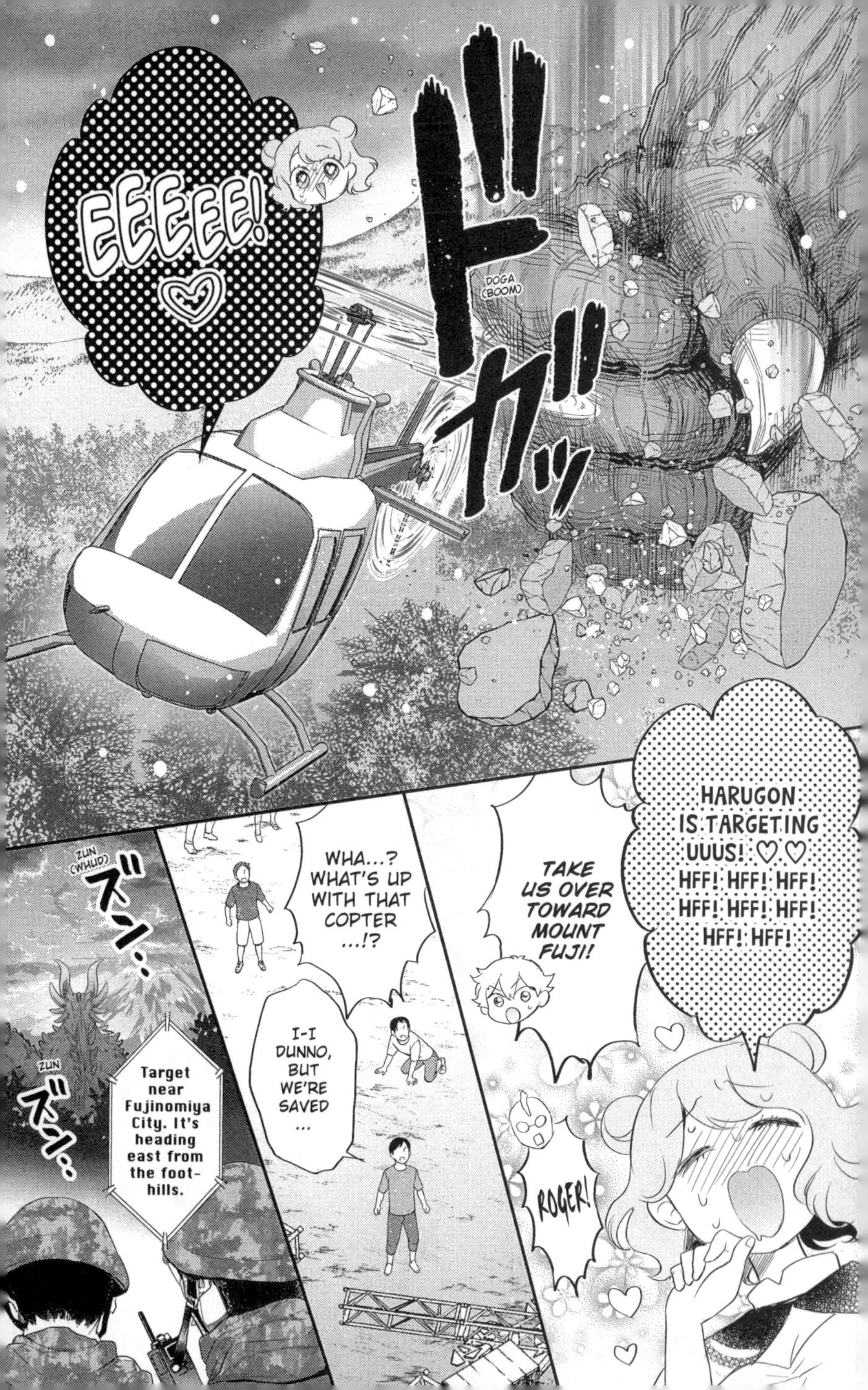

EEEEEE! ♡
ドガッ
DOGA (BOOM)
HARUGON IS TARGETING UUUS! ♡♡ HFF! HFF! HFF! HFF! HFF! HFF! HFF! HFF!
TAKE US OVER TOWARD MOUNT FUJI!
ROGER!
WHA...? WHAT'S UP WITH THAT COPTER ...!?
I-I DUNNO, BUT WE'RE SAVED ...
ズン..
ZUN (WHUD)
ズン..
ZUN
Target near Fujinomiya City. It's heading east from the foot-hills.

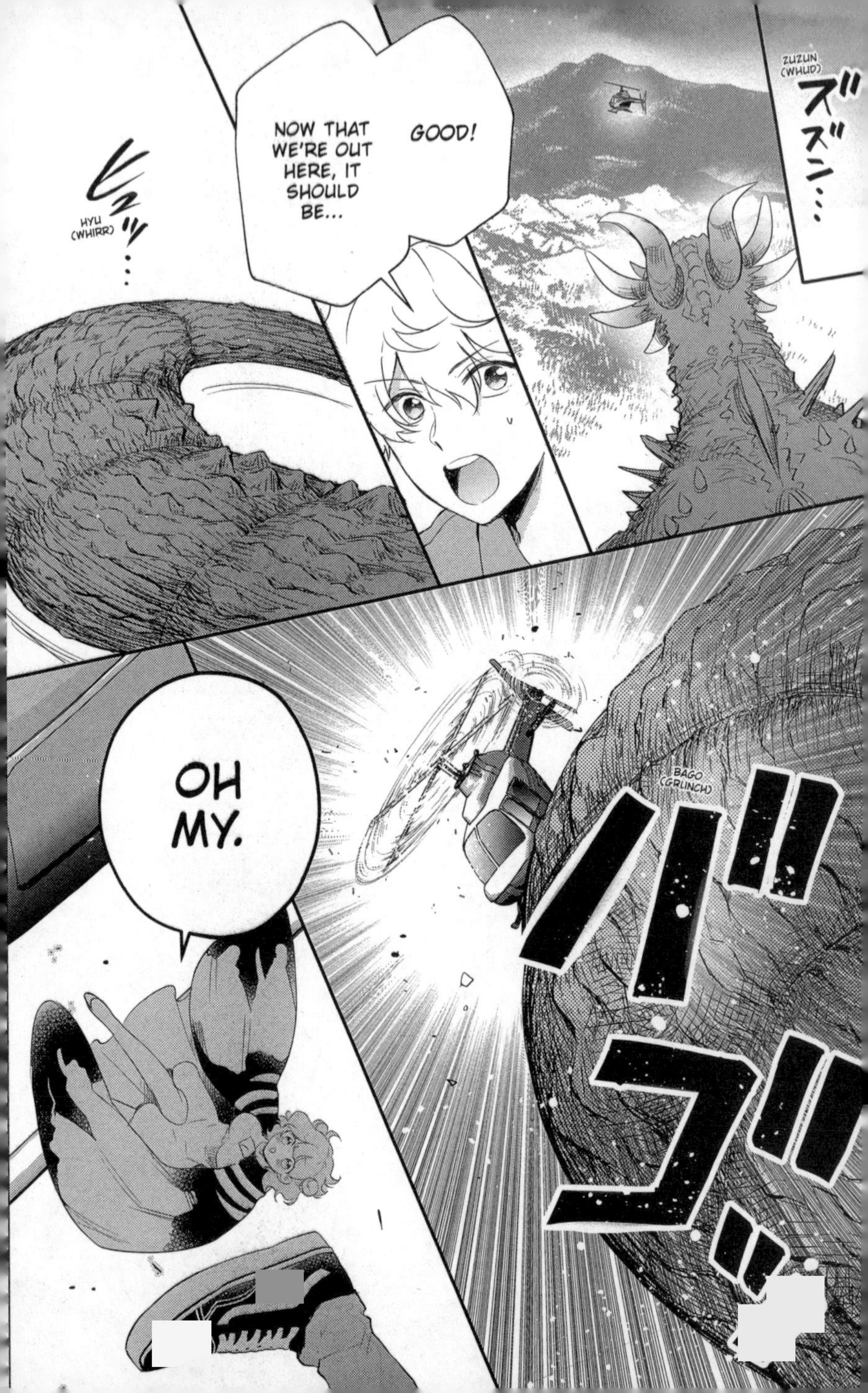
ZUZUN (WHUD)
ズズン…
GOOD!
NOW THAT WE'RE OUT HERE, IT SHOULD BE...
HYU (WHIRR)
ヒュッ…
BAGO (GRUNCH)
OH MY.

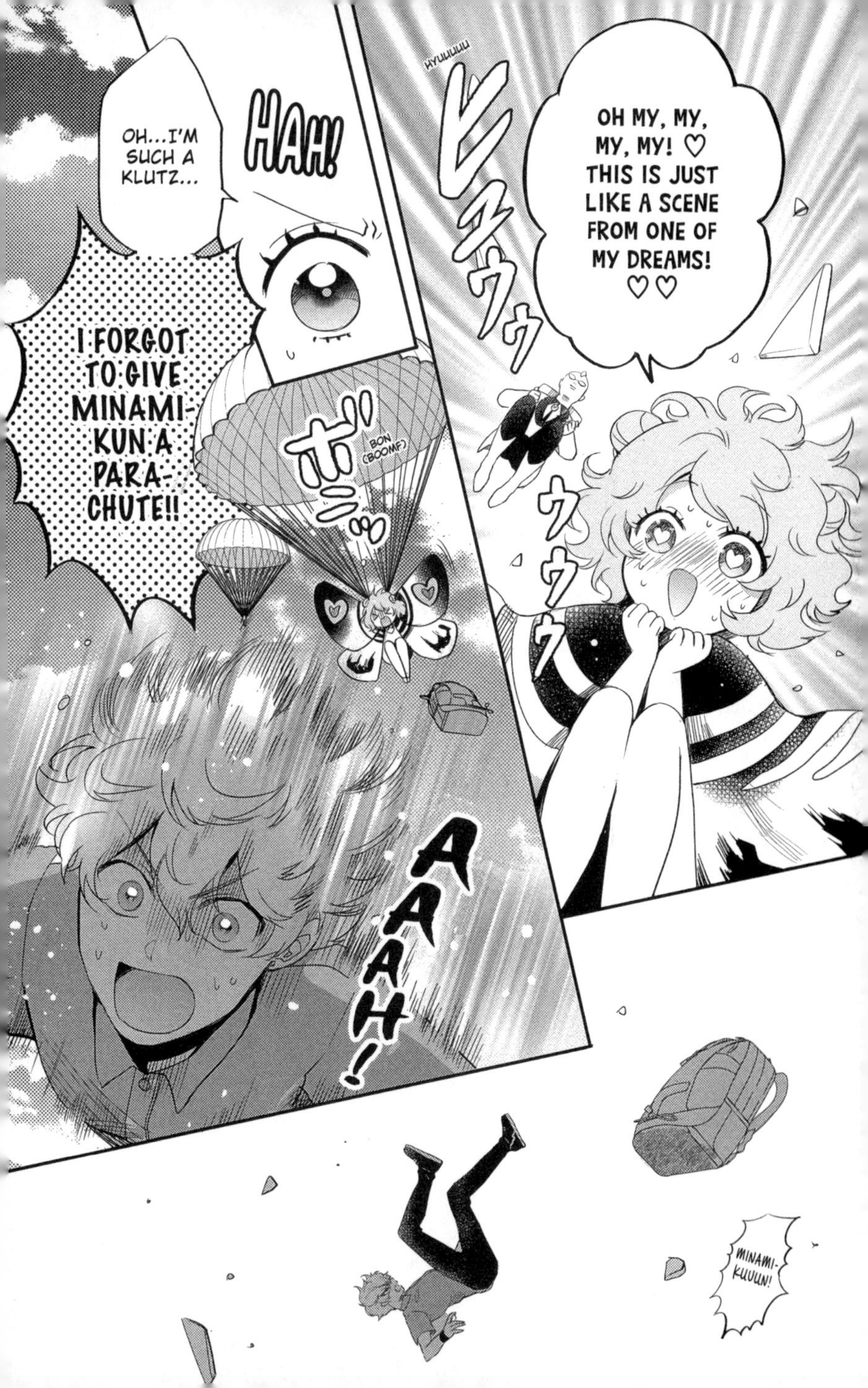
HYUUUUU
OH MY, MY, MY, MY! ♡ THIS IS JUST LIKE A SCENE FROM ONE OF MY DREAMS! ♡♡
OH...I'M SUCH A KLUTZ...
HAH!
I FORGOT TO GIVE MINAMI-KUN A PARA-CHUTE!!
BON (BOOMF)
AAAAH!
MINAMI-KUUUN!

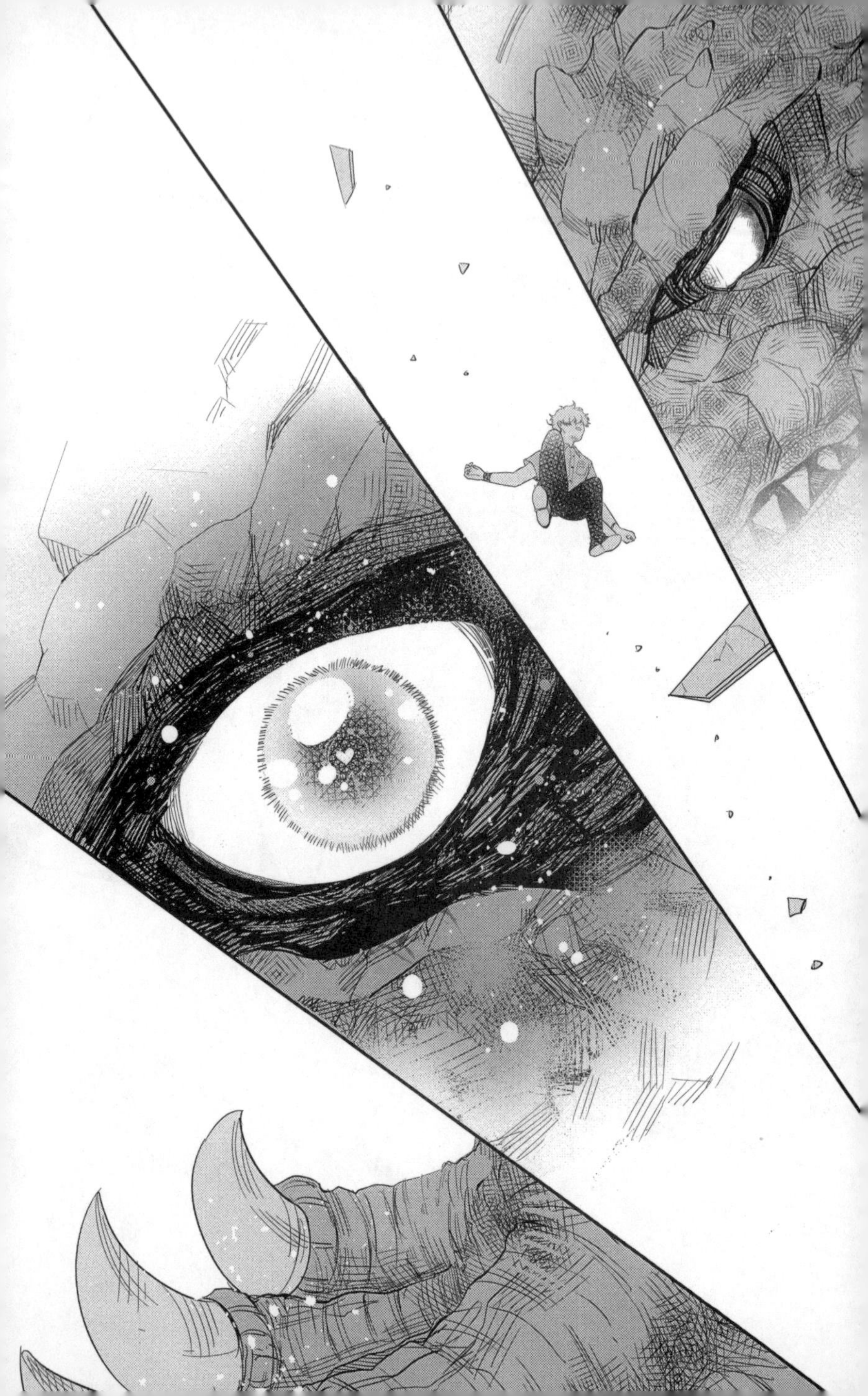

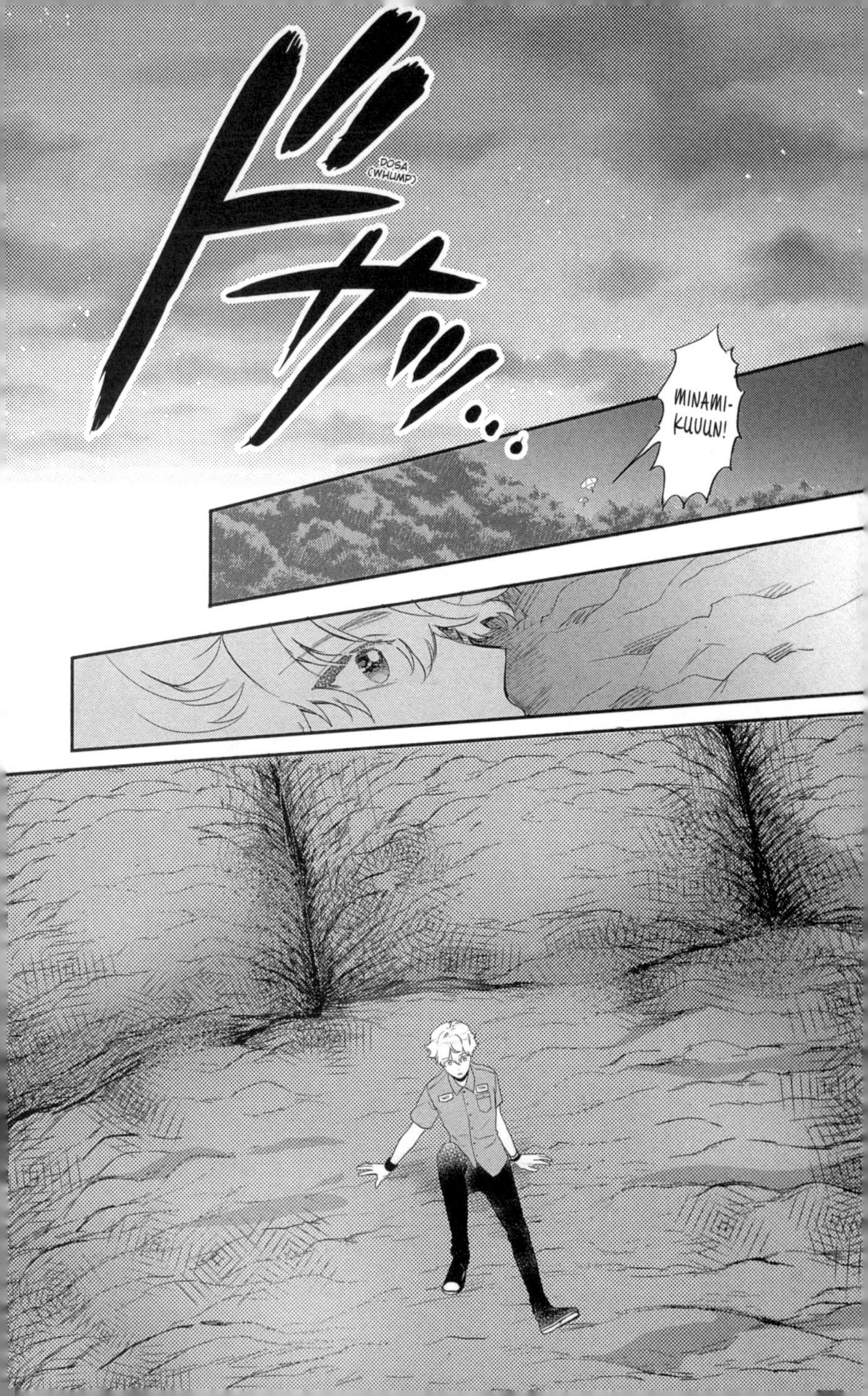
DOSA (WHUMP)
MINAMI-KUUUN!

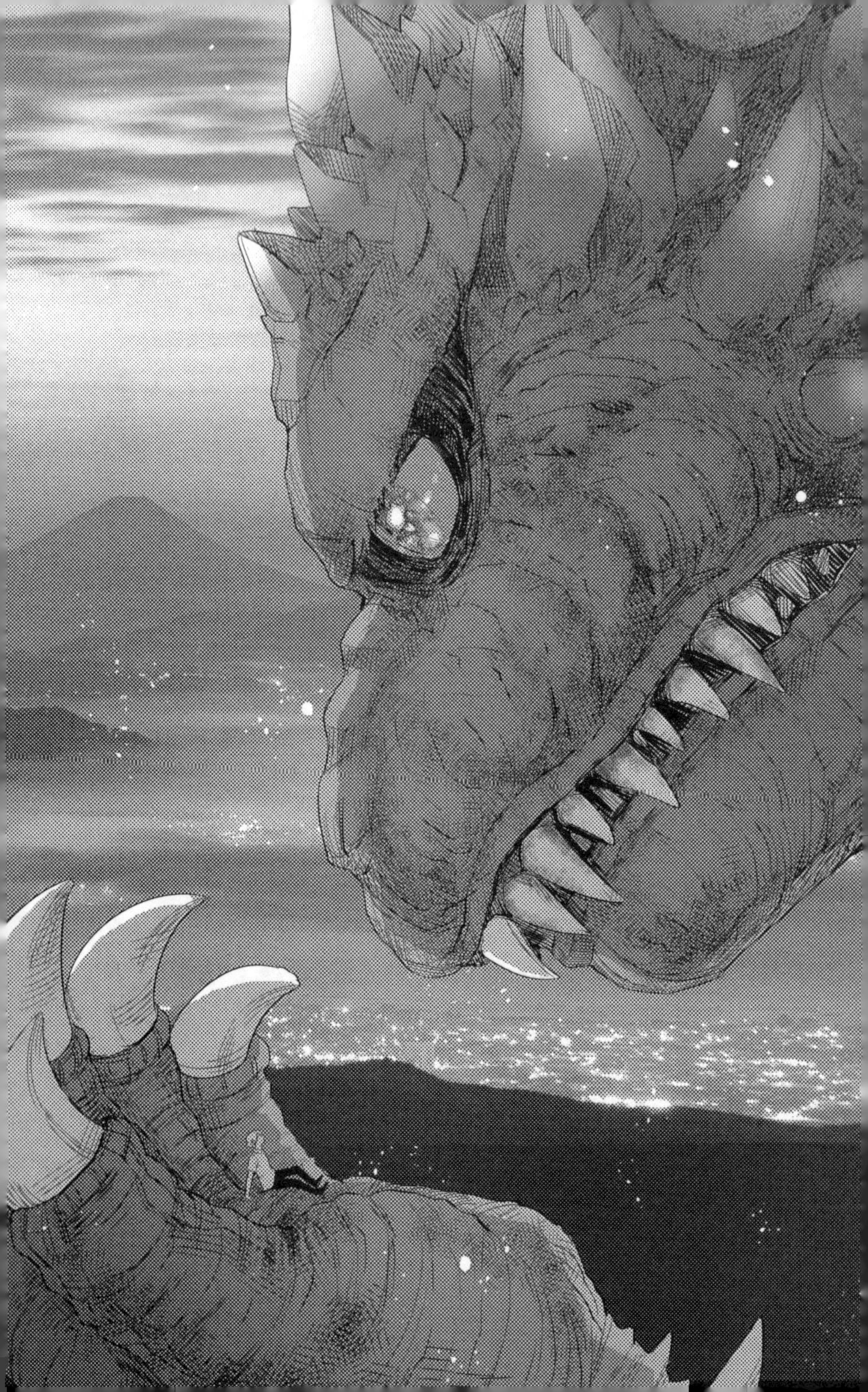

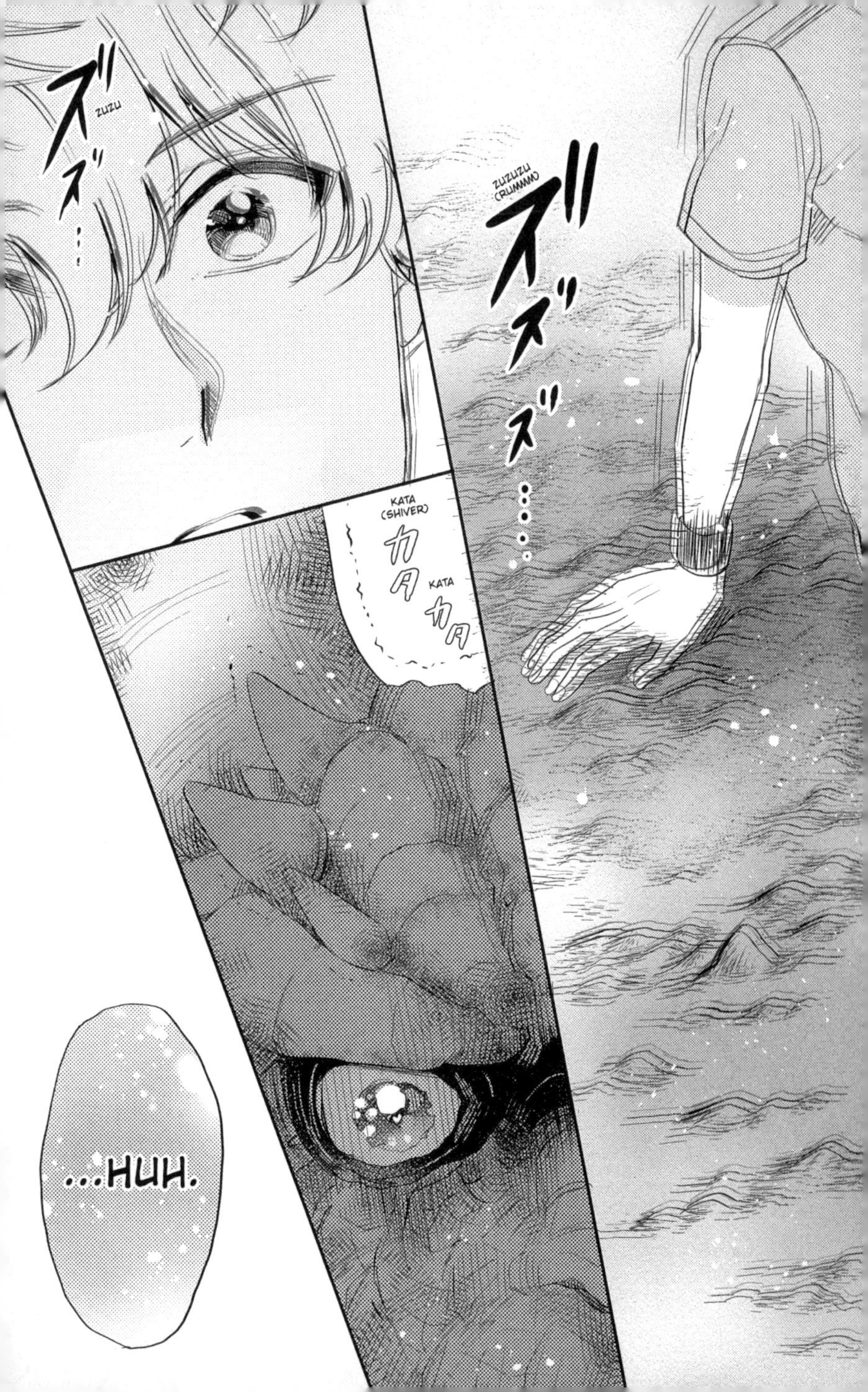

ズズズズ……
ZUZUZU (RUMMM)
ズズ…
ZUZU
カタ
KATA (SHIVER)
カタ
KATA
...HUH.

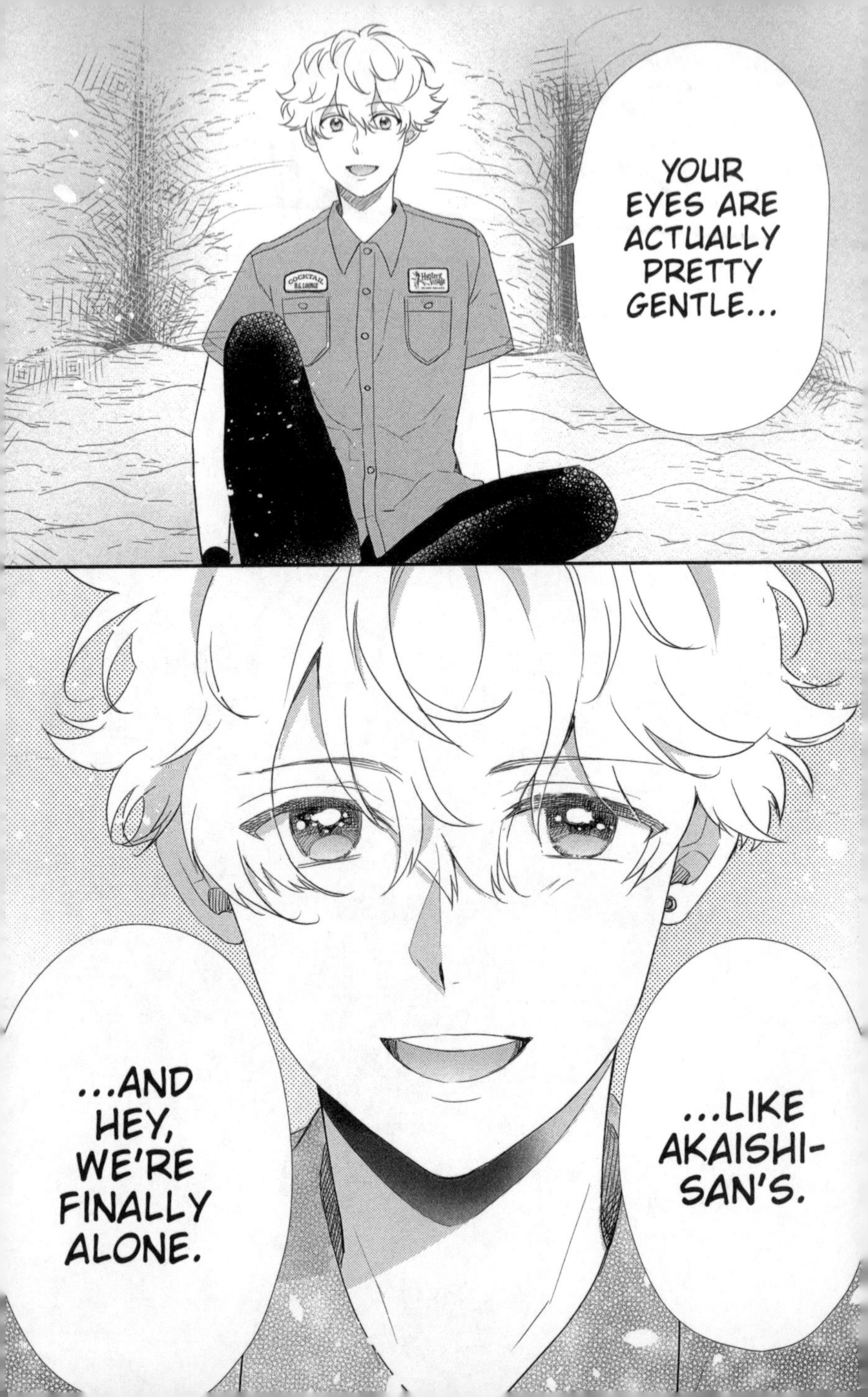
YOUR EYES ARE ACTUALLY PRETTY GENTLE...
...LIKE AKAISHI-SAN'S.
...AND HEY, WE'RE FINALLY ALONE.

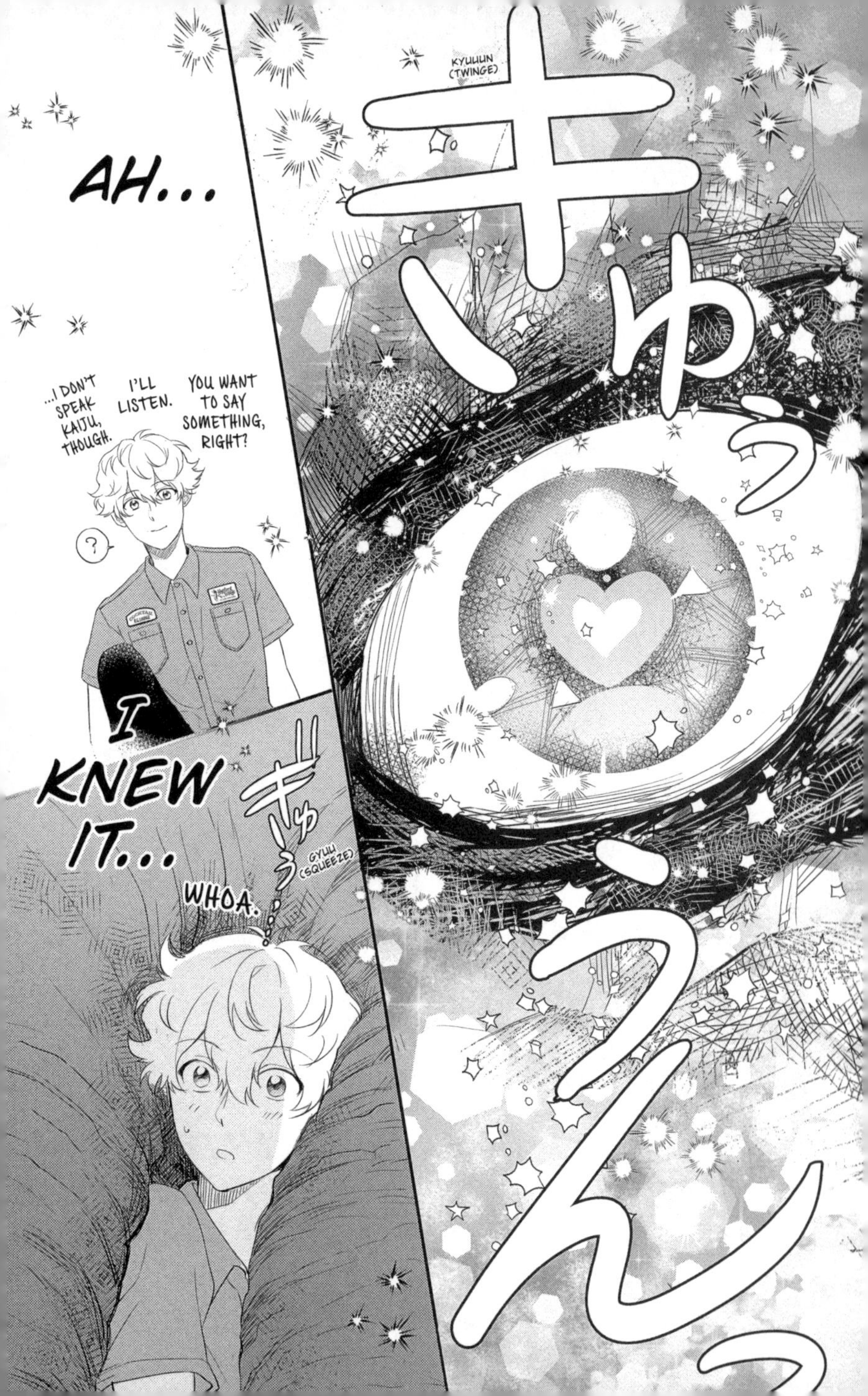
キゅううんっ
KYUUUN (TWINGE)
YOU WANT TO SAY SOMETHING, RIGHT?
I'LL LISTEN.
...I DON'T SPEAK KAIJU, THOUGH.
?
AH...
I KNEW IT...
ぎゅう
GYUU (SQUEEZE)
WHOA.

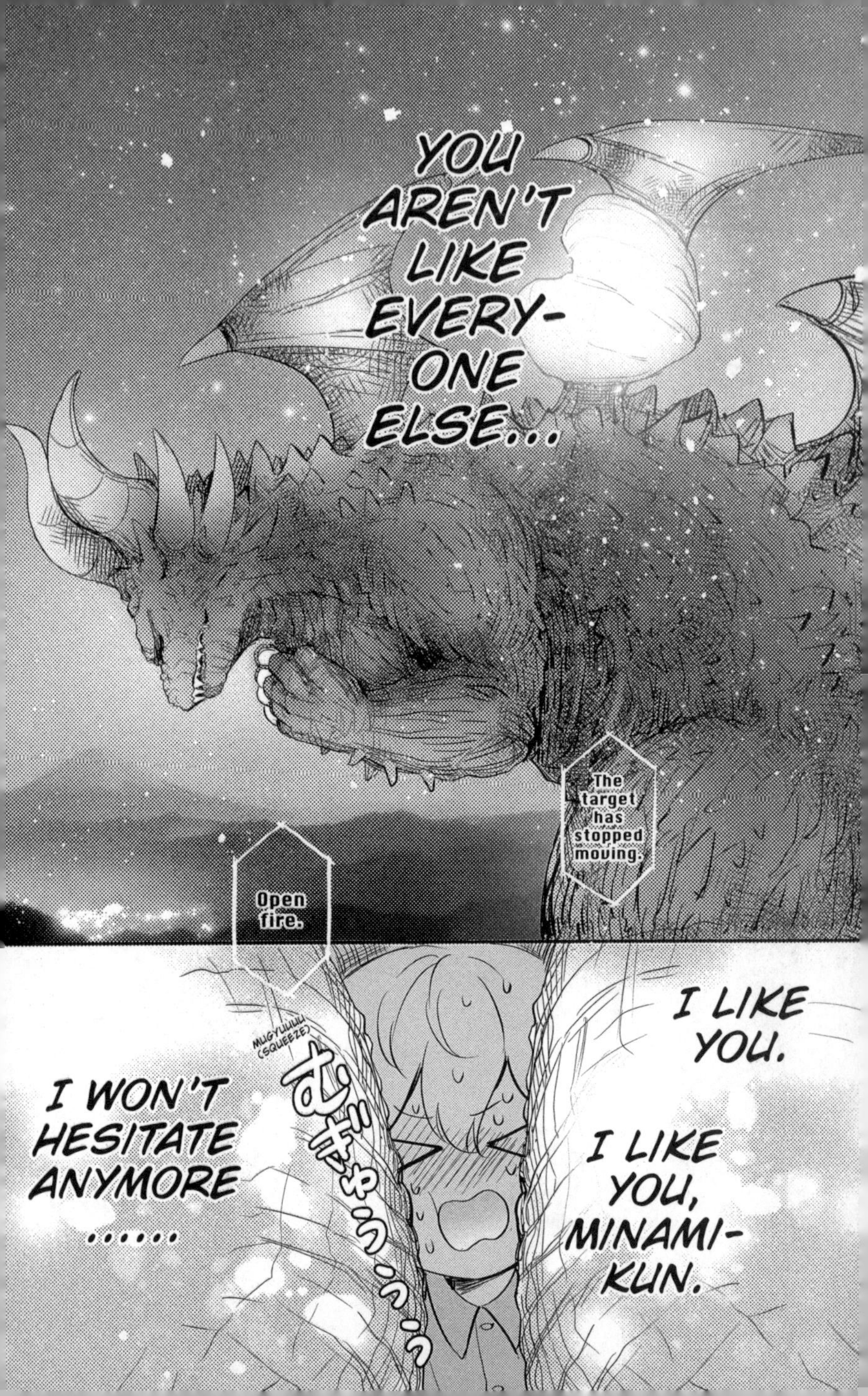
YOU AREN'T LIKE EVERY-ONE ELSE...
The target has stopped moving.
Open fire.
I LIKE YOU.
I LIKE YOU, MINAMI-KUN.
MUGYUUUU (SQUEEZE)
むぎゅううう
I WON'T HESITATE ANYMORE......

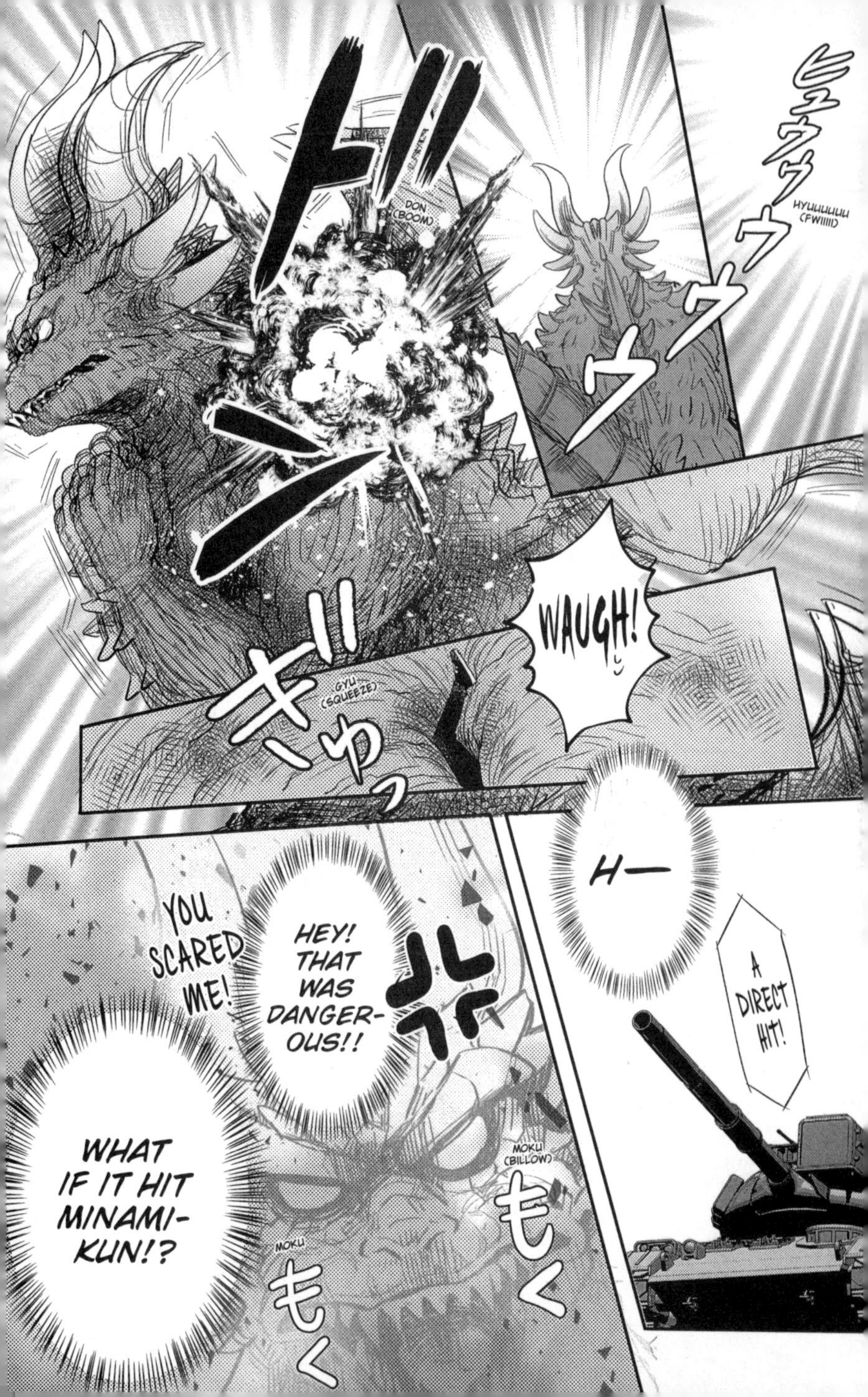
ヒュウウウウ
HYUUUUUU (FWIIIII)
ドーン
DON (BOOM)
WAUGH!
ぎゅっ
GYU (SQUEEZE)
H—
A DIRECT HIT!
HEY! THAT WAS DANGER-OUS!!
YOU SCARED ME!
もく
MOKU (BILLOW)
WHAT IF IT HIT MINAMI-KUN!?
MOKU
もく

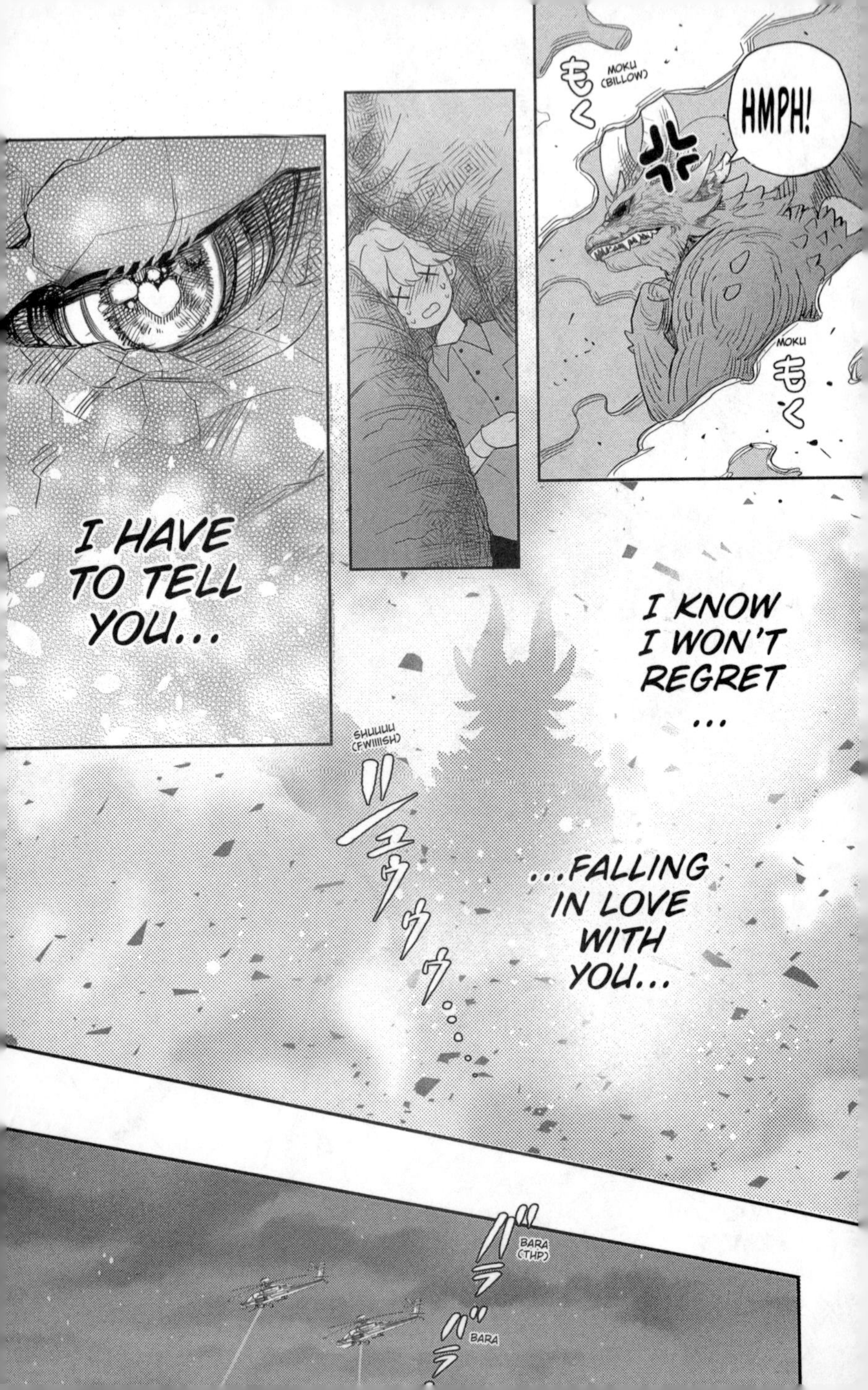

もく
MOKU (BILLOW)
HMPH!
もく
MOKU
I HAVE TO TELL YOU...
I KNOW I WON'T REGRET ...
...FALLING IN LOVE WITH YOU...
ジュウウウ
SHUUUU (FWIIISH)
バラ
BARA (THP)
バラ
BARA

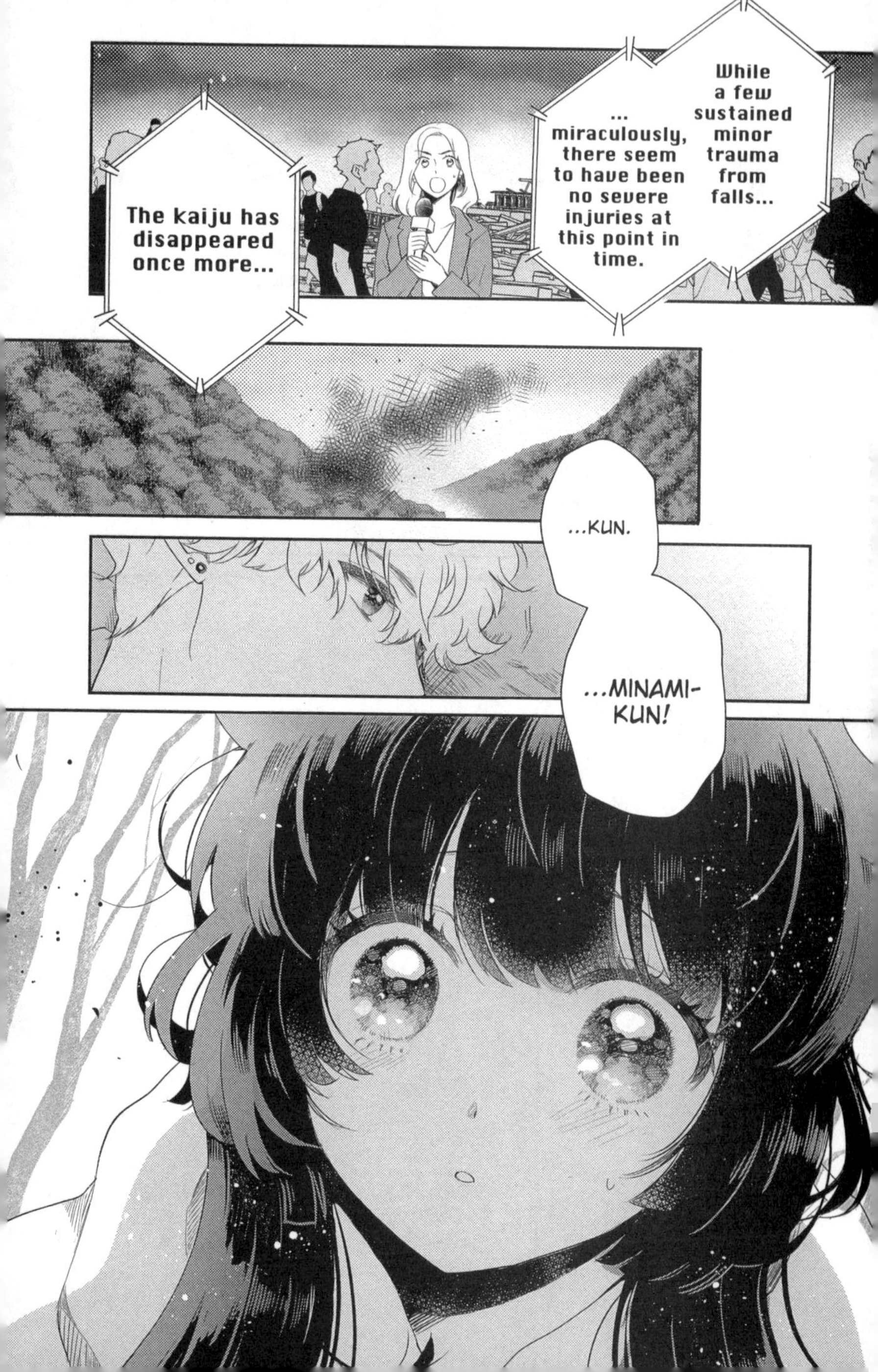
While a few sustained minor trauma from falls...
...miraculously, there seem to have been no severe injuries at this point in time.
The kaiju has disappeared once more...
...KUN.
...MINAMI-KUN!

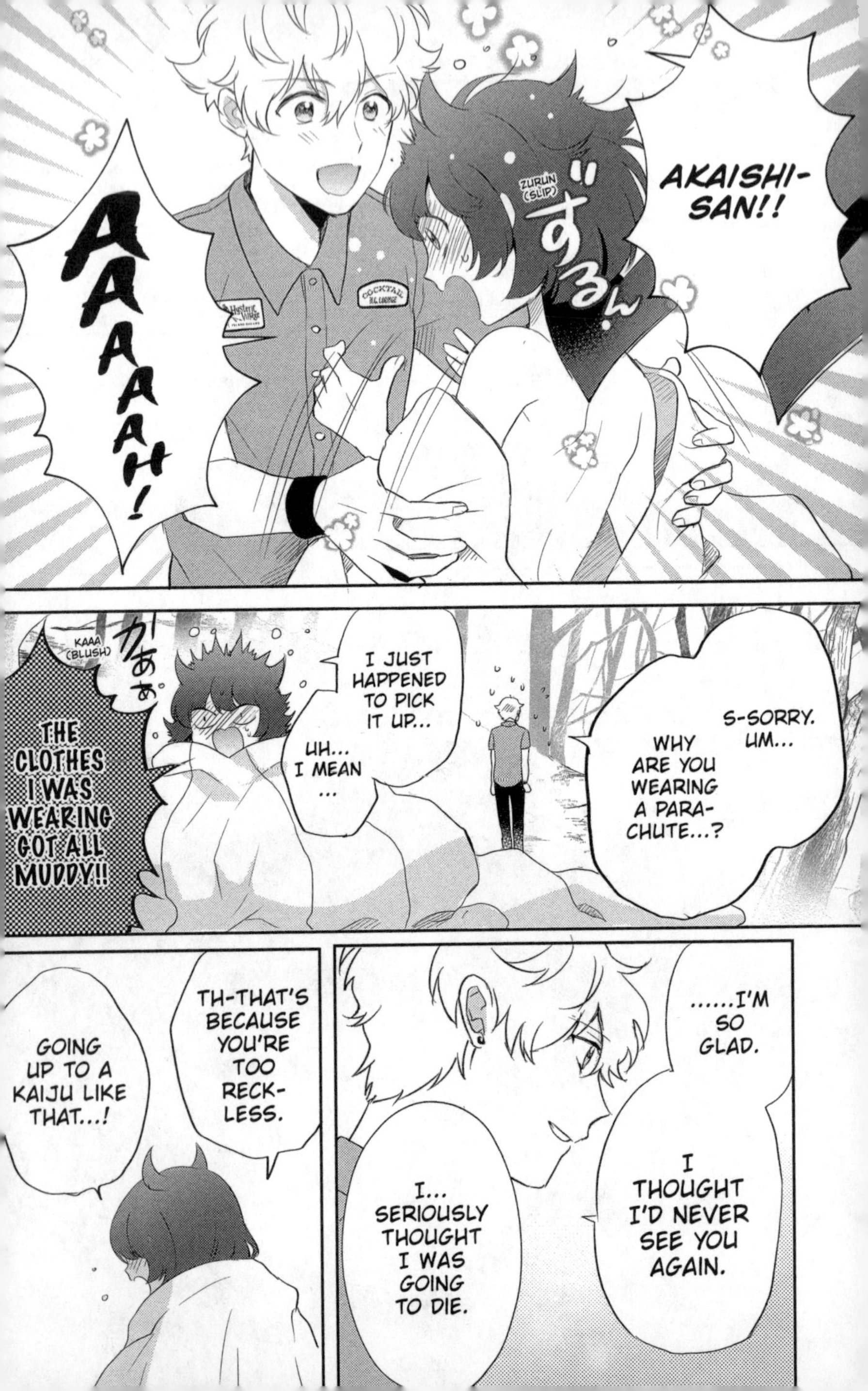
AKAISHI-SAN!!
ZURUN (SLIP)
するん
AAAAAH!
S-SORRY. UM...
WHY ARE YOU WEARING A PARA-CHUTE...?
I JUST HAPPENED TO PICK IT UP...
UH... I MEAN ...
KAAA (BLUSH)
かぁあ
THE CLOTHES I WAS WEARING GOT ALL MUDDY!!
......I'M SO GLAD.
I THOUGHT I'D NEVER SEE YOU AGAIN.
I... SERIOUSLY THOUGHT I WAS GOING TO DIE.
TH-THAT'S BECAUSE YOU'RE TOO RECK-LESS.
GOING UP TO A KAIJU LIKE THAT...!

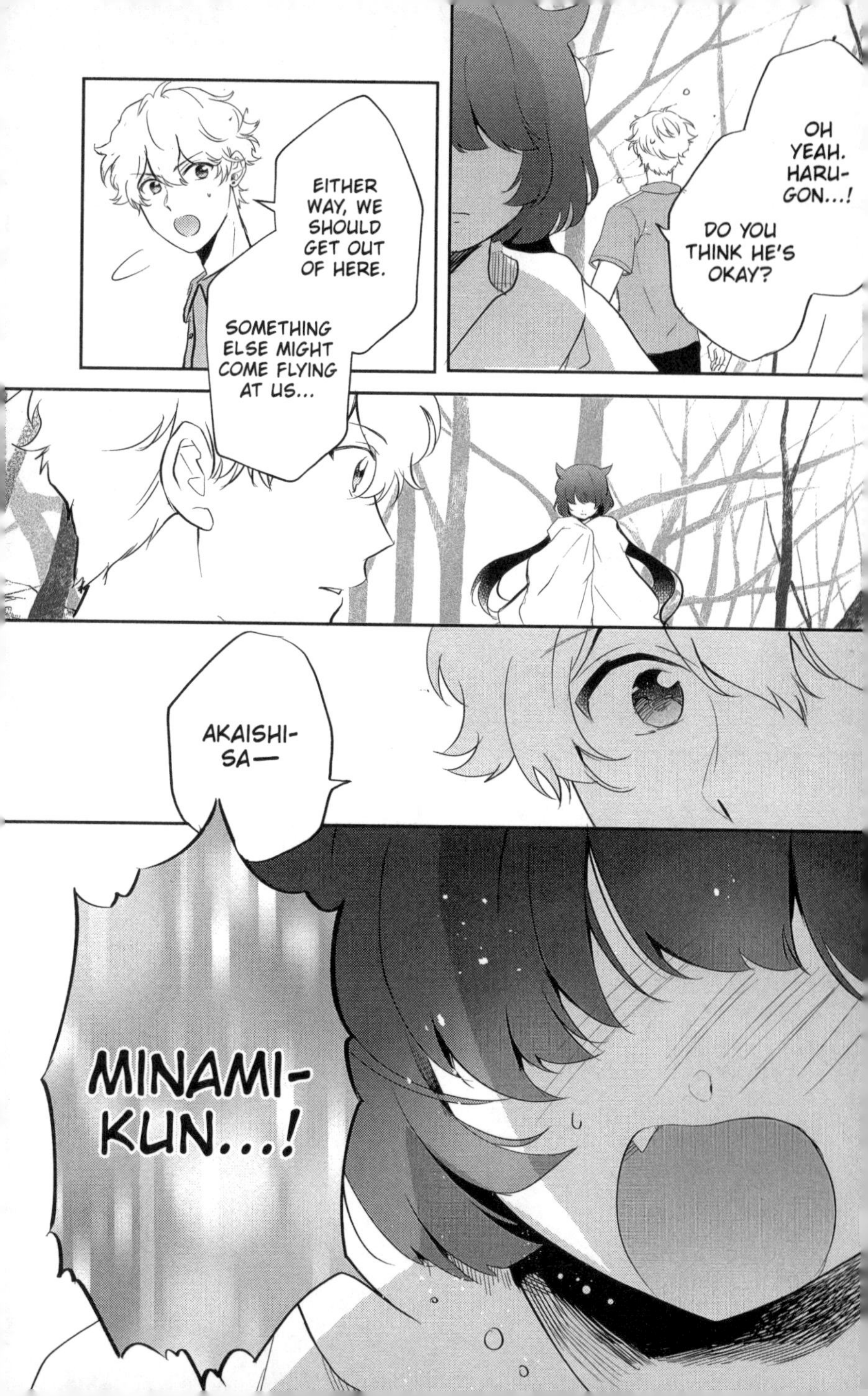
OH YEAH. HARU-GON...!
DO YOU THINK HE'S OKAY?
EITHER WAY, WE SHOULD GET OUT OF HERE.
SOMETHING ELSE MIGHT COME FLYING AT US...
AKAISHI-SA—
MINAMI-KUN...!

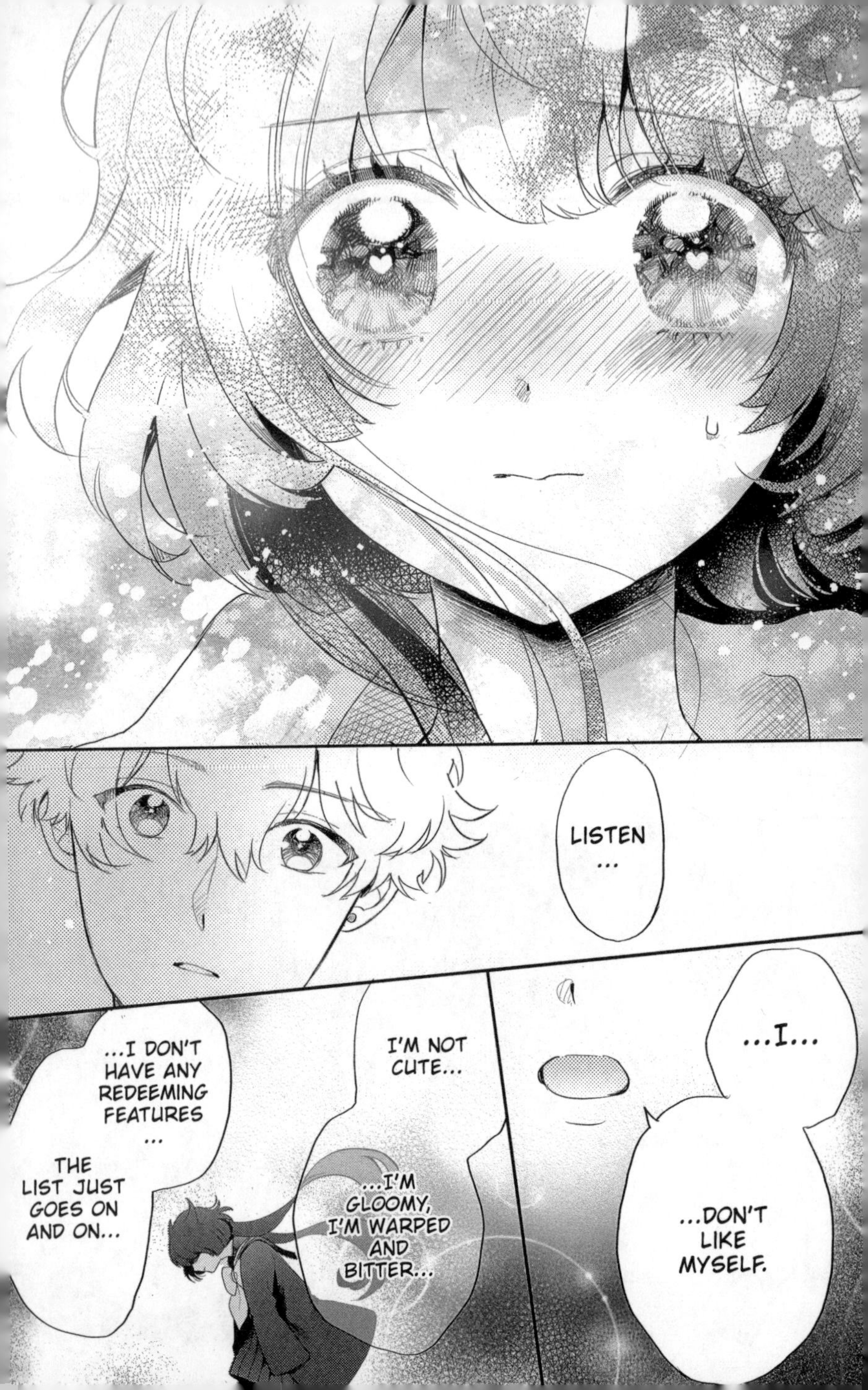
LISTEN ...
...I...
...DON'T LIKE MYSELF.
I'M NOT CUTE...
...I DON'T HAVE ANY REDEEMING FEATURES ...
...I'M GLOOMY, I'M WARPED AND BITTER...
THE LIST JUST GOES ON AND ON...

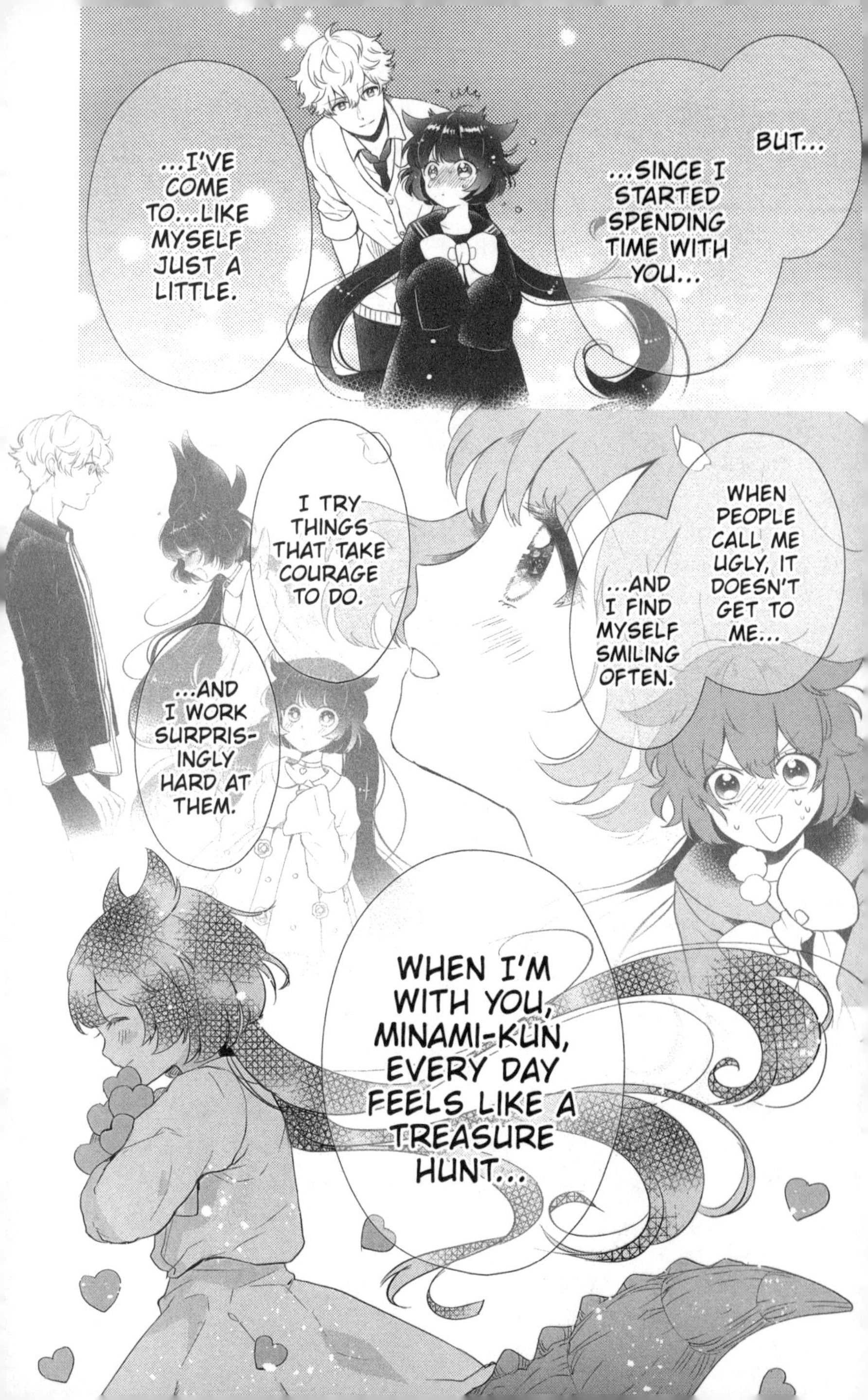
BUT...
...SINCE I STARTED SPENDING TIME WITH YOU...
...I'VE COME TO...LIKE MYSELF JUST A LITTLE.
WHEN PEOPLE CALL ME UGLY, IT DOESN'T GET TO ME...
...AND I FIND MYSELF SMILING OFTEN.
I TRY THINGS THAT TAKE COURAGE TO DO.
...AND I WORK SURPRIS-INGLY HARD AT THEM.
WHEN I'M WITH YOU, MINAMI-KUN, EVERY DAY FEELS LIKE A TREASURE HUNT...

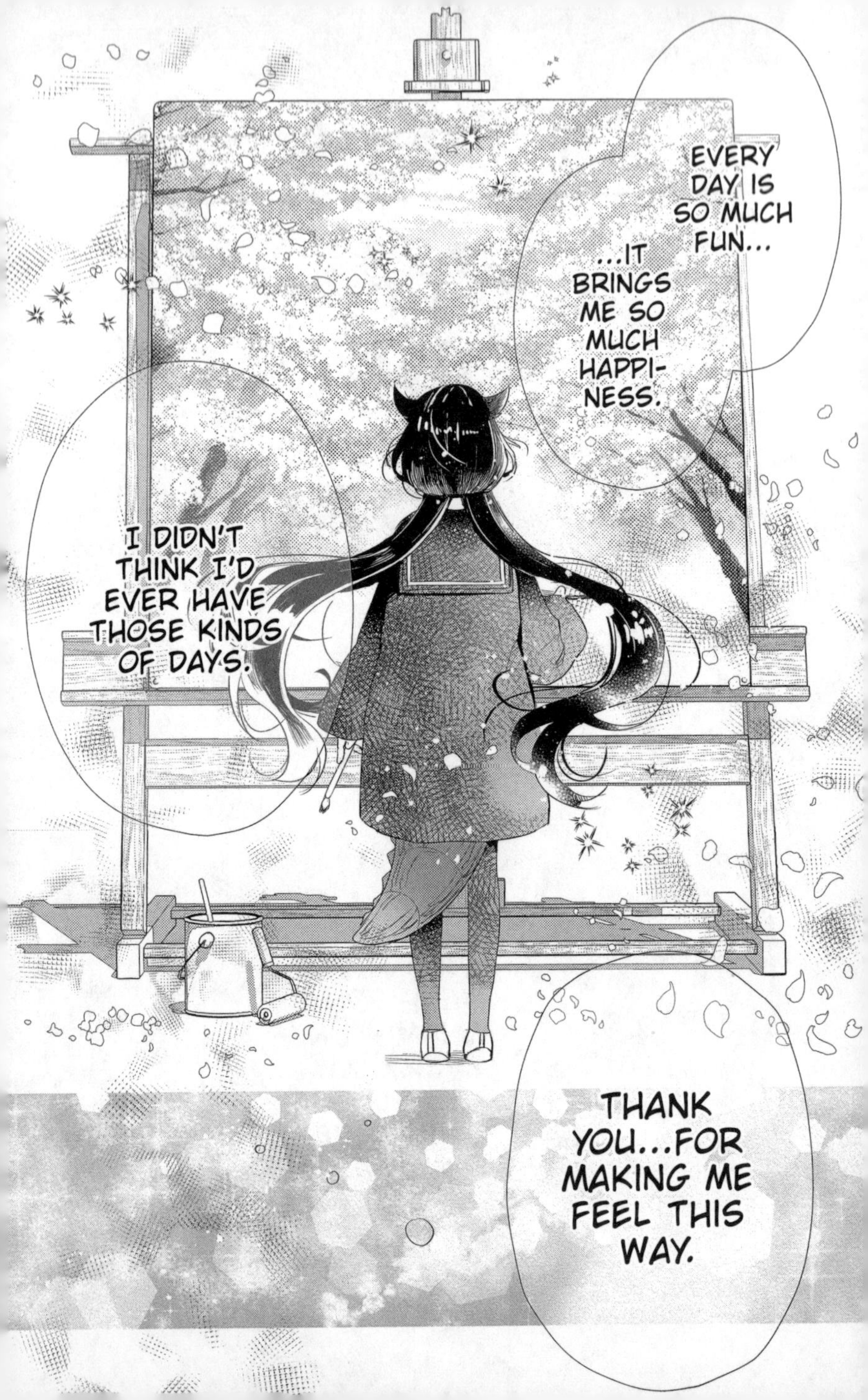
EVERY DAY IS SO MUCH FUN...
...IT BRINGS ME SO MUCH HAPPINESS.
I DIDN'T THINK I'D EVER HAVE THOSE KINDS OF DAYS.
THANK YOU...FOR MAKING ME FEEL THIS WAY.

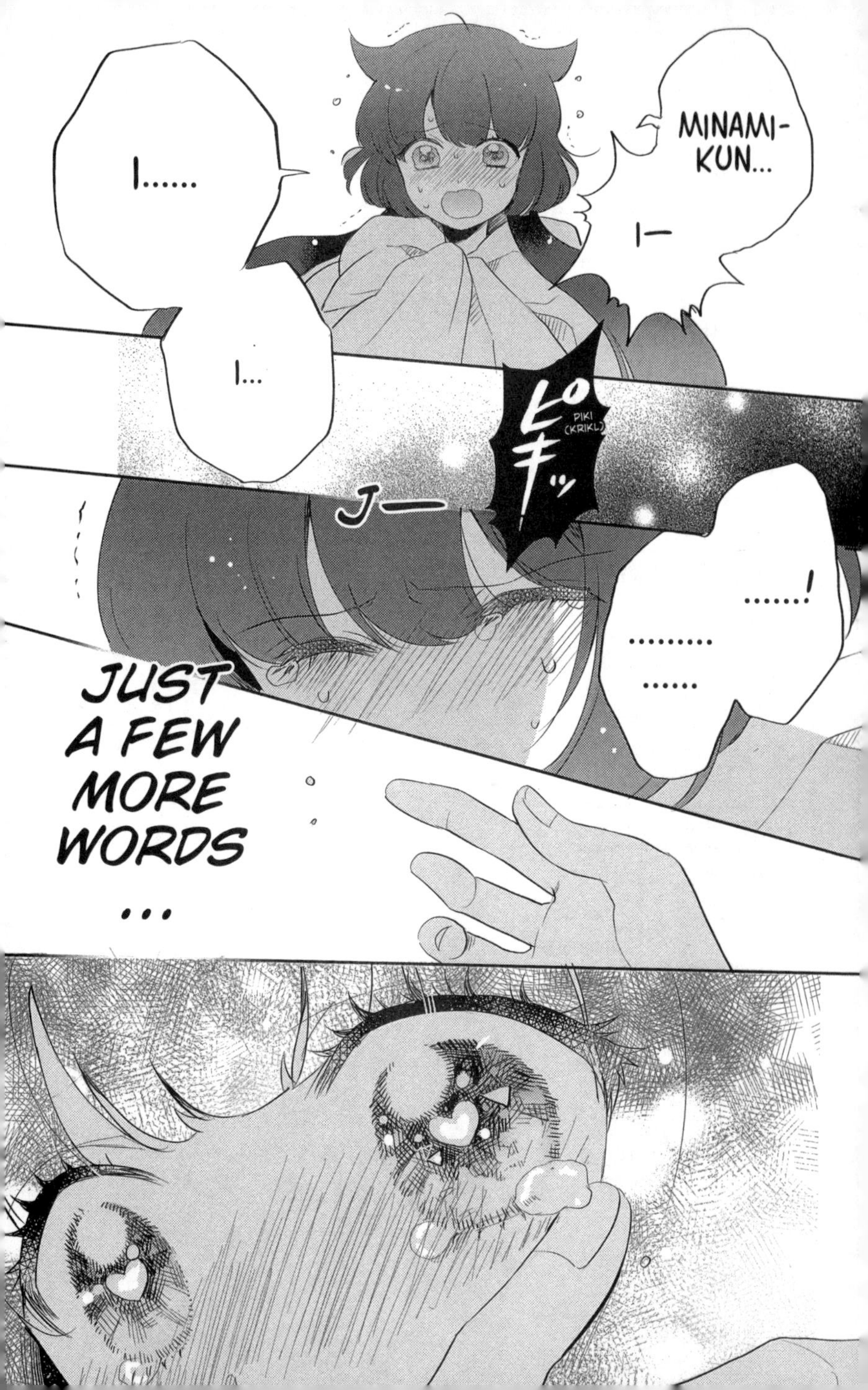
MINAMI-KUN...
I—
I......
I...
PIKI (KRIKL)
J—
......!
....
......
JUST A FEW MORE WORDS ...

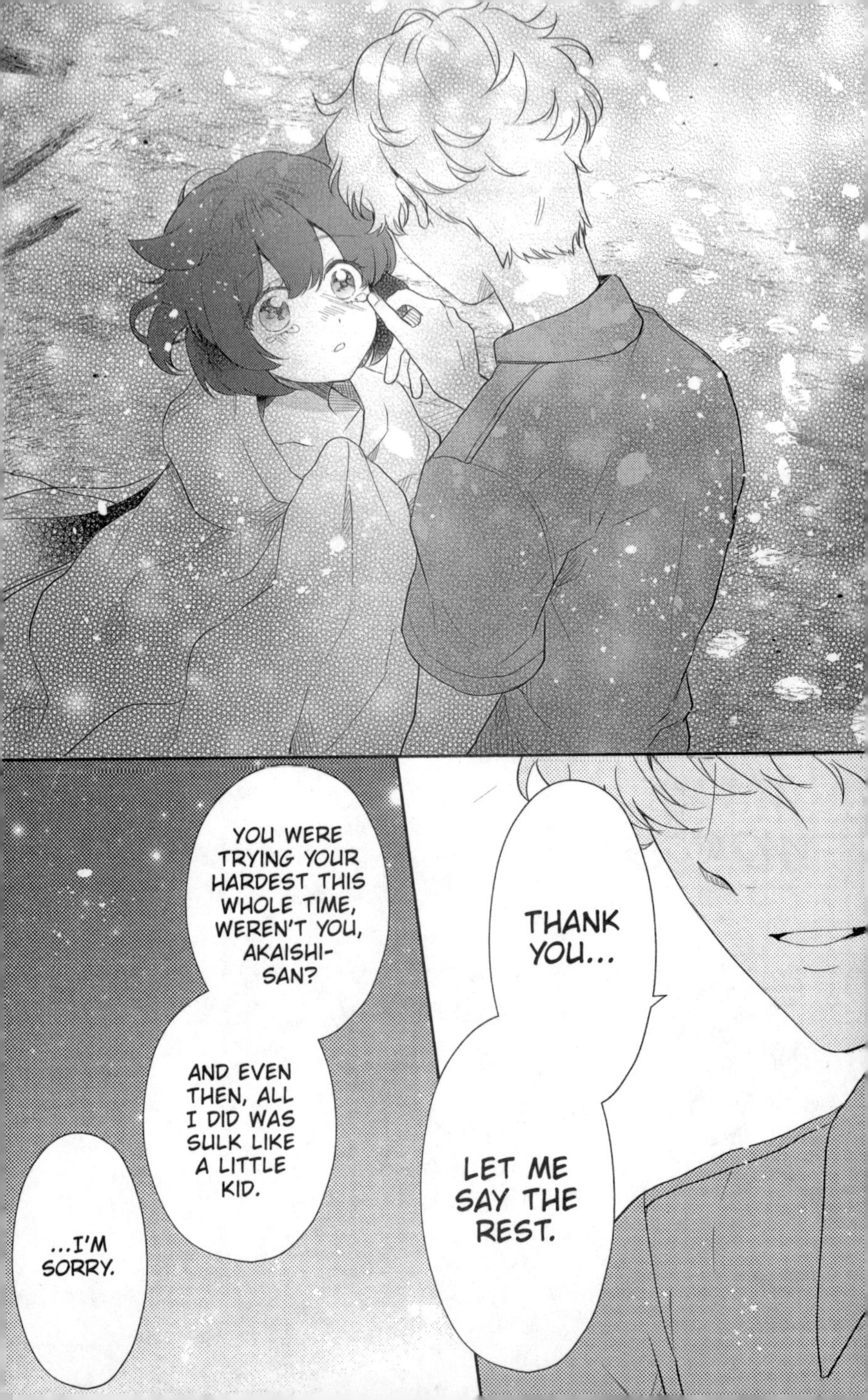
THANK YOU...
LET ME SAY THE REST.
YOU WERE TRYING YOUR HARDEST THIS WHOLE TIME, WEREN'T YOU, AKAISHI-SAN?
AND EVEN THEN, ALL I DID WAS SULK LIKE A LITTLE KID.
...I'M SORRY.

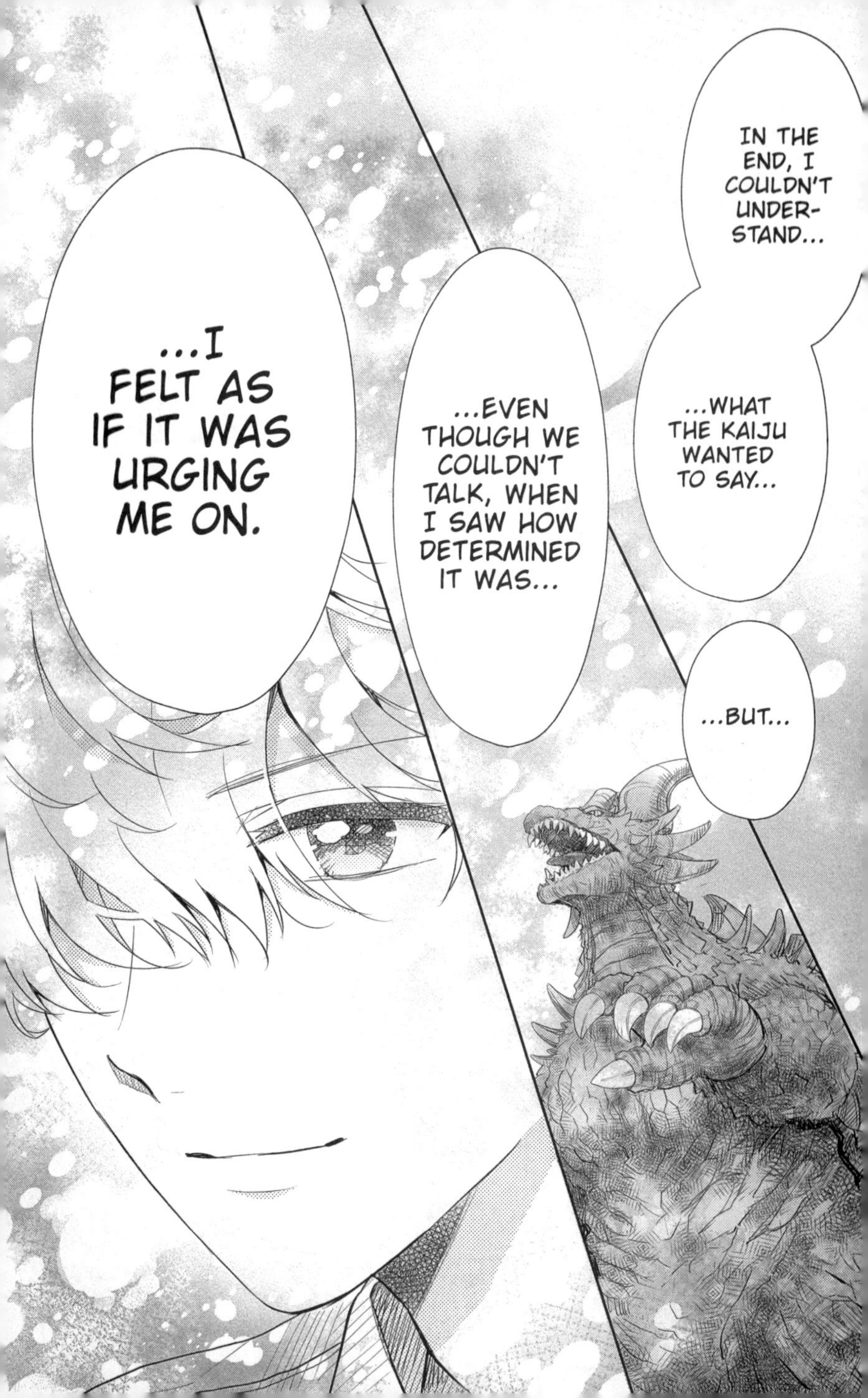
IN THE END, I COULDN'T UNDER-STAND...
...WHAT THE KAIJU WANTED TO SAY...
...BUT...
...EVEN THOUGH WE COULDN'T TALK, WHEN I SAW HOW DETERMINED IT WAS...
...I FELT AS IF IT WAS URGING ME ON.

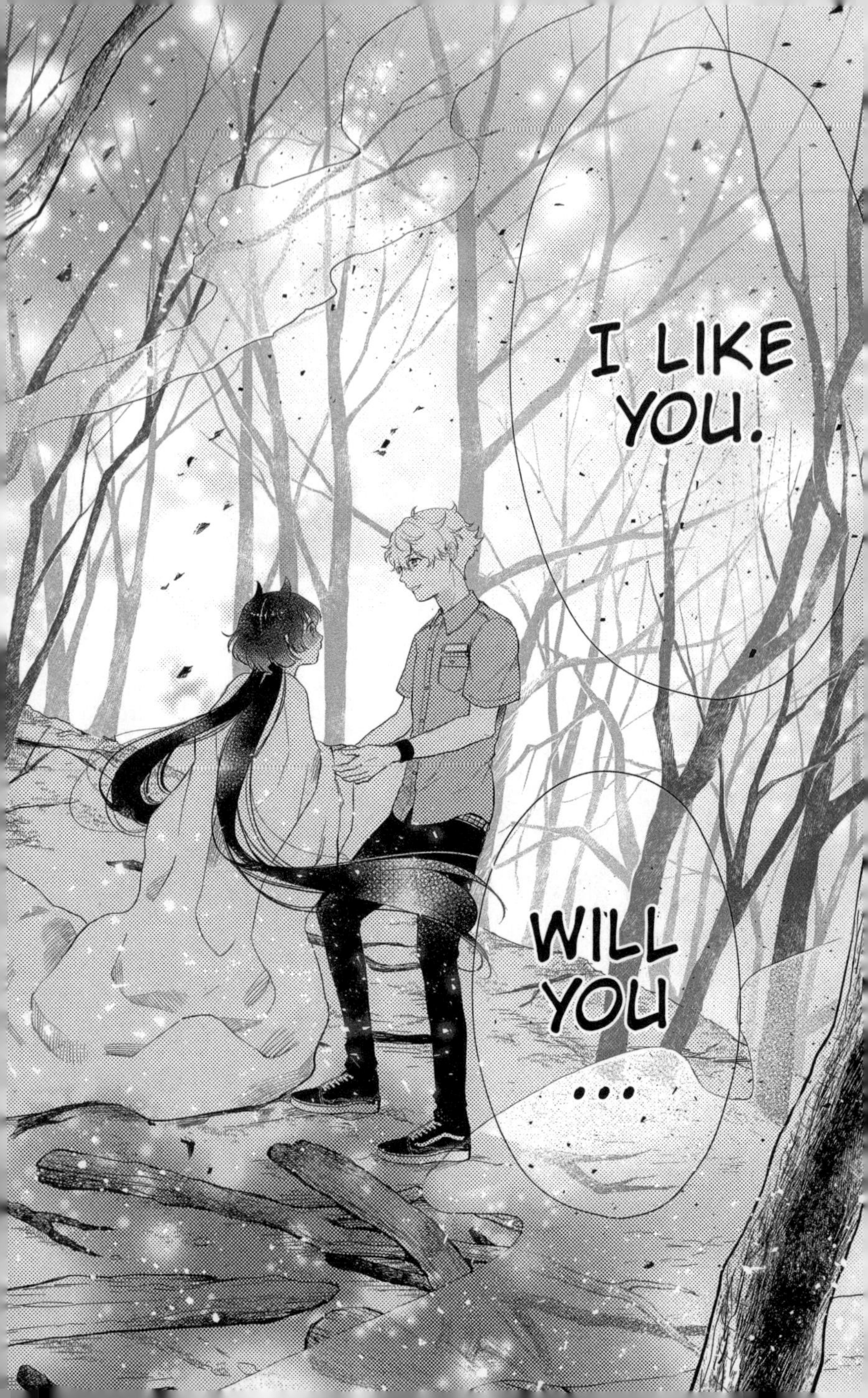
I LIKE YOU.
WILL YOU
...

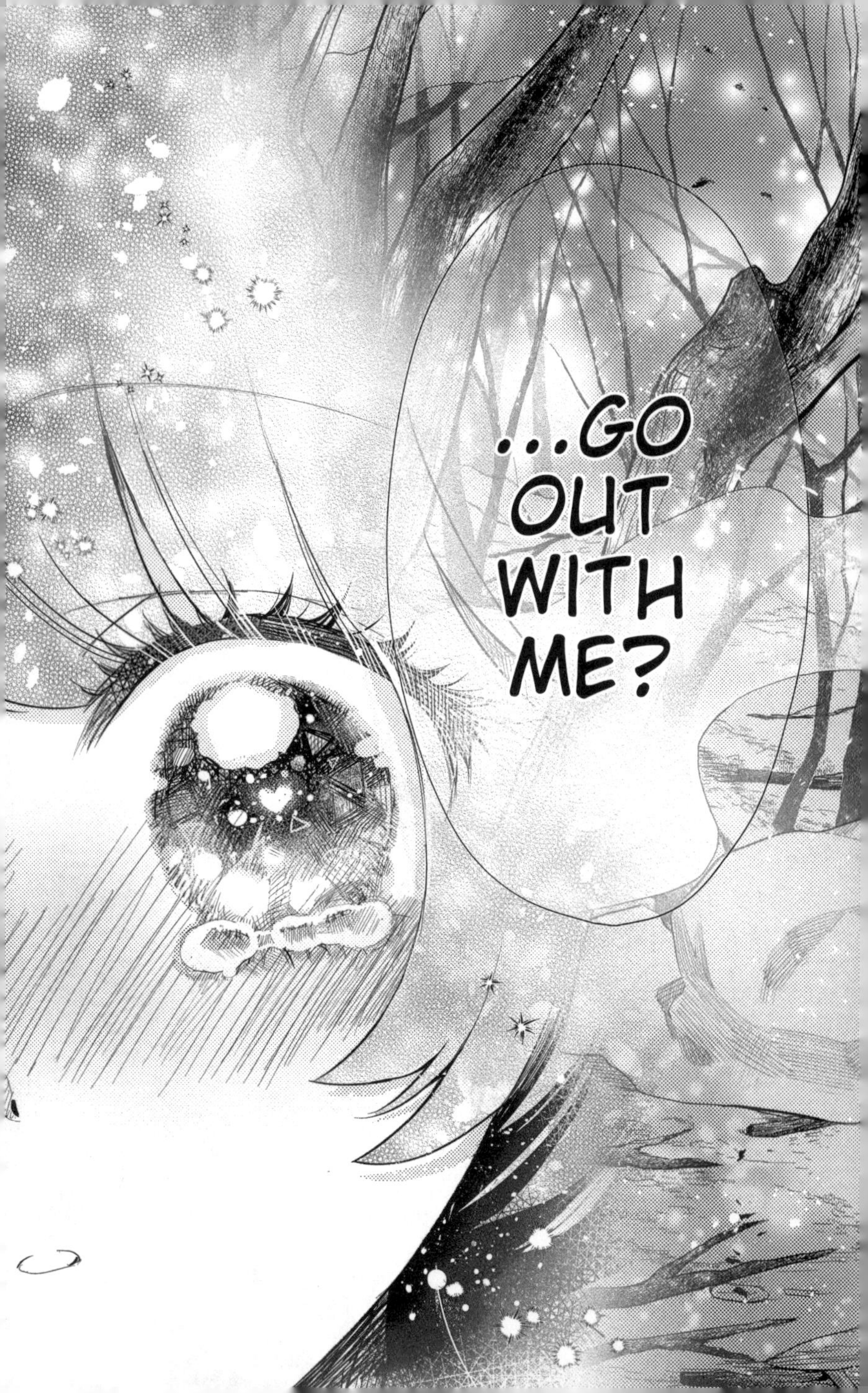
...GO OUT WITH ME?

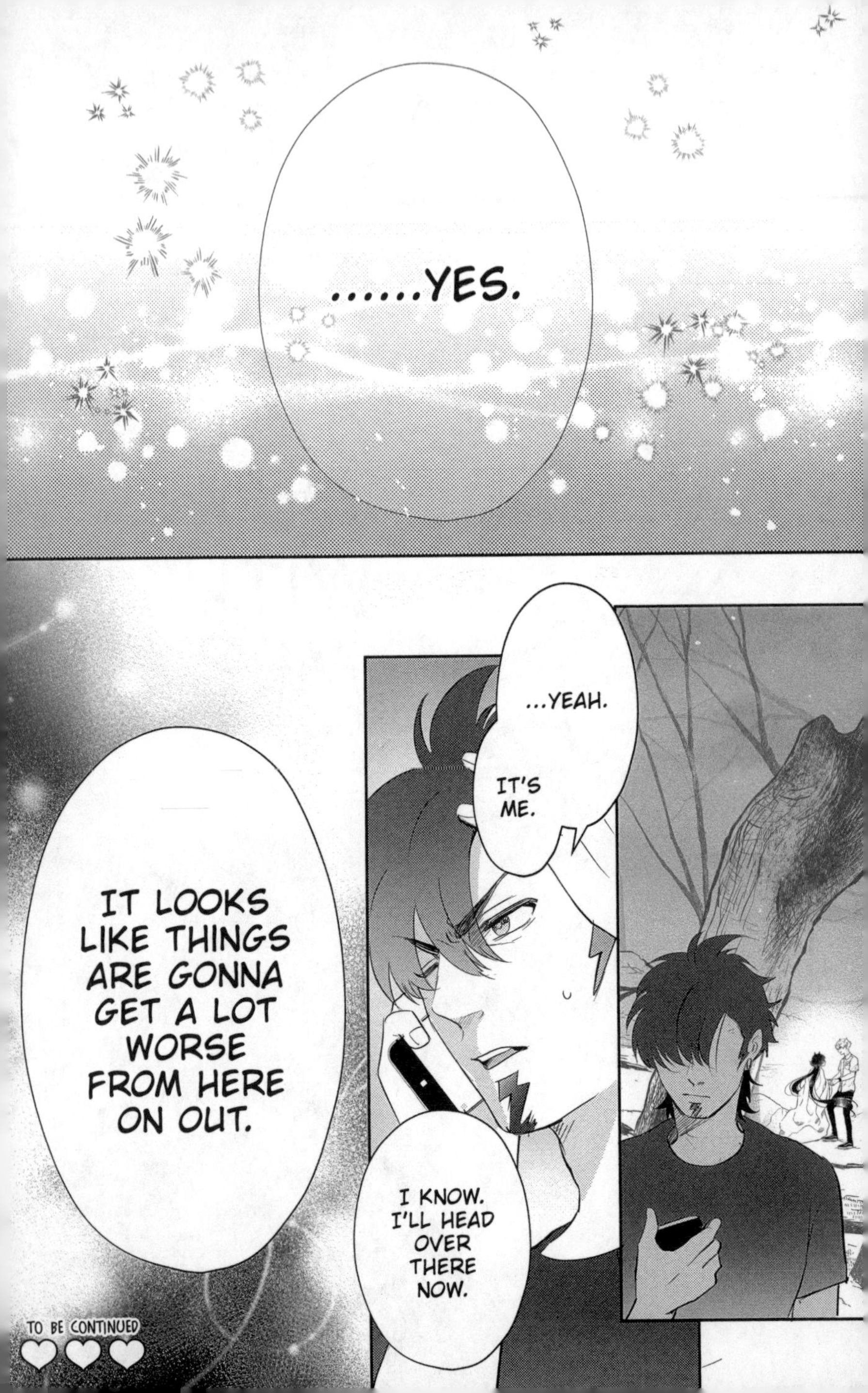
......YES.
...YEAH.
IT'S ME.
IT LOOKS LIKE THINGS ARE GONNA GET A LOT WORSE FROM HERE ON OUT.
I KNOW. I'LL HEAD OVER THERE NOW.
TO BE CONTINUED

KAIJU♥GIRL
CARAMELISE

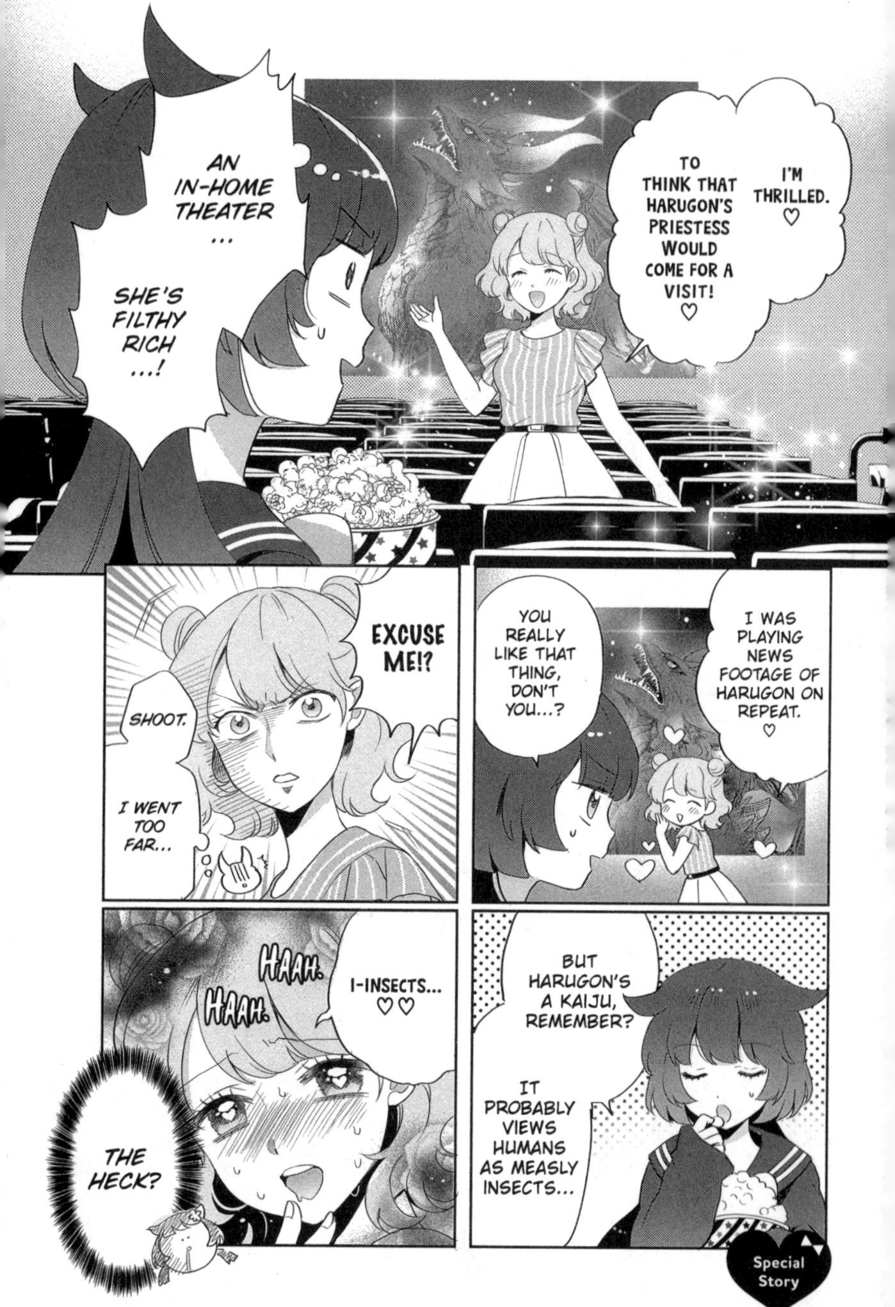
TO THINK THAT HARUGON'S PRIESTESS WOULD COME FOR A VISIT! ♡
I'M THRILLED. ♡
AN IN-HOME THEATER...
SHE'S FILTHY RICH...!
I WAS PLAYING NEWS FOOTAGE OF HARUGON ON REPEAT. ♡
YOU REALLY LIKE THAT THING, DON'T YOU...?
EXCUSE ME!?
SHOOT.
I WENT TOO FAR...
BUT HARUGON'S A KAIJU, REMEMBER?
IT PROBABLY VIEWS HUMANS AS MEASLY INSECTS...
I-INSECTS... ♡♡
HAAH.
HAAH.
THE HECK?
Special Story

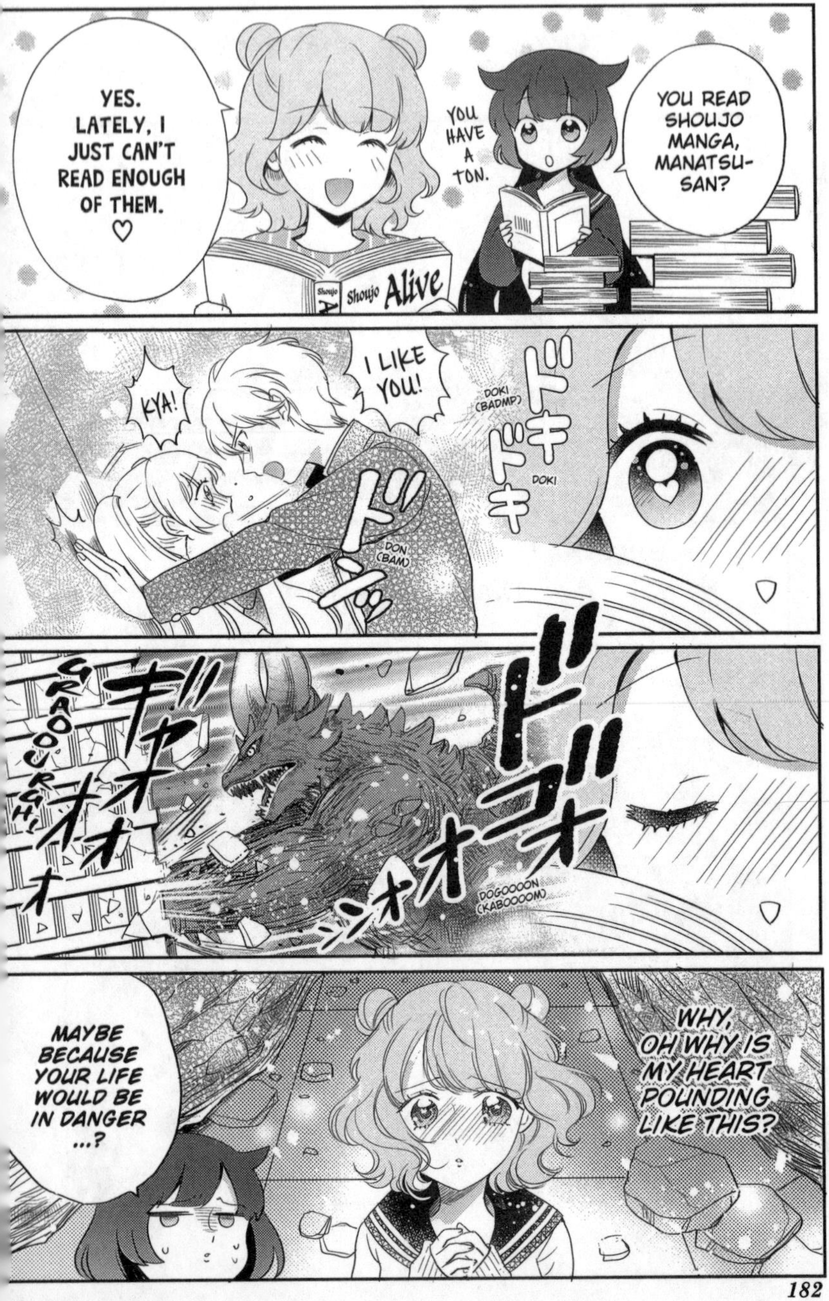

YOU READ SHOUJO MANGA, MANATSU-SAN?
YOU HAVE A TON.
YES. LATELY, I JUST CAN'T READ ENOUGH OF THEM. ♡
Shoujo Alive
DOKI (BADMP)
DOKI
I LIKE YOU!
KYA!
DON (BAM)
DOGOOOON (KABOOOOM)
GRAOOURGH!
WHY, OH WHY IS MY HEART POUNDING LIKE THIS?
MAYBE BECAUSE YOUR LIFE WOULD BE IN DANGER ...?

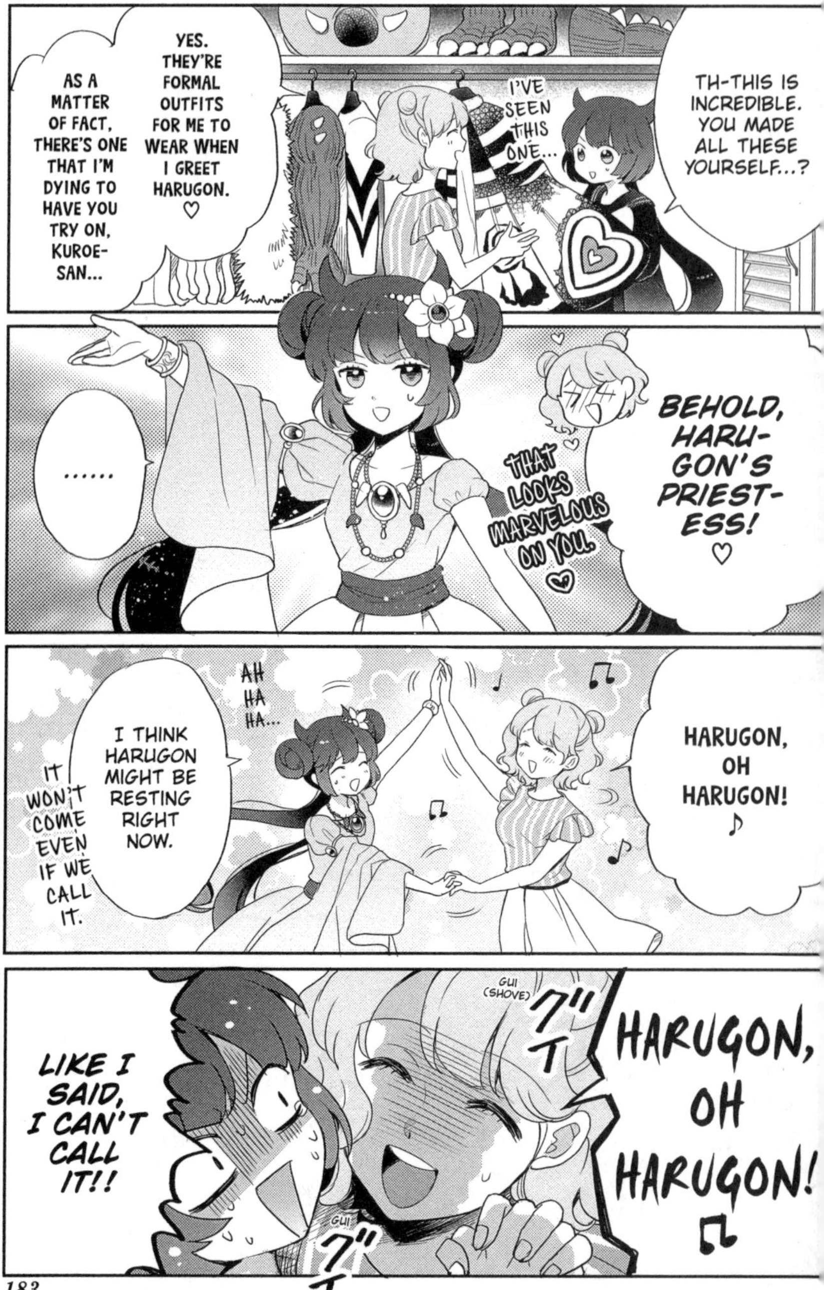

TH-THIS IS INCREDIBLE. YOU MADE ALL THESE YOURSELF...?
I'VE SEEN THIS ONE...
YES. THEY'RE FORMAL OUTFITS FOR ME TO WEAR WHEN I GREET HARUGON. ♡
AS A MATTER OF FACT, THERE'S ONE THAT I'M DYING TO HAVE YOU TRY ON, KUROE-SAN...
BEHOLD, HARUGON'S PRIESTESS! ♡
THAT LOOKS MARVELOUS ON YOU.
......
HARUGON, OH HARUGON! ♪
AH HA HA...
I THINK HARUGON MIGHT BE RESTING RIGHT NOW.
IT WON'T COME EVEN IF WE CALL IT.
HARUGON, OH HARUGON!
GUI (SHOVE)
グイ
GUI
グイ
LIKE I SAID, I CAN'T CALL IT!!

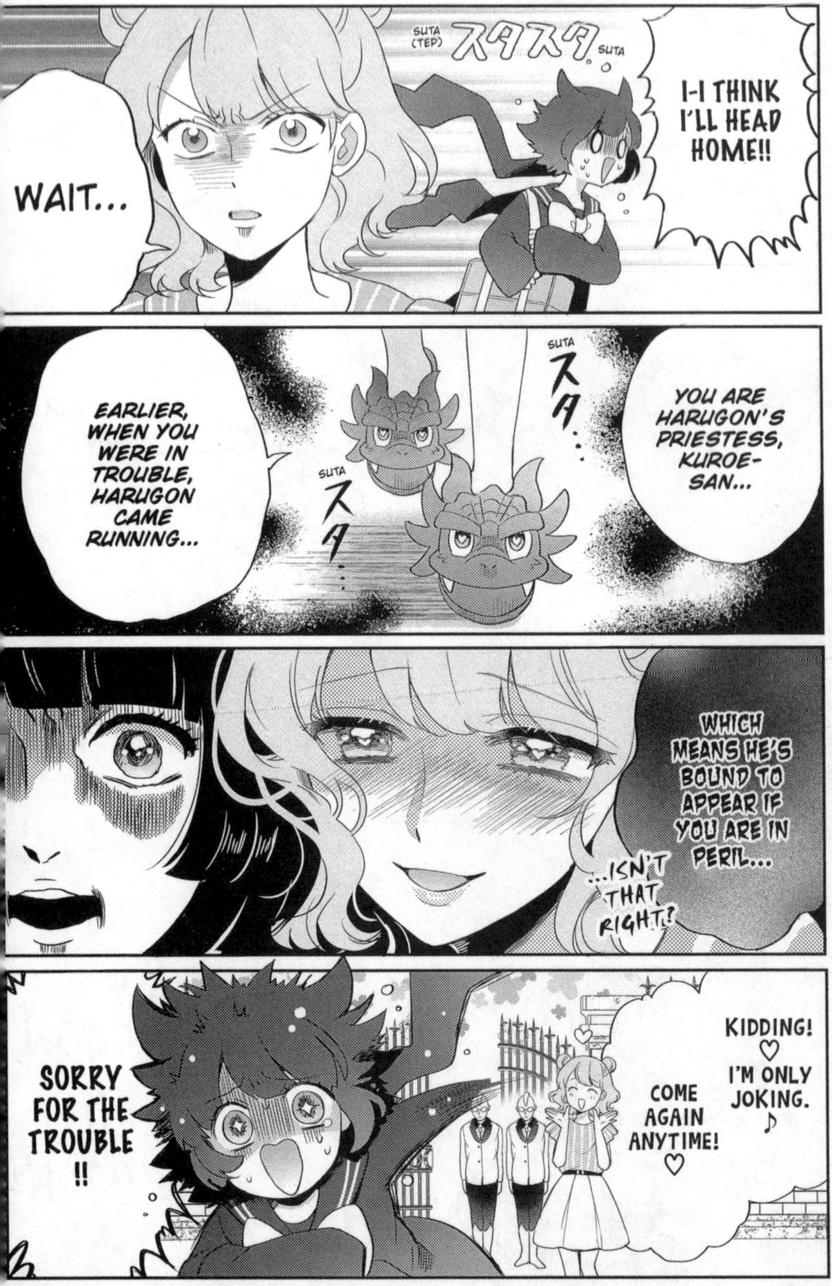
I-I THINK I'LL HEAD HOME!!
SUTA (TEP) スタスタ SUTA
WAIT...
YOU ARE HARUGON'S PRIESTESS, KUROE-SAN...
SUTA スタ...
SUTA スタ...
EARLIER, WHEN YOU WERE IN TROUBLE, HARUGON CAME RUNNING...
WHICH MEANS HE'S BOUND TO APPEAR IF YOU ARE IN PERIL...
...ISN'T THAT RIGHT?
KIDDING! ♡ I'M ONLY JOKING. ♪
COME AGAIN ANYTIME! ♡
SORRY FOR THE TROUBLE!!

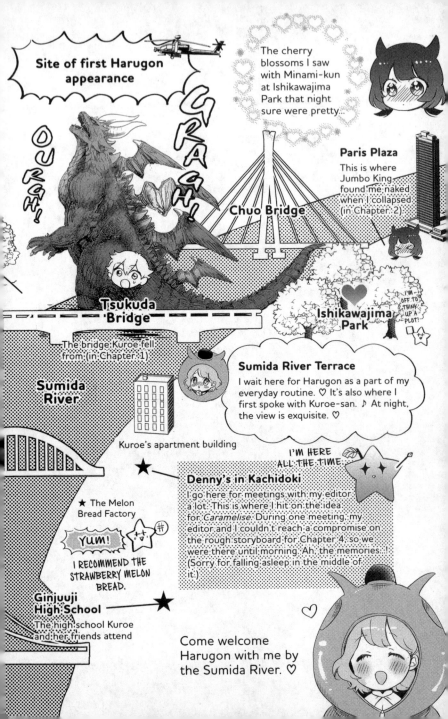

Site of first Harugon appearance

OURGH!

GRAGH!

The cherry blossoms I saw with Minami-kun at Ishikawajima Park that night sure were pretty...

Paris Plaza
This is where Jumbo King found me naked when I collapsed (in Chapter 2).

Chuo Bridge

Tsukuda Bridge
The bridge Kuroe fell from (in Chapter 1)

Ishikawajima Park

I'M OFF TO THINK UP A PLOT!

Sumida River

Sumida River Terrace
I wait here for Harugon as a part of my everyday routine. ♡ It's also where I first spoke with Kuroe-san. ♪ At night, the view is exquisite. ♡

Kuroe's apartment building

I'M HERE ALL THE TIME.

Denny's in Kachidoki
I go here for meetings with my editor a lot. This is where I hit on the idea for *Caramelise*. During one meeting, my editor and I couldn't reach a compromise on the rough storyboard for Chapter 4, so we were there until morning. Ah, the memories! (Sorry for falling asleep in the middle of it.)

★ The Melon Bread Factory

YUM!

I RECOMMEND THE STRAWBERRY MELON BREAD.

Ginjuuji High School
The high school Kuroe and her friends attend

Come welcome Harugon with me by the Sumida River. ♡

SPECIAL THANKS

To everyone involved in *Caramelise*, including the readers, my editor, the designer, my mom and dad, and my friends.

★Art Assistants
Sakamoto-san
Nakanishi-san

★Screentone Assistant
Yamaguchi-san

Thank you so much for picking up Volume 2! Please keep an eye out for the next volume as well!

Aoki Spica

Find the latest information on Twitter.
@nakiringo

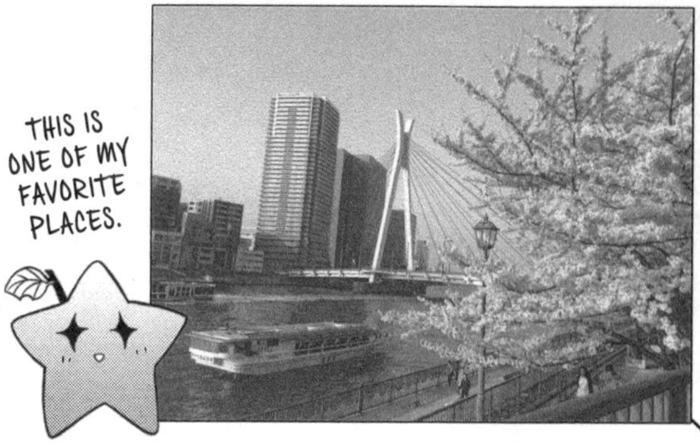
THIS IS ONE OF MY FAVORITE PLACES.

This is the area around the Chuo Bridge where Harugon first appeared. It's fun to see all the sightseeing and party boats cruise by. There are far fewer people than you'd expect, and I think it's a great semisecret spot for flower-viewing!

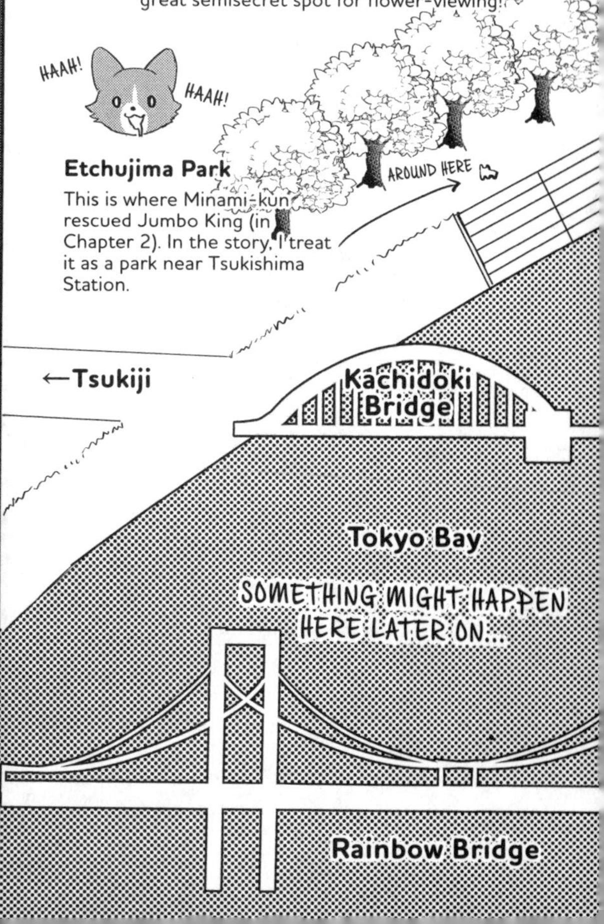
HAAH!
HAAH!
AROUND HERE
←Tsukiji
Kachidoki Bridge
Tokyo Bay
SOMETHING MIGHT HAPPEN HERE LATER ON...
Rainbow Bridge

Etchujima Park

This is where Minami-kun rescued Jumbo King (in Chapter 2). In the story, I treat it as a park near Tsukishima Station.

TRANSLATION NOTES

COMMON HONORIFICS

no honorific: Indicates familiarity or closeness; if used without permission or reason, addressing someone in this manner would constitute an insult.

-*san*: The Japanese equivalent of Mr./Mrs./Miss. If a situation calls for politeness, this is the fail-safe honorific.

-*senpai*: A suffix used to address upperclassmen or more experienced coworkers.

-*kun*: Used most often when referring to boys, this indicates affection or familiarity. Occasionally used by older men among their peers, but it may also be used by anyone referring to a person of lower standing.

-*chan*: An affectionate honorific indicating familiarity used mostly in reference to girls; also used in reference to cute persons or animals of either gender.

-*tan*: A casual honorific that expresses closeness and affection; it is similar to *chan* in that it is used in reference to cute persons.

PAGE 5

Mayumi Hamasaki is a fictional celebrity based on a legendary Japanese pop queen and songwriter by the name of Ayumi Hamasaki who debuted in 1998 and is one of Japan's bestselling artists of all time.

PAGE 77

Cosplay, or costume play, is an activity in which people dress up as a character from a specific cartoon, manga, anime, video game, or television series. You will often see fans cosplaying as their favorite character at conventions.

PAGE 98

Bakuon in Japanese means an "explosive sound," or "insanely loud."

PAGE 182

Shoujo manga is a genre of manga aimed toward young female readers. The word *shoujo* in Japanese means "young girl."

KAIJU♥GIRL
CARAMELISE

Two girls, a new school, and the beginning of a beautiful friendship.

Volumes 1-9 available now

Kiss & White Lily for My Dearest Girl

In middle school, Ayaka Shiramine was the perfect student: hard-working, with excellent grades and a great personality to match. As Ayaka enters high school she expects to still be on top, but one thing she didn't account for is her new classmate, the lazy yet genuine genius Yurine Kurosawa. What's in store for Ayaka and Yurine as they go through high school...together?

Kiss and White Lily For My Dearest Girl © Canno / KADOKAWA CORPORATION

Yen Press

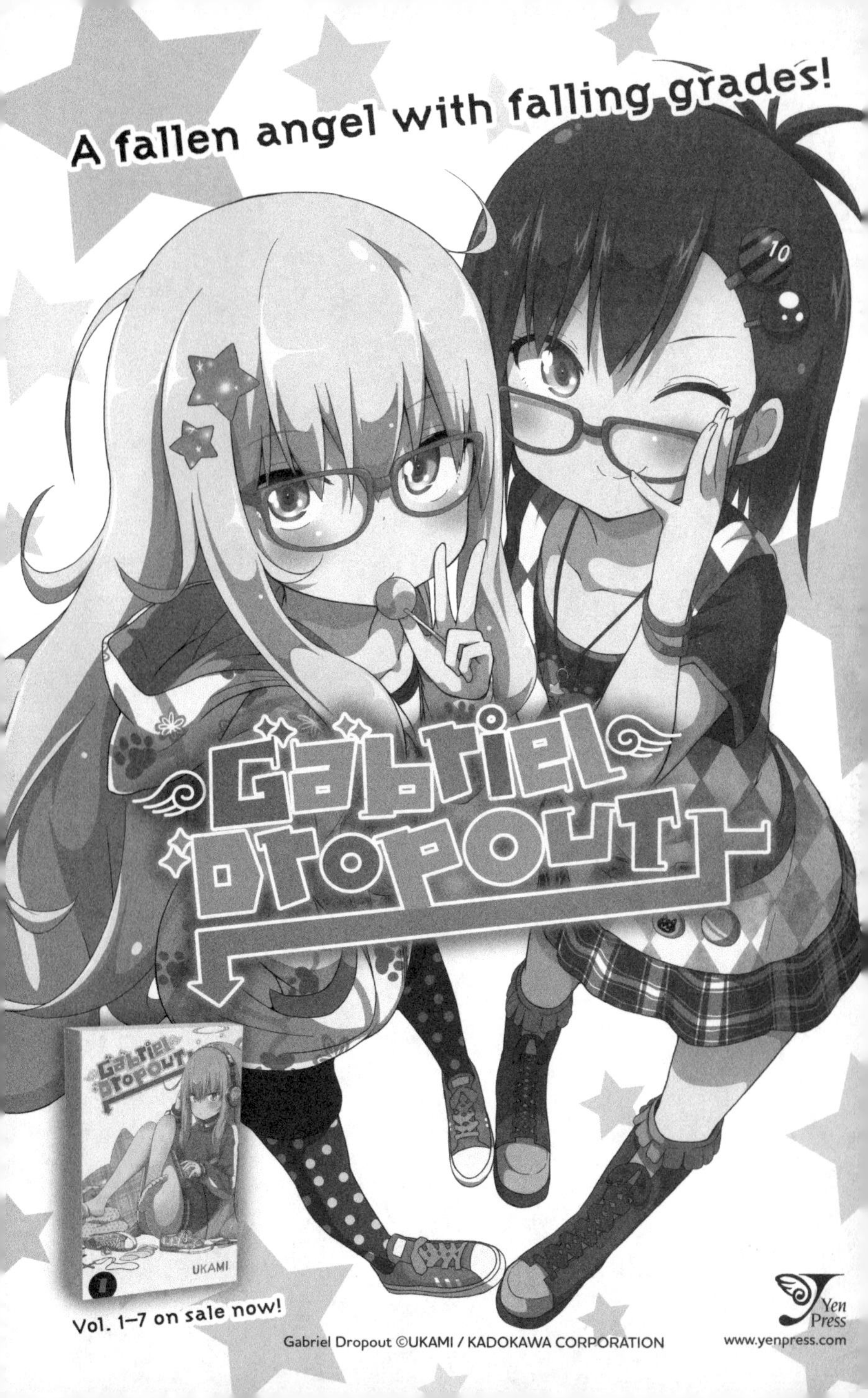

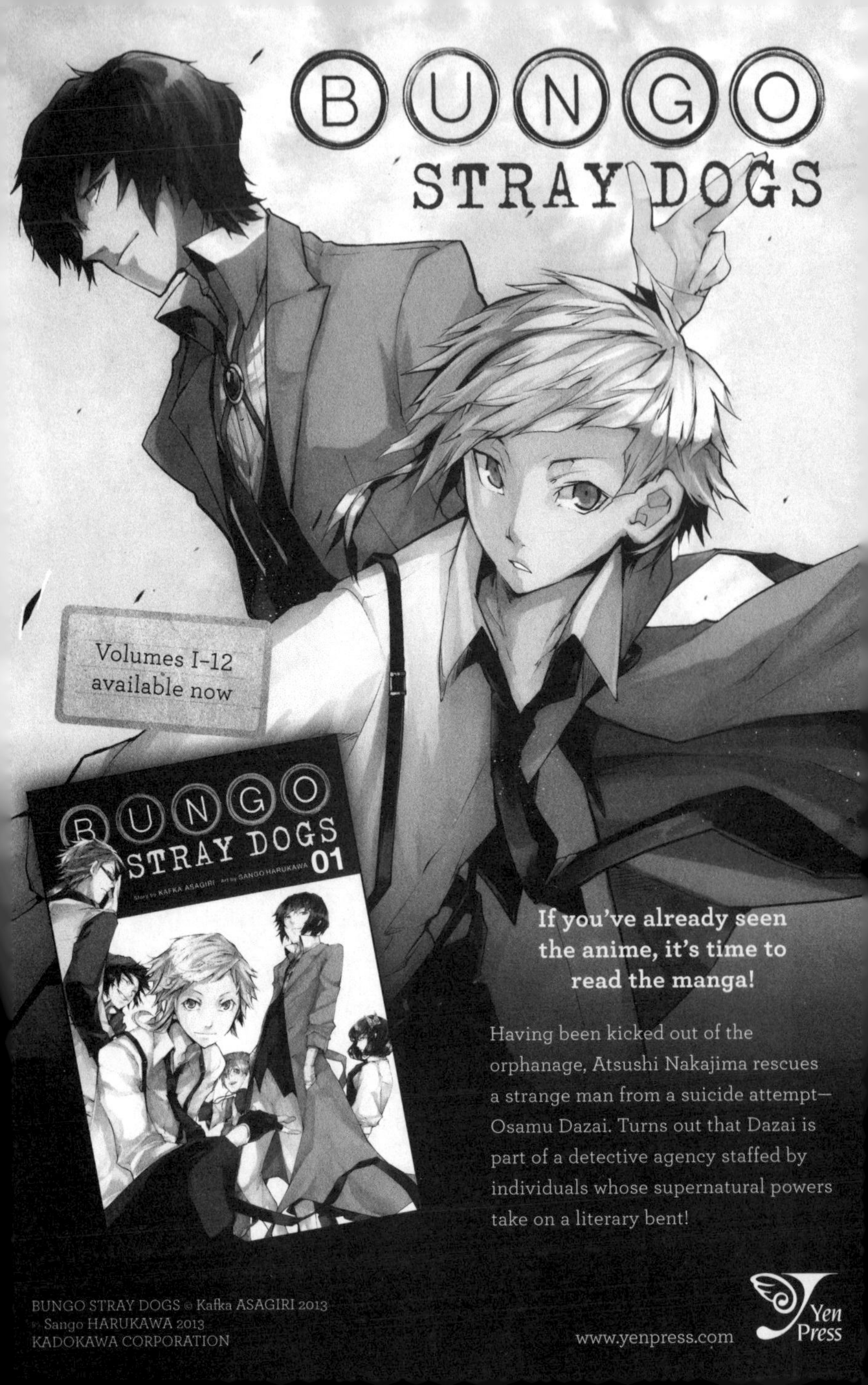
BUNGO
STRAY DOGS
Volumes 1–12 available now
BUNGO
STRAY DOGS
01
Story by KAFKA ASAGIRI · Art by SANGO HARUKAWA
If you've already seen the anime, it's time to read the manga!
Having been kicked out of the orphanage, Atsushi Nakajima rescues a strange man from a suicide attempt—Osamu Dazai. Turns out that Dazai is part of a detective agency staffed by individuals whose supernatural powers take on a literary bent!
BUNGO STRAY DOGS © Kafka ASAGIRI 2013
© Sango HARUKAWA 2013
KADOKAWA CORPORATION
www.yenpress.com
Yen Press

Death doesn't stop a video game-loving shut-in from going on adventures and fighting monsters!

KONOSUBA: GOD'S BLESSING ON THIS WONDERFUL WORLD!

IN STORES NOW

Yen Press

LIGHT NOVEL

MANGA

Konosuba: God's Blessing on This Wonderful World! (novel) © 2013 Natsume Akatsuki, Kurone Mishima KADOKAWA CORPORATION

Konosuba: God's Blessing on This Wonderful World! (manga) © MASAHITO WATARI 2015 © NATSUME AKATSUKI, KURONE MISHIMA 2015 KADOKAWA CORPORATION

ENJOY EVERYTHING.

Join Yotsuba as she delights in the things many of us take for granted in this Eisner-nominated series.

VOLUMES 1-14 AVAILABLE NOW!

Visit our website at www.yenpress.com.
Yotsuba&! © Kiyohiko Azuma / YOTUBA SUTAZIO

Hello! This is YOTSUBA!

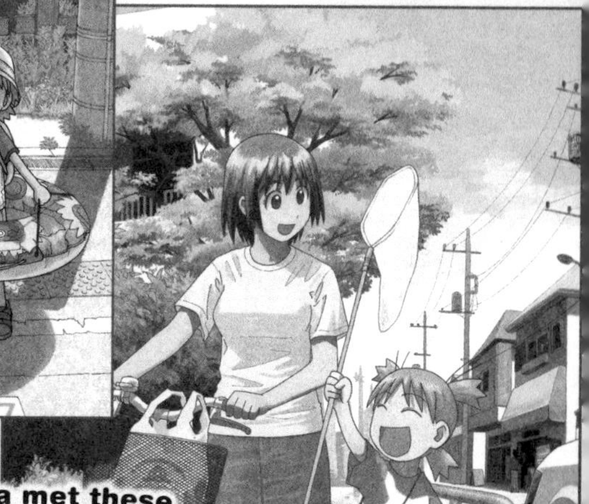

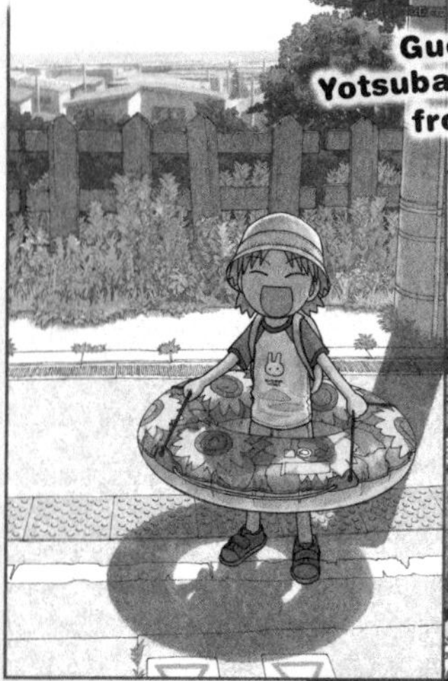

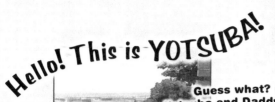

Guess what? Guess what?
Yotsuba and Daddy just moved here
from waaaay over there!

And Yotsuba met these
nice people next door and made
new friends to play with!

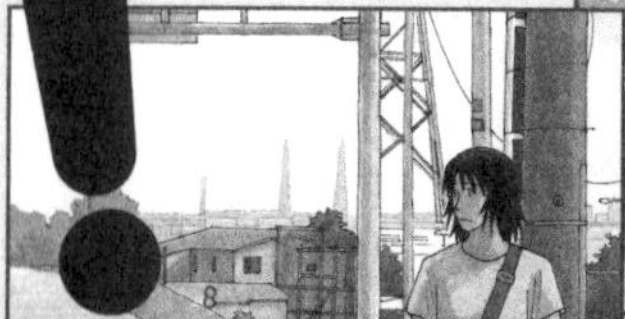

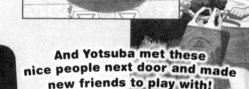

The pretty one took
Yotsuba on a bike ride!
(Whoooa! There was a big hill!)

And Ena's a good drawer!
(Almost as good as Yotsuba!)

And their mom always
gives Yotsuba ice cream!
(Yummy!)

And...
And...
OHHHH!

KAIJU GIRL CARAMELISE 2

Spica Aoki

TRANSLATION: Taylor Engel 💕 LETTERING: Lys Blakeslee

This book is a work of fiction. Names, characters, places, and incidents are
the product of the author's imagination or are used fictitiously. Any resemblance
to actual events, locales, or persons, living or dead, is coincidental.

OTOMEKAIJU CARAMELISE Vol. 2
©Spica Aoki 2019
First published in Japan in 2019 by KADOKAWA CORPORATION, Tokyo.
English translation rights arranged with KADOKAWA CORPORATION,
Tokyo through TUTTLE-MORI AGENCY, INC., Tokyo.

English translation © 2019 by Yen Press, LLC

Yen Press, LLC supports the right to free expression and the value of copyright.
The purpose of copyright is to encourage writers and artists to produce the
creative works that enrich our culture.

The scanning, uploading, and distribution of this book without permission is a theft
of the author's intellectual property. If you would like permission to use material
from the book (other than for review purposes), please contact the publisher.
Thank you for your support of the author's rights.

Yen Press
150 West 30th Street, 19th Floor
New York, NY 10001

Visit us at yenpress.com ♡ facebook.com/yenpress ♡
twitter.com/yenpress ♡ yenpress.tumblr.com ♡
instagram.com/yenpress

First Yen Press Edition: November 2019

Yen Press is an imprint of Yen Press, LLC.
The Yen Press name and logo are trademarks of
Yen Press, LLC.

The publisher is not responsible for websites (or
their content) that are not owned by the publisher.

Library of Congress Control Number: 2019935205

ISBNs: 978-1-9753-5946-1 (paperback)
        978-1-9753-8674-0 (ebook)

10 9 8 7 6 5 4 3 2

BVG

Printed in the United States of America